THE TRUTH PILL

THE TRUTH PILL

The Myth of Drug Regulation in India

DINESH S. THAKUR

PRASHANT REDDY T.

SIMON & SCHUSTER

London · New York · Sydney · Toronto · New Delhi

First published in India by Simon & Schuster India, 2022

3 5 7 9 10 8 6 4 2

Simon & Schuster India
818, Indraprakash Building,
21, Barakhamba Road,
New Delhi 110001.

www.simonandschuster.co.in

Hardback ISBN: 978-93-92099-17-5
eBook ISBN: 978-93-92099-22-9

Typeset in India by SÜRYA, New Delhi
Printed and bound in India by Replika Press Pvt. Ltd.

FSC
www.fsc.org
MIX
Paper from responsible sources
FSC® C016779

To Dr Raj Kumar,
who is a mentor and a role model to me

– Dinesh S. Thakur

~

For my friend and mentor,
the Late Dr Shamnad Basheer

– Prashant Reddy T.

CONTENTS

Prologue

An Epidemic of DEG Poisoning and Regulatory Failure

As the year 2019 drew to a close, doctors at two North Indian hospitals were grappling with a mysterious condition that had affected approximately 21 children, several of whom were infants. The weather had started to turn as winter began to set in and all of these children had been suffering from a cough or a cold which were typical for this time of the year; but these children then progressed to vomiting and ultimately suffering from kidney failure. Most of these children came from Ramnagar in Jammu.[1]

It is a remarkable medical event for a cluster of otherwise healthy children from the same neighbourhood to suddenly suffer from acute kidney failure. The first response of the government in such circumstances is to put together a team of doctors, microbiologists, and epidemiologists from various institutions to conduct an epidemiological investigation.[2] The Government of India rushed a group of experts to trace the source of the mystery affliction before it affected even more children in the area. At the time, the media reported that the children had died of a "mystery disease" and the government was looking at the usual suspects, such as contaminated water, to establish the cause of death.[3]

At the highly regarded Post-Graduate Institute of Medical Education & Research (PGIMER), Chandigarh, where many of the sick children had been admitted for treatment, doctors ran a battery of tests on their young patients to diagnose their ailments. The medication consumed by the children prior to their admission to the hospital was also sent for testing. One of these medications was a cough syrup called COLDBEST, which is a fixed dose combination of Paracetamol, Phenylephrine Hydrochloride, and Chlorpheniramine Maleate manufactured by Digital Vision, a pharmaceutical company with its manufacturing base in Himachal Pradesh, which is the national hub for most pharmaceutical companies due to a generous tax exemption policy introduced by the Government of India to bolster industrial development in the hilly region. The parents of the children in Jammu had bought this cough syrup from a local pharmacy after their children had exhibited signs of a fever along with either a cough or a cold.

The Regional Drug Testing Laboratory, Chandigarh, which tested three different samples of the same batch of COLDBEST alleged that the samples of the cough syrup tested positive for 34.24%, 34.97%, and 35.87% of diethylene glycol (DEG) which is a powerful industrial solvent that is used in the manufacture of anti-freeze, brake fluid etc.[4] It is never used in the manufacture of medicine and can be fatal to humans who consume it.[5] It causes the kidneys to fail and that can eventually lead to death. In cases of DEG poisoning due to manufacturing errors, children tend to suffer the most because their smaller body size causes them to be more vulnerable to the toxic effects of DEG when compared to adults. As one academic paper put it "...children often seem to be the sentinels in this cruel and unintended form of toxic surveillance".[6] Finally, the doctors at PGIMER had a probable answer to explain the renal failure leading to death of the children from Ramnagar.

By the time the mystery was solved by the doctors at PGIMER, approximately 11 children from Ramnagar between the ages of two months and six years died due to renal failure.

The youngest was not yet named. The names of the remaining were Annirudh, Akshu Kumar, Ashish, Pranav, Amit Kumar, Surabhi Sharma, Kanishk Dogra, Varuni, Jannu Kumar, and Shriyansh. They were born to parents who were daily wage labourers, a truck driver, a school teacher, and a soldier in the Indian Army. One of the parents was so distraught upon hearing the news of the death of his child, he reportedly demolished his own house.[7]

Though these children were all equal citizens of a democratic India, the news of their deaths struggled to get the attention of the Delhi-centric-English-language media which often sets the national agenda. It is virtually guaranteed that these deaths would have received far more media attention and perhaps even some public outrage if they were from the middle class and residing in New Delhi. Ultimately, just two English language Indian newspapers based in New Delhi, *The Tribune*, and the *Indian Express*, gave the story the required attention.[8]

The larger tragedy was the fact that the deaths of these twelve children from Jammu were entirely preventable. After all, DEG poisoning is a well-known and a well-documented problem within the pharmaceutical industry since 1937, when the first mass DEG poisoning event took place in the United States. At the time, a company called S.E. Massengill of Bristol, Tennessee, was just getting into the business of selling a new wonder drug called Sulfanilamide, which was one of the first antibiotics that could treat a broad spectrum of bacterial infections. Massengill wanted to sell Sulfanilamide in liquid form, as a sweetened syrup because it anticipated that such a formulation would lead to higher sales in the pediatric market. The chief chemist at the company experimented with various solvents that could dissolve Sulfanilamide into a syrup and ultimately ended up using diethylene glycol (DEG) as a solvent without being aware that DEG was toxic for humans. The formulation had not been tested for toxicity because it was not mandatory to do so under the law at the time.[9]

The first batch of "Elixir Sulfanilamide" entered the American market in October, 1937, and in a matter of a few days, doctors reported the death of six patients who consumed Massengill's drug. Despite a frantic recall effort, a total of 105 patients, including 34 children, were killed in the United States after consuming Massengill's cough syrup. An additional "victim", was the Chief Chemist at Massengill who killed himself while awaiting a trial before a court of law for his role in the incident.[10] The deaths of those patients provoked an overhaul of the Federal Food, Drug and Cosmetics Act in 1938 with an increased focus on safety.[11] The United States has never experienced another mass DEG poisoning event after 1937.

The rest of the world, especially countries in the developing world, have however experienced several DEG poisoning events: seven children died in South Africa in 1969[12], 47 children died in Nigeria in 1990[13] and another 84 children died in 2008[14], 236 children died in Bangladesh between 1990–92[15], 29 people died in Argentina in 1992, 88 children died in Haiti in 1996[16], and 365 people died in Panama in 2007[17].

India has the uniquely depressing record of having had at least 5 major DEG poisoning events. The first took place in Madras in 1972, killing 15 children after they consumed a cough syrup called Pipmol C that had been adulterated with DEG.[18] The second event took place in Mumbai in 1986 at the famous J.J. Hospital killing 14 patients after they consumed glycerin that had been adulterated with DEG.[19] The third mass DEG poisoning event took place in Bihar in 1988 killing 11 patients.[20] The fourth event took place in Gurgaon, a district neighbouring Delhi, in 1998 when 33 children between the ages of two months and six years died after consuming a cough syrup adulterated with DEG.[21] The event in Jammu in December, 2019 was therefore the fifth such mass-poisoning event in India.

In each of the above cases, the actual death toll is most certainly higher than what has been publicly reported. The reason for this discrepancy in reported numbers is the fact that DEG poisoning is difficult to diagnose. For example, the doctors probing the 33 deaths of children in Gurgaon, remarked in their study that: "At the beginning of the investigation we never imagined that contaminated medicine was causing acute renal failure in children."[22] Only when deaths take place in a cluster are doctors more likely to study common medications taken by all of the deceased and have them tested.

So, why does DEG adulteration recur with such frequency in India?

The simple answer is that Indian pharmaceutical companies quite often fail to test either the raw materials or the final formulation before shipping it to the market. This is despite Good Manufacturing Practices (GMP) as prescribed in Indian law requiring mandatory testing of both the raw material before it is used in production and the final formulation before it is shipped to the market. Such testing is required to ensure that the company has in fact received the correct solvent from the supplier and that it is of the correct purity. In many of these disasters, traders responsible for supplying chemicals such as propylene glycol have either mislabeled DEG as propylene glycol by mistake, or alternatively, have adulterated propylene glycol with DEG either on purpose to reduce costs or by mistake due to poor quality control measures.

In the case of the mass poisoning event in Jammu, the Himachal Pradesh Drug Control Administration (HPDCA) which has jurisdiction over the manufacturer of the alleged adulterated cough syrup—Digital Vision—alleged before the Himachal Pradesh High Court that Digital Vision lacked an appropriate facility to test the finished formulation for DEG contamination and that the analysis report from Digital Vision's quality control department indicating the absence of DEG in dangerous quantities was "misleading". Digital Vision itself has completely refuted all these allegations and has claimed that an independent laboratory as well as government laboratories concluded that its samples were of standard quality and not adulterated.[23]

If these allegations about the lack of an adequate testing facility are established to be true, it is necessary to question the HPDCA on its failure to notice such deep-rooted egregious violations during its previous inspections of Digital Vision's manufacturing facility. How could it have missed the lack of testing equipment in past inspections? Going by Digital Vision's past record, it is obvious that the HPDCA had multiple opportunities to inspect the firm's manufacturing facilities.

According to a government-maintained database called XLN, Digital Vision had been cited at least 13 times for violation of quality standards by just three state drug controllers in Maharashtra, Gujarat, and Kerala between 2012 and 2019 prior to the tragedy in Jammu, due to its drugs failing quality testing standards during random sampling and testing conducted by drug inspectors from those states.[24] The CDSCO's drug alerts, which report testing by central government laboratories, mention another five instances of Digital Vision's drugs failing quality testing in the years prior to the tragedy in Jammu.[25] An investigation by a journalist alleged that the company's drugs failed quality testing on 19 occasions in total![26] (Legally speaking, Digital Vision has a right to challenge the test reports from the state government laboratories before the Central Drug Laboratory, Kolkata, in case it is faced with a criminal prosecution for failing to meet the prescribed quality of standards but the XLN database does not display the results of possible testing before the CDL or whether the allegations of sub-standard drugs made by the drug inspectors have been proved in a court of law.)

Thus, by a conservative estimate, the HPDCA must have received at least 19 notices across a decade from other state drug controllers or its own drug inspectors informing it that Digital Vision's drugs had failed quality testing. This also meant that the HPDCA had 19 different opportunities to conduct inspections of Digital Vision's manufacturing facilities. In addition, the HPDCA would have also had to conduct yearly inspections of Digital Vision's facility as required by Rule 52 of the Drugs & Cosmetics Rules, 1945. Since the HPDCA, is not required to proactively publish reports of its inspections on its website, we simply do not know whether HPDCA ever inspected Digital Vision's facility on those 19 occasions. In an ideal scenario, the lack of quality control equipment to test for DEG poisoning at Digital Vision's facility, as alleged before the High Court, should have been spotted during these inspections, leading to an immediate cancellation of the company's manufacturing licence for failing to comply with GMP standards prescribed in the law. Why did that not happen? Did the drug inspectors look the other way due to political pressure? Or did the HPDCA not take any serious action because of good old-fashioned corruption? While there is no specific evidence of corruption in this case, the Indian press regularly reports about rampant corruption amongst drug inspectors.[27]

Separate and apart from the question of why exactly the drug regulatory system missed the warning signs at Digital Vision, is the response of the Indian state to the death of the 11 young children from Ramnagar. Historically, the Indian state responds to such incidents in one of two ways. The first is the criminal prosecution of the persons responsible for manufacturing and selling the adulterated drugs in question. This is a question of delivering justice to the deceased and their families. Shockingly, more than two years after the incident, Digital Vision is yet to be prosecuted for reasons that are not entirely clear.[28] It appears that nobody will be held accountable for the deaths of those 11 children from Ramnagar.

The second response by the State should ideally involve the commissioning of a broader investigation into the failure of the regulator and the shortcomings in the law, so that policy can be reformed in order to prevent a similar tragedy in the future. Unfortunately, neither the state government nor the central government thought it necessary to commission a deeper investigation into the regulatory failure that led to the fifth mass death event due to DEG poisoning in the history of independent India. It is not like there was no such demand for an investigation. In August 2020, one of us petitioned the Minister of Health, requesting the Ministry to conduct a transparent investigation into the entire incident.[29] The Minister did not even bother acknowledging the petition, let alone act on it.

We then followed up with a request for information under the RTI Act, asking the Ministry of Health whether it had conducted any investigation into the regulatory failures that led to the deaths of those 11 children.[30] The Ministry did not bother answering the question. It preferred to simply transfer the request for information to the Central Drug Standards Control Organisation (CDSCO) which is India's national drug regulator. The CDSCO in turn transferred the blame for the entire issue to the state drug controller on the grounds that it was the latter's responsibility to regulate Digital Vision.[31] Technically speaking, it was not an incorrect response but it is also a fact that only the Ministry of Health can initiate any amendment to the Drugs and Cosmetics Act 1940, and the rules therein. State governments cannot affect policy changes at the national level. Under India's convoluted drug regulatory law, the Government of India is responsible for imports and approving new drugs based on safety and efficacy data but the licensing of manufacturing units and prosecutions of pharmaceutical companies is primarily the responsibility of the state governments. Thus, for a policy reform exercise to be undertaken, the Ministry of Health needed to understand what exactly went wrong in this case from a regulatory perspective. The Ministry, however, was not interested in getting to the bottom of the issue. There can be no cure without a diagnosis.

Governance in India has not always been this incompetent. Back in 1986, after the deaths of 14 patients at the J.J. Hospital in Mumbai due to DEG poisoning, the Chief Minister of Maharashtra appointed Justice Lentin, a sitting judge of the Bombay High Court, to head a Commission of Inquiry into the events leading to the deaths of the 14 patients. The resulting report of this Commission of Inquiry is the stuff of legend.

To begin with, Justice Lentin held rigorous, marathon hearings in an open courtroom, something that is seldom seen today. Justifying the need for holding a public inquiry, Justice Lentin wrote:

> Secrecy breeds suspicion, and suspicion breeds contempt. A public inquiry would therefore ensure public confidence in the work of the commission to arrive at the truth without fear or favour, regardless of power, position, influence and importance of witnesses.[32]

In less than a year, Justice Lentin produced a report that ran into 300 pages, holding a powerful Joint Commissioner of the Maharashtra Food & Drug Administration (FDA) and even the Health Minister of the State of Maharashtra accountable for a dysfunctional regulatory system that created the environment for the tragedy at J.J. Hospital. The foreword to his scathing report was as follows:

> These pages describe and illustrate the ugly facets of the human mind and human nature, projecting errors of judgment, misuse of ministerial power and authority, apathy towards human life, corruption, nexus and quid pro quo between unscrupulous license holders, analytical laboratories, elements in the Industries department controlling the awarding of rate contracts, manufacturers, traders, merchants, suppliers, the FDA and persons holding ministerial rank. None of this will be palatable in the affected quarters. But that cannot be helped.[33]

In the pages that followed, Justice Lentin laid out reams of evidence painting a figure of an utterly broken system of drug regulation within the State of Maharashtra. Since Justice Lentin had held public hearings, the proceedings and the final report received widespread media coverage, thereby focusing public attention on the issue.

Documenting what it described as "amazing facts" dug out by Justice Lentin, the *India Today* news magazine described the manner in which the Maharashtra FDA failed to take action against the 582 formulations that were found to be substandard in the year 1986, the fact that 250 drug manufacturing units in Maharashtra were operating without any analytical laboratories, the manner in which Health Ministers regularly intervened to prevent honest bureaucrats at the State FDA from prosecuting erring pharmaceutical companies; evidence of doctors at J.J. Hospital and Ministers receiving money from pharmaceutical companies and finally, concrete evidence on how family members of S.M. Dolas—the powerful Joint Commissioner of the Maharashtra FDA responsible for much of drug regulation in Maharashtra—acquired a stake in pharmaceutical companies in Maharashtra.[34]

Summarizing the commission's report, *India Today* concluded:

> The commission's investigations have uncovered the horrifying spectacle of a watchdog health agency totally surrendering

> to the manipulations of people like Dolas. ...And the FDA has continued its lawless reign even after agencies from other states like Gujarat and Tamil Nadu complained about the quality of drugs emanating from the FDA's fiefdom.

Daily newspapers like the *Indian Express*, the *Times of India* and the *Sunday Observer* were the ones that maintained constant pressure on the government to act on the findings of the report. These newspapers published reports under the following headlines: "FDA still shielding guilty", "Name of game is favouritism", "Of ministerial incompetence, graft and neglect", "Labs hand-in-glove with FDA", "Sinister gangs of merchants of death", "Proxy payment behind glycerol contract", "Never before such lies", "Criminal silence".[35]

The media pressure worked and Bhai Sawant, the Health Minister of the State of Maharashtra, resigned from the state cabinet on March 10, 1988. The State Government suspended senior doctors of J.J. Hospital and three officials from the state FDA, including the powerful Joint Commissioner S.M. Dolas who was severely indicted by Justice Lentin. The State Government also endorsed most of the points made in the Commission's report.[36]

Recognizing the monumental work done by Justice Lentin, one doctor called upon the medical profession to "build upon Justice Lentin's labours" and "convince politicians and bureaucrats that the recommendations made by the learned judge can be neglected only at our peril".[37] Unfortunately, those lessons from 1988 were never learnt by the Indian drug regulatory framework at the national level as evident from the deaths of 33 children in Gurgaon in 1998 and the deaths of the 11 children from Ramnagar in 2019 due to the scrouge of DEG poisoning.

It is, however, also important to understand that the problem with Indian drug regulatory framework is not limited to corruption, as was the focus of the Lentin Commission in

1988. There is also the question of poor regulatory design. These range from the lack of regulatory transparency to the absurdly complex distribution of regulatory powers in India across 38 authorities spread across each state and union territory plus the CDSCO which works under the Union Government. For example, inspection reports of pharmaceutical facilities are not made publicly available without which there is no way to assess whether drug inspectors are actually doing their job as required. On the jurisdictional issue, since each state and union territory has its own drug controller who issues licences to manufacturing facilities, there is often little information sharing and coordination amongst them. Further, inter-state investigations are extremely difficult because a drug inspector working for the Maharashtra FDA lacks jurisdiction to enter and inspect Digital Vision's facility in Himachal Pradesh unless accompanied by a drug inspector from the HPDCA. The HPDCA, however, has its own reasons to not permit such inspections, the most important of which is the fact that the state government wants to continue pitching the state as a hub for pharmaceutical manufacturing. Together, these various flaws cause catastrophes like the deaths of these 11 young children.

For a country like India, which has earned itself the moniker of being "the developing world's pharmacy", such regulatory failures impact not just Indian citizens but also the citizens of all its trading partners. This makes it all the more necessary to revamp regulation governing the Indian pharmaceutical industry but as we will explain in the rest of this book, the Government of India is more interested in propping up the Indian pharmaceutical industry—the only manufacturing success story for India to showcase on the global stage—and towards this end, it will always resist tightening the regulatory screws.

We began this book with the DEG poisoning cases in

order to highlight the worst possible consequences of the lackadaisical, if not negligent approach of the Ministry of Health, the CDSCO, and HPDCA, all of whom were more interested in protecting themselves than the citizens of this country. However, what worries us more than this particular incident are the consequences of regulatory lethargy on the more mundane aspects of drug regulation; where although regulatory failure may not directly lead to deaths, it could still lead to a significant adverse impact on public health in a manner where it is difficult to draw direct connection between poor regulation and its consequences. Take for example, the approval of dubious new drugs with little to no evidence to justify the therapeutic claims made by the manufacturer, the refusal to upgrade regulations for generic drugs to guarantee therapeutic equivalence with the innovator drug, or the manner in which drug inspectors try to work around the law to avoid prosecutions of erring pharmaceutical companies. These are issues that do not necessarily lead to deaths but contribute in the long term to poor outcomes for public health.

The primary challenge in discussing many of these regulatory issues is that drug regulation as a policy issue lies at the intersection of regulatory science and public law, two areas that are not exactly popular amongst the common citizenry or politicians.

The secondary challenge is the difficulty in measuring and explaining the harm caused to patients due to poor regulatory policies and ineffective practices. The consequences of an inadequate scheme of drug regulation are much like climate change—not everybody can see the linkages in real time; its consequences cannot be easily measured, but it is most definitely causing harm to public health. In this book, we take a stab at explaining some of these crucial regulatory issues in a prose that is hopefully palatable to the ordinary consumer of 'Made in India' medicine.

Notes

1. Deepanker Gupta, '6 infants die due to unknown illness' *The Tribune* (16 January 2020) <https://www.tribuneindia.com/news/j-k/6-infants-die-due-to-unknown-illness-27436> accessed 28 May 2021; Prabha Raghavan and Arun Sharma, 'Behind killer cough syrup Coldbest: Glaring gaps in regulation and its manufacture' *The Indian Express* (12 March 2020) <https://indianexpress.com/article/india/behind-killer-cough-syrup-glaring-gaps-in-regulation-and-its-manufacture-6310065/> accessed 28 May 2021.
2. 'Central team to probe kids' death', *The Tribune* (18 January 2020) <https://www.tribuneindia.com/news/j-k/central-team-to-probe-kids%E2%80%99-death-28309> accessed 28 May 2021.
3. Press Trust of India, '10 Children Die Of "Mysterious Disease" In J&K's Udhampur, Say Officials', *NDTV* (18 January 2020) <https://www.ndtv.com/india-news/10-children-die-of-mysterious-disease-in-jammu-and-kashmirs-udhampur-say-officials-2166041> accessed 28 May 2021.
4. CDSCO Drug Alerts for March 2020: https://cdsco.gov.in/opencms/opencms/en/Notifications/Alerts/
5. HT Correspondents, 'HP pharma unit booked for infants' death due to contaminated syrup', *Hindustan Times* (3 March 2020) <https://www.hindustantimes.com/cities/hp-pharma-unit-booked-for-infants-death-due-to-contaminated-syrup/story-K02StB2Byi2OupRrT2CVTI.html> accessed on 28 May 2021.
6. Alan D Woolf, 'The Haitian Diethylene Glycol Poisoning Tragedy: A Dark Wood Revisited' (1998) 279 *Journal of the American Medical Association* 1215.
7. Arun Sharma, "Killer chemical" in cough syrup: Udhampur parents got medicine from local chemist', *The Indian Express* (26 February 2020) < https://indianexpress.com/article/india/jammu-cough-syrup-children-death-digital-vision-local-chemist-6286929/> accessed 28 May 2021. Replies from PGIMER to RTI Application No. APC/2021/550 dated 23.06.2021.
8. ibid.
9. William Rosen, *Miracle Cure: The Creation of Antibiotics and the Birth of Modern* (Penguin 2017) 76.
10. ibid 75.
11. Peter Barton Hutt, 'Drug Regulation in The United States' (1986) 2 Intl J of Technology Assessment in Health Care 619, 621.
12. Paul M Wax, 'It's Happening Again-Another Diethylene Glycol Mass Poisoning' (1996) 34 Clinical Toxicology 517.

13. HO Okuonghae and others, 'Diethylene Glycol Poisoning in Nigerian Children' (1992) 12 Annals of Tropical Pediatrics 235.
14. Lydia Polgreen, '84 Children Are Killed by Medicine in Nigeria', *The New York Times* (6 February 2009) <https://www.nytimes.com/2009/02/07/world/africa/07nigeria.html> accessed 28 May 2021.
15. Mohammed Hanif and others, 'Fatal renal failure caused by diethylene glycol in paracetamol elixir: the Bangladesh epidemic' (1995) 311 *BMJ* 88.
16. Woolf (n 6).
17. Walt Bogdanich and Jake Hooker, 'From China to Panama, a Trail of Poisoned Medicine' *The New York Times* (6 May 2007) <https://www.nytimes.com/2007/05/06/world/americas/06poison.html> accessed 28 May 2021.
18. V.R. Ravi Kumar, 'When a Drug Turned Killer' *The Hindu* (9 February 2020) <https://www.thehindu.com/opinion/open-page/when-a-drug-turned-killer/article30770710.ece> accessed 28 May 2021.
19. M. Rahman, 'Investigation exposes corruption in drug control in Bombay', *India Today* (31 August 1987) <https://www.indiatoday.in/magazine/living/story/19870831-investigation-exposes-corruption-in-drug-control-in-bombay-799245-1987-08-31> accessed 28 May 2021.
20. Salil Tripathi, 'Justice Lentin Commission report indicts Maharashtra public health administration', *India Today* (30 April 1988) <https://www.indiatoday.in/magazine/indiascope/story/19880430-justice-lentin-commission-report-indicts-maharashtra-public-health-administration-797183-1988-04-30> accessed 28 May 2021.
21. Jagvir Singh and others, 'Diethylene glycol poisoning in Gurgaon, India, 1998' (2001) 79 Bull World Health Organ 88.
22. ibid 92.
23. *M/S Digital Vision vs State of Himachal Pradesh And Others* CWP No.2572 of 2020 before the High Court of Himachal Pradesh (14 August 2020) [para 4(ii)(b)] <https://indiankanoon.org/doc/115798745/> accessed 30 May 2021. (The judgment makes the following observation pending the completion of an investigation and trial: "The Certificate of Analysis dated 23.09.2019 of Quality Control Department of the petitioner in respect to finished product COLDBEST-PC Syrup certified this product to be of standard quality and compliant of Ethylene Glycol and Diethylene Glycol norms. However, admittedly the petitioner-firm does not possess the testing facility for checking its drugs formulations

for presence of adulterant DEG. Therefore, analysis reports of petitioner's Quality Control Department with respect to COLDBEST-PC Syrup cannot be relied upon. Same goes for test reports of petitioner's Quality Control Department with respect to analysis of sample of PG. It cannot be said to have been tested for presence of poisonous adulterant DEG in absence of such testing facility available with the petitioner.")

24. 'XLN—Xtended Licensing, Laboratory & Legal Node' <https://xlnindia.gov.in/> accessed 30 May 2021.
25. CDSCO Drug Alerts for June, 2014; January, 2017; September, 2018; March, 2019; December, 2019; March, 2020.
26. Priyanka Pulla, 'How weak drug laws are costing lives', *Mint* (27 September 2021) < https://www.livemint.com/politics/policy/how-weak-drug-laws-are-costing-lives-11632761831130.html> accessed 29 September, 2021.
27. Divya Rajagopal, 'CBI Arrests Deputy Drug Controller over Graft Charges', *The Economic Times* (18 August 2019) <https://economictimes.indiatimes.com/news/politics-and-nation/cbi-arrests-deputy-drug-controller-over-graft-charges/articleshow/70728107.cms> accessed 30 May 2021; TNN, 'Drug Inspector's Rs 1 Lakh Diwali "Gift" Lands Her in ACB Trap', *The Times of India* (Hyderabad, 13 October 2019) <https://timesofindia.indiatimes.com/city/hyderabad/drug-inspectors-rs-1l-diwali-gift-lands-her-in-acb-trap/articleshow/71560435.cms> accessed 30 May 2021; Press Trust of India, 'Drug Inspector with His Peon Caught Accepting Rs 60,000 Bribe', *Business Standard* (29 November 2018) <https://www.business-standard.com/article/pti-stories/drug-inspector-with-his-peon-caught-accepting-rs-60-000-bribe-118112901153_1.html> accessed 30 May 2021; Press Trust of India, 'Drug Inspector Caught Taking Bribe in District Collectorate', *India Today* (Muzaffarnagar, 27 January 2017) <https://www.indiatoday.in/pti-feed/story/drug-inspector-caught-taking-bribe-in-district-collectorate-864487-2017-01-27> accessed 30 May 2021; Khomba Singh, 'Dogged with Corruption, Drug Regulation Is in Poor Health and Ineffective' *The Economic Times* (10 July 2012) <https://economictimes.indiatimes.com/industry/healthcare/biotech/pharmaceuticals/dogged-with-corruption-drug-regulation-is-in-poor-health-and-ineffective/articleshow/14790795.cms?from=mdr> accessed 30 May 2021.
28. Priyanka Pulla, 'How the regulator failed to bring killer cough syrup maker to task', *Mint* (5 April, 2022) https://www.livemint.com/science/hp-regulator-yet-to-bring-maker-of-killer-cough-syrup-to-book-11649095840263.html accessed 12 April, 2022.

29. Petition requesting transparency in the investigation and recall of DEG contaminated cough syrup that has killed 12 children from Dinesh Thakur to Union Minister of Health, Government of India, August 29, 2020 <https://casemindia.org/wp-content/uploads/2020/08/Recall-Petition-For-Coldbest-Final.pdf> accessed on September 23, 2021.
30. Reply to RTI appliction dated 1 June 2021, Ministry of Health. (Application no. MOHFW/R/T/21/02075, 1 June 2021) .
31. Reply to RTI application, dated 6 July 2021, CDSCO (Application no. CDSCO/ R/T/21/00410, 1 June 2021).
32. Justice B. Lentin, *Report of the Commission of Inquiry (Re. Deaths of Patients in J. J. Hospital at Bombay in January-February 1986 due to alleged reaction of drugs)* (1988) v.
33. ibid iii.
34. Rahman (n 19).
35. Sunil K Pandya, 'Letter from Bombay: An Unmitigated Tragedy' (1988) 297 *BMJ* 117.
36. ibid.
37. Sunil K Pandya, 'Medicine and Society: A Review of the Lentin Commission Report on the Glycerol Tragedy at the J.J. Hospital, Bombay' (1988) 1 *The National Medical Journal of India*, 144.

CHAPTER ONE

The Birth of Modern Medicine and Drug Regulation

Until the 19th century, the theory and practice of medicine, whether in the East or the West, was based on theories propounded more than 2,000 years ago. Western medicine was based mostly on the humoral theory. This theory, attributed to Hippocrates (approx. 4th BCE to 3rd BCE) and widely popularized by Galen (129–210 AD)[1] theorized that all illness in humans was caused due to an imbalance of the four main humors in the human body—black bile, yellow bile, phlegm, and blood, each of which were individually associated with four elements—earth, fire, water, and air.[2] For example, local inflammations in any part of the body were presumed to be caused by excess blood and hence the remedy of "blood-letting", where the presumed "excess" blood was drained from the body through "medical intervention" in an effort to restore the humoral balance.[3]

At the time, there was a limited understanding of human anatomy because of cultural and legal restrictions against the dissection of human bodies.[4] Later, French doctors like Giovanni Battusta Morgagni and Xavier Bichat began conducting autopsies identifying specific organs and tissues affected by disease. This vastly improved the depth of knowledge about the functioning of the human body. However, despite these advances, there was little scientific consensus in the West on the cause and nature of diseases.[5]

Even in the early 19th century, when Europe was facing outbreaks of cholera, the prevailing theory about the cause of the disease was the primitive Miasma theory. It attributed the spread of diseases like cholera to the inhalation of noxious forms of "bad air", especially the air polluted by decomposing matter.[6] This conclusion was possibly influenced by the observation that epidemics and the plague tended to occur during hot summer months in European cities which had rotting garbage and waste. Maintaining cleanliness and avoiding "bad air" was seen as key to avoiding illnesses.[7]

In the East, where Ayurveda was one of the prevalent medicinal systems in the Indian sub-continent over several centuries, the main underlying theory was that of tri-doshas. The three doshas—vata, pita, and kapha—are presumed to be the energy centers of the human body. One interpretation presumes each dosha to draw its energy from a combination of the elements that constitute the pancha bhoota—space, air, water, fire, and earth.[8] Another interpretation presumes vata to be wind, pitta to be bile, and kapha to be phlegm.[9] These three doshas were presumed to be influenced by environmental factors, age, and food.[10] As with the humoral theory, an imbalance of doshas was presumed in Ayurveda, to be the cause of most illnesses. In fact, there are Ayurvedic practitioners who insist that Greek theory of humoral medicine was in fact inspired by Ayurveda. Some therapeutic strategies underlying Ayurveda are similar to ancient Greek medicine and include enemas, blood-letting, emesis, purgation, and nasal purging as means to restore the balance.[11]

Needless to say, ancient medicine, whether in the East or the West, was not particularly effective in curing humans of painful diseases.

The birth of the cell theory and germ theory

The theory of medicine was finally transformed only in the late 19th century, less than 200 years ago, when pioneering research by European scientists laid the foundations of the "Cell Theory" and the "Germ Theory of Disease".

While the discovery and naming of "cells" per se is attributed to English scientist Robert Hooke who described 'cells' in 1665 in his book *Micrographia,*[12] the "Cell Theory" by itself owes its existence to German scientists Mathias Schleiden and Theodor Schwann, who in the 1830s proposed that cells were the basic constituent building blocks for all plants and animals. The theory contributed to the understanding that all diseases were caused by an alteration of cells in organisms.[13]

The ultimate breakthrough which revolutionized medical science was the conception of the "Germ Theory". This theory postulated that diseases were caused by bacteria, many of them present in the air as proved by Louis Pasteur through his experiments. After being called upon to investigate an outbreak of an infectious disease in the silk industry, he was able to identify two microorganisms that were causing the disease. This led him to believe that microorganisms could cause disease and for that era, this was a revolutionary theory.[14]

Soon thereafter, the German scientist, Robert Koch, was able to prove in a scientifically rigorous manner the infectious nature of disease-causing bacteria in living organisms. He first infected lab mice with fluids extracted from the spleen of cows and sheep that had died of anthrax poisoning. When the mice contracted the disease, he had proof that something in the blood of the dead animals was carrying the disease. He then managed to isolate and purify the element from the blood, by culturing it and injecting it into healthy animals leading them to contract the disease thereby proving the link between a specific pathogen and a particular disease.[15] This experimental research by Koch firmly established the "Germ Theory" and led to him laying down what are known as "Koch's postulates" to establish whether a disease was in fact caused by microorganisms. In the years that followed,

Koch identified the specific bacteria responsible for causing tuberculosis (tubercle bacillus) in 1882 and cholera in 1884, thereby transforming scientific understanding of these diseases which had claimed a large number of lives in Europe and the rest of the world.[16] These breakthroughs would change the way mankind searched for possible cures.

The birth of modern medicine

Historically, various civilizations across the earth have been known to experiment with plants and herbs to find cures for diseases and other medical conditions. Many of these civilizations documented in various herbal pharmacopeia, the herbs and plants that had the potential to cure various diseases. In ancient Greece, Dioscorides wrote a treatise called *De material medica*, in which he compiled a list of plants with medical properties that were discovered in the past and through his own research. Ancient Rome had a similar text called *Natural History*, written by Pliny, which compiled an extensive list of herbal and other natural remedies. The Chinese too had several herbal pharmacopeias. The earliest of which, called *Shen-Nung Pen T'sao Ching*, published during the time of the Han dynasty in the 2nd century CE, listed over 365 herbal medicines.[17] Similarly, India has ancient Ayurvedic texts which list the potential medicinal properties of certain herbs and plants.[18]

Humanity's eternal search for medical cures changed in the 19th century after the "Germ Theory" led to breakthroughs in the understanding of disease-causing bacteria, as well as advances in understanding the functioning of the human immune system. These theoretical breakthroughs combined with other scientific breakthroughs by German chemists opened a new door beyond just plants and herbs in the search for new cures. This new world of medical research evolved into two different branches of science—biologicals and chemicals.

In the 19th century, biologicals consisted of only vaccines, which could prevent infections and anti-sera which could for the first-time cure otherwise life-threatening diseases. Until the discovery of the "Germ Theory", the only vaccine that existed was Edward Jenner's smallpox vaccine which he had developed in 1796 by inoculating a child with material taken from a cowpox sore on the hand of a milkmaid. Prior to Jenner's vaccine, there existed a practice called variolation which was used widely across the world, which involved infecting people with small quantities of the smallpox virus, a process which worked to confer immunity on the recipient but was dangerous, often leading to deaths.[19] These were medical innovations that resulted from the powers of observation and correlation without a deep understanding of the science of causation. However, a better understanding of infections and human immunology helped scientists like Pasteur to lead the way in creating a new line of vaccines.

The first of these vaccines were developed in 1880 after Pasteur discovered that the virulence of a pathogen could decrease on its exposure to air or other elements and that injecting such weaker pathogens into healthy humans would stimulate a long-lasting immune response from the human body. Pasteur's theory was proved through his much-publicized experiment in which he administered on some animals a new anthrax vaccine that he had developed. Animals that he had inoculated with his vaccine survived anthrax infections while those in the control group that did not receive the vaccine were infected and perished. Soon Pasteur used the same theory to make the first rabies vaccine, which if administered soon after a dog bite could significantly reduce the chance of infection.[20]

Apart from the development of vaccines, there was also the development of the first antiserum that could cure diphtheria by Emil Behring and Kitasato Shibasaburo, both scientists at Koch's institute. They were able to demonstrate that animals infected with weakened diphtheria toxins were able to produce antibodies which when injected in an infected animal could neutralize the diphtheria toxins in the latter. The first antiserum for diphtheria, cultured in horses and then administered on humans, was an exceptional medical success story. A clinical trial in 1894 with this antiserum on 220 children suffering from diphtheria demonstrated a 77% cure rate. These were extraordinary test results for a disease which at the time was called the "strangling angel" in Europe because of the high toll it took on children and infants.[21] In 1901, Behring was awarded the first ever Nobel Prize in Physiology for his work on the diphtheria and tetanus antiserum.

A second new source of medicines that was tapped into by the Germans were chemicals and dyes. In the 19th century, Germany was a world leader in chemicals and dyes. This was due to a superbly rigorous higher educational system that produced highly skilled chemists.[22] It was these skilled German chemists who were first able to isolate pure chemical ingredients, also known as the "active ingredient", from herbs and plants. For example, morphine was isolated from opium in 1803 and used as a painkiller while quinine was isolated from the bark of the cinchona tree in 1820 and used to treat fevers, especially those caused by malaria.[23] Isolating the active chemical ingredient had enormous advantages since it meant that it would be possible to standardize doses depending on the severity of the medical problem, the physical characteristics of the patient, and also help devise means to stabilize the medicine in a manner that allowed for it to be stored for longer periods of time.

More importantly, German scientists began studying chemicals as a source of new medicines. They turned to chemicals as a source of new medicine because during the course of experiments, German scientists noticed that many synthetic chemicals being produced by Germany's booming chemical industry could have potential medical applications. They came to this realization when they noticed that different cells and tissues of the human body had affinities for different chemicals. This technique of visualizing different cells and tissues through the use of chemicals came to be known as "staining" and led to the development of a new field called "histology" which was crucial to developing diagnostic tools in medicine. One of the key figures in the development of "staining" techniques was the future Nobel Laureate Paul Ehrlich who was able to develop staining techniques to visualize red and white blood cells in leukemia and anemia. He also developed the diazo colour reaction to identify the presence of bilirubin in the urine of patients with jaundice.[24]

Ehrlich's understanding of the chemical interactions between chemical dyes and human cells led to future breakthroughs in the search for new medicines.[25] It was correctly hypothesized at the time that if specific chemicals interacted in particular ways with cells and tissues, these chemicals could also be a source of new medicines for various infections and medical conditions by interfering with disease-causing bacteria. Proving this hypothesis meant testing hundreds of chemicals to identify the ones with potential curative properties. This was an expensive proposition because it involved a "trial and error" approach and success was never guaranteed.

Securing funding for such research was not an easy task because of which the latter half of the 19th century was witness to a new funding model for scientists engaged in the search for new drugs. This new model involved German scientists entering into agreements with German chemical corporations, where the latter would fund research and provide their chemical "library" to scientists, in exchange for the intellectual property rights in the resulting inventions. As one commentator put it, "...the most significant innovation of the great German biochemical revolution was neither drugs not vaccines themselves but the creation of a durable funding source for ongoing lab research."[26]

The funding model and the decision to tap into chemicals and dyestuffs proved to be very fruitful. By the end of the 19th century, the biggest German chemical corporations like Hoescht, Bayer, and BASF had introduced to the market the first analgesics and antipyretics such as Aspirin, Kairin, Phenacetin, Antipyrine, Antifebrin etc.[27] By 1910, Paul Ehrlich had discovered arsphenamine, the first real antibiotic and "miracle cure". Known internally in Ehrlich's laboratory as Compound 606, the drug which was developed with support from Cassella, a German company, was eventually sold under the brand name "Salvasaran" by Hoescht, another Germany chemical company.[28] It was found to be highly effective against syphilis, a sexually transmitted disease that was highly contagious and deadly. The disease affected millions across Europe. Needless to say, the drug was a huge commercial success. It presumably made Hoechst AG significant profits and laid the foundations for the modern pharmaceutical industry to pour resources into the discovery of new drugs in exchange for patent rights.

In 1932, a different set of German scientists, led by future Nobel Laurate Gerhard Domagk, and supported by Bayer, followed Ehrlich's approach of testing thousands of chemicals on disease-infected mice before discovering the effectiveness of a specific variant of sulfanilamide. The new drug demonstrated astounding curative effects on laboratory mice that were infected with streptococci, which is a type of bacteria that causes many life-threatening infections in humans. It was soon discovered that this new drug could also cure a number of non-strep infections such as spinal meningitis, gonorrhea, and childbed fever, all of which were caused by different kinds of disease-causing bacteria. This new "wonder drug" was first marketed as Protonsil by Bayer and proved to be a true blockbuster.[29]

Given all these medical breakthroughs, it was no surprise that Germany soon came to be known as the "pharmacy of the world".[30]

This era of medical breakthroughs laid the foundations for the modern pharmaceutical industry and drug innovation. The challenge now for governments across the world was to ensure the consistent supply of quality drugs while keeping in check the fantastical claims being made by the pharmaceutical industry about their new inventions. This was easier said than done given the fact that many of these pharmaceutical corporations grew rapidly to become very profitable and powerful. Older models of self-regulation had to give way to a more direct intervention by the state.

The nation state steps in to regulate the science of drugs

Historically, in most societies, medicine was formulated by individual apothecaries or pharmacists or *vaids* or *hakims* as they were known in different jurisdictions. These solo practitioners would usually prepare various concoctions from mainly herbs, and sometimes alcohol, which was the common solvent available to extract the "active ingredients" from the herbs. The ingredients of these concoctions would only rarely be disclosed to the public. State regulation of these drugs was limited in the 19th century. For example, in the United Kingdom, the state did not directly regulate the quality of drugs. Rather it enacted legislation such as the Apothecaries Act 1815, or the Pharmacy Act 1868, which vested the right to manufacture certain specific drugs in apothecaries and pharmacies, who in turn would regulate themselves through their professional guilds or societies.[31] The other form of regulation was via penal laws which prohibited the adulteration of drugs. For example, the Indian Penal Code 1860, which was enacted by the British after the Crown took over the administration of India from the East India Company had a specific clause penalizing the adulteration of food and drugs.[32]

These prevalent models of regulation evolved with the discovery of new and effective therapies. Once mass manufacture of these new drugs began, it was necessary to create a new regulatory model especially since biologicals like vaccines and anti-sera were injected directly into the bodies of human beings. Even slight contamination during the manufacturing process could be fatal for the patient. Germany led the way in creating a new regulatory model. A key inspiration for the proactiveness of the German government was the "tuberculin" scandal in the preceding decade where Robert Koch's much anticipated new treatment—tuberculin—for treating tuberculosis failed to prove effective in curing the disease.[33] Eager to ensure the availability of high-quality anti-diphtheria serum, imperial Germany proactively put in place a new regulatory system in 1895 to ensure quality control of serum.

There were two components to the new German regulatory model created specifically for anti-diphtheria serum. The first was the creation of legally binding standards to ensure the potency and purity of the serums meant for use as treatments on humans. This was the first-time standards were being created for serums and it was a complex task. It had to begin with the very basic task of creating units to measure serum. Once standards were created and included in the legally recognized pharmacopeia, they were made binding on all future manufacturers. The ultimate aim of creating standards was to ensure consistency in the purity and potency of anti-diphtheria serum across the industry.

Adherence to these standards by manufacturers was then monitored at two sites. The first was at the site of production where an officer appointed by the state monitored the production process, and the second was at the state-run Institute for Serological Research and Serological Survey

(ISRSS), which functioned under the leadership of Paul Ehlrich, where each batch would be tested by a team of experts for adherence to quality standards.[34] This would include testing the serum on infected guinea pigs. If the serum was potent, it would only show a mild reaction at the spot where it was injected. If not, the guinea pig would die in four days.[35] By the standards of the day, this was a remarkably rigorous regulatory set-up.

Like the Germans, the French took a proactive approach to regulating these new anti-sera. The French enacted a legislation in 1895, covering a whole range of biologicals including any "...attenuated viruses, therapeutic sera, modified toxins and analogous products that can serve as prophylaxis against or therapy for contagious diseases..." All such products would require prior authorization from the Ministry of Interior, which relied on inputs from members of the Academy of Sciences and a Consultative Committee on Public Health.[36]

Both the German and French regulatory models were pathbreaking because they ensured perhaps for the first time in history, an assurance from the state regarding the quality of a drug that was being supplied to patients. Not only did this relieve pharmacists of their traditional job of guaranteeing quality but it also acted to boost public confidence in these new therapies.[37]

Not all countries were as proactive as the Germans and the French when it came to regulating these exciting new drugs. An interesting contrast to the proactive regulatory approach of the German and French, is the American approach to regulation. Till 1962, the American attempt to regulate the pharmaceutical industry has generally been on the heels of death and scandal. The first mass deaths due to contaminated vaccines and anti-sera occurred in the United States in the year 1901. In the first case, anti-diphtheria serum, which was unknowingly contaminated with tetanus, caused the death of

13 children in St Louis, Missouri. The horse that had been bled for the serum had a tetanus infection and was killed on discovery of the infection but the vials of serum drawn from the infected horse had not been destroyed or tested on guinea pigs. When administered on children, the anti-diphtheria serum infected them with tetanus causing their deaths. These deaths received a lot of publicity in the national press. As a result, there was a drop in confidence in this new treatment leading to an increase in deaths due to diphtheria in some cities. In that same year, there were 11 deaths in Camden, New Jersey, of people who recently received small pox vaccinations. They had died of tetanus infections and it was suspected that some of the vaccines were contaminated.[38]

These deaths in St Louis and Camden were the first instances of mass deaths from mass manufactured drugs and served as a reminder that these new life-saving and disease-preventing biologicals could be dangerous if not manufactured and tested properly in completely sterilized premises. The United States at the time did not regulate biologicals. These deaths, along with other cases of bacterial contamination of biological products, led to American doctors and the press demanding some form of regulation of biological products. The very next year, in 1902, the American Congress enacted into law the Biologics Control Act 1902, with an intent to guarantee the safety and efficacy of new biologics.

While most commentators view the Biologics Control Act as a reaction to the deaths in St Louis and Camden, there are academics who argue otherwise, stating that it was the biologics industry that pushed for the legislation. As per this theory, the privately owned pharmaceutical industry was worried that any more incidents of contaminations and death would cause various state and municipal governments in America to expand their existing manufacturing facilities for biologicals in order to better control quality of the biologicals available in their jurisdictions. Unlike today, America in the early 19th century had a public sector manufacturing biologicals. If that manufacturing process expanded further, it would reduce the private sector's market share. Better regulation was thus in the interest of the private sector, since it would check the "bad players" in the private sector and protect the reputation of the private sector.[39]

While the enactment of the Biologics Control Act 1902, brought regulation to the American pharmaceutical industry, it was limited to only "biologicals" i.e., viruses, therapeutic serums, toxins etc. This law did not cover other drugs, such as the newly available anti-pyretic drugs or even the first antibiotics, which were derived from industrial chemicals and dyestuff. The rest of these drugs came to be regulated by another American law called the Pure Food and Drugs Act 1906. This legislation was enacted after being kept pending for 27 years and after muck-raking journalists like Samuel Hopkins Adam and Upton Sinclair shone light on the fraudulent claims by the "patent medicine" industry and the meat-packing industry.[40] This new law was focused on issues such as mandating proper disclosure of ingredients on labelling of drugs (in order to combat the secrecy of 'patent medicine'), as well as prohibiting the adulteration and misbranding of drugs with "false claims". The Pure Food and Drugs Act did not focus on either "safety" or "efficacy" of new drugs.

The shortcomings of the model of regulation under the Pure Food and Drugs Act 1906 for non-biological drugs made itself obvious in 1937 when an American drug manufacturer sold sulfanilamide in a liquid form after dissolving it in diethylene glycol, without realizing the dangerous side-effects of diethylene glycol on humans. This mistake caused the deaths of more than 100 Americans when they drank the poisoned syrup. The tragedy invited a swift legislative response from the American Congress in the form of the Food, Drug and Cosmetic Act

1938, which amended the existing drug regulatory law to make it mandatory for manufacturers to submit safety data to the United States Food and Drug Administration (USFDA) before they could sell new drugs in America.[41]

Four years after the sulfanilamide disaster in 1941, tragedy struck once again, this time due to poor manufacturing practices within the American pharmaceutical industry. A batch of sulfathiazole tablets had been contaminated with a sedative called phenobarbital at a manufacturing plant owned by Winthrop, leading to over 300 deaths in the United States.[42] The episode led to the birth of modern Good Manufacturing Practices (GMPs) in the United States. As therapies and the pharmaceutical supply chain got more complex, the formulation and enforcement of GMPs by the state became even more crucial. For example, a key concern across the board, especially with injectables has been the challenge of maintaining sterility of all ingredients, including water. Even minor microbiological contamination can lead to serious infections. Given these challenges, GMP regulations have become progressively more detailed with almost every aspect of manufacturing and record-keeping covered by these regulations.

Across the Atlantic, European countries who did not learn from the American reforms of 1938 were about to face one of the most shocking tragedies in the history of the pharmaceutical industry because of a new drug called thalidomide. Initially marketed as a tranquilizer, thalidomide was also being prescribed to pregnant women in Europe as a remedy for morning sickness. Unknown to doctors at the time, the drug was teratogenic i.e., it had an adverse effect on the fetus, resulting in the birth of thousands of disabled babies in Europe in the late 50s and early 60s. In most cases, the limbs of the baby failed to develop properly while in some other cases, the eyes and ears were not developed properly. While the global toll of thalidomide is unknown, it is estimated Germany alone saw the birth of 10,000 babies affected by thalidomide.[43] There were also countless miscarriages across countries where pregnant women had been prescribed thalidomide. The United States on the other hand saw the birth of only 17 babies affected by thalidomide and even those births were because of the distribution of samples to doctors who had passed them on to their patients. This was because a heroic and diligent USFDA inspector, Frances Oldam Kelsey, had persistently rejected the marketing application filed by the manufacturers of thalidomide due to their failure to submit the safety data required by the amendments in 1938.[44]

Kelsey would go on to receive the President's Award for Distinguished Federal Civilian Service from American President J.F. Kennedy. She is considered to be one of the most significant personalities in the history of the USFDA, where she worked until the age of 91 years. On her passing at the age of 101 years, the *New York Times* in an obituary for her described her as a, "...20th-century American heroine for her role in the thalidomide case, celebrated not only for her vigilance, which spared the United States from widespread birth deformities, but also for giving rise to modern laws regulating pharmaceuticals."[45]

The silent heroes of the thalidomide episode were the policy makers who had amended American regulatory law in 1938 to mandate the submission of safety data as one of the conditions for approving new drugs in the United States. The episode was a stark reminder of the dangers of new medicines and the need to scientifically vet new drugs prior to their introduction in the market.

A new law and the demand for proof of "efficacy"

The timing of the thalidomide tragedy coincided with a scathing American Congressional inquiry into the workings of the American pharmaceutical industry. This inquiry which was held by the Senate Subcommittee on Anti-trust & Monopoly, from the years 1957 to 1961, was presided by Senator Estes Kefauver.[46]

By the time of this inquiry, the pharmaceutical industry had been transformed by a series of brilliant scientific discoveries. This included the discovery of a range of broad-spectrum antibiotics such as penicillin, ampicillin, streptomycin, neomycin, aureomycin, and erythromycin, all of which revolutionized medicine and slashed mortality rates from bacterial infections in less than a decade.[47] Apart from these antibiotics, scientists also discovered painkillers, anti-psychotropic drugs, hormonal therapies, and cardio-vascular drugs. Most of these discoveries were by private pharmaceutical corporations who were able to ringfence their inventions with patents and then market them under exclusive brand names. The resulting patent monopolies and the fantastical marketing claims quickly resulted in these pharmaceutical corporations becoming the most profitable businesses in America. The monopolistic nature of the pharmaceutical industry, the pricing of these drugs, and the manner in which they were marketed became the focus of the Senate anti-trust committee.

While investigating marketing practices of the pharmaceutical industry, the committee was particularly concerned with the issue of "efficacy" of new drugs given the wildly exaggerated claims being made by their manufacturers and their salesmen, often without scientific basis. The blitzkrieg of advertisements and marketing efforts assumed the form of visits to doctors by "detail men" (the terminology for sales persons employed by the pharmaceutical industry), mailing of brochures and samples, advertisements in medical journals, and exhibits at marketing conference.[48] The challenge for American doctors at the receiving end of these advertisements was to determine for themselves the claims of efficacy of these advertisements.

As explained by a Dr Weinstein who deposed before the Committee:

> ...a number of drugs have been put on the market with efficacy claims based on extremely meager and unobjective observations by people not truly qualified to make such observations. Also, there is absolutely nothing in the law to prevent the manufacturer from completely ignoring unfavourable reports. One company in its advertising for one of its products blithely states that there have been over 200 reports in the literature about this particular drug. They neglect to say that 60 per cent are not entirely favourable or pertinent.[49]

At that point in time, as explained earlier, American law did not require manufacturers to submit evidence of therapeutic efficacy. It only prohibited companies from making false therapeutic claims. This prohibition could be effectively circumvented by referencing vague scientific and experimental studies, the veracity of which was never verified by the state. As a result, many of the doctors deposing before Kefauver's committee suggested that independent agencies like the USFDA or the National Institute of Health (NIH) play a role in determining the efficacy of each new drug. A Dr Dowling testified as follows before the Committee:

> First, the Food and Drug Administration should be empowered to examine the efficacy as well as the toxic effects of all new drugs. It should be obvious to everyone that insufficient knowledge on the part of the doctor regarding the efficacy of a drug can react to the detriment of a patient just as much as toxic action by the drug, which the Food and Drug Administration now has the power to regulate.[50]

This point was belabored by other doctors who warned the committee that questions of efficacy had a direct bearing on safety and that it made no sense for the FDA to evaluate only safety without also examining efficacy of the drugs in question.

The hearings of the Senate anti-trust committee were widely publicized in the press with several newspapers providing daily updates to the public on Kefauver's confrontations with the heads of the biggest pharmaceutical corporations, as he hauled them over coals over their astonishing profit margins. By the time the final report was tabled, there was support for a new law to regulate the pharmaceutical industry.

Initially, political differences between the Kennedy administration and Kefauver almost gutted the law that was meant to reform many of the issues that came to the fore during the committee hearings, including the issue of regulatory reform. The thalidomide tragedy however brought them together to enable the enactment of far-reaching reforms on October 10 1962. Known as the Kefauver-Harris Amendments, after the senators who sponsored the bill to amend the Federal Food, Drug and Cosmetic Act, these amendments empowered the FDA to seek efficacy data in addition to safety data before approving a new drug for marketing in the United States. This data would have to be collected through "controlled" clinical trials.[51]

The enactment of this law was widely welcomed by the press. The *New York Times* declared it a "Victory on Drug Regulation", calling Senator Kefauver the "hero of this victory" for doggedly pushing the "...legislation despite widespread public apathy, lack of Administration interest and bitter opposition from some industry and Congressional sources."[52] As correctly noted by the *New York Times,* Kefauver's efforts would have been in vain if it was not for the unfortunate thalidomide tragedy that awoke the public, the government, and the legislature to the dangers of this new era of medical innovation. Commenting on the indifference of the elected representatives on such an important issue until the precipitation of a crisis, the editorial remarked on how it did "...not speak too well for Congressional responsiveness to a public need that it took such an unpredictable and chance occurrence as the thalidomide tragedy to secure passage of this law so clearly related to the general welfare." This lack of responsiveness by politicians to the demands of drug regulation is unfortunately a feature in democracies around the world. Nevertheless, given the thalidomide tragedy, the Kefauver-Harris amendments enacted in the United States were eventually replicated in Europe and other developed countries in the following decades. This new model of regulation was extraordinary for its time because the state for the first time was playing a role in guaranteeing efficacy of all new drugs on the basis of scientific data and expert opinion.

Lessons from history

There are four important takeaways from this discussion on the evolution of medicine and drug regulation in the democracies of the United States and Europe.

The first is that much of drug regulatory law has been written with the blood of citizens who died in hundreds, many of them, children. This tells us that if a country is governed by a poorly designed and enforced drug regulatory system, people will die. The pharmaceutical industry cannot be trusted to regulate itself.

The second takeaway is that even robust democracies with a free press have not always taken proactive steps to ensure efficient drug regulation. The major drug regulatory milestones in the United States and Europe over the last century were triggered mostly by mass deaths or scandals caused by experimental or poorly manufactured medicines. The Germans wanted to regulate the anti-diphtheria serum because of their past experience with Koch's failed tuberculin. The Americans were forced to act in 1902, 1938, and 1941 only because of mass deaths of their citizens due to contaminated drugs. Again in 1962, the thalidomide disaster forced sweeping reforms in both the United States and Europe because of the deaths and deformities caused by the new drug. There are few other areas of regulatory law where reforms have been catalyzed primarily due to the mass death of citizens.

The third takeaway is that debates around drug regulation have progressively become more scientifically complex. The 1901 scandal in St Louis was because the contaminated sera was due to an infected horse from which the serum was extracted. The thalidomide tragedy however was because the drug in one particular isomeric form was dangerous to the unborn fetus. The complexity of these issues has increased progressively over the decades. Any regulatory system meant to deal with cutting edge pharmaceutical innovation needs to be upgraded regularly, both in terms of qualified personnel and regulations every time technology makes a leap ahead. Given the lethargy and red-tape of most bureaucracies, the regulator is likely to remain one step behind the industry unless elected representatives crack the whip.

The fourth takeaway is that it is in the interest of the pharmaceutical industry as a whole to welcome better regulatory standards. A major fallout of the above scandals, apart from deaths and lawsuits, is the loss of consumer confidence and this can be a setback for both public health and profitability of the pharmaceutical sector. There are examples from the early 20th century where big players in the American and German pharmaceutical industries welcomed regulation because they were worried that unregulated players may lead to more public sector involvement in manufacturing of new drugs. They expected consumer confidence in their medicines to improve significantly if state regulators played an active role in guaranteeing the safety and efficacy of all drugs in the market. This enthusiasm amongst the pharmaceutical industry towards regulation has fluctuated over the decades but the core sentiment likely remains the same.

The point of discussing the regulatory history of Europe and the United States is to demonstrate, through the course of this book, how little India has learnt from the history of these other countries. The price of this ignorance is often paid by not just Indian citizens but also the citizens of India's trading partners who import copious amounts of medicine from the "pharmacy of the developing world".

Notes

1. William Bynum, *The History of Medicine: A Very Short Introduction* (OUP 2008), 5.
2. ibid 10.
3. ibid 12–13.
4. ibid 11.
5. ibid 53–55.
6. ibid 75–76.
7. Marianna Karamanou and others, 'From Miasmas to Germs: A Historical Approach to Theories of Infectious Disease Transmission' (2012) 1 *Le Infezioni in Medicina*, 58, 59.
8. Priya Vrat Sharma, *History of Medicine in India, from Antiquity to 1000 A.D.* (Indian National Science Academy 1992), 382.
9. MR Raghava Varier, *A Brief History of Ayurveda* (OUP 2020), 61.
10. Sharma, (n 8), 383.
11. Varier, (n 9), 52.
12. Bynum, (n 1), 93.
13. Paolo Mazzarello, 'A Unifying Concept: The History of Cell Theory' (1999) 1 *Nature Cell Biology*, E13.
14. Bynum, (n 1), 99.
15. William Rosen, *Miracle Cure: The Creation of Antibiotics and the Birth of Modern* (Penguin 2017), 23.
16. Bynum, (n 1), 103–104.
17. Les Iversen, *Drugs: A Very Short Introduction* (OUP 2016), 2–3.
18. Syal Kumar, Gustav J Dobos and Thomas Rampp, 'The Significance of Ayurvedic Medicinal Plants' (2017) 22 *Journal of Evidence-based Complementary & Alternative Medicine*, 494.
19. Stefan Riedel, 'Edward Jenner and the History of Smallpox and Vaccination' (2005), 18 *Baylor University Medical Centre Proceedings*, 21.
20. ibid.

21. Stefan HE Kaufmann, 'Remembering Emil von Behring: From Tetanus Treatment to Antibody Cooperation with Phagocytes' 8 mBio e00117.
22. Rosen, (n 15), 40.
23. Iversen, (n 17), 5.
24. Michael Titford, 'Paul Ehrlich: Histological Staining, Immunology, Chemotherapy' (2010) 41 *Laboratory Medicine*, 497.
25. ibid.
26. Rosen, (n 15), 57.
27. Kay Brune and Burkhard Hinz, 'The Discovery and Development of Antiinflammatory Drugs' (2004) 50 *Arthritis & Rheumatism*, 2391.
28. Rosen, (n 15), 57.
29. Rosen, (n 15), 67.
30. Tobias Cramer, 'Building the "World's Pharmacy": The Rise of the German Pharmaceutical Industry, 1871–1914' (2015) 89 *Business History Review*, 43.
31. Jon Merrills, *Pharmacy Law and Practice* (Elsevier 2013), 363.
32. Indian Penal Code 1860, s. 272.
33. Axel C Hüntelmann, 'Evaluation as a Practical Technique of Administration: The Regulation and Standardization of Diphtheria Serum' in Jonathan Simon and Christoph Gradmann (eds), *Evaluating and Standardizing Therapeutic Agents, 1890—1950* (Palgrave Macmillan 2010) ch 2, 44.
34. ibid 35.
35. ibid.
36. Jonathan Simon, 'The Politics of Serum Production in France', in Jonathan Simon and Christoph Gradmann (eds), *Evaluating and Standardizing Therapeutic Agents, 1890—1950* (Palgrave Macmillan 2010) ch 5, 96.
37. ibid.
38. Ross E DeHovitz, 'The 1901 St Louis Incident: The First Modern Medical Disaster' (2014) 133 *Paediatrics*, 964.
39. Terry S Coleman, 'Early Developments in the Regulation of Biologics' (2016) 71 *FOOD AND DRUG LAW JOURNAL*, 544.
40. Bryan Denham, 'Magazine Journalism in the Golden Age of Muckraking: Patent-Medicine Exposures Before and After the Pure Food and Drug Act of 1906' (2020) 22(2) *Journalism & Communication Monographs*, 100; James H Cassedy, 'Muckraking and Medicine: Samuel Hopkins Adams' (1964) 16 *American Quarterly*, 85.
41. Suzanne White Junod, 'FDA and Clinical Drug Trials: A Short

History' (US Food & Drug Administration 2008) 5 < https://www.fda.gov/media/110437/download> accessed 28 June 2021.

42. John P Swann, 'The 1941 Sulfathiazole Disaster and the Birth of Good Manufacturing Practices' (1999) 41 *American Institute of the History of Pharmacy*, 16.
43. 'What's Happened to Thalidomide Babies?—BBC News' (3 November 2011) <https://www.bbc.com/news/magazine-15536544> accessed 28 June 2021.
44. Katie Thomas, 'Pursuing an Untold Story of Thalidomide', *The New York Times* (23 March 2020) <https://www.nytimes.com/2020/03/23/reader-center/insider-thalidomide-fda.html> accessed 27 June 2021.
45. Robert D McFadden, 'Frances Oldham Kelsey, Who Saved U.S. Babies From Thalidomide, Dies at 101', *The New York Times* (7 August 2015) <https://www.nytimes.com/2015/08/08/science/frances-oldham-kelsey-fda-doctor-who-exposed-danger-of-thalidomide-dies-at-101.html> accessed 28 June 2021.
46. United States Senate (Sub-committee on Antitrust and Monopoly), *Study of Administered Prices in the Drug Industry* (Rep No 448, 1961).
47. Rosen (n 15).
48. United States Senate (Sub-committee on Antitrust and Monopoly) (n 46), 156.
49. ibid 187.
50. ibid.
51. Jeremy A Greene and Scott H Podolsky, 'Reform, Regulation, and Pharmaceuticals—The Kefauver—Harris Amendments at 50' (2012) 367 *The New England Journal of Medicine*, 1481.
52. 'Victory on Drug Regulation', *The New York Times* (5 October 1962) <https://www.nytimes.com/1962/10/05/archives/victory-on-drug-regulation.html> accessed 28 June 2021.

CHAPTER TWO

Controlling the Craze for Medicinal Drugs in Colonial India

One of the earliest public debates in India on the need for regulating the manufacture and sale of pharmaceutical drugs took place in 1927 in the Council of States of the bi-cameral Indian Legislature when India was still under British rule. A legislator from the Bombay Presidency, Sir Haroon Jaffer, had moved a resolution on the 9 March 1927, before the Council of States, titled "control of the craze for medicinal drugs".[1] The short text of resolution was as follows:

> This Council recommends to the Governor General in Council to urge all Provincial Governments to take immediate measures to control the craze for medicinal drugs by legislation for the standardisation of the preparation and sale of such drugs.

In his address to the Council, Sir Jaffer took aim at four issues pertaining to medicinal drugs.

The first was the indiscriminate availability of all kinds of medicines of doubtful efficacy. In his words, several of the new drugs made "claims that were never properly demonstrated and which are prepared merely to put money into the pockets of the manufacturers".[2]

The second issue was "the indiscriminate use of drugs by doctors in their prescriptions".[3] These included the so called "patent & proprietary drugs" whose ingredients were kept confidential and not disclosed to the public. This problem was greatly magnified in India, according to Sir Jaffer, by the number of "unqualified or only partly qualified and very inexperienced doctors" practising in India.

The third issue was the growing demand from the public for all kinds of powders, tonics, serums, vaccines, and injections, regardless of the absurd claims made by the manufacturers of such medicines. Sir Jaffer jokingly remarked[4]:

> I have not yet heard of any case in India where the monkey gland has been grafted on to an old person to make him as frisky as a full-blooded boy, but I presume it is possible that many enthusiasts getting on in years have atleast made inquiries about it based on what they have read of so called successful graftings in the West.

The fourth issue was the problem of adulteration and substandard drugs. He explained how there were many cases where a local drug was "absolutely useless" and "inactive, if not adulterated" and boosted by the "un-solicited testimonials" from "non-existent individuals".[5]

The bleak picture painted by Sir Jaffer was not surprising since at the time there was no uniform law in British India regulating the manufacturing standards and sale of medicinal drugs. Although some provinces like Bengal, the Central Provinces, Assam, Ajmer-Merwara, and United Provinces had provincial legislations to regulate the sale of adulterated drugs, none of them dealt with standardisation of drug quality or efficacy of drugs. These were presumably very basic laws, since it is almost impossible to guarantee quality without the creation of binding legal standards. Some of the remaining provinces, like Madras, had enacted legislation only on the issue of food adulteration.[6]

Of the four speakers that followed Sir Jaffer, two supported the resolution with amendments and two others opposed it. One of the supporters was Major General T.H. Symons who was then the Director General of the Indian Medical Service (IMS), which although primarily a military service, played an important role in influencing public health policies in British India until 1947 when it was disbanded.[7] General Symons described to the Council an inspection of dispensaries and mofussil hospitals in the Madras Presidency by experts which had revealed certain dispensaries to contain expensive drugs that he had never heard of during his career as a doctor. Supporting the urgent need for standardisation of drugs in India, General Symons pointed out how both the United States and the United Kingdom had already enacted legislation to regulate the manufacture and sale of pharmaceutical drugs.[8] The United States had enacted two laws to regulate the manufacture and sale of medicinal drugs: the Biologics Control Act 1902, and the Pure Foods and Drugs Act 1906.[9] The British had enacted The Sale of Food and Drugs Act 1875, which was limited in its scope, and the more thorough Therapeutic Substances Act 1925, which regulated only biologics.[10]

Opposing the motion was Dr U. Rama Rau, a legislator from Madras who was outraged by Sir Jaffer's criticism of doctors, describing the speech as "nonsense and libel".[11] Dr Rau blamed the "craze" for medicines not on doctors but unregulated advertisements in the press. Addressing the Council, he said:

> Sir, the craze for patent medicines is not because of doctors. It is because of numerous advertisements appear in the papers, not only the Indian papers but also the English and other papers, in which the patent medicines are advertised to cure every illness on the face of the earth. If my Honourable friend had moved a Resolution to prevent these patent medicines from being advertised in India I could understand it, or if he had said that advertisements must not appear in the papers regarding patent medicines, I would have entirely supported him. Or if he had moved that there should be no importation

> of patent medicines from foreign countries to India, I would have entirely supported him.[12]

The second speaker opposing the motion was Mr P.C. Desi Chakra, a representative from Burma. His opposition was borne from the fact that such regulation would lean in favour of Western medicine and against Ayurvedic medicine.[13] According to him, doctors trained in Western medicine had a "natural bias" that would tend to put out of the market all Unani and Ayurvedic preparations which at the time were popular choice of medicine in British India.[14] This concern is not entirely surprising because there was always some tension between Western medicine and traditional Indian medicine in the pre-independence era not only for commercial reasons but also because of cultural conflicts over practices such as dissection of the human body.[15]

Notwithstanding the opposition, the motion ultimately was adopted by the Council of States after some amendments, notably to drop the word "craze for medicinal drugs" which was replaced with "indiscriminate use of medicinal drugs".[16] It was a momentous occasion for British-ruled India because until this motion was adopted, the interest of India's British rulers in the issue of drug quality was motivated by their desire to control the trade in narcotics and taxation. The government laboratories that existed at the time were primarily affiliated to the tax authorities because they were meant to check the amount of opium or alcohol in food and drug products so as to determine the excise duty payable. The issue of adulteration or drug quality from a safety perspective was not on the radar of India's colonial rulers until this motion by Sir Jaffer forced the British Government to take note.[17]

The debate preceding the vote on the resolution is fascinating because of the many parallels it has to the debate on drug regulation in India of the 21st century. This includes the perception of a problematic nexus between doctors and pharmaceutical companies, the issue of misleading advertisements by an assorted group of charlatans selling all kinds of concoctions as medicines, the tension between traditional medicine and modern evidence-based medicine, and lastly, the continuing problem of adulterated and sub-standard medicine.

The colonial government drags its feet on the issue

Despite Sir Jaffer's resolution being adopted by the Council of States, the British administrators of India continued dragging their feet on the issue. In 1928, yet another motion was moved in the Legislative Assembly of the Indian Legislature; this time asking for an adjournment of the proceedings of the House to discuss the urgent issue of "quinine fraud".[18] The legislator behind that motion was Lt Colonel H.A.J. Gidney. A prominent member of the Anglo-Indian community and formerly a member of the IMS, he was a nominated member to the Legislative Assembly.[19] He was no stranger to the debate on regulating medicinal drugs. Many years before his motion to discuss the "quinine fraud", in 1921, when Gidney was a member of the Legislative Assembly, he had attempted to convince the government during a discussion on the budget that the customs duty on import of patent medicines from the United Kingdom. and other countries should be increased to 20% from 7.5% because many of these drugs (whose composition was secret at the time) were perpetuating false claims through their "cure-all" advertisements. That amendment to the budget failed because the government did not think that customs tariffs were the best solution to the problem described by Gidney.[20]

But returning to his address to the House, on 4 September 1928 demanding an adjournment, Gidney warned the government that the mortality due to malaria in India was a staggering four million patients a year and that "spurious" quinine was likely one of the reasons for the large number of avoidable malarial deaths in India. At the time, quinine, which was first isolated in 1920 from the bark of the cinchona tree found originally in Peru, was the most effective treatments for malaria. In Gidney's words, the quinine fraud was "the most terrible fraud that has ever been perpetrated on this country and the unrestricted sale of this spurious drug has, I submit, been largely responsible for the steady high mortality from malaria".[21]

Illustrating with an example, Gidney described the results of an examination of quinine by a Chemical Examiner of the Punjab Government who certified that a sample advertised to have 5 grains of quinine bisulphate actually had only 1 grain or less of quinine and 3.5 grains of chalk, along with 1 grain of alum or some other substance to lend taste! He also made the sensational claim that "most of the quinine offered in the bazaars for sale to the public...is not quinine but chalk".[22] This was no exaggeration. Earlier that year, the *Indian Medical Gazette* had published a small survey documenting the quality of quinine sold in India by J.W.D Megaw, an officer in the IMS along with Sudhamoy Ghosh and N.R. Chatterjee who were both professors at the Calcutta School of Tropical Medicine. They drew 90 samples of quinine tablets from the market and tested them for the quantity of quinine in each sample. They discovered that 23 samples were 25% weaker than the stated strength. More than 40% of the samples had a deficiency of more than 10%. Some 11 samples had more quinine content than advertised. Although the survey was quite small, it was the first empirical evidence of the quinine fraud in India at the time.[23]

According to Gidney, the problem was not limited to quinine since India was "par excellence the dumping ground for every variety of quack medicine and adulterated drug manufactured in all parts of the world".[24] The sole responsibility for the sale of such spurious medicine according to Gidney, was the failure of the government to take steps to regulate the sale of medicinal drugs at a time when even countries like Egypt, Palestine, and Mesopotamia had drug regulatory laws in place.[25]

Reminding the government of Sir Jaffer's motion that was adopted by the Council of States, on 9 March 1927, Gidney upbraided the government for dragging its feet on the issue despite the widespread support for such a law from both the medical profession and the industry. He rattled off the following names of eminent personalities who supported the enactment of such a law:

> The Tropical School of Medicine in Calcutta has also pronounced its opinion about the danger of this drug adulteration and pressed for legislation. The Senior Trade Commissioner has also exposed these dangers and advised a Food and Drugs Act. Mr. J.C. Ghosh of Calcutta has also exposed these dangers and pressed for legislation. The Indian Chambers of Commerce in Bombay have also written to the Government of India, Education, Health and Lands Department, and asked for a Food & Drugs Act and standardisation of all drugs manufacturers or imported into India. Representatives of well-known drug manufacturers and the public Press have also widely ventilated the fraud and dangers. I ask the Government, what has it done? Nothing! When it was clearly its duty to act at once and save India. Why has it failed to do its duty? Why has it not introduced a Food and Drugs Act, a Pharmacy and Poisons Bill and other remedial measures?[26]

There indeed appeared to have been a groundswell of support at that time in the Indian press across the industry and the medical profession on the issue of legislation to improve the quality of drug supply. It was a topic of discussion at the recent Indian Science Congress held at Lahore, where in Sir

Jaffer's words "...the drug craze in India and the tendency for it to reach dangerous proportions were ...fully discussed and... it was unanimously agreed that some control was urgently needed."[27] Similarly, the Secretary of Indian Merchants Chamber of Bombay complained to the government that the uncontrolled sale of inferior quality drugs was creating a bad name for the pharmaceutical industry and that the Chambers was of the view that "the introduction of a Food and Drugs Act in this country would be desirable from the point of view of both dealers and consumers, as some continental and English firms are known to make a practice of wilfully adulterating their goods for shipment into India in response to trade demands for such goods".[28]

Similarly, medical journals like the *Indian Medical Gazette*, the *Indian and Eastern Druggist*, and the *Pharmaceutical Journal of England*, as also newspapers like the *Statesman* and the *Civil and Military Gazette* had voiced their support for governmental regulation of the sale of drugs.[29]

Despite this popular support for the government to regulate the manufacture and sale of medicinal drugs, the British administrators of India appeared to be indifferent to the issue. In its response to Gidney's motion for adjournment, the British India Government speaking through Mr G.S. Bajpai, the Secretary of the Department of Education, Health and Lands and a bureaucrat belonging to the Indian Civil Service (ICS), managed to successfully convince the President of the Council of States to dismiss Gidney's motion for adjournment because it dealt with a vintage issue rather than a recent event as required by the rules of the house.[30] In other words, the issue was not urgent enough because it had been raised in India repeatedly and for a long time.

Regardless of Gidney's failed, yet heroic, effort to pin the government into a corner, it is worth reflecting on the possible reasons for the delay in the government's lethargic response to unregulated sale of medicinal drugs.

The first and most likely reason is that the British colonial project in India was focussed on extracting economic resources from India rather than governance for the well-being and improvement of lives of the average Indian citizen. In the eloquent (and famous) words of John Sullivan, an Englishman who had headed the Board of Revenue, "Our system acts very much like a sponge, drawing up all the good things from the banks of the Ganges, and squeezing them down on the banks of the Thames." Not only did India serve as a base for raw materials like cotton required by the textile mills of Manchester, England, it also served as a market for finished goods from England and this included medicinal drugs such as the quinine sample referenced by Gidney during his address to the Legislative Assembly. The British, therefore, had very little incentive to create a regulatory framework in India to regulate the import of medicinal drugs from their very own country in order to protect their colonial subjects. For their own citizens in Great Britain, the British Parliament had enacted the Sale of Food and Drugs Act 1875, and the Therapeutics Substances Act 1925. In India however, the extent of the British interest in drug quality was guided by its desire to regulate the narcotics trade and levy excise duties. Protecting Indians from the detrimental effect of substandard and adulterated drugs did not feature on the British agenda.

The second likely reason for the delay in enacting a new drug regulatory law was the federal scheme brought in by the Government of India Act 1919. This law devolved legislative powers regarding medicine from the Indian Legislature to the various provincial legislatures. Gidney had referred to this aspect in his speech, saying, "I know that medicine is a transferred subject and that the Devolution Rules state that food adulteration is also a provincial matter."[31] However, as Gidney pointed out, the "Government [could not] evade direct responsibility in this quinine fraud because this spurious drug is imported into India at various seaports" and the regulation of imports fell within the purview of the Government of India and the Indian Legislature.[32] Regulation of imports could have had a substantive impact on the quality of drugs available in India because it was clear from government records in 1931 that most of these medicinal drugs were imported rather than domestically manufactured.[33] While it is likely that convincing provincial legislatures to act on this issue with haste may have been a difficult exercise, there is little doubt that the British could have moved swiftly to curb imports of adulterated medicine from the United Kingdom and the other countries if the Governor General appointed by the British Government had the political will to do so.

The Chopra Committee—The Report of the Drugs Enquiry Committee, 1930–31

Although slow to react, the Government of India finally did take note of the resolution moved by Sir Jaffer in 1927 and after consultations with the provincial governments issued an order on 11 August 1930, appointing an expert committee to study the magnitude of manufacture and sale of "impure or defective" medicine in India and to make recommendations to improve the situation as well as to enquire into the necessity of legislation to restrict the profession of pharmacy to only "duly qualified persons".[34]

This committee was headed by Lt Col R.N. Chopra who was a member of the IMS and a Professor of Pharmacology, School of Tropical Medicine and Hygiene, Calcutta. Educated at Cambridge, Chopra is often referred to as the "Father of Pharmacology" in India because of his contributions and illustrious scientific career in the field of Pharmacology at the Calcutta School of Tropical Medicine.[35] The other members were Rev. Fr. J.F. Caius, a pharmacologist at the Haffekine Institute, Bombay, Mr H. Cooper of Messrs Smith, Stanistreet

& Co. Ltd., Manufacturing Chemists, Calcutta, and Maulvi Abdul Matin Chaudhury.

The Committee conducted extensive consultations, issuing over 2,180 questionnaires to the medical profession, pharmacists, medical universities, medical journals, industry experts, government analysts responsible for testing medicine, and other assorted experts, soliciting both opinions and recommendations on the quality of medicinal drugs being sold in India. It received 638 replies, 392 from official sources and 246 from non-official sources, making it an incredible consultative exercise even when compared to most contemporary law-making exercises in independent India.[36]

Much of the testimony to the Committee painted a terrifying picture of the situation on the ground, especially with regard to the quality of quinine that was much required to combat malaria. It appeared that the legislators in the Council of State and Legislative Assembly had been correct about the extent of the problem. Prof. P.S. MacMahon, a public analyst to the Government of the United Provinces, explained to the committee that "...it is not surprising to find 'quinine' pills sold with impunity on the market composed of clay and chalk, and containing less than half per cent of quinine."[37]

A Mr W.J. Campbell of Smith & Campbell, Pharmaceutical Chemists, who was a chemist from Lahore with 24 years of experience, was of the opinion that: "The Indian market is flooded with spurious drugs and chemicals which are certainly cheap, but worthless as medicinal agents." He then proceeded to give a list of examples of drugs that had failed testing due to either adulteration or lack of the advertised active ingredient.[38]

Another pharmacy from Lahore, by the name Beli Ram & Brothers, described to the committee how "locally" made quinine tablets often contained chalk with a bitter taste of quassia or burnt alum and were sold in considerably large quantities throughout Sindh. Imported drugs were no better according to them, as they cited examples of German-made drugs failing quality testing after import because these drugs were only one-fourth of the advertised strength on the labels.[39]

Yet another testimony from Punjab came from Major G.C. Maitra, of the IMS. He presented particularly worrying examples from the quality testing performed by the army on drugs that it purchased. According to Major Maitra:

> In the last 18 months, 39 samples of Sulfarsenol and 3 of Neosalvarsan were tested. About 40 per cent of the former and 100 percent of the latter were found to have become toxic on injection into the experimental animal—a specially bred strain of English white mice.

A second problem according to Major Maitra, were the "very extravagant claims" being made in advertisements. One remedy, titled "Conquest of death", was accompanied by literature which claimed that, "In case the medicine has reached the patient too late and he has breathed his last, he may be revived if made to inhale this remedy within three hours of death by artificial respiration."[40]

The committee heard similar complaints from across the country. From down south in Madras, it heard from Mr D.R. Mawnay, a wholesale chemist who supplied to several southern pharmacies and who was of the opinion that "legislation must be enacted to put an immediate stop" to adulteration of medicines and that "central laboratories must be established where all drugs must be tested before they are allowed to enter the market".[41]

Another voice from Madras was Dr Lakshmanaswami Mudaliar, who was a physician at the Government Hospital for Women and Children. He informed the committee that:

> ...it may be stated from clinical experience of the therapeutic value of certain well-known drugs, that at present the market

> is flooded with a large number of preparations of inferior quality and doubtful purity, which must necessarily be deleterious to the patients. There are certain preparations, such as Extract Ergot Liquidum, preparations of Digitalis and certain preparations of Quinine, which have been found defective from clinical experience. Even in regard to well-known British Pharmacopial preparations, the clinical results of drugs obtained from different firms, vary. It is also a fact that there are certain drugs sold in the market at rates which are so widely different that it is but reasonable to infer that the cheaper drugs are probably of doubtful quality.[42]

Similarly, from Bangalore, Dr C.V. Natarajan, who was the Superintendent of the Health Institute, Bangalore, stated in his testimony to the Committee that:

> The necessity for controlling drug traffic and drug adulteration is a long desired want. Locally manufactured indigenous preparations as well as imported preparations fall very often very low regarding their potency...Another unknown factor is the period of maintenance of the full potency of such extracts and tinctures during transportation and storage at the existing temperature of tropical climate.[43]

From Bombay, Colonel B. Higham, IMS, who was a Chemical Analyser at the Government Laboratory in Byculla, Bombay, and tested drugs for the Collector of Customs and others, also narrated instances of several drugs failing testing. Expanding on one particular episode he informed the committee that:

> In 1928, I was sent several samples of quinine tablets and the amounts of quinine present were found to be very much less than those shown on the labels...I regarded this as so important that I addressed the Surgeon General in the matter and suggested that an *ad interim* Quinine Act should be introduced in the legislature pending the introduction of the General Drugs Act that I considered must eventually be required.[44]

The testimony from an academic in Calcutta, Mr P. Neogi, Professor of Chemistry, Presidency College, Calcutta, spoke out against "secret remedies". Many patent and proprietary medicines at the time were "secret" with no obligation under the law to disclose their ingredients. In his words:

> I am of opinion that secret remedies should be banned. The approximate composition of each patent medicine must be disclosed to the public. A legislation should be passed requiring manufacturers of patent medicines to disclose on the labels of the phials containing those medicines their approximate composition.[45]

Also, from Calcutta was the Editor of the *Indian Medical Gazette*—Lt Col E. Knowles. The *Indian Medical Gazette* had been reporting about the crisis of counterfeit and adulterated drugs in India and the need in India for a legislation like the Therapeutic Substances Act which was enacted in the United Kingdom. in 1925. Like the others, Knowles rattled off a long list of examples of how santonin, quinine, and cinchona febrifuge were being heavily adulterated in the Indian market. In no uncertain terms, Knowles told the committee that, "There can be no question as to the imperative necessity of legislation to deal with this situation."[46]

The Drug Inquiry Committee thus received testimony from literally all four corners of the country and there appeared to be a near consensus that the drugs being supplied to the Indian market were of poor quality and marketed through grossly exaggerated advertisements. There were, however, some contrary views from Indians who were worried that the attempt to impose regulation was nothing but a strategy to stifle the nascent but growing pharmaceutical sector in India. The key proponent of this argument was the Indian Medical Association (IMA), which continues to be the pre-eminent association of medical doctors in India.

In its testimony to the Committee, the IMA claimed that its members had "considerable misgivings" about the enquiry being conducted by the committee and that they apprehended that that the committee's findings would be "...used with the ulterior purpose of prejudicing the position of the infant drug industry in this country" so as to benefit the British drug industry at a time when there were "...manifestations of a strong national desire for using indigenous preparations and drugs." The IMA also claimed that "...though the Food and Drugs Act in the United Kingdom makes it compulsory to examine all drugs and food substances consumed in the United Kingdom, the products for export to India are beyond the provisions of this Act."[47] Regarding the specific allegation contained in the Committee's questionnaire that there was widespread sale of inferior quality drugs in India, the IMA stated that it could not "...accept this statement in the absence of accurate and proper evidence."[48]

It most certainly did not help the Government's case, as the IMA pointed out in its testimony, that although the membership of the Committee consisted of a representative of a British firm, no Indian firm was given similar representation on the Committee. This, according to the IMA, lent credence to its claim that the enquiry was a pretext to stifle the growth of the Indian pharmaceutical industry.[49]

It must be remembered that this was the era of the independence struggle and the Swadeshi movement which had been initiated in 1905 by Indian nationalists. This movement called upon Indians to boycott British goods in favour of swadeshi or domestically manufactured products, was meant to protest the British plan to divide the province of Bengal on communal lines. The simple strategy behind the call to purchase only swadeshi goods was to hurt British economic interests and thus undermine one of the main motivations of its colonising mission in India. It should also be noted that the year 1930 was also witness to the famous Dandi March which involved Gandhi leading a march of satyagrahis from Sabarmati Ashram in Ahmedabad to Dandi in order to "produce" salt and sell it without paying the salt tax imposed by the British. The Dandi March is considered to be one of the most iconic civil disobedience moments of the Indian freedom struggle and is today considered to be a pivotal moment in the struggle for Indian independence from the British Empire. It is thus no surprise that nationalist sentiment was making an appearance in the debate regarding the regulation of the pharmaceutical industry.

On the other hand, it should also be remembered, as pointed by Sir Jaffer's speech in the Council of States in 1927, that doctors of that era were likely playing a major role in prescribing dubious medicines to their patients. It is possible that the IMA had financial incentives to resist any new law or authority that would interfere with the authority of their members to prescribe drugs of their choice to their patients.

The IMA's view on the topic was, however, the minority opinion. A majority of the testimony received by the Committee weighed overwhelming in favour of a legislation to control the sale of drugs, with several terming it as an "urgent" requirement in the Indian context.

After reviewing all the testimony and drug control legislation in other countries, the Committee recommended in its final report dated 29 March 1931, that a drug control legislation be enacted for India. Although the Committee did not submit a draft bill, it did recommend that any future law should ensure standardization of medicine through the creation of an Indian Pharmacopeia, prohibit misleading advertisements of drugs, regulate the sale of patent and proprietary remedies (whose ingredients were secret at the time), ensure better regulation of the profession of pharmacists, the licensing of manufacturers, importers and retailers of medicinal drugs, the setting up of laboratories at the central and provincial level to undertake testing of quality of drugs, the creation of an advisory council, and most importantly, criminalising the sale of adulterated or misbranded drugs.[50]

In a move that appeared to be designed to pre-empt any criticism that the Committee was attempting to throttle the rise of the local drug industry, the Committee also made recommendations for "fostering" the growth of the Indian drug industry.[51]

On the most important issue of whether there should be one central law or a multitude of provincial legislations addressing drug regulation, the Committee recommended the route of a single central law to ensure uniformity across British-India. It made this recommendation despite the fact that as per the Devolution Rules framed under Section 45-A of the Government of India Act 1919, the subjects of medical administration, public health, and administration of justice would fall within the purview of the provincial legislatures. The Committee argued that it was possible under Section 67(2) of the Government of India Act 1919, for the Indian Legislature to pass legislation on subjects devolved to the provincial legislature with the prior sanction of the Governor General.[52]

In its concluding remarks, the Committee acknowledged that some of its proposals would "...strike at vested interests and are sure to arouse vigorous opposition" but that it was "...impressed with the sincerity, force and earnestness of the general demand for reform." It signed off by asking for "energetic action on the part of the Government".[53]

The wait for a new law continues

Despite the thorough investigation by the Drugs Inquiry Committee and the near unanimous consensus that the issue of drug control urgently required legislative action, the government of the day continued to drag its feet while Indian legislators grew increasingly impatient. On 18 September 1935, an Indian legislator in the Council of State, Sir Nasarvanji Choksy, frustrated with the slow pace of reforms, moved a resolution before the Council calling upon the Governor General in Council to initiate "early measures" to implement the recommendations made by the Drugs Inquiry Committee. While moving the motion, Sir Choksy informed his peers that the matter of poor quality or adulterated medicine had become far worse since the submission of the report of the Drugs Inquiry Committee, providing several recent examples where spurious or adulterated medicine had been detected in India.[54]

The Government representative tasked with resisting Choksy's resolution was Mr Ram Chandra who tried placating the Council by explaining the reasons for the delay. Chandra explained to the House that the problem was not a lack of a law since several provinces or in some cases municipalities had local laws to deal with drug adulteration. In addition, he pointed out that the Indian Penal Code (IPC) had provisions penalising the sale of adulterated drugs. The challenge according to Chandra, was the lack of standardisation of drugs and the lack of laboratories and experts to test the quality of drugs and the funding these laboratories and experts would require to enforce a new legislation. Apparently, many of the provinces like Bombay, Bengal, United Provinces, and Madras had told the Government of India that they lacked the funds to run drug testing laboratories. This lack of co-operation from the provinces was a key problem in enacting any legislation for the entire country, according to Chandra. He said that the Government of India itself, although "unable to incur any substantial expenditure", would try to provide an effective solution to this problem if the provincial governments were more co-operative on this issue.[55] In other words, the

Government of India simply passed along the blame to the provincial governments, ignoring the fact that the Drugs Inquiry Committee had actually recommended that a central law be enacted for this purpose.

The Government of India's defence before the Council of State did not win it much support. The suggestion that the lack of funds was stalling the creation of an effective drug control system rankled some of the legislators. Mr Hossain Imam, a legislator from Bihar and Orissa, was one such legislator who sought to remind the Government of India that there existed a "Silver Jubilee Fund" which had sufficient funds to create the necessary infrastructure under a new drug control legislation.[56] The "Silver Jubilee Fund" was likely a reference to a fund created by the British to celebrate King George V's 25th coronation ceremony on 6 May 1935. Many other legislators spoke in favour of Choksy's resolution and a majority of the Council of State voted in favour of the following, slightly amended resolution:

> This Council recommends to the Governor General in Council to initiate early measures to implement the conclusions of the Report of the Drugs Inquiry Committee, or, if for financial or other reasons he has to delay giving effect to all the conclusions of the Committee, to take early steps to pass legislation which would effectively prevent the sale of spurious drugs.[57]

A failed legislative attempt

Perhaps due to the above resolution, the Government of India finally introduced, on 7 October 1937, the Import of Drugs Bill, in the Legislative Assembly. As obvious from the title, the legislation dealt with only the import of drugs and kept away from regulating domestically manufactured drugs. The reason for limiting the scope of the bill to only imported drugs, as pointed out by Secretary Girja Shankar Bajpai who introduced the bill in the Legislative Assembly, was apparently a legal limitation in the new Government of India Act 1935 (which had replaced the old Government of India Act 1919). Under the old Government of India Act 1919, as pointed out by the Drugs Inquiry Committee (1931), the Indian Legislature could override the provincial legislature with the prior approval of the Governor General. However, the Government of India Act 1935 envisaged a stricter separation of legislative powers between the Federal Legislature and the provincial legislatures. Under the new scheme, the legislative powers were identified in three lists under Schedule VII to the Act. List I contained subjects for the Federal Legislature, List II contained subjects for provincial legislatures and List III contained subjects on which both the federal and provincial legislatures could enact laws.

As per the government of the day, the issue of legislation to control the quality of drugs manufactured and sold within India fell within the powers of the provincial legislature and thus the Federal Legislature could not enact a new law in this regard. As a result, the Government of India passed the buck on regulation of domestically manufactured drugs to the provinces, hoping that the Bill under consideration would "serve as a stimulus" for the provinces to enact their own legislation.[58] This strategy however did not pan out. Ultimately the Import of Drugs Bill 1937, was referred to a Select Committee of the Legislative Assembly for further examination which predictably ended with the recommendation that the Bill be reworked to regulate even the domestic manufacture and distribution of drugs.[59] This was not a surprising ask given that this issue of a uniform law across India had been raised repeatedly in the legislature in previous years.

Finally, a new comprehensive drug law

After the rejection of the Import of Drugs Bill 1937 by the Select Committee, the Government of India adopted a new strategy for creating a uniform legislation across British India. This strategy involved a request to all the provincial legislatures to pass a resolution under Section 103 of the Government of India Act 1935 empowering the Federal Legislature to pass a drug control law to regulate the domestic manufacture and sale of drugs, including those in their provinces. Once all the provincial legislatures passed such resolutions under Section 103, the Federal Legislature could enact a legislation even on those legislative subjects that fell within List II.[60]

The new law, which came to be known as the Drugs Act 1940, separated the powers and responsibilities of the federal and provincial governments, allowing both provinces and the federal government to set their own pharmacopeial standards. In simple English, "pharmacopeial standards" are standardized methods of testing the identity, purity, and quality of drugs. Drugs that fail to pass these standards are considered to be substandard drugs. Imports would be regulated only by the Federal Government. The domestic manufacture and sale of drugs were to be regulated by provincial governments who were required to appoint their own drug inspectors and government analysts to staff their laboratories.[61] Similarly, rule-making powers were distributed between the federal and provincial governments to correlate with the distribution of powers under the legislation. For example, the provincial governments were at liberty to make their own rules regarding qualifications for hiring their own drug inspectors and government analysts and prescribing the format of manufacturing licences, regulating the mode of labelling of drugs etc.[62] The federal government could make similar rules with respect to imported drugs.[63] In order to ensure some coordination and expertise on the issue of standards and the various rules drafted by different governments, the law also created two bodies—the Drugs Technical Advisory Board (DTAB), which had a mix of interdisciplinary expert members to advise on technical issues, and the Drugs Consultative Committee (DCC), which had as its members representatives from the various provincial governments.[64]

This new version of the Bill was largely welcomed by weary legislators who had been seeking legislative action on this issue for more than a decade. There was the inevitable criticism about the significant delay in enacting such law during the legislative debates. Sir Gidney, who had repeatedly raised the need for legislative action against adulterated and counterfeit medicine since 1921 was thankful to the government and effusive in his praise of Colonel Chopra who had headed the Drugs Inquiry Committee.[65] However, like many of his colleagues, he called upon the government to take similar actions and regulate the profession of pharmacists since they played a crucial role in providing medicine to consumers. That was an era where pharmacists actually "manufactured" or "compounded" some of the medicines meant for patients.

Others like Mr J.D. Boyle, a legislator from Bombay, were critical of the fact that manufacturers and importers of drugs were being given representation on the DTAB. In his opinion, it was "...to a certain degree improper that those who will be bought within the mischief of this Act should find a seat on the technical board which will formulate the policy."[66] This was an important articulation of the possible "conflict of interest" between the DTAB's role in protecting public health and the pharmaceutical industry's goal of increased profits. Other legislators like Pandit Lakshmi Kant Maitra had the polar opposite view. He argued that there should be more representation of persons from the Indian pharmaceutical industry on the board, as was the case in other countries and that it could not be presumed that they would "pollute" the atmosphere of the advisory board.[67] This line of argument was not entirely out of place in that era where the most prevalent form of regulation was "self-regulation". In those times, most professions and trades were regulated by self-representative bodies such as guilds and councils. The idea of regulation of a trade or profession by the state was still in its infancy.

Notwithstanding the criticism posed by some legislators, the government's bill was passed in both chambers of the Federal Legislature, thereby giving India its first ever Drugs Act 1940, more than 13 years after Sir Jaffer's resolution in the Legislative Assembly had called upon the government to pass such a law.

Many of the issues raised during the debate on Sir Jaffer's motion in 1927 were not addressed by the new law. These include issues such as the lack of requirement for the pharmaceutical industry to provide any clinical proof of safety and efficacy of new drugs, lack of regulation of traditional medicinal industries like Ayurveda and Unani, exaggerated and misleading advertisements by the pharmaceutical industry, and finally, the unhealthy nexus between the pharmaceutical industry and the medical profession. Some of these issues continue to plague India almost a century after being raised in the legislative debate of 1927.

During the course of the 20th century, the global pharmaceutical industry has seen an explosion of innovation as well as tremendous growth. The Indian pharmaceutical industry has grown exponentially earning itself the moniker of being the "pharmacy of the developing world" because of its ability to manufacture low-cost generic drugs. Despite leaps in medical innovation and the dramatic growth of the industry, India's drug regulatory infrastructure has evolved at snail's pace because of the reluctance of successive governments to improve the quality of regulation, lest it muzzles the growth of the pharmaceutical industry. The cost of this inaction is felt by not just India but by all countries importing drugs from India, especially those countries with weak domestic regulatory systems.

Notes

1. At the time though India was still a colony of the British Empire, the Government of India Act 1919 which was enacted by the British Parliament, provided for a small measure of self-government in India wherein Indians could elect their own representatives to a bicameral central legislature as well as provincial assemblies. The Council of States was the upper house of the Indian Legislature. Council of State Debates, 9 March 1927, vol I, 515.
2. ibid 516.
3. ibid 515.
4. ibid 516.
5. ibid 517.
6. Government of India, *Report of The Drugs Enquiry Committee* (1930–31) 24–31.
7. Donald McDonald, 'The Indian Medical Service. A Short Account of its Achievements 1600–1947' (1955) 49 *Proceedings of the Royal Society of Medicine* 13, 17.
8. Council of State Debates (n 1) 522.
9. Peter Barton Hutt, 'Drug Regulation in The United States' (1986) 2 *International Journal of Technology Assessment in Health Care* 619.
10. RG Penn, 'The State Control of Medicines: The First 3000 Years' (1979) 8 *British Journal of Clinical Pharmacology*, 293.
11. Council of State Debates (n 1) 519.
12. ibid 520.
13. ibid 523.
14. ibid 524.
15. David Arnold, *Colonizing the Body: State Medicine and Epidemic Disease in Nineteenth-Century India* (University of California Press 1993) 5–6.
16. Council of State Debates (n 1) 543–44.
17. Patricia Barton, '"The Great Quinine Fraud": Legality Issues in the "Non-Narcotic" Drug Trade in British India' (2007) 22 *The Social History of Alcohol and Drugs*, 1, 11.
18. Legislative Assembly Debates, 4 September 1928, vol III, 154.
19. Esther Mary Lyons, 'THE TWO GREAT ANGLO-INDIANS' (2000) 5 *International Journal of Anglo-Indian Studies*, 37.
20. Legislative Assembly Debates, 19 March 1921, 1364–65.
21. Legislative Assembly Debates, (n 18).
22. ibid 155.

23. JWD Megaw, Sudhamoy Ghosh and NR Chatterjee, 'Stock Solutions of Quinine' (1928) 63 *The Indian Medical Gazette*, 244.
24. Legislative Assembly Debates, (n 18).
25. ibid.
26. ibid 156.
27. Sir Jaffer, Council of State Debates, (n 1) 515.
28. *Report of The Drugs Enquiry Committee*, (n 6) 2.
29. ibid 2–3.
30. Legislative Assembly Debates, (n 18) 157.
31. ibid 156.
32. ibid.
33. *Report of The Drugs Enquiry Committee*, (n 6) [para 29] 14.
34. ibid 3, 4.
35. Harkishan Singh, 'Ram Nath Chopra (1882-1973)—A Visionary in Pharmaceutical Science.' (2008) 43 *Indian Journal of History of Science*, 231.
36. *Report of The Drugs Enquiry Committee*, (n 6) 16.
37. ibid 247.
38. ibid 251–52.
39. ibid 254–56.
40. ibid 285.
41. ibid 256, 279.
42. ibid 286.
43. ibid 289.
44. ibid 279.
45. ibid 280.
46. ibid 267.
47. ibid 262.
48. ibid 263.
49. ibid.
50. ibid 158–70.
51. ibid 173.
52. ibid 172.
53. ibid 173.
54. Council of State Debates, 18 September 1935, vol II, 128.
55. ibid 134–35.
56. ibid 139.
57. ibid 143.
58. Legislative Assembly Debates, 7 October 1937, vol VII, 3213–4.
59. JD Tyson (Education, Health and Lands Secretary), Council of State Debates, 10 April 1940, vol I, 558.

60. ibid.
61. The Drugs and Cosmetics Act 1940, ch III and IV.
62. ibid, s 33.
63. ibid, s 12.
64. ibid, ch II.
65. Legislative Assembly Debates, 4 April 1940, vol III, 2171.
66. ibid 2181.
67. Legislative Assembly Debates, 5 April 1940, vol III, 2208.

CHAPTER THREE

Of Botched Investigations, Dodgy Prosecution Guidelines, and Lenient Judges

In August 2013, government analysts working at the Drug Testing Laboratory in Chennai under the Tamil Nadu Drug Control Administration received as a matter of routine, drug samples from the Drug Inspectors in Gudiyattam, Vellore. The samples in question were supposedly of Glipizide, a drug used to treat Type 2 diabetes. Drug inspectors routinely purchase such samples and send them to government laboratories for testing as prescribed in the Drugs and Cosmetics Act 1940. These particular tablets were allegedly manufactured by the Tamil Nadu-based Alfred Berg & Co. Pvt Ltd and had been purchased in bulk by the Tamil Nadu Medical Services Corporation, a government company responsible for purchasing and distributing drugs to government-run hospitals across the state of Tamil Nadu.[1]

The most usual adverse outcome during the testing process by government analysts is for the drug to be declared as "Not of Standard Quality" (NSQ) because of its failure to comply with the standards laid down in the Indian Pharmacopoeia. Except in this case, the government analysts made the shocking allegation that the tablets in question contained not Glipizide as mentioned on the labelling of the samples sent to them but instead another drug called Glibenclamide! While Glibenclamide is also used to treat Type 2 diabetes, it should not be used as a substitute for Glipizide without the advice of a doctor. It takes the human body three to four times longer to metabolize Glibenclamide when compared to Glipizide, thereby increasing the possibility of hypoglycemia in patients who unwittingly take one drug instead of the other.[2]

The allegations in question were so scandalous that the drug inspectors from the Tamil Nadu Drug Control Administration, instead of merely summoning manufacturing records as is the usual practice during such investigations in India, visited the manufacturing premises of Alfred Berg & Co. to inspect the manufacturing facility for regulatory compliance. The inspection allegedly revealed shocking lapses at the facility. Not only did the drug inspectors accuse the facility of lacking a "separate quality assurance department" as mandated by the GMP code laid down in Schedule M to the Drugs and Cosmetics Rules 1945, but also alleged that the staff were unable to produce quality control records that they were mandated to retain under the law.[3] The staff had apparently claimed to the drug inspectors that they had sent their quality control records to their headquarters and did not maintain records at the manufacturing facility. Similarly, when the raw materials register and packing material register were sought by the inspectors, the director of the company produced a compact disk that was supposed to contain these records but which allegedly did not open on the computer.[4] In other words, the most critical records documenting the manufacturing process were not accessible to the drug inspectors and in the records that were accessible, the inspectors alleged several discrepancies.

Subsequently, a criminal complaint filed before the Judicial Magistrate at Gudiyattam on December 8 2014 by the Drug Inspector Mrs S.L. Dheivanar alleged that Alfred Berg & Co.'s manufacturing facility did not adhere to the GMP code; that the premises were congested with raw material that was not properly labelled and that required records were not being maintained by the company. The complaint filed in court also "observed" that Alfred Berg & Co. was "simply manufacturing the drugs first and then creating records thereafter" and that the investigating team was of the opinion that "the manufacturer did not produce the proper and genuine records" in order to cover their mistakes.[5]

The drug inspector also accused Alfred Berg & Co. of substituting Glipizide with Glibenclamide for purely profit motives; the cost of Glipizide was ₹9,000 per kg, while the cost of Glibenclamide was only ₹1,900 per kg. If these allegations against the company were in fact true, Alfred Berg & Co. presumably profited enormously from this substitution (regardless of whether it was a mistake) because as per the complaint filed in court, it had sold a whopping total of 5,67,000 Glipizide tablets to the Tamil Nadu Medical Services Corporation![6]

Given the seriousness of the allegations, it was no surprise that the drug inspectors sought to prosecute Alfred Berg & Co. under a provision of the Drugs and Cosmetics Act 1940 that carries a maximum punishment of life in prison and a fine that could go up to three times the value of the consignment seized.[7] In an ideal world, this was exactly the kind of case that should have been swiftly prosecuted. The Indian legal system, however, has its own logic. As we discovered to our utter astonishment, this case which was filed in December 2014, had not proceeded to trial as of March 2022! According to the e-courts record for this case, the court was unable to serve summons on the company despite the fact that Alfred Berg & Co. is headquartered in Chennai, merely 167 kilometers away from Gudiyattam. At some point in 2016, the Judicial Magistrate finally issued non-bailable warrants against the company, thereby clearing the path for the police to arrest the accused management personnel in charge of the company.

Yet as of 2022, according to the e-courts record, these warrants had not been executed.[8] In order to double check the accuracy of the e-courts records, we filed an application under the RTI Act 2005 with the Drug Inspector, Vellore, who confirmed that the case continues to be pending before the court.[9] During this very time period, we discovered that Alfred Berg & Co. has been actively litigating before the Madras High Court in three different criminal cases filed against it by the Tamil Nadu Drug Control Administration over quality issues.[10] In a fourth case, we discovered that four representatives of the management of Alfred Berg & Co. appeared before the Metropolitan Magistrate at Sadiapet, Chennai in May 2016, to plead guilty in a prosecution filed by the Tamil Nadu Drug Control Administration under the Drugs and Cosmetics Act 1940.[11] It is thus a mystery to us as to why the state has not been able to secure the presence of the management of Alfred Berg & Co. in the prosecution before the court at Gudiyattam.

The allegations against Alfred Berg & Co. are extraordinary even by Indian standards. Typical allegations made by Indian drug inspectors against the members of the Indian pharmaceutical industry are better captured in the criminal complaint filed before the Chief Judicial Magistrate, Pune, in August 2009, by drug inspectors from Maharashtra against Olcare Laboratories, a Gujarat-based pharmaceutical firm. In this case, the drug inspectors alleged that Azithromycin tablets manufactured by the firm sent to a government laboratory for testing were declared to be NSQ by a government analyst after it was found to contain only 25.69 mg of Azithromycin instead of the 200 mg advertized on the label i.e., 12.85% of the advertized amount.[12]

After the case bounced around in the judicial system for a period of seven years, the proprietor of Olcare Laboratories, along with the manufacturing chemist and analytical chemist who oversaw the manufacturing process at the manufacturing facility of the firm, finally pled guilty before the Chief Judicial Magistrate to the charge of manufacturing NSQ drugs. The judge now had to decide an appropriate punishment for the guilty parties in this case. The punishment prescribed by the Drugs and Cosmetics Act 1940, for the manufacture and sale of NSQ drugs is a minimum of one year imprisonment and a maximum imprisonment of two years, with a small monetary fine of ₹20,000. The law allows the judge to impose a prison term of less than one year for "adequate and special reasons to be recorded in the judgment". In the circumstances of this case, the Chief Judicial Magistrate hearing the case decided that it would be adequate punishment to sentence the guilty in this case, to "simple imprisonment till the rising of the court" along with a paltry fine of ₹70,000.[13]

A sentence of "simple imprisonment till the rising of the court" is exactly as it sounds. It basically allows the convicted persons to go free once the judge "rises" from the court for the day. Technically, if the judge rises 15 minutes after passing the sentence, the guilty can leave court in 15 minutes. This is the most lenient form of sentencing. The reason offered by the Chief Judicial Magistrate for this lenient punishment in this case was that at most a prospective patient consuming the NSQ drug would not have received immediate relief and would simply have had to consume more of the medicine. Thus, as per the court's logic, it was okay to let the accused off with a lenient fine since "They have undertaken that they will take proper care in future."[14] A key factor in the court arriving at this conclusion was a statement by the prosecuting drug inspector before the judge that the NSQ drug would not be injurious to health and that a "heavy fine" would be sufficient in the facts of the case.[15]

The above reasoning is deeply problematic for two reasons. First, the provisions of the Drugs and Cosmetics Act 1940, invoked in this case do not require such an assessment of the possible adverse impact of a NSQ drug on patients. Second, the judge and drug inspector were completely wrong in concluding that the drug with only 12.85% of the active ingredient would not pose any harm to patient. The fact of the matter is that Azithromycin is a broad-spectrum antibiotic that is used to treat a wide range of life-threatening infections. If a patient battling a serious life-threatening infection was administered the defendant's NSQ tablets that contained only 12.85% of the active ingredient advertized on the labeling of the drug, there is a high possibility of the patient dying because the tablet simply did not have enough of the active ingredient to control the infection. Dosage of antibiotics is usually decided by doctors based on factors such as the weight of the patient. If a doctor prescribed a 200 mg tablet keeping in mind specific body weight and metabolism, the infection will not be cured if the tablet has only 25.69 mg of the antibiotic. Apart from the issue of the possible death of patients administered such NSQ drugs, it should be noted that substandard antibiotics contribute to a rise in antimicrobial resistance, which is one of the biggest public health issues facing the world today.[16] Yet, the manufacturing firm in this case escaped with a slap on the wrist from the judge without the management of the firm having to spend any time in prison. Such judicial outcomes are unfortunately quite routine in prosecutions under the Drugs and Cosmetics Act 1940.

Even in cases where it is obvious that a NSQ drug poses a danger to public health, Indian courts are known to have been very lenient. Take for example the case filed by drug inspectors of the Tamil Nadu Drug Control Department in 2019 against Tamman Titoe Pharma Pvt Ltd after vials of a drug manufactured by the company allegedly failed both the assay test and the bacterial endotoxin test (BET). The presence of endotoxins in a drug can have dangerous consequences for patients, ranging from aseptic shock to death. After a relatively speedy trial that concluded in April 2021, the XV Metropolitan Magistrate, Georgetown, Chennai found the company guilty of manufacturing the NSQ drug in question. However, as a punishment, the judge merely sentenced the management of the company to "simple imprisonment till the rising of the court along with a paltry fine of ₹50,000".[17] The court also ordered the company to pay the charges for an advertisement in the paper publishing details of the conviction in the newspaper. The court justified this leniency on the grounds that the prosecution did not argue that the drug caused any "injury or harm" to the public.[18] As mentioned earlier, most provisions of the Drugs and Cosmetics Act 1940 do not require the prosecution to establish possible adverse effects of a substandard drug on patients. In a similar case in neighbouring Kerala, when the Chief Judicial Magistrate of Thalassery, found the Madhya Pradesh-based Modern Laboratories guilty of manufacturing an Ampicillin injection that failed the tests for bacterial endotoxin, sterility and assay, it sentenced the management to simple imprisonment for three months and a fine of ₹10,000 each.[19] (This sentence was stayed by the Sessions Court pending the outcome of an appeal.[20]) The reason for the leniency offered by the judge to circumvent the minimum sentencing requirement of one year in the Drugs and Cosmetics Act 1940 was the fact that the accused had been appearing before the court over a period of 13 long years![21]

It is not unknown for such prosecutions to take more than a decade to conclude. Take for example in Maharashtra, we were able to collect from the e-courts database, a set of 95 judgments in prosecutions against pharmaceutical manufacturers under the Drugs and Cosmetics Act 1940, that were filed between 1993 and 2015. For this dataset, the median time to disposal was 10.5 years with the average being 11.35 years! These figures would have actually been much higher if it was not for one particular judicial magistrate in whose courtroom, pharmaceutical companies suddenly began pleading guilty to manufacturing NSQ drugs after having contested their cases for several years. In all these cases, the manufacturers received only a light fine without having to serve any jail time. In cases where the pharmaceutical manufacturers decide to slog it out through an entire trial, a typical case can take up to 20 years only to result in an acquittal. Take for example the criminal complaint filed by a Drug Inspector of the Maharashtra Food and Drug Administration on September 1 1994, against Macleods Pharmaceuticals and its management personnel before the Judicial Magistrate First Class at Palghar district in Maharashtra. The drug inspector accused the company of manufacturing and selling Ampicillin, an antibiotic, that had been declared to be NSQ by a government analyst in a government laboratory on the grounds that it contained only 47.50% of the active ingredient advertized on the label of the drug. After a trial and arguments that dragged on for 23 years, 5 months and 25 days, the Judicial Magistrate on February 26 2018, acquitted all the accused on a host of procedural grounds, including the fact that the drug inspectors were not able to establish whether the drug was properly stored in the dispensary, from where it was drawn by the Drug Inspector.[22]

But the situation is not the same across all states. In Karnataka for example, cases were being disposed in a matter of a few months. We discovered that the Special Court for Economic Offences, Bangalore, Karnataka was concluding similar prosecutions in a matter of months in judgments spanning three pages without even a mention of the nature of the defect that led to the drug being declared NSQ. This appears to have been possible because this court was content with handing out paltry fines and "simple imprisonment till the rising of the court". By way of illustration, this particular court took cognizance of a criminal complaint filed by a Drug Inspector on November 6 2012, against BRD Medilabs, accusing it of manufacturing NSQ drugs. The management of the company pled guilty to all charges on December 15 2012, and on the same day was "sentenced till the rising of the court" along with a fine of ₹20,000! The judgement does not even mention the name of the drug that was declared NSQ or the nature of the defect.[23] There are several such judgments where the same court dealt with such cases in the same manner as it would deal with the prosecution of traffic offences.

Separate and apart from these cases where pharmaceutical manufacturers are prosecuted after their drug samples fail the prescribed quality testing standards are cases of pharmaceutical companies manufacturing drugs without having the requisite manufacturing licences under the Drugs and Cosmetics Act 1940. The purpose of licensing manufacturing facilities is to allow for drug inspectors to verify that the manufacturing facility is in compliance with GMP requirements in Schedule M to the Drugs and Cosmetics Rules 1945, that it has qualified personnel to oversee the manufacturing process and that it is capable of manufacturing the drugs. To manufacture drugs without first procuring a manufacturing licence is a very serious issue since it robs the drug inspectors of a chance to verify compliance of the manufacturing facility with the law. Yet, there have been instances where companies have been prosecuted for manufacturing drugs without first procuring the necessary manufacturing licences from the state drug controller. In one such case from Andhra Pradesh, drug inspectors from the Andhra Pradesh Drug Control Administration accused Krebs Biochemicals Industries Ltd, a publicly listed bulk drugs manufacturer of engaging in the bulk manufacture of the active pharmaceutical ingredients (API) used to make several drugs, including anti-retroviral drugs used in the treatment of HIV patients, without having the requisite manufacturing/ testing licences mandated under the Drugs and Cosmetics Act 1940. The bulk drugs were being manufactured for Ranbaxy Laboratories, which was also prosecuted, but the case against it was subsequently split from the case against Krebs Biochemicals.[24] The modus operandi in this case for the HIV drugs was simple. Ranbaxy procured "test licences" for the manufacture of Emtricitabine, Atazanvir Sulphate and Lopinavir on the premises of Krebs Biochemicals. Such test licences are meant to facilitate the manufacture of small quantities of drugs as required for the purpose of "examination, test or analysis". Generally, these test quantities are used to generate data required for regulatory approval. It is far easier to get a "test licence" when compared to a "manufacturing licences" since the law lays down a long list of requirements and inspections before the grant of a "manufacturing licence". No such requirements exist for the grant of "test licences". Once Krebs Biochemicals and Ranbaxy procured these test licences, the former allegedly manufactured industrial quantities of each drug: 51.20 kgs of Emtricitabine, 117.965 kgs of Lopinavir and 495.85 kgs of Atazanavir Sulfate. Not only were these quantities far in excess of "test quantities" but the drug inspectors also alleged that the drugs Atazanvir and Lopinavir were manufactured prior to the grant of even the test licence by the drug controller. The batch of Emtricitabine was manufactured after the expiry of the test licence granted by the drug controller. In addition to these three drugs, the drug inspectors had alleged violations in the manufacture of two other drugs, one of which involved Ranbaxy.

This case filed in 2011 against Krebs Biochemicals before the Additional Judicial Magistrate of First Class, Kovur, Andhra Pradesh, ended in 2019 with the court convicting Krebs Biochemical Industries and its Managing Director for the "manufacture and sale" of 495.85 kgs of Atazanavir Sulfate (treatment for HIV), 117.965 kgs of Lopinavir (treatment for HIV), 51.20 kgs of Emitracitabine (treatment for HIV), and two other drugs without first obtaining the valid licences thereby violating section 18 (c) Drugs and Cosmetics Act". The trial against Ranbaxy is still pending.

The Managing Director of Krebs Biochemicals was sentenced to prison for a period of one year and a fine of ₹20,000 for the crime of manufacturing drugs without having valid licences.[25] The conviction and sentence are currently pending appeal before the Sessions Judge.[26] On 22 March 2022 the Sessions Judge hearing the appeal noted in his order "The Appellant tried to influence in respect of judgment on 21.03.2022. Hence it is not safe to pronounce, the judgment and appellant is warned not to repeat such acts..." With those words the judge transferred the case to another court.

Of the various types of cases discussed above, the case against Macleods Pharmaceuticals which involved NSQ drugs is the most representative of the typical case filed by a Drug Inspector in India, both in terms of facts and outcomes.

Subverting parliamentary will through prosecution guidelines

While the acquittals and lenient sentencing discussed in the cases above is worrying, what worries us more is the fact that only a very small percentage of cases where the system detects NSQ drugs are actually prosecuted by the drug inspectors. This is not due to the corruption or negligence of individual drug inspectors but due to the dubious prosecution guidelines laid down by the Drugs Consultative Committee (DCC); a committee consisting of representatives from all the state drug control administrations, the Drug Controller General of India (DCGI) who heads the CDSCO and the top brass of the Ministry of Health.[27] This committee does not have any rule making authority and the prosecutions guidelines formulated by it are not legally binding on drug inspectors. These guidelines are only meant to offer guidance to drug inspectors on the type of cases under the Drugs and Cosmetics Act 1940, that they must prosecute. Except that, these guidelines are not in tune with the letter or spirit of the law. In fact, it can be argued that the DCC guidelines actively undermine the Parliamentary will expressed in the bare reading of the Drugs and Cosmetics Act 1940, by advising drug inspectors to consider administrative measures such as licence suspensions in lieu of criminal prosecutions for certain offences. What follows is an explanation of how the prosecution guidelines drafted by the bureaucracy have subverted the Drugs and Cosmetics Act 1940.

Under the Drugs and Cosmetics Act 1940, any drug sample tested in a government laboratory that fails quality parameters prescribed in the officially recognized pharmacopoeias can be prosecuted for one of the following offences: misbranding, adulteration, being declared spurious, or being NSQ.

The actual legal definitions of these offences are complicated, but here is a simple explainer of each term. Adulterated drugs usually involve cases where the drug is contaminated with foreign substances that are harmful or reduce its quality or when the drug is manufactured in unsanitary conditions.[28] Spurious drugs generally mean counterfeit drugs where a drug is an imitation of another company's drug and is meant to deceive customers of the true source of manufacture.[29] This includes using a name or a packaging that belongs to another drug. Misbranded drugs are those which make false claims on the labelling of the drug or which fail to follow the law on labelling.[30] A drug which fails quality testing prescribed in the recognized pharmacopoeia but does not fall in any of the previous categories is declared as NSQ.[31] Majority of the quality problems with Indian drugs fall in this last category where drugs manufactured by licenced manufacturers fail quality testing due to poor formulation practices or failure to follow GMP standards. These drugs tend to have too little of the active ingredient to be effective or fail dissolution tests thereby indicating their inability to dissolve in bloodstream of potential patients. In some cases, where government laboratories have the capacity to test for contamination, there have been instances where drugs fail tests for microbial contamination as well.

The punishment for each offence listed above differs. In 2008, the punishment under this law was increased dramatically by Parliament to extend to life in prison with a minimum punishment of 10 years, if such adulterated, spurious or NSQ drugs caused or were likely to cause "grievous hurt" or death.[32] The same provision also allows for the imposition of a fine of ₹10 lakhs or three times the value of the drugs confiscated, whichever is higher.

The manufacture of spurious or adulterated drugs unlikely to cause death or "grievous hurt" is punishable with a minimum punishment of seven years and a maximum punishment of life in prison, along with a fine that is not less than ₹3 lakhs or three times the value of the drugs confiscated, whichever is higher.[33]

On the other hand, manufacturers of NSQ drugs that do not cause death or "grievous hurt" is punishable by a minimum imprisonment of one year and a maximum imprisonment of two years, along with a fine of up to a maximum of ₹20,000.[34]

In each of the provisions mentioned above, the law allows the court the discretion to impose a lesser sentence for special reasons which are to be recorded in writing.

For most of the offences mentioned above, such as the manufacture of NSQ drugs, the state is not required to establish either "criminal negligence" or "criminal intent" in order to secure convictions. The mere fact that the drug has failed testing is sufficient to secure a conviction. Such provisions reflect Parliament's zero-tolerance policy towards the issue of drug quality. This is quite an imposing standard for the pharmaceutical industry since it mandates imprisonment of the responsible personnel and the management of the pharmaceutical company even if a single drug it manufactured is found to be NSQ. While it is always open to the pharmaceutical industry to lobby the Parliament asking it to reform the law and lower punishments, it is not open for a body of bureaucrats like the DCC to ignore the law laid down by the Parliament by directing drug inspectors to wink at the standards laid down in the Drugs and Cosmetics Act 1940. Yet, this is exactly what has happened with the DCC's prosecution guidelines.

The original guidelines published by the DCC in 1993 advised drug inspectors across the country that "The weapon for prosecution should be used sparingly and judiciously but due regard to merits of the case be given as a prudent measure. Prosecution should be launched where administrative measures have failed to have desired effects."[35] The administrative measures in context of the Drugs and Cosmetics Act 1940, involve "suspension" or "cancellation" of manufacturing licences and were created by the government through the Drugs and Cosmetics Rules 1945, through powers delegated to it by Parliament.[36] Suspension or cancellation of a manufacturing licence is a response to a violation of the terms and conditions of the grant of a manufacturing licence. In other words, such a suspension or cancellation is the withdrawal of a privilege extended by the state to a pharmaceutical company. In form and substance, such a suspension or cancellation of a manufacturing licence is no substitute under the law for criminal punishment that is meant to punish a manufacturer for endangering the life of common people. Yet, the DCC's guidelines recommended to drug inspectors across the country to consider suspension of manufacturing licenses in lieu of criminal prosecutions.

In 2008, after the Parliament amended the Drugs and Cosmetics Act 1940 to significantly increase punishments for the manufacture or sale of adulterated and spurious drugs or NSQ drugs that could result in harm to patients, the DCC replaced the guidelines from 1993 with a new set of guidelines.[37] Similar to the guidelines that it replaced, the new guidelines in 2008 recommended vigorous prosecution *only* in cases of spurious or adulterated drugs. For NSQ drugs that were so declared because of a failure to pass quality testing in a government laboratory, the new guidelines create two categories: "grossly substandard" and "minor defects". The Drugs and Cosmetics Act 1940 itself does not draw this distinction. As per the law, any drug that fails standards in the Indian Pharmacopeia is to be declared NSQ. In any event, based on this artificial distinction between "grossly substandard" and "minor defects", the DCC's prosecution guidelines prescribe the following course of action:

> In the case of drugs manufactured by a licensed manufacturer under a valid manufacturing licence has been found grossly sub-standard, the matter may be investigated at the manufacturer's end, and where criminal intent or gross negligence has been established and if the merits of the case so demand, and where it is felt that administrative measures would not be sufficient to meet the ends of justice, the recourse to prosecution should be resorted to.

Simply put, even if the drug inspector detects "grossly substandard" drugs as defined in the guidelines, "the weapon of prosecution" is to be "used judiciously" only where the "criminal intent or gross negligence" of the manufacturer had been established and only if "administrative measures" were not sufficient to "meet the ends of justice".[38] This guidance in the DCC guidelines is deeply problematic for three reasons.

First, the Drugs and Cosmetics Act 1940 does not require any assessment of "criminal intent" or "gross negligence" for prosecuting manufacturers of NSQ drugs.

Second, the Drugs and Cosmetics Act 1940 also does not require a drug inspector to choose between administrative measure and criminal punishment. As explained earlier, one is not the substitute for the other. It is simply shocking therefore that this statutory committee consisting of the bureaucracy responsible for enforcing a law enacted by Parliament took it upon itself to frame these guidelines to undermine the express intent of elected lawmakers.

Third, the definition of "grossly substandard" drugs in the DCC guidelines includes the following categories: injectables that failed sterility or endotoxin testing or toxicity testing, tablets that fail disintegration and dissolution tests (meaning that these tablets will not dissolve in the blood of patients), liquid preparations that contain fungus etc., and only drugs with less than 70% of the active ingredient.[39] These are all categories of defects that can cause terrible treatment outcomes for patients. Drugs that fail endotoxin testing, toxicity, or sterility testing can cause death. Drugs that contain less than 70% of the active ingredient can fail to deliver the required dosage especially if these drugs are Narrow Therapeutic Index (NTI) drugs. The Indian Pharmacopeia generally permits a variation of only 10% in the content of active ingredient.

Given the potential of all the aforementioned defects to cause serious illness, if not death to patients, it is stunning that the DCC guidelines do not advise vigorous, mandatory prosecutions in all cases of "grossly substandard" drugs, especially when the 2008 amendments prescribe a sentence of life in prison for NSQ drugs that have the potential to cause "grievous hurt" or death. The advice in the "guidelines" to drug inspectors to look at "administrative measures" as the first resort in such cases and to consider prosecution only "judiciously" is simply unacceptable.

Equally worrying is the approach of the DCC guidelines

to the issue of "minor defects" which it defines as including quality issues such as "broken or chipped tablets", "presence of spot/dis-colouration/uneven coating", "clear liquid preparations showing sedimentation" etc.[40] These kinds of defects are generally a result of poor manufacturing processes that escape quality-control measures at the manufacturing facility. To classify some of these issues as "minor defects" is misleading to say the least. For example, tablet discolouration is often due to contaminants in raw materials or from interactions between excipients that may occur during storage. The chemical composition of a poorly formulated product reacts with surrounding air and light if not stored under the conditions specified on the label resulting in molecular conversion and possible changes in colouration. Similarly, liquid formulations may degrade over time resulting in visible sedimentation. Such degradation often causes drug-drug interactions which may causally be linked to potential adverse events. Classifying such degradation as "minor defects" is unscientific.

For "minor defects", the DCC guidelines recommend "administrative measures" such as the cancellation or suspension of manufacturing licences as the first response, with prosecution being the exceptional response, reserved for cases "where it is justifiably felt that above measures would not meet the ends of justice".[41] This, despite the fact that most of the "minor defects" as described in the DCC guidelines are likely to be a result of poor formulation capacity of the manufacturer and serious lapses in the quality control process.

Despite the DCC guidelines lacking the force of law (since the DCC has no rule-making powers) there is conclusive evidence from some states which demonstrates that drug inspectors in deference to the DCC's prosecution guidelines, use criminal prosecutions as the last resort against erring pharmaceutical companies. We were able to access via the RTI Act 2005, consolidated state-level data on the frequency of prosecutions in cases where NSQ drugs were detected during varying time periods, for five states: Karnataka, Maharashtra, Uttarakhand, Delhi, and Gujarat. Scrutiny of this data revealed that criminal prosecutions were ordered only in a small fraction of the cases where NSQ drugs were discovered.

In Maharashtra, between 2010 and 2015, of the 2,176 drugs found to be NSQ by the state laboratories, only 293 prosecutions were ordered by the department. (Prosecution data for 18 months was unavailable in the registers).[42] Similarly in Karnataka, between the years 2009 and 2013, of the 755 drugs that were found to be NSQ by the state laboratories, the department ordered prosecutions in only 81 cases.[43] In Uttarakhand, during the period of January 2010 to May 2015, of the merely 68 drugs found to be NSQ by the state laboratory, only four prosecutions were ordered.[44]

For the city of Delhi, publicly available data on the website of the Delhi Drugs Control Department, indicates that of the 130 drugs declared NSQ by the state laboratory between 2012 and 2018, prosecutions were ordered in merely 29 cases.[45]

Lastly, the Commissioner for Food and Drugs Control Administration, Gujarat, in response to a request we made under the RTI Act revealed that between January 1 2016, and December 2021, a mere 65 prosecutions were ordered.[46] During the same time period, as per the XLN website, the state laboratories in Gujarat declared a total of 1,617 drugs as NSQ. This would mean that Gujarat is prosecuting approximately 4% of the NSQ cases that it detects.

In the remaining cases, where the state drug controllers do not prosecute the erring manufacturer, they fall back on "administrative measures" such as suspension or cancellation of licences. Gujarat, for example suspended a total of 1,318 licences in the same time period that it ordered only 65 prosecutions. In cases where the manufacturer of the NSQ drug is located outside the jurisdiction of the state drug inspector who has detected the NSQ drug, the general practice is for the drug inspector to refer the test report to the state drug controller who has issued the manufacturing licence for further action. The Karnataka NSQ Register provided more details in this regard, since it also recorded the response from other states after they were informed by the Karnataka Drug Control Department that a drug manufactured in a facility under their jurisdiction tested NSQ. For example, drug inspectors from Himachal Pradesh, which is the primary source of NSQ drugs in Karnataka, typically informed the Karnataka Drug Control Department that they punished the company in question by "suspending" their manufacturing licence for the drug in question for a time period ranging between 10 days and 180 days.

Technically speaking, if a manufacturing licence has been suspended, the pharmaceutical company cannot manufacture the drug for the duration of the "suspension" but we have serious doubts as to whether these licence "suspensions" amount to a punishment at all. A typical pharmaceutical manufacturer likely holds multiple manufacturing licences for different drugs at the same facility. It is perfectly profitable for these companies to stop a manufacturing line for one drug temporarily while continuing to manufacture other drugs during the suspension period. A better indicator of the extent to which such licence suspensions actually punish or hurt erring pharmaceutical manufacturers is whether they litigate these licence suspensions before a court of law. A search of all High Court judgments across India over a period of 75 years threw up only two judgments dealing with the issue of suspension of manufacturing licences under the Drugs and Cosmetics Act 1940.[47] The most likely reason there is no substantial litigation on the issue of licence suspension is because such suspensions are either not enforced or even if enforced, are not materially hurtful to the business interests of these erring pharmaceutical companies.

It is more likely that only a cancellation of a manufacturing licence will hurt their business interests. These cancellations however appear to be rarer than suspension of a manufacturing licence. In the registers that we were able to access, Uttarakhand cancelled manufacturing licences only in five cases, Delhi cancelled manufacturing licences only in two cases across eight years and Karnataka cancelled 18 manufacturing licences across three years. Gujarat did not cancel any manufacturing licences. In any event, there is no bar under the law against reissuance of the cancelled manufacturing licence on payment of the required licence fee and fulfilment of required conditions.

From the data presented above, it is very clear that the DCC guidelines are actually followed by drug inspectors and that these guidelines have effectively subverted the Drugs and Cosmetics Act 1940, to create a parallel legal framework that is exceptionally lenient towards errant pharmaceutical companies manufacturing NSQ drugs. Given the farce of licence suspensions and the reluctance to institute criminal prosecutions, it is very likely that most pharmaceutical companies found to be manufacturing NSQ drugs do not face any serious legal or financial liability when they are found to be manufacturing NSQ drugs. In no other country in the world is the business of manufacturing pharmaceutical drugs such a low-risk enterprise.

Of faulty investigations and prosecutorial errors

Presuming that a drug inspector receives permission to prosecute a case where a NSQ drug was manufactured and sold by a particular pharmaceutical company, despite the high thresholds set in the aforementioned DCC guidelines, it is the responsibility of the drug inspector to conduct an investigation, decide the charges, and file a criminal complaint before a court of law.

For successful prosecutions of a case involving a NSQ drug,

the law does not really require a very detailed investigation. A conviction can be procured solely on the basis of the government analyst's report declaring the drug to be NSQ, provided the drug inspector complies with all procedural safeguards. As a result, most drug inspectors conduct a limited investigation, generally aimed at establishing the chain-of-custody between the manufacturing facility where the drug was manufactured and the pharmacy from where it was purchased by the drug inspector. This is usually done by sourcing the trail of invoices from the wholesaler, retailer etc.

Once the journey of the drug through the supply chain is established, the focus of the criminal investigation shifts to the manufacturer of the drug. In an ideal world, this aspect of the investigation should begin by reviewing past inspection reports of the manufacturing facility along with any information on past investigations or prosecutions against the same drug manufacturer. Unfortunately, such information is not available in consolidated public databases, which is a big problem due to the federal nature of India's regulatory system wherein each individual state drug controller issues its own manufacturing licences for facilities within its territorial jurisdiction (which only it can inspect) and conducts its own testing, investigations, and prosecutions. There is no unified database save for the XLN website which contains testing data from just a handful of states. Given the lack of such consolidated databases, the only way to collect such information about manufacturing facilities located in other states is to contact the respective drug controller in that state and make a request for such information. Such coordination can be time consuming and inefficient, especially since most Indian drug controllers prefer using snail mail even in this digital age.

An ideal investigation into the manufacture of a NSQ drug should also include a surprise inspection of the manufacturing facility in order to inspect for GMP compliance and conduct a "root-cause analysis", which is industry lingo for identifying the specific reasons for failure in the manufacturing controls that caused the drug to be NSQ. This is very important from a public health perspective because only once the manufacturer is forced to identify the cause of the defect, will it rectify the same, thereby ensuring that future batches of the drug meet quality specifications or alternatively it can be mandated by the regulator to put procedures in place to avoid such failures in the future. Surprisingly however, Indian drug inspectors rarely, if ever, conduct inspections of facilities as part of their investigations. In an overwhelming number of the approximately 225 criminal complaints, investigation reports, and judgments that we researched upon, the drug inspector in charge would simply write to the pharmaceutical company that manufactured the NSQ drug, asking for a copy of the manufacturing records of the batch in question. Only a few enterprising drug inspectors turn up at the manufacturing facility to ask for a copy of the records and conduct an inspection in person.

Only in a small minority of cases, like the Alfred Berg & Co. case discussed in the beginning of this chapter, do drug inspectors actually carry out a "surprise inspection" or "raid" of facilities suspected of flouting quality norms. Even in these small number of cases, drug inspectors can run into jurisdictional issues because of the federal nature of India's drug regulatory framework wherein each state appoints its own drug inspectors to carry out licensing and enforcement. Due to this distribution of powers which dates back to 1940, the Drugs and Cosmetics Act 1940 limits the search and seizure powers of drug inspectors to the jurisdiction of the area for which they have been appointed by the state government. Most states usually appoint a drug inspector for a district or to oversee a couple of districts. For the drug inspector to enter and search facilities outside her jurisdiction, she will have to coordinate with the drug inspector who has jurisdiction over the facility that manufactured the NSQ drug. This may be relatively easy in case the manufacturer is located within the same state, since both drug inspectors work for the same drug controller. However, if it turns out that the manufacturing facility is located in a different state, matters can get severely complicated since it involves coordination between two different regulators working under different state governments and with different political aims. For example, a state like Himachal Pradesh, which has consciously worked to turn into a hub for pharmaceutical manufacturing, may not be interested in permitting inspections of its facilities by drug inspectors from other states. In his book on the functioning of the India drug regulatory system, K.L. Sharma, who was a former joint secretary in the drug regulation section of the Ministry of Health, documents the extreme resistance of states like Himachal Pradesh and Tamil Nadu in allowing drug inspectors from the CDSCO to conduct joint inspections of manufacturing facilities along with the respective state drug inspectors.[48] In his words, "...it particularly proved to be a Heculean task to convince the Government of Himachal Pradesh who agreed to the state participating in inspections after detailed discussions on the condition that the modalities of inspection were to be first discussed by the inspecting team with the State Drug Controller." Similarly, he notes "The Tamil Nadu Government also refused to cooperate initially; however on persuasion, the state government reluctantly agreed."[49]

Perhaps for the above reasons, most Indian drug inspectors limit themselves to asking for the manufacturing records to be sent to them by mail. There are two problems with this approach. First, asking pharmaceutical manufacturers to send the records via mail gives them ample time to manipulate the manufacturing records to paper over any wrongdoing on their part. There is great incentive for them to do so in face of a possible criminal prosecution. In her book *Bottle of Lies*, Katherine Eban documents in detail the scale of data fabrication discovered by the USFDA during its surprise inspections at manufacturing facilities owned by Indian pharmaceutical companies. Indian companies have even had to cough up fines for destroying documents. Take for example Fresenius Kabi, an Indian manufacturer of cancer drugs which pled guilty to concealing and destroying records prior to an inspection conducted by the USFDA in 2013. It agreed to pay $50 million in fines to the United States government.[50]

The second problem with this approach of asking for manufacturing records via mail is that merely perusing manufacturing records does not give the drug inspector a reasonable idea of the physical conditions at the manufacturing facility. Take for example the allegations against Alfred Berg & Co.; of congested premises without proper labeling and the lack of a separate quality assurance department or the allegations made by the USFDA against Indian manufacturing firms related to lack of sterile manufacturing conditions. These issues go to the heart of compliance with GMP and can be discovered only through a physical inspection of the facilities.

In any event, under the Drugs and Cosmetics Act 1940, even without a physical inspection of the premises or an in-depth scrutiny of the manufacturing records, it is possible for the drug inspector to secure a conviction of the manufacturer solely on the basis of the government analyst's test report *unless* the accused company is able to establish a failure of the drug inspector to comply with all the procedural safeguards laid down in the law. If and when pharmaceutical companies decide to contest the charges and take the case to trial, their chances of getting acquitted are very high.

For example, in Maharashtra, of the 95 judgments that we were able to access through the e-courts database, in cases against pharmaceutical companies between 1993 and 2016 on the charges of manufacturing NSQ drugs, drug inspectors of the Maharashtra Food and Drug Administration were able to secure convictions only in five cases where the accused contested charges. In another 54 judgments where the accused contested the charges, the trials ended in acquittals. In another 28 of these 95 cases, the pharmaceutical companies pled guilty in exchange for no jail time and a small monetary fine. The remaining ended in discharge of the accused before charges could be framed.

In Andhra Pradesh, of the 54 judgments that we were able to access through the e-courts database between 1999 and 2017 in cases filed against pharmaceutical companies on the charges of manufacturing NSQ drugs, drug inspectors of the Andhra Pradesh Drug Control Administration were able to secure convictions in only eight cases. In another 38 cases, the courts acquitted the pharmaceutical manufacturers after the trial, and in the remaining cases the accused were discharged even before charges were framed.

In Telangana, of the 24 judgments that we were able to access through the e-courts database in cases filed against pharmaceutical companies between 2002 and 2015 on the charges of manufacturing NSQ drugs, drug inspectors of the Telangana Drug Control Department managed to secure four convictions.

Based on an analysis of the above judgments from Maharashtra, Andhra Pradesh, and Telangana, we were able to identify eight common errors that were committed by drug inspectors during the investigation and prosecution of the cases under the Drugs and Cosmetics Act 1940 which eventually led to the acquittal of the accused pharmaceutical company.

To begin with, a drug inspector is required to file a copy of the Gazette notification establishing her appointment and jurisdiction to investigate and prosecute the case. Failure to provide such evidence, especially the notification outlining the drug inspector's jurisdiction, can be fatal to the case. Despite being such a basic requirement, we have seen a few judgments where the courts acquitted pharmaceutical companies because it was not convinced that the drug inspector had the jurisdiction to investigate or prosecute the case.

Second, the drug inspector must absolutely file as evidence a receipt showing purchase of the drug samples of the impugned drug from a pharmacy as well as documentation demonstrating that the pharmacy purchased the drug from the manufacturer, even if it is through wholesale dealers. This is necessary to establish that the sample was in fact manufactured by the manufacturer. Failure to file this paperwork will lead to the case falling apart.

Third, when a sample of a drug is purchased by the drug inspector, she is required under Rule 4 of the Drugs and Cosmetics Rules 1945, to send the drug sample in a sealed packet via registered post to the government analyst in the government laboratory for testing. Rule 4 also requires that the "specimen impression" of the "seal" affixed on the packet containing the drug, be sent separately to the government analyst. This is to reduce scope for manipulation of the sealed package in transit. A failure to comply with this requirement can lead to the case falling apart. On receipt of the sample, the Director of the government laboratory, or a person authorized by the Director is supposed to match the specimen of the seal impression to the seal on the sealed packet containing the drug sample in order to compare and check for any signs of tampering and record the same in the test report. When a prosecution is filed before a court, during the course of the trial, the drug inspectors need to lead evidence before the court proving that all of these procedural requirements have been met. For example, the receipt from the post office acknowledging that the sample was sent by registered post to the laboratory needs to be filed before the court to prove that the sample was sent to the laboratory in the prescribed mode. If the drug inspector fails to provide evidence on these issues, the entire prosecution case can fall apart.

A fourth set of errors typically made by drug inspectors is the failure to record the condition of the storage of the drug sample being purchased, both at the pharmacy from where it is purchased and during the process of transit of the sample to the government laboratory. Recording the conditions of storage is very important because many pharmaceutical companies will try to argue in their defense that the sample degraded during transit or at the pharmacy because it was not stored properly. For example, if the drug in question is known to be sensitive to temperature, the drug inspector must produce documentation to show that the drug was properly stored during transit to the government laboratory. Yet, many drug inspectors fail to address this issue while leading evidence during the course of a prosecution. Failure to do so can lead to the prosecution's case collapsing because in a criminal trial, the court will give the accused pharmaceutical company the benefit of the doubt.

A fifth set of errors which is the predominant reason for acquittals in most states we studied, is the failure of the drug inspectors and government analysts working in the government laboratory to complete the testing process of the drug sample before the expiry date printed on the label of the drug. In fact, the first round of testing, usually in the state government laboratory, needs to be completed with enough time left to facilitate an "appeal" by the accused manufacturer before the Central Drug Laboratory (CDL), Kolkata. This "appeal" is the statutory right of the manufacturer under the Drugs and Cosmetics Act 1940, and it allows the manufacturer to request the court to send the sample stored with it to CDL for a second round of testing. All of this has to take place before the expiry date printed on the drug packaging. If the accused-pharmaceutical company is denied this right to have the sample tested at CDL prior to the expiry date of the drug, the court will dismiss the prosecution because a statutory right granted to the accused pharmaceutical company has been frustrated by the government. The reasons for these delays are multifold. It could be sloppiness on part of the drug inspector or due to delays at the state government's laboratory. The delay at the state laboratory or the CDL could be due to a backlog at either laboratory or because of difficulties in procuring reference standards or impurity standards from the Indian Pharmacopoeia Commission.

A sixth set of errors, which are quite rare, are attributable to government analysts who conduct the testing. Rule 6 of the Drugs and Cosmetics Rules 1945 requires government analysts to disclose in the form sent back to the drug inspector the complete protocols used to test the drug sample along with test results. A failure to disclose the test protocols can lead to acquittals.

The seventh set of errors, although relatively rare, is the failure to serve a copy of the report of the government analyst on the pharmaceutical company in order to enable them to prepare for their defense.

The eighth set of errors that are made generally at the stage of prosecution, involves "panch witness". These "public witnesses" are supposed to be independent citizens who can verify that the sample has been seized and sealed properly by the drug inspector. This is not a procedural requirement in the Drugs and Cosmetics Act 1940 but a general practice during criminal investigations in India. The aim is to have someone outside of the investigating agency verify seizures and sign the "panchanamma" or "seizure memorandum". These "panch witnesses" are then supposed to turn up during the course of the trial and corroborate their signature, the items seized, the placement of the seals etc. Very often these "panch witnesses" do not turn up or do not "remember" crucial facts—this could be attributed to the long gaps between the sampling/seizure and the conduct of the trial. Despite the Drugs and Cosmetics Act 1940 not requiring these "panch witnesses" to be present, we noticed that some Judicial Magistrates can be quite pedantic and acquit the defendants if these "panch witnesses" fail to provide the expected testimony. In our opinion, if the aim is to protect against tampering of evidence, then these "panch witnesses" are not required because most modern drugs have tamper-proof packaging and a government analyst can easily tell if the drug inspector has tampered with the packaging.

It is obvious from the above analysis that there is a lot of scope for errors during the course of a criminal prosecution against a pharmaceutical company charged with manufacturing NSQ drugs. These lapses by drug inspectors during investigations and prosecutions have not missed the attention of judges in the High Courts, who are often asked to quash criminal prosecutions under the Drugs and Cosmetics Act 1940 due to the failure of drug inspectors to comply with procedure under the law. In one such instance in 2012, the Rajasthan High Court made the following remarks about the conduct of drug inspectors, even alluding to possible corruption:

> This Court has been coming across numerous matters wherein in the prosecutions involving the offences and violations of law affecting the health and life of public at large, like the offences under the Prevention of Food Adulteration Act, Drugs and Cosmetic Act, Essential Commodities Act, Insecticides Act and Seeds Act, N.D.P.S. Act etc., the accused escape the clutches of law because of deliberate non-compliance of the technical provisions and safeguards prescribed in the Acts, viz., as in the present case, this Court is being led to quash the prosecution against the manufacturers of the medicinal preparation just

> because of unjustified delay committed by the Drugs Inspector in sending the mandatory intimation under Section 25 (2) of the Drugs and Cosmetics Act to the manufacturing company. The endeavour of the concerned authorities should be to see that the manufacturers/ all the responsible persons are brought to book by proceeding expeditiously, but sadly enough, the prosecutions are deliberately left ridden with loop-holes so that the manufacturers or the big fish escape the clutches of law taking resort to the technical flaws. This Court feels that the possibility of such loop- holes being deliberately left so that the big fish may go scot-free cannot be ruled out. Obviously, the objective behind such an approach can either be due to negligence or can be aimed at achieving some gain. In any event, in order to prevent such wrong-doings on the part of the concerned officials in future and to see that the erring officials are brought to book, a direction is hereby issued to all the lower courts in the State of Rajasthan that whenever such inaction resulting into the prosecution being stifled because of technical irregularities committed by the concerned officials, caused to notice, the Court shall, after giving an opportunity to show cause to the concerned official, proceed to report the matter to the Disciplinary Authority of such official under rule 66 of the Criminal (General) Rules, 1980...[51]

Similarly, the Bombay High Court in 1994, while hearing a case involving spurious drugs, made the following scathing remarks on the depressing state of affairs regarding prosecutions under the Drugs and Cosmetics Act 1940:

> Cases involving racketeering in life saving drugs or trading in spurious medicinal preparation for that matter, require special consideration particularly where it is demonstrated that there has been a compromise in quality or adulteration of the Drugs. Many precious lives have been lost due to the spurious preparations having been administered and it is a matter of little consequence whether the fault can be traced

> to the manufacturer, to the intermediary or to the dealer. These are crimes against humanity and the law must approach them with a degree of utmost firmness if the rackets are to be contained and snuffed out. Even at the risk of sounding ruthless, it will have to be stated that if a gradation of anti-social offences were to be done, this category would probably top the list.
>
> The situation becomes all the more distressful when it is disclosed that the offender is being shown sympathetic consideration by the very public authorities in whom the sacred task of safeguarding public safety is entrusted. Instances are not wanting where an unscrupulous trader even after having been booked, approaches the top authorities in the Government and they in turn agree to condone the lapse for reasons that are not difficult to understand. The conduct of such Government authorities in whitewashing grave crimes requires to be taken serious note of by the Courts because on the one hand it is completely demoralising to a point of total frustration for the Enforcement Officers who see the criminal go scot-fee because of the contacts at the higher level and more importantly because it is an assurance and an insurance to that and all other similarly placed criminals that such lucrative rackets are quite safe.[52]

In another judgment, albeit one involving food adulteration in Maharashtra, the Bombay High Court made the following scathing remarks against the entire Maharashtra Food and Drug Administration:

> I conclude that the Food and Drugs Department and its officers right from the cadre of Food Inspectors to Joint Commissioner do not have any legal knowledge, legal skill and seriousness with which the provisions of these Acts concerning human health is required. They are casual, callous and hardly concerned. Relevant and concerned provisions/amended provisions of Code of Criminal Procedure are not even known to them to make use thereof. They are making cases only to show that cases are being prepared and instituted

> in courts and finally tell the people that courts have discharged or acquitted the accused persons and thus save their skin. In my opinion, Government is simply wasting money on Food and Drugs Department and serious view for revamping this department will have to be taken by the Government with strict `accountability' to be fixed for each and every officer.[53]

Most of the above condemnations by the High Courts are likely informed by a number of similar petitions asking for the quashing of criminal proceedings on the grounds that the drug inspectors fail to comply with relatively simple procedural safeguards. The subtext of much of this condemnation by these judges is a suspicion that those responsible for the investigation and prosecution of offences under the Drugs and Cosmetics Act 1940 are willfully committing errors because they have been bribed. It is always difficult to corroborate such suspicions but there is likely some truth to these allegations given the frequency of news reports of drug inspectors being arrested on allegations of corruption.

Of easy convictions and lenient sentencing

The only aspect of the enforcement mechanism which is more astonishing than the acquittal rate in prosecutions of the pharmaceutical companies charged with manufacturing NSQ drugs, is the rate at which pharmaceutical companies plead guilty in some states to charges of manufacturing NSQ drugs. The incentive for such guilty pleas lies in the fact that many judges are only too eager to ignore the minimum mandatory punishment of one year prescribed in the Drugs and Cosmetics Act 1940, by invoking a special exception in the law, to sentence the management of these companies to "simple imprisonment till the rising of the court" along with a paltry fine which is usually ₹20,000 as prescribed in the law.[54] In some cases the fines may be higher but rarely above ₹1 lakh.

As mentioned earlier, "simple imprisonment till the rising of the court" is literally how it sounds—the accused has to be in court till the judge rises, after which the accused is deemed to have served the sentence and is free to go, provided the fine has been paid. The wide prevalence of this sentencing practice across the Indian states that we surveyed was astonishing.

In Maharashtra, of the total 95 judgments in our dataset, accused pharmaceutical companies pled guilty in 28 cases! In each of these cases, the courts handed out sentences of "simple imprisonment till the rising of the court" along with paltry fines in the range of ₹5,000 to ₹80,000.

In Maharashtra, in almost all the cases, the Judicial Magistrates justified these lenient sentences on one (or a combination) of the following grounds: *first*, that the accused had pled guilty voluntarily, *second*, since the case had languished in court for several years, the accused had already spent much time and money in court[55], and *third*, that the drugs in the matter were not "dangerous to life" since it was not adulterated or spurious but "only the required ingredient is found to be less than the standard prescribed". Judges in Maharashtra made such statements in cases where Azithromycin tablets tested for only 12.85% and 13.05% of the quantity advertized on the label and where Glimepiride tablets for diabetic patients had less than 33.85% of the quantity advertized on the label.[56] In all three cases, patients could have been seriously harmed if the drugs failed to perform as expected.

For the state of Karnataka, we managed to get access to some interesting data for a period of seven years from 2015 to 2021. We got this information in the form of a photocopy of an untitled handwritten register from the Karnataka Drug Control Department that was given to us under the RTI Act 2005 when we sought information from it on the number of NSQ drugs etc. in the state. On perusing the contents of the register, it became clear to us that it contained the details of all prosecutions filed by the drug inspectors of the Karnataka Drug Control Department over a period of seven years across the entire state of Karnataka.[57] These included prosecutions filed against manufacturers of NSQ drugs, pharmacists and a tiny number of cases pertaining to the violation of price control laws.

The conviction-related data from the registers revealed some stunning information. Of the 285 cases in which the accused were convicted, the courts in Karnataka sentenced the guilty to "simple imprisonment till the rising of the court" in a total of 248 cases! In the remaining cases, fines were imposed just in 23 cases and prison terms were awarded only in 14 cases. We were also able to access 13 judgments delivered by a court in Bangalore between 2010 to 2018 in cases against pharmaceutical manufacturers under the Drugs and Cosmetics Act 1940 for manufacturing NSQ drugs. In these 13 judgments, the pharmaceutical companies pled guilty and were merely sentenced to "simple imprisonment till the rising of the court" with fines ranging from ₹5,000 to ₹35,000. In almost all the judgments, the judges justified going below the minimum prescribed punishment of one year on grounds that the accused either had a family that they had to support or alternatively that the NSQ drugs were not spurious or adulterated, or the fact that the accused employ a large number of employees who will go unemployed in case of his imprisonment.

Similarly, we were able to access 30 judgments from Tamil Nadu in prosecutions against pharmaceutical companies on the charges of manufacturing NSQ drugs. In 27 of these cases, the accused pled guilty either before trial or during the trial after the prosecution led its evidence. In the remaining three cases, the pharmaceutical companies were found guilty of manufacturing NSQ drugs (in one case the company only failed to maintain records) after a trial. In all 30 cases, the courts in Tamil Nadu passed sentences of "simple imprisonment till the rising of the court" accompanied with fines that were significantly higher than those imposed in Maharashtra or Karnataka. This is because the courts in Tamil Nadu imposed the statutory fine of ₹20,000 on each of the accused charged in the case. Depending on the number of accused, the cumulative fines could go up to ₹1,20,000. As with the courts in Karnataka and Maharashtra, the courts in Tamil Nadu justified awarding sentences lesser than the one-year mandatory prison term prescribed in the Drugs and Cosmetics Act 1940 on the grounds that the accused had families to support or that the case had taken years to resolve itself or more misleadingly, that there was no harm caused to anyone by the NSQ drugs. In many cases, the judicial magistrates appear to have been misinformed on the nature of the defect. For example, as discussed earlier in one case, the vials of a drug had tested positive for bacterial endotoxins, which can be dangerous for humans. Yet, the court justified the lesser sentence on the grounds that the drug in question did not harm anyone.[58]

The manner in which the courts in these states routinely circumvent the minimum mandatory imprisonment terms in the law runs against previous Supreme Court rulings in cases under laws that have a similar minimum sentencing clause as the Drugs and Cosmetics Act 1940, with the same "special reasons" exception. In the words of the Supreme Court, "'Special reasons' have to be distinguished from 'good' or 'other reasons'."[59] The Supreme Court has also ruled that "pendency of criminal case for over a period of time can... not be treated as a special reason" since "Prolonged litigation in the country is admittedly a general reason in criminal cases."[60] In another case, the Supreme Court cautioned judges on invoking the exception to the minimum imprisonment clause, stating the following:

> The court must exercise its discretion in imposing the punishment objectively considering the facts and circumstances of the case. The power under the proviso is not to be used indiscriminately in a routine, casual and cavalier manner for the reason that an exception clause requires strict interpretation ...The court while exercising the discretion in the exception clause has to record "exceptional reasons" for resorting to the proviso. Recording of such reasons is sine qua non for granting the extraordinary relief. What is adequate and special would depend upon several factors and no straight jacket formula can be laid down.[61]

Far from citing exceptional reasons, most of the judgments that we studied from the states of Maharashtra, Karnataka, and Tamil Nadu cited almost the same if not similar reasons to justify awarding less than the minimum of one year prescribed in the Drugs and Cosmetics Act 1940.

Such lenient sentencing, combined with a statutory cap on monetary fines at a mere ₹20,000 means that pharmaceutical companies found guilty of manufacturing NSQ drugs seldom face any material punishment for a crime that could seriously hurt or kill people, especially the most vulnerable patients.

Why is it that judges are so lenient towards pharmaceutical manufacturers? This trend is likely reflective of a larger structural flaw in the Indian justice system wherein judges tend to take a very lenient view of white-collar crime committed by the middle class. As far back as in 1978, the Supreme Court lamented upon this very issue in a case where a professor found guilty of forging university degrees was sentenced to "simple imprisonment till the rising of the court". In that case the Supreme Court had condemned such lenient sentencing practices in the following words:

> We are scandalized by this soft justice syndrome vis-a-vis white collar offenders. It stultifies social justice and camouflages needed severity with naive leniency... It is surprising that the

> Public Prosecutor has consented, on behalf of the State, to this unsocial softness to an anti-social offender on conviction for grave charges. Does the Administration sternly view white-collar offenders, or abet them by agreeing to award of token punishment, making elaborate trials mere tremendous trifles?[62]

Reversing this trend of lenient sentencing in prosecutions under the Drugs and Cosmetics Act 1940 will require public prosecutors to push back against such sentencing practices by judicial magistrates and if required appealing such decisions to higher courts. For this to happen, state governments must have the political will to order prosecutors to demand stricter sentencing or at the very least compliance with the minimum sentencing requirements in the law. The only other alternative is to completely eliminate any discretion to judges in the Drugs and Cosmetics Act 1940 to award punishments lesser than a year.

A roadmap for reform

If there is one relevant takeaway from this chapter, it should be the fact that India's Drugs and Cosmetics Act 1940 is barely enforced against the erring members of the pharmaceutical industry, thereby jeopardizing public health in not just India but also in countries that import medicine from the "pharmacy of the developing world".

It is clear that the pharmaceutical industry in India faces very few consequences, penal or otherwise, for manufacturing and selling NSQ drugs in India. The prosecutorial errors, delays in the judicial system and the leniency of courts in sentencing are systemic issues affecting the entire Indian legal system and are not unique to the enforcement of the Drugs and Cosmetics Act 1940. Better training for drug inspectors and instructions to prosecutors to push back against lenient sentencing through appeals to the High Courts can resolve some of the issues identified in this chapter.

It may also be time to rethink the nature of criminal punishments prescribed under the Drugs and Cosmetics Act 1940. There are many in India who believe that the state must refrain from criminal punishments in what are essentially economic activities. However, given the potential of drugs to cause hurt or even death, we believe that criminal punishments must certainly be retained in the law. There is, however, a valid case to argue for greater flexibility for drug inspectors to choose between criminal punishments that involve imprisonment or a system of monetary fines. This would of course need a relook at the paltry fine of ₹20,000 in the current law. Ideally, fines should be linked to the turnover of the company. The choice between a lengthy sentence in prison versus punishing fines should be well-defined in the law so that there is no ambiguity. For example, if a drug drawn from the market is declared NSQ and a subsequent investigation of the manufacturing facility demonstrates a failure to comply with GMPs, a criminal prosecution with jail time should be mandatory. Similarly, if inspections reveal a poor adherence to legally mandated GMPs, a prosecution should be mandated regardless of whether the drugs resulting from such a manufacturing process fails a quality test.

We are apprehensive of default criminal prosecutions for all pharmaceutical manufacturers whose drugs test NSQ because the supply chain in India is the regulatory equivalent of the "wild west", as we discuss later in this book. The pharmaceutical industry, thus, has a valid point when they claim that their products can get degraded as they traverse through this unregulated supply chain. To send them to prison because a drug drawn from some point in a poorly regulated supply chain fails quality testing may not be fair. That said, better investigations that focuses on reference samples that each manufacturer is required to retain of each batch shipped into the market will help clarify whether the error was with the manufacturer or in the supply chain. Such corroborative testing should be required to establish that the manufacturer and not the supply chain was responsible for the drug being declared NSQ.

In any circumstance, the reforms that we speak of above must be carried out only with the blessing of the Parliament. It is unacceptable, in our opinion, for unelected bureaucrats like those sitting in the DCC to formulate prosecution guidelines that completely subvert parliamentary will in the Drugs and Cosmetics Act 1940. It is astounding that a committee like the DCC, which comprises basically of state drug controllers to collude in this fashion to essentially give the very industry that they are charged with regulating, a reprieve from a law enacted by the Parliament. In political science, this phenomenon where the regulators serve the interests of the industry they are meant to regulate, rather than public interest, is called "regulatory capture".

The DCC guidelines are the perfect example of "regulatory capture". It would, however, be a mistake in our opinion to blame this issue solely on the bureaucracy of drug inspectors who staff the drug regulatory apparatus at the level of state governments. There is very likely a political angle to this "capture" involving elected state level politicians. As argued even by K.L. Sharma, the former joint-secretary responsible for drug regulation policy in the Ministry of Health in his book, state governments are in competition with each other to attract investment from the pharmaceutical industry in their respective states.[63] One way to do so is to go slow on enforcement activities. As long as this competition exists, it makes no difference even if better governed states like Maharashtra, Tamil Nadu, or Karnataka ramp up their enforcement mechanisms because India will always be a common market that allows drugs manufactured in poorly regulated states like Himachal Pradesh or Uttarakhand to be sold across the country.

One way to end this "competition" between states is to centralize the entire licencing and enforcement mechanism with a single regulator that functions under the Government of India. This may also help resolve the issue of uneven enforcement of the law across the country. In many Indian states, due to local politics, poor "state capacity", and budgetary priorities, drug regulation is not a priority because of which there is little attention paid to the issue of enforcing the Drugs and Cosmetics Act 1940. Take for example Nagaland, which confirmed to us in a RTI reply to not having prosecuted any pharmaceutical company since January 1 2016 for manufacture of NSQ drugs![64] Centralizing regulation with the Government of India, which has much deeper pockets than the states, could help resolve this uneven enforcement of the Drugs and Cosmetics Act 1940, across the country but more on this in the last chapter.

Notes

1. Criminal Complaint filed by the Drug Inspector, Vellore under the Drugs and Cosmetics Act 1940 before the Judicial Magistrate, Gudiyattam on 8 December 2014.
2. World Health Organization, 'Should elderly patients with type 2 diabetes be treated with glibenclamide or different sulfonylurea?' <https://www.who.int/selection_medicines/committees/expert/19/applications/Sulfonylurea_18_5_A_R.pdf> last accessed 5 May 2022.
3. The Drugs and Cosmetics Rules 1945, sch M: para 6.2 (Independent QA) and para 12 (Documentation); Criminal Complaint (n 1) 4.
4. Criminal Complaint (n 1) 4.
5. Criminal Complaint (n 1) 5.
6. ibid.
7. The Drugs and Cosmetics Act 1940, s 17B read with s 27(c) (amongst other provisions).
8. *Drug Inspector, Gudiyatham vs Alfred Berg and Co Pvt Ltd & Ors* PRC/4/2016 before the Judicial Magistrate, Gudiyatham, Tamil Nadu (CNR No.: TNVL11-000414-2016).
9. ibid.
10. *State of Tamil Nadu vs Alfred Berg & Co & Ors* Crl.O.P. No.

27614 of 2016 before the Madras High Court decided on 21 April 2017.; *Alfred Berg & Co (I) Pvt Ltd vs State of Tamil Nadu* Crl.O.P. No. 27312 of 2013 before the Madras High Court decided on 10 January 2020; *Alfred Berg & Co (I) Pvt Ltd vs State of Tamil Nadu* Crl.O.P. No. 29269 of 2013 before the Madras High Court decided on 30 January 2020.

11. *Inspector of Police vs Alfred Berg & Co Pvt Ltd* CC No. 0003384 of 2014 before the IV Metropolitan Magistrate, Saidapet, Chennai decided on 20 May 2016.
12. *State of Maharashtra represented by Drug Inspector vs Jayesh Chandulal Mehta, proprietor of Olcare Laboratories* RCC No. 3771 of 2009 before the Chief Judicial Magistrate, Pune decided on 28 September 2016.
13. ibid 5.
14. ibid 4, para 10.
15. ibid 3, para 7.
16. Theodoros Kelesidis and Matthew E. Falagas, 'Substandard/ Counterfeit Antimicrobial Drugs' (2015) 28 *Clinical Microbiology Reviews* 443; Atholl Johnston and David W. Holt, 'Substandard Drugs: A Potential Crisis for Public Health' (2014) 78 *British Journal of Clinical Pharmacology*, 218.
17. *State represented by the Drugs Inspector vs Tamman Titoe Pharma Pvt Ltd & Ors* C.C. No. 1348 of 2020 before the Court of XV Metropolitan Magistrate, Georgetown, Chennai decided on 17 April 2021 at 5.
18. ibid 5, para 10.
19. *Drug Inspector vs Modern Laboratories & Ors* STC No. 107/2018 before the Chief Judicial Magistrate, Thalassery, Kerala decided on 21 January 2020.
20. *Modern Laboratories & Ors vs Drug Inspector* Crl.A/038/2020 before the Principal District & Sessions Judge, Thalassery, Kerala decided on 4 February 2020.
21. *Modern Laboratories* (n 19) 22.
22. *State of Maharashtra vs Dr Rajendra Agarwal, Director Macleods Pharmaceuticals & Ors* R.C.C. No. 230 of 1004 before the Court of Judicial Magistrate First Class, II Court, Palghar decided on 26 February 2018.
23. *Drug Inspector, Bangalore Circle-VI vs M/s BRD Medilabs & Anr* C.C. No. 134 of 2012 before the Special Court (Economic Offences), Bangalore decided on 15 December 2012.
24. *State of Andhra Pradesh represented by Drug Inspector vs Krebs*

Biochemicals Industries Ltd & Ors C.C. No. 399 of 2011 before the Court of the I Additional Judicial Magistrate of First Class, Kovur, Andhra Pradesh decided on 26 March 2019. Read with Criminal Complaint No. 399 of 2011 filed under Section 32 of the Drugs and Cosmetics Act 1940 by Drugs Inspector, Gudur, Nellore District before the Court of Hon'ble Judicial First Class Magistrate at Kovur, Sri Potti Sriamulu Nellore District on 16 September 2011. The case also involved Ranbaxy Laboratories Ltd. because of its commercial relationships with Krebs Biochemicals but the case against Ranbaxy was spun off into a different case: C.C. No. 517 of 2018 before the I Additional Judicial Magistrate of First Class, Kovur, Andhra Pradesh.

25. ibid 52.
26. *Krebs Biochemicals & Industries Ltd and Anr vs Drug Inspector, Gudur* :CRLA/0000125/2019 before the Principal District and Sessions Judge, District Court Nellore (filed on 16 April 2019).
27. Central Drugs Standard Control Organization, Drugs Consultative Committee (DCC), 'Guidelines for Taking Action on Sample of Drugs declared spurious or not of Standard Quality in the light of Enhanced Penalties under the Drugs and Cosmetics (Amendment) Act, 2008' (DCC Guidelines) <https://cdsco.gov.in/opencms/export/sites/CDSCO_WEB/Pdf-documents/Consumer_Section_PDFs/DCC_Guidelines_Spurious_Drugs.pdf> last accessed 5 May 2022.
28. The Drugs and Cosmetics Act 1940, s 17A.
29. ibid, s 17B.
30. ibid, s 17.
31. ibid, s 16.
32. ibid, s 27.
33. ibid, s 27(c).
34. ibid, s 27(d).
35. DCC Guidelines (n 27) 11.
36. The Drugs and Cosmetic Rules 1945, Rule 85.
37. DCC Guidelines (n 27) 1.
38. ibid 4.
39. ibid 2.
40. ibid 3.
41. ibid 4, 5.
42. Reply to RTI application dated 25 August 2015, Office of Commissioner Food and Drug Administration, Maharashtra (Application No D&C/MaAdhi./352/126-15/15, 17 July 2015).
43. Reply to RTI application dated 27 June 2015, Drugs Control

Department, Karnataka (Application No DCD/20/RTI/2015-16, 2 June 2015).

44. Reply to RTI application dated 28 October 2015, Drug Licensing and Controlling Authority, Uttarakhand (Application No 17/P/8/216/2015/26098, 29 September 2015).
45. Government of NCT of Delhi, Drugs Control Department, 'Not of Standard Quality Sample 2012 to 2018' <http://drugscontrol.delhigovt.nic.in/wps/wcm/connect/doit_drug/DoIT_Drug/Home/Not+of+Standard+Quality+Sample/> last accessed 23 March 2022.
46. Reply to RTI application dated 14 March 2022, Commissioner, Food and Drugs Control Administration, Gujarat (Application No RTI/ID-117-2021/2022, 14 February 2022).
47. *Digital Vision vs State of Himachal Pradesh & Anr* CWP No. 2572 of 2020 before the High Court of Himachal Pradesh decided on 14 August 2020; *Dr Louis Biotech vs State of Bihar* CWP No. 9487 of 2016 before the Patna High Court decided on 12 July 2016.
48. KL Sharma, *Healing the Pharmacy of the World: An Inside Story of Medical Products Manufacturing and Regulation in India* (Notion Press 2021) 102.
49. ibid 103.
50. The United States Department of Justice, Office of Public Affairs, *Indian Cancer Drug Manufacturer Agrees to Plead Guilty and Pay $50 Million for Concealing and Destroying Records in Advance of FDA Inspection* (Press Release No 21–137, 9 February 2021).
51. *Albert David & Ors vs State of Rajasthan & Anr* S.B. Criminal Misc. Petition No. 411 of 2008 before the Rajasthan High Court at Jodhpur decided on 13 April 2012.
52. *State of Maharashtra vs Jethmal Himatmal Jain & Anr* 1994 Cri.L.J. 2613 before the Bombay High Court decided on 22 March 1994.
53. *Shivkumar & Ors vs State of Maharashtra & Anrs* Criminal Application No. 3439 of 2006 & Ors before the Bombay High Court decided on 21 June 2010.
54. The Drugs and Cosmetics Act 1940, s 27(d).
55. *PP Mhanvar vs Ram Gulwady MD of Sanmour Pharma Pvt Ltd* R.C.C. No. 109/2009 before the Chief Judicial Magistrate, Thane decided on 16 January 2019.
56. *State of Maharashtra vs Vinod Ratilal Shah MD of Iatros Pharmaceutical Pvt Ltd & Ors* R.C.C. No. 1831 of 2006 before the Chief Judicial Magistrate, Pune decided on 21 November 2016; *State of Maharashtra represented by Drug Inspector vs Jayesh Chandulal Mehta proprietor of Olcare Laboratories* RCC No. 3771 of 2009

before the Chief Judicial Magistrate, Pune decided on 28 September 2016; *State of Maharashtra vs Harpreet Singh Kalra* R.C.C. No. 349 of 2007 before the Chief Judicial Magistrate, Satara decided on 11 February 2019.

57. Reply to RTI application dated 26 May 2022, Karnataka Drug Control Department (Application No DCD/RTI/114/2021-2022, 10 February 2022).
58. *Tamman Titoe Pharma* (n 17).
59. *State of Jammu & Kashmir vs Vinay Nanda* AIR 2001 SC 611. <https://indiankanoon.org/doc/492051/> last accessed 5 May 2022.
60. ibid.
61. *State of Rajasthan vs Vinod Kumar* [2012] 6 S.C.R. 1. <https://indiankanoon.org/doc/52875779/> last accessed 5 May 2022.
62. *Madhav Hayawadanrao Hoskot vs State of Maharashtra* 1978 AIR 1548. <https://indiankanoon.org/doc/513169/> last accessed 5 May 2022.
63. Sharma (n 48) 52, 53.
64. Reply to RTI application dated 2 March 2022, Directorate of Health & Family Welfare, Government of Nagaland (Application No DHFW-13/DC/RTI/116/2013-14/12479, 10 February 2022).

CHAPTER FOUR

Of Glass Particles and Bacterial Endotoxins in Drugs

In the decades following the enactment of the Drugs Act in 1940, as the Indian pharmaceutical industry grew by leaps and bounds, nobody in government paid much attention to the functioning of its drug regulators. At best, individual Members of Parliament would raise questions during "Question Hour" about the questionable approval and sale of certain drugs not authorized for sale in any developed countries.

The only expert committee constituted by the Government of India since independence to exclusively study the functioning of the drug regulatory framework was the Mashelkar Committee in 2003.[1] While this committee made useful recommendations to improve the existing system, it failed to conduct an empirical evaluation of the various components of India's complex regulatory system partly because it was chasing the red herring of spurious or counterfeit drugs. Given that nobody in India was really paying attention to the quality issues in the pharmaceutical industry, it was not surprising that the Indian pharmaceutical industry faced its first major scandal with Ranbaxy at the hands of a foreign drug regulator like the USFDA.

In June 2013, a few weeks after Ranbaxy finally pled guilty to the offence of selling adulterated drugs in the United States after a seven-year long investigation by the United

States government, the Ministry of Commerce of the Indian Government put out a boisterous press release claiming that the Indian pharmaceutical sector is a "highly regulated one" and that "vested interests are raking up isolated issues" to attack the reputation of the country's pharmaceutical industry.[2] In the following years, most senior government officials and even some public health activists adopted this position as foreign regulators began to discover a horrifying number of quality-related violations at manufacturing facilities of major pharmaceutical companies located in India.

Far away from the politics of trade and faux nationalism, the mostly ignored records of Indian drug inspectors and government drug laboratories narrated a completely different story about the quality woes of the Indian pharmaceutical industry. The records of just three of India's 28 state governments and nine union territories (each of which has its own drug controller to regulate manufacturing of drugs), which are available on xlnindia.gov.in reveal that between 2007 and December 2020, a total of 7,525 drugs sampled from the market in these states had been declared NSQ after failing quality testing in the state government laboratories run by Gujarat, Maharashtra, and Kerala.[3] Similarly, the drug alerts announced by the national regulator—the CDSCO—based on random testing conducted by central drug laboratories, reported 2,668 NSQ drugs between 2013 and 2021.[4] Tamil Nadu, which did share information under the RTI Act 2005, reported that its laboratories detected a total of 2,355 NSQ drugs between 2015 and 2021.[5] It is important to remember that each failed drug sample represents an entire batch of medicine; meaning that the entire batch which often runs into hundreds of thousands of tablets, capsules, injections etc., is NSQ; unless of course storage conditions at individual pharmacies have resulted in the degradation of the tested samples. It is thus evident from the official records that

India is staring at a tsunami of NSQ drugs circulating in its market. It is worth remembering here that these statistics do not include data from some of India's most heavily populated states like Uttar Pradesh, Madhya Pradesh, and Rajasthan (none of which co-operated with us under the RTI Act 2005). Much of this information is publicly available except nobody in the government or the media wants to acknowledge the magnitude of the problem.

It is also important to remember that since each of these samples have been drawn by drug inspectors from random pharmacies, these drugs were already in circulation and being consumed by patients when the government laboratories declared them to be NSQ. Yet, if you search the news archives for "drug recalls" being announced by the government, you are unlikely find much information on recalls. (More on this later.) As a result, we suspect that the total number of patients affected by these NSQ drugs possibly runs into hundreds of thousands, perhaps millions over the last decade given that each NSQ drug represents an entire batch of substandard/contaminated drugs that was most likely not recalled from the market. To truly understand the depth of the problem, it is also important to understand the nature of the defects due to which these drugs are declared NSQ.

In simple terms, a drug is declared to be NSQ when it fails the quality tests prescribed in the legally recognized pharmacopeia. For formulations sold as tablets, these tests usually include an assay test which determines the quantity of the active ingredient in the tablet. It is not uncommon for NSQ drugs in India to test for only 10% or 20% of the active ingredient advertized on the label. Depending on the medicine in question, failure to contain the advertized quantity of active ingredient can lead to a range of poor health outcomes, ranging from death of the patient (in case of life-saving antibiotics) to severe discomfort (in case of drugs like antacids). Then there is the "dissolution" and "disintegration" test which establishes the ability of the tablet to break down and dissolve in the bloodstream. Drugs declared NSQ on this count will fail to dissolve in the bloodstream and hence will therefore have no real therapeutic action on the patient. Once again, depending on the quality of drug, these failures can have implications ranging from death to discomfort. For formulations sold as liquids in vials to be administered as injections, there are other kinds of tests such as "sterility" testing meant to test the sterility of the drug in order to ensure it is free of any kind of contamination. Since these drugs are injected directly into the bloodstream, any contamination will have a severe outcome in the patient. Failure to use sterile water when formulating such injectables will result in contamination with bacteria and other microorganisms which will invariably result in severe illness and/or death of the patient. In many cases, such contaminated injectables will make otherwise healthy patients dangerously ill. An additional problem with injectables is the presence of "glass particles" in vials meant to be administered as injections. Needless to say, since injections deliver the drug directly into the bloodstream, it is dangerous for it to contain "glass particles".

For most but not all of these 7,525 drugs, the XLN database (which contains data from Gujarat, Maharashtra, and Kerala) discloses the reason for the drug samples being declared NSQ by government analysts. Approximately 2,332 of these samples failed to meet standard pharmacopeial tests for "assay" which aims to test for the quantity of active ingredient present in a drug formulation. Another 1,164 tests failed the "dissolution" test which is meant to test the ability of drug formulation to dissolve into the bloodstream and become bioavailable. A smaller set of approximately 463 drugs failed tests for sterility or were found to contain bacterial endotoxins or unidentified particulate matter. Another set of approximately 90 drugs, most of which were meant to be administered through injections (and in one case, eye drops) were found to be contaminated with glass particles. We do not know the number of samples that were actually tested by these labs since the data in the XLN database only reports those that failed testing. We could not perform a similar analysis on data from other sources such as replies to RTI applications and the CDSCO drug alert notices but it is clear that India is facing a systemic crisis from a public health perspective and not mere "isolated issues" as claimed by the Ministry of Commerce or public health activists speaking in support of the Indian pharmaceutical industry.

The question to ask is how exactly did things get so bad in India? Afterall, under current GMPs, including those recognized by Indian law since 1988, a pharmaceutical company is required to conduct quality testing at each stage of manufacture, including before shipping a batch of their drugs to the market.[6] In fact, the law requires continued testing of retained samples of batches shipped to the market through its expiry date in order to detect any degradation that may occur over time due to stability issues. Yet, given the sheer quantity of drugs detected as NSQ over the last decade from the open market, it is obvious that a number of Indian pharmaceutical manufacturing facilities are completely flouting quality and process control procedures that form the core of GMPs. This blatant disregard for GMP came to light originally during the Ranbaxy scandal when it was discovered that the company was indulging in both active data fabrication and brazen negligence by failing to withdraw NSQ drugs from the market despite knowing that the drugs failed stability testing. As we discuss later in this chapter with examples from actual inspection reports of drugs inspectors from Karnataka, the kind of violations of GMPs in India is terrifying from a public health perspective.

One of the likely reasons for Indian pharmaceutical companies ignoring GMP compliance in India is because the Indian drug regulatory machinery has always been more focused on surveiling and testing the quality of drugs sold in the market. This approach, which we describe as the "market surveillance" approach, depends purely on a lottery of whether a particular company has its sample drawn from the market in a state that has adequate testing facilities. As we explain in this chapter, the manner in which states conduct this sampling of drugs from the Indian market is chaotic at best. Further, many states simply do not have sufficiently well-equipped laboratories and trained analysts to conduct a full pharmacopeial analysis of samples procured by drug inspectors from the market. Even when these laboratories detect NSQ drugs, there is no mechanism to affect a nationwide recall of drugs.

Trying to protect public health through market surveillance, as described above, is less rigorous and efficient than focusing on GMP compliance during the manufacturing process. More importantly though, the market surveillance approach is inherently more difficult to enforce. Right from the stage of sampling drugs to testing the samples for quality and recall process, the Indian system is riddled with loopholes, shortage of infrastructure, and other inherent inefficiencies that leaves too much of the regulatory process to the mercy of lady luck. A deep dive into these issues is critical to understanding the severity of the failures of the Indian drug regulatory framework that has led to the flood of NSQ drugs in India.

The random sampling of drugs for market surveillance without any sense or strategy

Since its enactment in 1940, the Drugs and Cosmetics Act 1940, has given drug inspectors powers to draw samples of drugs from the market provided they follow a very specific procedure laid down in the law.[7] This procedure requires the drug inspector to intimate the seller of the drugs in writing that the drug was being purchased for the purpose for testing, tender the fair price for the drug and then divide the purchase into four portions in the presence of the seller. All four portions are then sealed and marked, with the seller being permitted to add his own seal. Of these four portions, one is returned to the seller, another is sent to the government analyst, a third is sent to the manufacturer, and the fourth is produced before the court before which proceedings may be instituted.

This practice of drawing four samples can be traced back to an old British law called the Sale of Food and Drugs Act 1875, and continues to exist in Indian law.[8] It is not the most efficient of methods to monitor drug quality in the market. In an ideal world, testing should be conducted on a statistically significant number of samples of a batch in order to determine the quality of the entire batch. Testing just one sample from a commercial batch which typically has hundreds, if not thousands of samples is not scientific and statistically indefensible because the batch may enter different supply chains with varying storage and dispensing conditions before it is drawn for testing. Yet, the fundamentals of this regulatory architecture have remained untouched 82 years after the enactment of the Drugs Act in 1940. As of 2022, drug inspectors still draw four samples from the open market for testing.

The second big problem with this sampling approach is the failure to cover a wide cross-section of the market both in terms of manufacturers and formulations. In an ideal world, the Ministry of Health should lay down a scientifically designed sampling methodology to guide drug inspectors across states on the type of drugs they should be drawing samples from different manufacturers for the purpose of quality testing at a predetermined frequency. The aim of such sampling should be to cover a large cross-section of different drugs sold in the open market and manufactured by different companies for different treatment regimens so that the results give a representative assessment of Indian drug supply across various therapeutic areas across the country.

As of today, state drug controllers, who conduct the bulk of testing in India, do not proactively disclose their sampling strategy. We filed applications under the RTI Act 2005, with a few state drug controllers as well as the CDSCO asking them whether they had specific sampling guidelines in place instructing their drug inspectors on the type of drugs/frequency to be drawn from the market for the purpose of testing. From their responses we discovered that none of them had any guidelines to ensure either wide or statistically meaningful sampling of drugs. At most, the CDSCO in one of its manuals and one state drug inspector in one district of Tamil Nadu had vague guidelines specifying "locations" from where drugs are to be sampled (i.e., government hospitals and dispensaries).[9] There was however nothing in these guidelines about the type of drugs to be sampled. States like Uttarakhand and Kerala had no guidelines for their drug inspectors on the types of drugs or locations from which drugs were to be sampled.[10] An independent study of the Kerala Drug Control Department also made similar observations, stating in pertinent part that, "The statutory sampling target for drugs seems arbitrary and there was no document to suggest risk-based sampling strategies."[11]

The lack of such guidelines means that drug inspectors in each district of the country are randomly sampling drugs of their choice without even a state-level strategy; forget a national strategy. A likely result of such a strategy is that certain categories of drugs are either under-represented or over-represented. We further suspect that limited budgets to purchase drugs (drug inspectors have to tender a fair price under the law while drawing samples from the market) may be further skewing the type of drugs that are bought by drug inspectors for the purpose of testing. Drug inspectors may be buying a larger number of cheaper drugs instead of a smaller number of more expensive drugs. An independent study conducted on the functioning of the Kerala Drug Control Department discovered that there was a state-wide ceiling of ₹400,000 in the year 2018 for purchase of drugs from private sellers, thereby making it difficult for the drug inspectors to buy the more expensive drugs.[12] Modern cancer medication can cost a few thousand rupees for a single dose.

It is difficult to confirm these suspicions for all states because government laboratories do not proactively publish the entire list of drugs that they test. They generally publish only the list of the drugs that failed quality testing and not a list of all drugs that were sent to them for analysis. For example, in the XLN database, we find a very small number of failed injectables—only Gujarat seems to be testing such injectables frequently. Does this mean that only a small number of injectable drugs fail testing in these government labs or that the samples procured by the drug inspectors do not include injectables as often as they do tablets and capsules? Similarly, we have never seen a single oncology drug being declared NSQ, while anti-acid medication seems to be failing tests quite often, most likely because they are tested more often. If we can consider this anecdotal evidence to be reliable, it is obvious that Indian drug inspectors need to be given statistically robust sampling guidelines, without which the "market surveillance" approach is doomed to fail.

As a result of the factors described above, in our opinion, the starting point of the "market surveillance" model of regulation under the Drugs and Cosmetics Act 1940 is deeply flawed. We had pointed this out in a report to the Ministry of Health in 2016 but regrettably no action has been taken by the government in this regard. One of us, Dinesh Thakur, even petitioned the Minister of Health in July, 2020, on the urgent need to put in place sampling guidelines.[13] As usual, the Health Ministry failed to even acknowledge receipt of the petition, much less act on it.

Dysfunctional state laboratories

The second limb of the "market surveillance" approach to drug regulation are the laboratories operated by both central and state governments. These laboratories are tasked with testing samples of drugs purchased from the market by drug inspectors. Samples that fail testing can lead to an investigation and prosecution of the manufacturer by the drug inspector. Thus, if these laboratories are dysfunctional or not fully functional, there is little hope of actually enforcing the quality standards prescribed in the Drugs and Cosmetics Act 1940.

In order to understand the functioning of these laboratories, we filed applications under the RTI Act with 15 state laboratories. Only a handful of them responded but those responses revealed worrying information.

The first point of worry is the almost negligible number of drugs tested in most states when compared to Tamil Nadu, a better governed state in the Union. For example the state of West Bengal, which has a population of 90 million people, tested just 2,637 samples in the six years between January 1 2016 and February 2022.[14] In the same time period, in the state of Delhi, with a population of 19 million people, drug inspectors sent merely 3,433 samples for testing—of these, the laboratory operated by the Drugs Control Department of Delhi claimed to have tested only 2,610 samples.[15] Bihar on the other hand, with a population of 128.3 million people tested merely 14,103 samples during the same time period.[16] These are paltry figures when compared to the 57,567 samples tested during the same time period in Tamil Nadu, a state with a population of 67.9 million people.[17]

The second problem and the reason that the above numbers do not tell us the complete story is the fact that many of these laboratories do not have the equipment required to conduct all the tests required to establish whether a drug is actually of standard quality. We asked all the laboratories whether they had basic testing equipment like High Performance Liquid Chromatography (HPLC) machines which are essential to separate, identify, and quantify each ingredient in a drug sample and a dissolution apparatus that is required to test whether the drug dissolves as intended. The answers many of these laboratories provided are simply shocking.

For example, the Combined Food and Drug Laboratory in Patna, which is responsible for testing drugs for the entire state of Bihar, informed us that it had only one HPLC machine which was 20 years old and non-functional and that it was instead using an outdated method involving a spectrophotometer for the assay test.[18] This despite it being well known that spectrophotometers are far less accurate than HPLC machines when it comes to identifying individual ingredients in the drug sample.

Two of the other states had HPLC machines which were ancient. The Composite Testing Laboratory located in Solan, Himachal Pradesh, which is responsible for testing drugs in the pharmaceutical hub of the country reportedly has just 1 HPLC machine which was 16 years old.[19] Similarly, in Delhi, the laboratory under the Drugs Control Department reported having only 1 HPLC machine, which was bought 18 years ago in 2004.[20] Only the state laboratories in Tamil Nadu and West Bengal were well-equipped with 16 and 8 HPLC machines, respectively, which were a mix of new and old.[21]

A second quality test required to be carried out in these laboratories is "dissolution testing"; this is a critical test because drugs formulated as tablets will not have any therapeutic effect if they do not dissolve as per specifications. Unless such testing is carried out, a drug cannot be declared to be of standard quality. We asked all the laboratories whether they had the necessary equipment to carry out dissolution testing for tablets. Once again, the answers from some of these laboratories were shocking. The Combined Food and Drug Laboratory in Bihar informed us that, "No Instruments is available for dissolution test."[22] Similarly, the Composite Testing Laboratory in Himachal Pradesh informed us that, "Dissolution testing not carried out in this Laboratory."[23] That the one state laboratory in the pharmaceutical manufacturing hub of India does not conduct such testing should worry us all. Only the laboratory in Tamil Nadu reported having nine such dissolution test apparatus.[24] West Bengal was close, with four dissolution testing apparatus.[25]

Apart from conducting assay and dissolution tests, state laboratories are also required to conduct a critical test called "impurity testing". Impurities in drugs can be organic or inorganic and are usually a result of problems with the manufacturing process. These impurities can be dangerous for patients, causing serious adverse effects. For example, a protein impurity in the antibiotic ampicillin was linked to a severe skin rash in some patients. There are several more examples where impurities in drugs were found to be causing anaphylaxis or injuries to specific organs.[26] Many of these impurities are known and classified and can be tested against "impurity standards" sold by the Indian Pharmacopeia Commission (IPC) which is the main standard-setting body in India. This is a critical test from a quality perspective but is not always conducted in India. In response to our query about whether it conducted impurity testing, the Combined Food and Drug Laboratory in Bihar informed us that it could not carry out impurity testing because it did not have HPLC machines.[27]

Similarly, the Composite Testing Laboratory in Himachal Pradesh replied with a one-line answer informing us that, "Impurity testing is not carried out in this Laboratory".[28] This is a shocking state of affairs, especially considering the fact Himachal Pradesh is the hub of pharmaceutical manufacturing in India.

It is thus clear that even when Bihar and Himachal Pradesh claim that they are testing 14,103 and 11,103 drug samples respectively, they are not actually performing all the tests that are legally required under the Indian Pharmacopeia to certify a drug as being of standard quality.

Given that testing is the basis of the entire regulatory framework under the Drugs and Cosmetics Act 1940 it is worth questioning the extent to which the Act is enforced across different states in India. We suspect the situation to be far worse in many states, a fact that we were not able to confirm because of their refusal to reply to our queries under the RTI Act 2005. Only a few states like Tamil Nadu and Gujarat appear to have well-equipped laboratories capable of testing even complex formulations like injectables. Similarly, the six central and regional laboratories set up by the Ministry of Health, were equipped with far better testing facilities, most likely because of the Ministry's deeper pockets and also because these facilities are relatively new.

The shaky foundations of the Indian Pharmacopoeia Commission and its impact on testing laboratories

One of the crucial elements of any regulatory framework is the issue of standards laid down in the pharmacopeia. A typical pharmacopeia will publish monographs detailing standardized testing protocol for each new drug formulation that enters the market. These include the testing protocols for identity, purity, dissolution, disintegration, and sterility. Only a drug that complies with all these tests and also passes a visual inspection, is considered to be of standard quality.

The pharmacopoeia being followed by a pharmaceutical company is generally printed on the packaging of its drugs. IP indicates that the company is following standards laid down in the Indian Pharmacopoeia which is published by the Indian Pharmacopoeia Commission. Similarly, the abbreviations such as BP, EP, and USP, expand into the British Pharmacopoeia, European Pharmacopoeia, and the United States Pharmacopoeia, respectively.

In addition to publishing a monograph, a pharmacopoeia will also manufacture and sell "reference standards" and "impurity standards" to both the pharmaceutical industry and government drug laboratories. A "reference standard" is essentially a small sample of the pure active ingredient of a particular drug. A useful analogy to understand the role of reference standards are the designated weights that were once used in grocery stores to weigh fruits or vegetables that were being bought. These weights, which were basically iron blocks of 250 gm, 500 gm, and 1 kg were used to weigh produce and confirm to the consumer the quantity being purchased. The reason consumers trust these weights is because they are calibrated against a standard that is guaranteed under the law. A similar process applies to the reference standards produced by the IPC. When a lab conducts drug testing, it compares the manner in which the sample of the drug being tested reacts when compared to its "reference standard". The lab conducts a test where both the reference standard and the drug samples are evaluated using a HPLC machine. The results of this test tells the analyst tasked with certifying the drug whether the test sample has the same "chemical" as the reference standard and the quantity of the "chemical" when measured against the reference standard.

Similarly, a pharmacopoeia is also required to supply "impurity standards". As the name suggests, these are critical to test for the presence of impurities that are known to be generated during the process of manufacturing a drug or while storing it as a by-product of degradation.

A well-functioning pharmacopeia that understands the science of standards and guarantees the supply of high-quality standards is critical for both the pharmaceutical industry and regulator. Prior to independence, the Drugs Act 1940 and the Drug Rules 1945 recognized only foreign pharmacopeias, some of which like the USP continue to exist as non-governmental, non-profit organizations. After independence, India setup the Indian Pharmacopoeia Committee in 1948 to act as India's standard-setting body for the pharmaceutical industry.[29] It published the first Indian Pharmacopoeia as a collection of all its monographs in 1955. In 2008, the Ministry of Health, acting on a proposal first put forward by the Drugs Technical Advisory Board (DTAB) in 1984,[30] converted the Indian Pharmacopoeia Committee into the supposedly more autonomous Indian Pharmacopoeia Commission (IPC), but for all practical purposes, the IPC operates under the administrative control of the Ministry of Health and the Secretary of the Ministry of Health and Family Welfare remains the Chairperson of the IPC.[31]

The IPC is the most important standard-setting body in India not due to its scientific acumen but because an amendment in 1977 to Rule 124 of the Drugs and Cosmetics Rules 1945 ensured that the standards in the Indian Pharmacopoeia are legally binding in India.[32] Only if a drug is not listed in Indian Pharmacopoeia, can a manufacturer adopt the standards laid down in other official pharmacopoeias such as the USP, BP etc.

Making the standards prescribed by the IPC mandatory would have been fine if it were not for one major problem. As per the government's own records, the IPC has been found to be lacking in its ability to ensure the timely availability of reference and impurity standards. We documented multiple instances of complaints by state drug controllers against the IPC starting in 2004 at the 35th meeting of the DCC which has as its members all state drug controllers. At this meeting, some of the state drug controllers complained that a shortage of both reference standards and impurity standards was making it difficult for government analysts in the state laboratories to conduct all the prescribed tests in the pharmacopoeia.[33] The minutes of the meeting also state this shortage rendered the entire exercise of drug inspectors drawing the samples from the market as "an exercise in futility". Instead of demanding more efficiency from the IPC, the committee resolved that in case of shortage of reference standards or chemicals, the government analyst should insert a disclaimer in the test report, mentioning the shortage as the cause for not conducting all the mandated tests in a monograph.[34] From a public health perspective, this was a disastrous decision because it meant that an otherwise NSQ drug would get a clean chit. Strangely, there was no discussion at that DCC meeting on how exactly to solve the issue of shortage of reference standards.

Again, in the 43rd meeting of the DCC that was held in 2011, the Karnataka Drug Controller complained about the non-availability of certain reference standards required for the purpose of testing some drugs.[35] The minutes record that the Secretary of the IPC, Dr G.N. Singh, who was present at the meeting, informed the DCC that the Commission had 230 reference standards that could be purchased but did not offer any concrete solutions to address the complaint made by the Karnataka Drug Controller.[36]

The issue came up again in the 45th meeting of the DCC held in 2013 when the Goa Drug Controller complained about the lack of reference standards with the IPC. The minutes record in pertinent part:

> It is observed that several times the Reference Standard which are mentioned in Indian Pharmacopeia for the analysis of

> various APIs are not available with the Indian Pharmacopeia Commission.[37]

The DCC once again simply passed the buck to the IPC instead of trying to get to the root of the issue and finding a permanent solution.

At the 48th meeting of the DCC held in 2015, the minutes note that while the government was auditing laboratories that were to be empanelled for the purpose of a government-funded drug-quality survey, it was discovered that many laboratories did not have either a copy of the Indian Pharmacopoeia (IP) or the IP Reference Standards.[38] The situation clearly did not improve over the years because the official minutes of the 56th meeting of the DCC held in 2019 stated the following with regard to the shortage of standards:

> The State Drugs Testing laboratories are continuously facing constraint of the reference and working standards for the regulatory analysis of the quality surveillance drugs samples and the test reports cannot be delivered in the prescribed time frame.[39]

Once again, the DCC did not attempt to get to the root of the problem except asking state laboratories to approach the IPC in this regard. Reporting in 2021 confirms that state testing laboratories continue to face difficulties in procuring reference standards as a result of which they are unable to conduct several types of testing, including for the presence of impurities.[40]

One of the possible reasons that the minutes of the DCC do not record a strong condemnation of the inefficient workings of the IPC is the simple fact that the DCC meetings are chaired by the Drug Controller General of India who in rank, is subordinate to the Secretary of the Ministry of Health and Family Welfare who is the Chairperson of the Governing Council of the IPC. To criticize the functioning of the IPC is in effect to criticize the Secretary of Health and Family Welfare and that is not how the Government of India functions.

Of course, when we asked the IPC, through an application under the RTI Act, whether it had received complaints from drug-testing laboratories about delays in supplying reference standards, it stated in no uncertain terms that it had not received any complaints from state drug controllers or government analysts about delays in the supply of standards.[41] Clearly, the complaints being raised during the DCC meetings were never communicated to the IPC, thereby demonstrating poor inter-agency coordination.

Separate and apart from the complaints raised at the DCC meetings against the IPC, there is also the fact that only four least-developed countries—Afghanistan, Nepal, Ghana, and Mauritius—recognize the standards laid down by IPC.[42] The fact that a country that likes to boast of itself as the "pharmacy of the developing world" is unable to convince more countries, to adopt its official standards speaks poorly of international confidence in the IPC. On the other hand is the USP, which is not even an official arm of the American government, whose standards are used in a whopping 140 countries![43]

Given its importance to public health in India, there is no denying that the IPC is in need of urgent reforms. Running the IPC is the equivalent of running a rather complex business enterprise involved in precision manufacturing of standards. It is well known that the Government of India has a terrible record of running business. There are several ways to increase efficiency within the government structure. One easy solution is to spin off the IPC into a statutory body not dependent on the Ministry of Health for every decision. This would also make it easier for the institution to hire talent from the private sector at competitive renumeration without being caught in the red-tape of government employment regulations and be more responsive toward the industry and the state drug testing laboratories. A more systemic reform effort will require the Ministry of Health to conduct transparent and open deliberations with stakeholders to identify the failings of the IPC. Sadly, history has demonstrated that the Ministry of Health rarely reflects or introspects on the many failings of its drug regulatory framework.

The murderous apathy of the Indian state in enacting a recall law

Presuming that a government analyst in a government laboratory is able to overcome all of the aforementioned obstacles to actually test the drug sample and determine that it is NSQ, the next logical step from a public health perspective should be to recall the entire batch of the drug from the market before it is consumed by any more patients and also inform patients who have already consumed the NSQ drug. This is especially true in cases like the one discussed in the prologue where a cough syrup adulterated with DEG caused deaths of at least 11 children from Jammu. A less discussed aspect of that case is the death of a two year old toddler in August 2020, approximately eight months after the deaths of the 11 children from Jammu. The toddler was admitted at PGIMER, Chandigarh with renal failure and the doctors at the hospital discovered that the child's parents had given her a different brand of cough syrup manufactured by Digital Vision, the same company whose cough syrup was allegedly responsible for the deaths of the 11 children from Jammu. The doctors at PGIMER then sent the cough syrup for testing to a laboratory which alleged that the sample was found to be adulterated with DEG. It is very possible that the same batch of adulterated ingredients was used to manufacture different brands of cough syrups but was not effectively recalled the first time. The doctors at PGIMER reported the adulteration to CDSCO asking it to take urgent steps.[44] The manufacturer for its part has denied these second set of allegations in interviews to the press.[45]

The CDSCO's response in this case was to simply write to different state drug regulators informing them of the brand name and asking them to take steps to withdraw the drug from the market.[46] This was the same modus operandi followed by the CDSCO after the first tragedy in Jammu. There was no attempt by the national drug regulator to co-ordinate a public communications strategy to inform the public, trace other potential victims or supply other state drug controllers with sales records so as to enable them to identify distributors and enable a swift recall of the entire batch of adulterated medicine from the market.

Contrast the above approach of the CDSCO with the following two incidents where doctors or regulators discovered adulterated cough syrup: the American government's response in 1937 after discovering that the DEG-adulterated cough syrup was killing patients and the response of Indian doctors in Chennai in 1972 who discovered the adulterated Pipmol cough syrup. In the first incident, the USFDA deployed its entire field force of drug inspectors to trace every bottle of the DEG adulterated syrup that had been manufactured and sold by the manufacturer. The USFDA made active efforts to track down all the salespersons involved in selling the adulterated formulations and contact all of their customers. In addition, shipping records and sales receipts of the company that manufactured the adulterated syrup were individually checked to trace the sales. Doctors and pharmacists joined the effort in large numbers. This effort was combined with public service announcements on the radio and television. The FDA inspectors did not stop until they traced each and every bottle of the syrup that had been sold in the market.[47]

In the second incident, the doctors in Chennai who discovered the DEG-adulterated Pipmol C took matters into their own hands by coordinating with All India Radio to make public announcements and holding a press-conference to publicize the poisoned batch before the media. They made sure that news of the adulterated Pipmol C was broadcast loud and clear to the general public.[48]

Contrast the above two examples with the flawed recall efforts in 1941 in the United States by a company called Winthrop which sold an entire batch of sulfathiazole tablets contaminated with phenobarbital, a sedative. After hearing of adverse reactions from doctors who had prescribed its drug, the company tested the batch in its labs and discovered the contamination. Its recall process was however too slow and ineffective, resulting in the loss of 64 lives and another 134 adverse reactions after the company discovered the contamination! A post mortem of the recall process noted that the company was not transparent with its own branch offices. Instead of informing them that the drug was contaminated, the company headquarters misled them by telling them that the batch had to be recalled because the tablets were not disintegrating properly. Further, the company had focused on recalling the drug at only primary distribution points and not the end consumers or hospitals. It was only when the USFDA stepped in, was Winthrop compelled to be transparent and notify all the stakeholders of the actual reason for the withdrawal. The USFDA also issued a press release to inform the general public and involved a range of stakeholders from state health boards to pharmacy organizations to conduct an efficient recall of the contaminated medicine.[49]

In contrast to the above examples, the CDSCO's lackadaisical approach in the Digital Vision case was boringly predictable for anybody familiar with the functioning of the Indian drug regulatory framework. Every year, hundreds, if not thousands of drugs fail testing in state and central government laboratories. Conducting a national recall of a particular batch of drugs in such cases is not easy in a country like India with complicated supply chains. A drug manufactured in Himachal Pradesh could reach states from Mizoram to Tamil Nadu in a matter of weeks after moving through a chain of intermediate distributors. To further complicate matters, once word gets out that a particular batch is adulterated or NSQ, nobody in the supply chain has an incentive to voluntarily report it to possible consumers or the regulatory authorities because of a fear of legal liability and loss of business reputation.

In such circumstances, where private players—be it pharmaceutical manufacturers or distributors—have little incentive to conduct a swift recall of NSQ drugs, the state must deploy both an effective public communication strategy and coercive investigative resources to not only trace unsold stock but also track down each and every patient who may have consumed the NSQ drug. To exercise such powers, India needs a law empowering and clearly fixing responsibility on the CDSCO—the national regulator—to conduct nationwide recalls. This responsibility cannot be palmed off to state drug controllers because they lack the authority and resources to operate outside their home state. Yet, India does not have such a law and the reason as to why it lacks such a law is a story of epic bureaucratic procrastination.

This is a story that begins with a meeting, in 1976, of the DCC, consisting of all state drug controllers, the DCGI, and representatives from the Ministry of Health and Family Welfare.[50] Item No. 11 on the agenda of that meeting was "To review the existing procedure of recall by manufacturers of drugs found deficient". The minutes of that meeting recorded the Chair's observation that, "When a drug is found deficient and is required to be withdrawn from the market, the instructions sent to manufacturers in this regard in many cases are not carried out with the result that the stocks of the defective drugs continue to move in the market."[51] Another participant at the meeting narrated an instance of how a drug declared NSQ because it contained phenol was found to be on sale in Rajasthan 18 months after the manufacturer had been ordered to withdraw it from the market.[52] For this reason, the Chair of the DCC warned against leaving the issue of withdrawals solely to the manufacturer and recommended drug inspectors verify whether withdrawals of NSQ drugs were actually taking place from the market.

At that meeting in 1976, it was also resolved that for future recalls, the state drug controller where the manufacturer was located would be responsible for gathering the names and addresses of all the distributors to whom the NSQ drug had been sold by the erring manufacturer and then transmitting those details to the state drug controllers in whose jurisdiction the distributor was located. It was then supposed to be the duty of those state drug controllers to communicate to dealers in writing to withdraw the stocks and destroy them in the presence of the state drug inspector.[53] All of this was fine except for the fact that this decision was never translated into law via an amendment to either the Drugs and Cosmetics Act 1940 or the Drugs and Cosmetics Rules 1945. In effect, the issue of recall was left entirely to the individual discretion of state drug controllers.

The issue of recalls came up once again in 1989 at the 26th meeting of the DCC. This time it was the Secretary of Health and Family Welfare who expressed his concern about the recall of drugs found to be toxic and hazardous to public health. He wanted in place a mechanism to ensure complete recalls of such drugs in a span of 72 hours. The minutes of the same meeting record the fact that a high-powered group under the Chairmanship of the Health Minister of Maharashtra had already been constituted by the Central Council of Health to make recommendations on a number of issues including "strengthening of procedure for quick recalls of drugs in emergency situations".[54] We do not know what became of these recommendations.

The issue then came up again in 1996, this time at a meeting of the DTAB which is another statutory body under the Drugs and Cosmetics Act 1940 with a mandate to advise the government on technical issues arising under the Act. Item No. 12 on the agenda was a proposal to ensure the swift recall of spurious, substandard or adulterated drugs, within a time span of 48 hours. The minutes specifically mention that this was an issue of concern that been "expressed in various fora". What followed was a perversion that would perhaps embarrass even the most cynical of bureaucrats. The minutes of the meeting record:

> During the course of discussion, the members felt that there would be practical problems both at the industry level as well as effective and uniform enforcement by the State Drugs Control Authorities in case the provisions giving a specific time-frame are incorporated in the Drugs and Cosmetics Rules, 1945. The members felt that the time is not yet ripe for incorporating a statutory provision relating to time bound recall of the drugs. However, the Drugs Controller General (India) may issue guidelines to the State Drugs Control Authorities on the ways and means that should be devised and the procedures to be followed for effective recall of the drugs.[55]

Simply put, the members of DTAB concluded that it would be too inconvenient for the industry and the bureaucracy if the law put in place mandatory mechanisms to ensure the recall of NSQ drugs within a period of 48 hours, despite it being known that NSQ drugs pose a grave threat to public health! An injection containing glass particles, or which has been found to have microbial contamination, or a life-saving drug that fails a dissolution or assay test can result in serious illness or the death of patients. Yet the very authorities tasked with protecting public health were of the opinion that "time is not yet ripe" for an amendment to the law to facilitate rapid recalls of drugs that were known to be NSQ.

Two years later, in 1998, the DCC once again discussed a proposal for amending the Drugs and Cosmetics Rules 1945 to ensure the expeditious recall of NSQ drugs. Like their counterparts in the DTAB, the members of the DCC decided that "... it is very difficult to incorporate any statutory provisions in the Drugs and Cosmetics Rules relating to the time-bound recall of the drugs at the present moment."[56] Instead like the DTAB, the DCC resolved that uniform non-binding guidelines by the DCGI would suffice.

The saga did not end in 1998. Six years later, in 2004, the issue of amending the law to guarantee effective recalls came up once again before the DCC at its 35th meeting and the matter was sent to a sub-committee for a more detailed discussion.[57] Since the Ministry of Health does not proactively publish the reports of the various sub-committees of the DCC, we have no idea as to the recommendations made by the sub-committee in this case but given that there is no mention of this sub-committee in future meetings of the DCC, it is safe to presume that the sub-committee never submitted a report.

Three years later in 2007, the DCC once again flagged the issue of recall guidelines at its annual meeting. This time the issue acquired some urgency, most likely because the World Health Organization (WHO) had conducted a National Regulatory Assessment (NRA) of the Indian regulatory framework and had possibly flagged the lack of recall and destruction guidelines as an issue to be remedied.[58] Yet, when the issue of time sensitive recalls of NSQ drugs came up once again four years later at its 43rd meeting in 2011, the DCC came to this following conclusion:

> The committee after deliberations felt that the issue is a complex one because of interstate withdrawal. It therefore, recommended that a committee may be formed to deliberate on various aspects of withdrawal of such drugs from the market and the difficulties faced by the regulatory authorities in monitoring the withdrawals. The committee may consider evolving a priority recall system in the cases of banned drugs and grossly substandard drugs as well as withdrawal of other categories of drugs declared as not of standard quality.[59]

And so, yet another sub-committee was set up to look into the issue. Its recommendations were never discussed in future meetings of the DCC, possibly because it never submitted a report.

The very next year, in 2012, the Parliamentary Standing Committee on Health and Welfare examined the issue of recalls while reviewing the functioning of the CDSCO in its now famous 59th report. The report made the following observation with respect to recalls:

> By the time a sample is tested, a large number of packs get sold out with undeterminable injury to patients. There is no effective method of recalling unsold stocks lying in the distribution network. This cannot be allowed to go on.[60]
>
> The Committee recommends that once a batch of a drug is found to be substandard and reported to CDSCO, it should issue a press release forthwith and even insert paid advertisements in the newspapers apart from uploading the information on the CDSCO website. Retail chemists should be advised to stop selling unsold stocks and return the same to local Drugs Inspectors as per rules.[61]

One would have expected the Ministry of Health and Family Welfare of the Government of India to respond to a demand by the highest law-making body with the utmost urgency and sincerity. Regretfully, this was not the case. Rather than put together a swift policy response, the bureaucracy of the Ministry of Health engaged in a lethargic game of passing the buck. The Ministry of Health in its Action Taken Report (ATR) assured Parliament that the "CDSCO had also formulated guidelines on recall and rapid alert for drugs and that the same was uploaded on its website".[62] While a document called "Guidelines on Recall and Rapid Alert System for Drugs" was made available on the CDSCO's website on November 23 2012, the Ministry simply omitted mentioning to Parliament, the crucial detail that those recall guidelines lacked the force of law and were hence not binding on any governmental authority.[63] A separate issue was the fact that the guidelines were very poorly drafted and lacking in detail. For the most part, these guidelines outline steps to be taken by the manufacturer, but as discussed in previous DCC meetings, it is clear that manufacturers have no incentive in executing effective recalls. Ultimately, it is the state drug controller or the CDSCO that has to play the more important role. The guidelines were also quite vague on fixing responsibilities. Take for example the guidelines' position on the tricky issue of "inter-state" recalls. It merely states: "For interstate co-ordination & communication, the zonal offices of CDSCO of their respective jurisdiction are responsible."[64] It is silent on the exact mechanics of the entire process. What happens when drug controllers of different states disagree with each other on recalls? What exactly is the role of the CDSCO in such a case? What does it mean to say that the CDSCO is responsible for "interstate co-ordination and communication" when the CDSCO has no administrative authority over state drug controllers? Who would be responsible for tracing patients who may have consumed the NSQ drugs?

At around the same time, the then DCGI, Dr G.N. Singh, was quoted in the press claiming that after the public comments were received, the guidelines would now be forwarded to the Ministry of Health and Ministry of Law to translate the same into binding law in three to four months.[65] This never happened. Instead, the same guidelines were circulated in 2013 for comments at a meeting of the DCC without any discussion of translating the guidelines into the law.[66]

A few years later, in 2015, we filed requests under the RTI Act, 2005 with several state drug controllers asking them whether they followed any specific guidelines to effect drug recalls. We received six different answers from six different state drug controllers—not a single one of those responses referred to the CDSCO's recall guidelines![67] Clearly, these state drug controllers did not even know that the CDSCO's recall guidelines even existed.

While this policy paralysis continued at the level of the Ministry of Health, some of the state drug controllers rang the alarm bells about the lack of an adequate recall law in India. In 2015, Ravi S. Menon, a Deputy Drugs Controller from Kerala made a public appeal in the media on the need for a more efficient recall system in India. In pertinent part, he stated:

> There is gigantic quantity of NSQ drugs in the Indian pharma market. They are marketed in several places by separate marketing companies. Most of these drugs are manufactured in the excise free zone areas in Uttarakhand and Himachal Pradesh. Those manufacturers should be accountable for withdrawing the batches immediately from the market. The state and central law enforcing agencies are helpless in weeding out these batches from circulation or imposing any fine on the manufacturers due to lack of adequate provisions in the law.[68]

In July 2016, exactly 40 years after the issue of recalls was first flagged at the meeting of the DCC in 1976, the issue was taken up once again at a meeting of the DTAB. Noting the importance of recall guidelines, the minutes referenced the version of recall guidelines drafted by the CDSCO and recorded the fact that "concerns about lack of proper implementation of recall and alert system in the country still exist". As a solution, the DTAB proposed translating the guidelines into the law by incorporating them into the Drugs and Cosmetics Rules 1945 and recommended that a group be setup to study the issue.[69]

The matter then went back to the DCC which took it up at its 50th meeting in November 2016. The minutes of this 50th meeting record the standard spiel on how "Concerns have been raised from time to time regarding lack of an effective recall system whereby drugs found to be NSQ by one State are mandatorily recalled across the country from all the States" (earlier that year, we had raised the issue of "drug recalls" in a report submitted to the Ministry of Health and Family Welfare) and that, "The present system of recalling drugs needs substantial improvement."[70] A two-pronged strategy was thus proposed to the members of the DCC. The first step was to amend the rules to create a legally binding framework for recall and second was for all states to display information about their NSQ drugs on the "SUGAM" portal which was the e-governance platform developed for drug controllers. These were both sensible recommendations, yet what followed was an example of not just bureaucratic apathy but pure malice.

Instead of fixing the responsibility to monitor recalls on state or central drug controllers, the DCC sought an amendment to the Drugs and Cosmetics Rules 1945 to basically impose on manufacturers the responsibility for withdrawing NSQ drugs from the market if their drugs failed quality testing. This was an utterly daft recommendation because Schedule M to the Drugs and Cosmetics Rules 1945 already placed such a duty on the manufacturers. Moreoever, the entire reason the issue of recall guidelines came up repeatedly before the DCC was because manufacturers were found to be reluctant to recall their NSQ drugs. As is usually the case when the DCC wants to kick the can down the road, this meeting of the committee wrapped up discussions by creating yet another sub-committee to review and update the existing recall guidelines.

The issue was clearly not resolved in 2016 because in 2018, at its 54th meeting, the DCC was once again discussing "obstacles on complete recovery of NSQ drugs from market". Rather than reflect and repent upon its earlier apathy, the DCC merely discussed one recommendation that each state have a dedicated officer to "... ensure that every single unit of the defective drugs is recalled by manufacturer from supply chain and proper reconciliation of the stocks of manufacture, distribution and recall" is maintained.[71] There was no mention of amending the law to actually create an accountable mechanism for recalls or to deal with retail withdrawals.

The next year in 2019, at its 55th meeting, the DCC minutes record that one of the earlier sub-committees set up for the purpose of reviewing the recall guidelines had not submitted its final report and hence another sub-committee was setup under the Chairmanship of the Drug Controller of Andhra Pradesh. Although this report was not proactively published by the Ministry, we managed to get a copy of the final report by filing a request under the RTI Act in 2021, after some initial resistance from the CDSCO.[72] This report made some useful recommendations on short and long-term reforms to facilitate recalls. However, on the issue of an actual amendment to the rules, this sub-committee proposed only one amendment to Rule 65 in order to create a time limit of 10 days within which any pharmacy or distributor of drugs would have to conduct a recall after being informed of a NSQ batch by a drug inspector. There was no mention of who in the government would be responsible for vetting whether the pharmacy or distributor was actually recalling the NSQ drug. The report was also woefully silent on addressing the challenges of fixing accountability for complex inter-state recalls or follow up with patients.

At its 57th meeting also held in 2019, the DCC agreed to most of the recommendations of the aforementioned sub-committee, including the need for better sharing of information about NSQ drugs but as usual none of the decisions at the meeting actually translated into amendments to the law.

As a result, *46 years* after the issue of recalls was first raised at the DCC meeting in 1976, India still lacks a robust law on recalling NSQ drugs. Stop reading for a second and reflect on what the above sentence says about the priority of the Indian state when it comes to protecting the health of its citizens! This, despite thousands of NSQ drugs being detected every year by government laboratories across India. Of what use is this costly exercise of market surveillance which involves funding laboratories and drug inspectors in every state, if it does not result in rapid recalls of NSQ drugs from across the market?

The continued opposition and lethargy of the DCC on the issue of robust recall guidelines can be pinned down to the fact that a well-designed and transparent recall system will shine a bright light on the rotten state of drug regulation in India. If the press and the common public were to be informed every other day of a batch of drugs that have to be recalled from the market because of quality concerns, they are bound to demand greater accountability of state drug controllers. Just imagine if you as a citizen heard or read of 12,548 recall notices (combined figures from XLN, the CDSCO's drug alerts, and Tamil Nadu) in the press over 10 years publicizing the recall of drugs that were NSQ—chances are that you would demand accountability from drug regulators and therein lies the nub of the issue. The average Indian bureaucrat will do anything to escape even an illusion of accountability, which is why India does not have any recall guidelines.

For our part, after a failed attempt by one of us, Dinesh Thakur, to raise the issue of recalls before the Supreme Court of India in 2016 via a broader public interest litigation, we sent a report to the Ministry of Health on the failures of the drug regulatory framework in India—one of the issues we discussed in the report was the lack of a law on drug recalls in India.[73] As you can guess, nothing much has happened.

The failure to guarantee good manufacturing practices

The reason that thousands of drugs have failed quality testing in government laboratories over the last decade is the simple fact that many Indian pharmaceutical companies regularly flout GMP's code that they are legally required to follow under Indian law. The history of GMPs can be traced to a tragedy in the United States in 1941, when approximately 300 people died or fell ill because of contamination of a batch of 410,000 sulfathiazole tablets with a powerful sedative called phenobarbital, at a manufacturing plant owned by a company called Winthrop.[74] That tragedy led to the USFDA bringing in the first GMP code for the pharmaceutical industry. Since its inception, GMP codes have evolved to put in place a set of highly sophisticated procedures which when followed, guarantees that only quality drugs are shipped to the market. Under the latest version of GMP, pharmaceutical companies are under a duty to maintain highly sanitized premises, to test inputs before these are used in the manufacturing process, to test batches before market release, and to also retain samples for future testing. The retained samples are meant to be subject to regular testing at different timepoints post sale to examine whether the drug has degraded due to stability issues. Given the manner in which the GMP code is written, it should be possible to catch most quality issues before the drug is shipped to the market. In case post-marketing stability testing of retained samples reveals degradation, the pharmaceutical company is expected to recall its drugs from the market.

Rigorous compliance with GMPs has made it possible for American pharmaceutical companies to avoid tragedies that have engulfed other countries. Take for example the glycerin poisoning incident in Panama in 2007, which killed over 365 children. The Chinese company implicated in the Panama scandal had earlier supplied counterfeit glycerin to an American pharmaceutical company. The American company followed cGMP standards and tested the shipment from the Chinese company for purity before using it for manufacturing purposes. It was thus able to detect the adulteration in time to discard it.[75] The deaths of the 11 children from Jammu due to DEG poisoning could easily have been avoided if the manufacturer had tested either the input chemical or the final syrup before marketing. Similarly, on the issue of post-sales testing, it is quite common to hear of pharmaceutical companies, including Indian companies, to announce recalls of drugs from the American market due to quality issues discovered after retained samples of each batch were subject to testing. Yet, we never hear of these same Indian pharmaceutical companies recalling drugs from India.

The centrality of GMPs to the American legal system can be understood by the fact that the definition of adulterated drugs in the United States extends to those drugs manufactured in a facility that do not follow GMPs during the process of manufacturing.[76] Therefore, if a pharmaceutical company is found to have shipped drugs to the market without complying with GMPs, the drugs are presumed to be adulterated. This regulatory framework places a heavy burden on pharmaceutical companies catering to the American market to ensure rigorous compliance with GMPs by maintaining detailed and meticulous documentation of testing conducted of both input materials and finished formulations at various stages of manufacture. From an enforcement perspective, ensuring GMP compliance is far more thorough and efficient compared to drawing samples of manufactured drugs from the market for testing. It is logistically possible to conduct at least one surprise inspection every year of every manufacturing facility in the country but it is certainly impossible for the government to sample every manufactured batch of drugs in the country in order to test it for quality.

Like the United States, India too has incorporated GMPs standards into the Drugs and Cosmetics Rules 1945 in the year 1988, via Schedule M, making it a precondition for issuing a manufacturing licence.[77] In 2001, these regulations were replaced with new regulations that brought Indian law closer to international standards and Rule 52 was amended to require yearly inspections of licensed premises for compliance with the terms of licence.

More worrying though, three years after the new GMP regulations were brought in, the government significantly watered them down by amending Schedule M. Many of these "dilutions" were simply shocking. For example, the original requirement inserted into the law in 2001 required that "all manufacturing activity shall be used exclusively for production of drugs and no other manufacturing activity shall be undertaken therein". Spelling this out in the law was likely required since it is possible that many Indian companies that manufacture pharmaceuticals also manufacture chemicals at the same premises. This is not the best idea given the sterility requirements at facilities manufacturing pharmaceutical drugs. In 2004, this clause was amended to create an exception for all manufacturing facilities that were licensed prior to December 11 2001, meaning that all the older units could continue to manufacture chemicals in the same premises that were manufacturing pharmaceuticals.[78] This was an absurd exception since it makes no rational sense to have different GMP standards based on the year in which the manufacturing facility was licenced by the government. Another amendment introduced in 2004 omitted the limits of microbiological and endotoxin levels in steam systems that were specified in the Schedule M as drafted in 2001. These steam systems are absolutely crucial to sterilize manufacturing surfaces used in pharmaceutical manufacturing facilities. It is critical for the steam to not contain bacteria or endotoxins in order to prevent contamination of manufacturing services. Yet, this critical requirement was deleted in 2004.

The reason for these amendments lowering standards can be found in an answer provided by the government to a Parliamentary Question in December 2004. In this response, the government basically admitted to receiving many "representations", including a memorandum from 34 Members of Parliament that the new GMP standards inserted into Schedule M were threatening the closure of thousands of small-scale pharmaceutical manufacturing units and that in response to these concerns, the government was in the process of "rationalizing" GMP standards contained in Schedule M.[79] The survival of the small-scale manufacturing units was clearly more of a priority than ensuring the quality of medicine for people of India.

The problem however does not stop with the quality of the GMP code followed in India but also the attitude of Indian regulators in enforcing the existing GMP code. Nothing captures their attitude better than the following statement by former DCGI G.N. Singh, who defended the lax standards in India when compared to those followed in the United States on the grounds that, "If I follow US Standards, I will have to shut down almost all drug facilities."[80]

Under Indian law, the state drug controllers who are responsible for issuing manufacturing licences are also required to carry out yearly inspections of the manufacturing facility. But are they actually carrying out these yearly inspections? This is a difficult question to answer because unlike the USFDA which publishes its inspections reports, the Indian state drug controllers who are supposed to carry out scheduled inspections do not make any information publicly available on their findings. However, from insider accounts by those familiar with the functioning of the Indian regulatory mechanism, it is quite clear that most state drug controllers are not inspecting Indian manufacturing plants for GMP compliance. One such account is in the book *Healing the Pharmacy of the World* written by K.L. Sharma, the former Joint-Secretary, Drug and Food Regulation, Government of India, who had the responsibility for setting the course of India's drug-regulatory policy for a few years. Sharma narrates the story of how the Ministry of Health ordered the CDSCO to conduct risk-based inspections after a national drug survey report had thrown up shocking results. Of the 170 manufacturing facilities that were jointly inspected (after much resistance by the state drug controllers) by the central and state drug inspectors, compliance with GMP standards in 33 facilities was found to be less than 25% with several plants having "critical deficiencies"![81]

A more revealing account of the state of affairs in Indian pharmaceutical facilities can be found in Katherine Eban's *Bottle of Lies: The Inside Story of the Generic Drug Boom.* As Katherine Eban documents in her book, Indian pharmaceutical companies exporting to the United States found ways to rig the entire system by fabricating quality data to paint a false and misleading picture of GMP compliance. One company was found to literally pull the plug on the testing equipment every time a sample failed testing so as to crash the software that would have logged the failed tests.[82] USFDA inspectors accused another large Indian company of having an entire testing laboratory, that was "off the books" and used only for the purpose of fabricating quality data.[83] The incentive for fabricating such data lies in the fact that ensuring strict compliance with GMPs is usually a time-consuming and expensive exercise. For example, if a batch fails accelerated stability testing before it is shipped to the market, it will have to be destroyed. Similarly, if a batch fails stability testing after it has been shipped to the market, the manufacturer will have to publicly announce a recall, account for every unit of that batch and destroy it. All of this entails huge financial losses because of which there is little incentive to comply with GMPs unless there is a strong deterrent under the law.

Separate and apart from the data integrity issues, Eban also casts a spotlight on issues like basic cleanliness and sanitation issues raised by the USFDA in its inspection reports. American inspectors came across bird infestations at a sterile manufacturing plant, bathrooms with pools of urine on the floor, gloves designated for use in sterile areas that were flaking, crushed insects in a shipping box for gloves, failure to maintain records of sterilization, and in one instance, a snake coiled on laboratory equipment![84] Similarly, Sharma in his aforementioned book, mentions how during an inspection in Tamil Nadu, inspectors found the "premises filthy with open drains".[85]

The more shocking observations in our opinion are the ones contained in 29 "stop production orders" issued by the Karnataka Drug Control Department between 2014–2021 and provided to us in response to an application under the RTI Act 2005.[86] The observations in these inspection reports reveal severe lapses in following GMP standards laid down in Schedule M to the Drugs and Cosmetics Rules 1945. In all 29 cases, the lapses were so serious that the manufacturers were ordered to stop production of the drugs that they had been licenced to manufacture by the Karnataka Drug Control Department. Many of the observations in these reports bear strong similarity to observations in USFDA Form 483 (which lists the observations made during an inspection) of other manufacturing facilities in India.

A common issue that cropped up in several of these inspection reports pertained to the quality of water being used in the manufacture of drugs. Pharmaceutical manufacturing requires the water used in the manufacturing process to be free of any microbiological contamination. But several of the 29 inspections reports clearly marked the quality of water as a quality issue.

In one report, the drug inspectors note: "Water system found under unhygienic condition and fungus found in water storage tank (sic)."[87] Another notes, "You have not provided water system for generation of purified water."[88] A third report noted how the manufacturer used "local municipality water" for operations at the plant since the water plant for demineralisation was not working for two years.[89] A fourth report notes "...water system for generation of purified water kept in unhygienic. Records related to periodic cleaning & microbiological testing is not maintained and there is no recirculation loop for water system (sic)."[90] A fifth report notes, "You have not provided the validated water system for potable water used for cleaning purposes & purified water used for manufacture of drugs. You have not maintained records or test reports. You have not complied with the requirements of Schedule M Part I (1.3) and Schedule M part I D(6)."[91] A sixth report noted, "You don't have purified water system and failed to produce qualification reports of purified water. (as per para 1.3 of Pt. I, Sch. M of Drugs & Cosmetics Rules, 1945)."[92]

It is because of such lapses in validating the quality of water being used in the manufacturing process that so many of the drugs (especially the injectables) we discussed earlier are found to be contaminated with bacterial endotoxins and other assorted particulate matter that could be dangerous to patients.

A second recurring observation in some of the "stop

production orders", is a problem with basic cleanliness and sanitation at facilities manufacturing drugs. GMPs require pharmaceutical manufacturing facilities to be meticulously clean. As important as maintaining actual cleanliness is the need to maintain records and documentation of the frequency at which sanitation procedures are carried out. Yet many of the "stop production orders" that we reviewed from Karnataka, had some variation of the following observations:

> You have not maintained the premises in clean and hygenic conditions. Cracks were observed and dust was accumulated in production area. You have not maintained the premises as required under Schedule M Part I (1.2)(iii).[93]
>
> You have not submitted the Cleaning validation reports. Dust was found accumulated on the floor, walls of manufacturing area and as well as on the equipments.[94]
>
> Open drains are found in production area.[95]
>
> ...you have provided open windows in manufacturing areas.[96]
>
> The spoons used to adjust fill weight after repacking into primary packing material found rusted. No precautions has been taken by the firm to prevent product contamination.[97]
>
> The roof of Production Blocks in the clean rooms meant for Active Pharmaceutical Ingredients (API) manufacturing are found to be leaking on rain water. It is not maintained to suit the manufacturing operations so as to permit production of drugs under hygienic condition. (Violation of Rule 74 (o) R/w Schedule Part-I M para 1.2).[98]
>
> The final stage of preparations of a drug isolation/filtration/drying/milling/sieve and packing operations are not provided with air filtration system with pre and finally with 5 micron filter. Air handling units to control air borne contamination are found to be not in working conditions.[99]
>
> You have not provided the Air Handling System or any other suitable system in the manufacturing area to control air borne contamination as required under Schedule M, Part I-F (1.2).[100]

> You have not provided exhaust system of suitable capacity to remove vapours, fumes, smoke & dust particles. You have not complied with the requirements of Schedule M Part I-D(2).[101]
>
> You are not carrying out disinfection as a routine procedure. No cleaning and sanitation procedures are adopted and followed for equipments and areas Sanitization conditions are not adequate as required under Schedule M Part I (9.3).[102]

A third series of problems that we observed in these "stop production orders" from Karnataka pertains to the non-compliance with the quality control requirements laid down in the GMP section of Schedule M. As per the law, pharmaceutical companies are supposed to conduct extensive testing throughout the manufacturing process, starting from the input material to the final formulation by qualified personnel in the quality control department which is supposed to be independent from the manufacturing department. As some of these "stop production orders" reveal, several of the inspected companies did not even have a quality assurance department and even when such a department existed, it was often found that they were not conducting adequate testing, or that they lacked the equipment for testing, or that they were not retaining samples for post sales testing, or that the authorized personnel meant to supervise manufacturing were not present on the premises. A few such observations are reproduced below:

> In GC System, you have provided access to analyst to delete the chromatogram [data], to change the time of system and you have not enabled audit trial in GC system, which may leads to modification of data (Data integrity)(as per 12.5 of Pt.I, Sch. M of Drugs & Cosmetics Rules, 1945). (sic)[103]
>
> You have not established Quality Assurance department to have a control over the preparation, checking procedures and approval of standard documents. (as per 14 of Pt.I, Sch. M of Drugs & Cosmetics Rules, 1945).[104]

You have not provided adequate training to employees working in QC and also not produced training records. (as per 6.6 of Pt.I, Sch. M of Drugs & Cosmetics Rules, 1945).[105]

You are not testing 100% API before release of materials for repacking. On review of documents (COAs) submitted, it is observed that you are not testing all the parameters for Finished Goods as per I.P. (As required under Rule 74-A(f) if D&C Act, 1945 & Rules thereunder).[106]

In GC system, you have provided access to analyst to delete the chromatogram [data], to change the time of system and you have not enabled audit trial in GC system, which may leads to modification of data (Data Integrity).[107]

You don't have Quality assurance section to control starting material, intermediaries, to control finished product process and to verify the quality of product before release. (as per para 14 of Pt.I, Sch. M of Drugs and Cosmetics Rules, 1945).[108]

You have not maintained sufficient quantity of control sample to carry out all tests and also not maintained control sample register. (as per para 16.7 of Pt.I, Sch. M of Drugs & Cosmetics Rules, 1945).[109]

You have not maintained the reference samples (control samples) from each batch as required in Schedule M, Part I (23.1).[110]

You have not appointed/authorized any quality control personnel. You have manufactured, repacked & released the drugs for distribution & sale in the absence of approved quality control personnel. You have not complied with the requirements of Schedule M part I (6.2) & (25.1).[111]

You are not carrying out tests for raw materials before release for production and not maintained any test reports as required under Schedule M Part I (10.9) & (16).[112]

You have not provided separate QA department (As per 14 of Sch.M Pt-1 of Drugs and Cosmetics Rules, 1945.[113]

The firm has not maintained staff required for manufacture of drugs as per rule 71 of Drugs and Cosmetics Rules, 1945 to manufacture the permitted products.[114]

> HPLC found [to be] not [in] working condition and also not furnished qualification documents for HPLC.[115]

These examples are merely representative and not exhaustive. There are several other violations described in these stop production orders which are too complicated to discuss here. These findings, however, broadly corroborate the findings of the USFDA as described in *Bottle of Lies* of other manufacturing facilities located in India. We have not been able to access similar inspection reports issued by other drug controllers in India but if those reports were to be proactively published by the government, we are quite sure these reports would reveal similar problems with pharmaceutical manufacturing units across the country.

Clearly then, the issue of GMP compliance is not an isolated issue as made out by the Government of India post the Ranbaxy scandal. It is a systemic issue and there is a very simple explanation for these violations. Modern GMPs made a relatively late entry into Indian law. While a version of mandatory GMPs was introduced into the law in 1988, it was the version in 2001 that represented a significant upgrade in the quality of GMPs. This meant that existing pharmaceutical manufacturing units had to make a transition to the new system and it is very likely that many of them lacked the resources or inclination to do so in a resource-scarce environment. Since 1988, the job of ensuring compliance has been left to state drug controllers who likely lack the resources or political backing to carry out the required inspections that were necessary to cancel the manufacturing licences of pharmaceutical companies that failed to make that transition to the new GMPs standards.

One way to force Indian pharmaceutical companies to pay more attention to GMP standards is to follow the American model of presuming all drugs manufactured through a compromised GMP process as "adulterated". As it stands currently in India, the law does not provide for any punishment despite the grave consequences of NSQ drugs. It only allows for the cancellation of the manufacturing licence since following GMP standards is a condition of the manufacture licence. However, Indian law does not recognize the violation of GMP standards as a specific offence. There is a residuary clause which basically states that violation of any rule under the Drugs and Cosmetics Act 1940 can lead to imprisonment for a year but we have come across only one case where this clause has been invoked to charge a pharmaceutical company with violation of GMP standards.[116] If Parliament clearly articulates such an offence, it would make it easier for a drug inspector to charge pharmaceutical companies with violation of GMP standards, especially in relation to the failure to maintain records or indulging in data fabrication. Any such change in the law will also have to be accompanied by augmenting the human resources required to conduct GMP compliance.

Conclusion—Transparency and Recall Guidelines

One of the reasons why boisterous press releases like the one referenced at the start of this chapter were never challenged by journalists or even well-meaning public health activists is because there is a complete lack of transparency in the way the law is enforced. As mentioned earlier, only three states took it upon themselves to upload their test results to the XLN database. Even this data on the XLN website is very messy; there is no consistency in the way data is catalogued, making it difficult to perform any meaningful analysis. And asking for this information from the CDSCO and the state drug controllers via the RTI Act is an abject lesson in how the bureaucracy lives to frustrate anyone asking for accountability. Requests for information are routinely transferred to "other" offices and denied on illegal grounds which then lead to appeals that go on forever.

A simple reform measure that can dramatically alter the present status-quo is to force drug controllers to disclose more information proactively to the general public. This should include proactive publication of all test reports prepared by government laboratories and all inspection reports prepared by drug inspectors. This data should be released in an organized, searchable format. Such transparency would make it possible for doctors, journalists, and regular citizens to understand the levels of efficiency of different state drug controllers and identify the problematic pharmaceutical companies.

The more complicated reforms will require auditing state government laboratories in order to gauge their testing capability, reforming the IPC and putting in place a special law on nationwide recalls. None of this is going to happen without sustained public pressure.

Notes

1. Government of India, Ministry of Health and Family Welfare, *Report of The Expert Committee on a Comprehensive Examination of Drug Regulatory Issues, including the problem of Spurious Drugs* (hereinafter the *Mashelkar Committee Report)* (No Z.28015/112/2002-D/DMS&PFA, 2003). Two other reports which studied the entire pharmaceutical industry touched upon the workings of the regulator.
2. Government of India, Ministry of Commerce and Industry, '*Clarifications on Reports of Malpractices of Pharma Manufacturing in India*' (Press Information Bureau, 3 June 2013).
3. The Gujarat Food and Drug Control Administration which pioneered the XLN website in 2007, The Maharashtra Food and Drug Administration which joined in 2011 and the Kerala Drugs Control Department which joined in 2013. 'XLN—Xtended Licensing, Laboratory and Legal Node' <https://xlnindia.gov.in/> accessed 23 Jan 2022
4. CDSCO Drug Alerts: https://cdsco.gov.in/opencms/opencms/en/Notifications/Alerts/.
5. Reply to RTI application dated 23 March 2022, Drug Testing Laboratory, Chennai, Government of Tamil Nadu (Application No 379/A1/2022, 17 February 2022).

6. Reply by the Minister of State (Ministry of Health & Family Welfare) Kumari Saroj Khaparde to question raised by Shri Dharanidhar Basumatari, Rajya Sabha Deb 2 May 1989, Question No 737, 140–141.
7. The Drugs Act 1940, s 23.
8. The Sale of Food and Drugs Act 1875, s 14.
9. Central Drugs Standard Control Organization (CDSCO), 'Guidelines for the Zonal, Sub-zonal and Port Offices of the Central Drugs Standard Control Organization' (2011) 15–16; Reply to RTI application dated 30 November 2011, Office of the Director of Drugs Control, Tamil Nadu (Application No 17436/E1/2011).
10. Reply to RTI application dated 04 January 2016, Office of the Chief Medical Officer (Application No SU/A/2015-16/14287-88, 14 December 2015).
11. Dr Ravi Prasad Varma P, 'Effectiveness of Drugs Control and Regulating Mechanism of the Drugs Control Department in Kerala State' (Kerala State Planning Board 2021).
12. Ibid at 29.
13. Dinesh Thakur to the Union Minister for Health, 'Petition to setup Expert Committee to examine the sampling and testing protocols of drugs withdrawn under Section 23 & Section 25 of the Drugs & Cosmetics Act, 1940' (3 July 2020) <https://casemindia.org/wp-content/uploads/2020/07/Samplying-Testing-Petition-Unsgned.pdf> accessed 12 January 2021.
14. Reply to RTI application dated 7 March 2022, State Drugs Control & Research Laboratory, Government of West Bengal (Application No SDCRL/29, 17 February 2022).
15. Reply to RTI application dated 25 March 2022, Drugs Control Laboratory, Government of NCT, Delhi (Application No (0019)/2022/RTI/DC/6700, 17 February 2022).
16. Reply to RTI application dated 17 March 2022, Joint Food and Drugs Laboratory, Government of Bihar (Application No 709, 17 February 2022).
17. Reply to RTI application dated 23 March 2022, Drug Testing Laboratory, Chennai, Government of Tamil Nadu (n 5).
18. Reply to RTI application dated 17 March 2022, Joint Food and Drugs Laboratory, Government of Bihar (n 16).
19. Reply to RTI application dated 16 March 2022, Composite Testing Laboratory, Khandagat, District Solan, Directorate of Health Safety and Regulation, Government of Himachal Pradesh (Application No HSR-H (RTI) 2022-IX-9528, 17 February 2022).

20. Reply to RTI application dated 25 March 2022, Drugs Control Laboratory, Government of NCT, Delhi (n 15).
21. Reply to RTI application dated 7 March 2022, State Drugs Control and Research Laboratory, Government of West Bengal (n 14); Reply to RTI application dated 23 March 2022, Drug Testing Laboratory, Chennai, Government of Tamil Nadu (n 5).
22. Reply to RTI application dated 17 March 2022, Joint Food and Drugs Laboratory, Government of Bihar (n 16).
23. Reply to RTI application dated 16 March 2022, Composite Testing Laboratory, Khandagat, District Solan, Directorate of Health Safety & Regulation, Government of Himachal Pradesh (n 19).
24. Reply to RTI application dated 23 March 2022, Drug Testing Laboratory, Chennai, Government of Tamil Nadu (n 5).
25. Reply to RTI application dated 7 March 2022, State Drugs Control and Research Laboratory, Government of West Bengal (n 14).
26. US Department of Health and Human Services, Food and Drug Administration, Center for Drug Evaluation and Research (CDER), *Guidance for Industry—ANDAs: Impurities in Drug Substances* (November 1999); Priyanka Pulla, 'Inside the Fight to Decide How Pure India's Drugs Need To Be', *The Wire Science* (25 June 2022) available at https://science.thewire.in/india-drug-impurities-fight accessed 16 July, 2022; Alexander Cartwright, 'Toxicology of Impurities in Organic Synthetic Drugs' (1990), *International Journal of Pharmacy*.
27. Reply to RTI application dated 17 March 2022, Joint Food and Drugs Laboratory, Government of Bihar (n 16).
28. Reply to RTI application dated 16 March 2022, Composite Testing Laboratory, Khandagat, District Solan, Directorate of Health Safety and Regulation, Government of Himachal Pradesh (n 19).
29. Indian Pharmacopoeia Commission, 'Annual Report 2010–11' (Ministry of Health and Family Welfare, Government of India 2011) 1.
30. Drugs Technical Advisory Board (DTAB), *'MINUTES OF THE THIRTYNINTH DRUGS TECHNICAL ADVISORY BOARD MEETING HELD ON DECEMBER 19, 1984 AT NEW DELHI'* (1984). <https://cdsco.gov.in/opencms/opencms/system/modules/CDSCO.WEB/elements/common_download.jsp?num_id_pk=NTcz> accessed 13 January 2022.
31. Vide resolution: Resolution (F.No.X.11035/2/06-DFQC, 8 May 2008); Indian Pharmacopoeia Commission, 'Annual Report 2019–20' (Ministry of Health and Family Welfare, Government of India 2020) 16.

32. The Drugs and Cosmetics Rules 1945, Rule 124.
33. Drugs Consultative Committee (DCC), '*MINUTES OF THE 35TH MEETING OF THE DRUGS CONSULTATIVE COMMITTEE HELD ON 29TH & 30TH APRIL, 2004*' (2004) 483. <https://cdsco.gov.in/opencms/opencms/system/modules/CDSCO.WEB/elements/common_download.jsp?num_id_pk=Nzk3> accessed 13 January 2022.
34. ibid 484.
35. Drugs Consultative Committee (DCC), '*MINUTES OF THE 43rd MEETING OF THE DRUGS CONSULTATIVE COMMITTEE HELD ON 14th NOVEMBER*' (2011) 19.
36. ibid.
37. Drugs Consultative Committee (DCC), '*REPORT OF THE 45TH MEETING OF THE DRUGS CONSULTATIVE COMMITTEE HELD ON 4TH AND 5TH FEBRUARY 2013 AT THE HOTEL METROPOLITAN NEW DELHI-110001*' (2013) 32. <https://cdsco.gov.in/opencms/opencms/system/modules/CDSCO.WEB/elements/common_download.jsp?num_id_pk=ODA3> accessed 13 January 2022.
38. Drugs Consultative Committee (DCC), '*REPORT OF THE 48TH MEETING OF THE DRUGS CONSULTATIVE COMMITTEE HELD ON 24TH JULY, 2015 AT NEW DELHI*' (2015) 38. <https://cdsco.gov.in/opencms/opencms/system/modules/CDSCO.WEB/elements/common_download.jsp?num_id_pk=ODEw> accessed 13 January 2022.
39. Drugs Consultative Committee (DCC), '*MINUTES OF 56TH MEETING OF DRUGS CONSULTATIVE COMMITTEE HELD ON 01ST JUNE, 2019 AT NEW DELHI*' (2019) 18 <https://cdsco.gov.in/opencms/opencms/system/modules/CDSCO.WEB/elements/common_download.jsp?num_id_pk=OTE1> accessed 13 January 2022.
40. Priyanka Pulla, 'India's Drug Testing Has a Big Blind Spot: Officials Rarely Check for Impurities', *The Wire Science* (3 November 2021) <https://science.thewire.in/health/india-drug-testing-blind-spot-imprity-test-rare-pharmacopoeia-commission/> accessed 13 January 2022.
41. Reply to RTI application dated 22 March 2022, Indian Pharmacopeia Commission (Application No CIPGZ/R/E/22/00017 dated 9 March, 2022).
42. 'Four countries accept IP as book of standard', *Express Pharma*, (29 June 2022) < https://www.expresspharma.in/four-countries-accept-ip-as-book-of-standard/> accessed 16 July 2022.

43. 'Legal Recognition of USP Standards' (*USP*) <https://www.usp.org/about/legal-recognition> accessed 23 January 2022.
44. Email from Bhavneet Bharti to Chandigarh CDSCO titled "Regarding child with Renal failure at PGI Chandigarh & Contamination of Syp Cofset-At with Diethylene Glycol", provided under the RTI Act in response to RTI application no. APC/2021/550 (On file with authors); Priyanka Pulla, 'How weak drug laws are costing lives' *Mint* (27 September 2021) <https://www.livemint.com/politics/policy/how-weak-drug-laws-are-costing-lives-11632761831130.html> accessed 13 January 2022.
45. Savita V Jayaram, 'Digital Vision under DGCI Scanner: Renaming Coldbest to Cofset AT Cough Syrup Didn't Help Manufacturer' *IB Times* (10 August 2020) <https://www.ibtimes.co.in/digital-vision-under-dgci-scanner-renaming-coldbest-cofset-cough-syrup-didnt-help-manufacturer-826143> accessed 28 March 2022.
46. Usha Sharma, 'DCGI asks drug controllers to prevent sale, distribution of DEG contaminated cough syrup, Cofset' *Express Pharma* (7 August 2020) <https://www.expresspharma.in/latest-updates/dcgi-asks-drug-controllers-to-prevent-sale-distribution-of-deg-contaminated-cough-syrup-cofset/> accessed 30 May 2021.
47. Carol Ballentine, 'Sulfanilamide Disaster' [1981] FDA Consumer Magazine 144.
48. V R Ravi Kumar, 'When a Drug Turned Killer' *The Hindu* (9 February 2020) <https://www.thehindu.com/opinion/open-page/when-a-drug-turned-killer/article30770710.ece> accessed 13 January 2022.
49. JP Swann, 'The 1941 Sulfathiazole Disaster and the Birth of Good Manufacturing Practices' (1999) 53 PDA *Journal of Pharmaceutical Science and Technology*, 148.
50. Drugs Consultative Committee (DCC), '*REPORT OF THE 19TH MEETING OF THE DRUGS CONSULTATIVE COMMITTEE HELD ON 12TH & 13TH APRIL, 1976 AT NEW DELHI-110001*' (1976) Item No. 11 <https://cdsco.gov.in/opencms/opencms/system/modules/CDSCO.WEB/elements/common_download.jsp?num_id_pk=ODUy> accessed 13 January 2022.
51. ibid 20.
52. ibid 21.
53. ibid.
54. Drugs Consultative Committee (DCC), '*MINUTES OF THE 26TH MEETING OF THE DRUGS CONSULTATIVE COMMITTEE HELD ON 14TH & 15TH SEPTEMBER 1989*' (1989). <https://cdsco.gov.in/opencms/opencms/system/modules/CDSCO.WEB/

elements/common_download.jsp?num_id_pk=Nzg4> accessed 13 January 2022.

55. Drugs Technical Advisory Board (DTAB), *'MINUTES OF THE FORTY-FIFTH DRUGS TECHNICAL ADVISORY BOARD MEETING ON FEBRUARY 1, 1996 AT NEW DELHI'* (1996) 7 <https://cdsco.gov.in/opencms/opencms/system/modules/CDSCO.WEB/elements/common_download.jsp?num_id_pk=NTgw> accessed 13 January 2022.
56. Drugs Consultative Committee (DCC), *'MINUTES OF THE 32ND MEETING OF THE DRUGS CONSULTATIVE COMMITTEE HELD ON 22ND & 23RD SEPTEMBER, 1998'* (1998) <https://cdsco.gov.in/opencms/opencms/system/modules/CDSCO.WEB/elements/common_download.jsp?num_id_pk=Nzk0> accessed 13 January 2022.
57. Drugs Consultative Committee (DCC), *'MINUTES OF THE 35TH MEETING OF THE DRUGS CONSULTATIVE COMMITTEE HELD ON 29TH & 30TH APRIL, 2004'* (2004) 470. <https://cdsco.gov.in/opencms/opencms/system/modules/CDSCO.WEB/elements/common_download.jsp?num_id_pk=Nzk3> accessed 13 January 2022.
58. Drugs Consultative Committee (DCC), *'MINUTES OF 38TH MEETING OF DRUGS CONSULTATIVE COMMITTEE HELD ON 4TH JUNE 2007 AT NEW DELHI UNDER THE CHAIRMANSHIP OF DR. M. VENKATESWARLU. DRUGS CONTROLLER GENERAL OF INDIA'* (2007) 5.
59. Drugs Consultative Committee (DCC), *'MINUTES OF THE 43rd MEETING OF THE DRUGS CONSULTATIVE COMMITTEE HELD ON 14th NOVEMBER'* (n 35) 10.
60. Department-Related Parliamentary Standing Committee on Health and Family Welfare, *The Functioning of The Central Drugs Standard Control Organisation (CDCSO)* (Fifty-Ninth Report) (RS 2012) para 15.5.
61. ibid para 15.11.
62. Ministry of Health and Family Welfare, *Final Action Taken Report on the observations/recommendations contained in the 59th report of the department related parliamentary standing committee on Health & Family Welfare on the functioning of the Central Drugs Standard Control Organisation (CDSCO)* (2012) 25.
63. Central Drugs Standard Control Organisation, *Guidelines on Recall and Rapid Alert System for Drugs (Including Biologicals & Vaccines)* (2012).

64. ibid para 3.4, 16.
65. Usha Sharma, 'CDSCO drafts guidelines on recall and rapid alert system for drugs' *Express Pharma* (22 November 2012) <https://www.expresspharma.in/cdsco-drafts-guidelines-on-recall-and-rapid-alert-system-for-drugs/> accessed 30 May 2021.
66. Drugs Consultative Committee (DCC), *'REPORT OF THE 45TH MEETING OF THE DRUGS CONSULTATIVE COMMITTEE HELD ON 4th AND 5th FEBRUARY 2013 AT THE HOTEL METROPOLITAN NEW DELHI-110001'* (2013) <https://cdsco.gov.in/opencms/opencms/system/modules/CDSCO.WEB/elements/common_download.jsp?num_id_pk=ODA3> accessed 30 May 2021.
67. Dinesh S. Thakur and Prashant Reddy T., *A report on fixing India's broken drug regulatory framework* (4 June 2016) (on file with authors).
68. Peethaambaran Kunnathoor, 'Amend D&C Act to make manufacturers accountable for prompt recalling of NSQ drugs from market: Kerala deputy DC' *Pharmabiz* (12 October 2015) <http://www.pharmabiz.com/PrintArticle.aspx?aid=91059&sid=1> accessed 30 May 2021.
69. Drugs Technical Advisory Board (DTAB), *'MINUTES OF THE 72ND MEETING OF THE DRUGS TECHNICAL ADVISORY BOARD HELD ON 27TH JUNE, 2016 AT NIRMAN BHAWAN, NEW DELHI-110001'* (2016) <https://cdsco.gov.in/opencms/opencms/system/modules/CDSCO.WEB/elements/common_download.jsp?num_id_pk=Nzcy>
70. Drugs Consultative Committee (DCC), *'REPORT OF 50TH MEETING OF DRUGS CONSULTATIVE COMMITTEE HELD ON 04 & 05TH NOVEMBER, 2016 AT NEW DELHI'* (2016) 22 <https://cdsco.gov.in/opencms/opencms/system/modules/CDSCO.WEB/elements/common_download.jsp?num_id_pk=ODEy> accessed 13 January 2022.
71. Drugs Consultative Committee (DCC), *'REPORT OF 54TH MEETING OF DRUGS CONSULTATIVE COMMITTEE HELD ON 30TH JULY, 2018 AT NEW DELHI'* (2018) 7 <https://cdsco.gov.in/opencms/opencms/system/modules/CDSCO.WEB/elements/common_download.jsp?num_id_pk=ODE2> accessed 13 January 2022.
72. Reply to RTI application dated 16 December 2021, Ministry of Health and Family Welfare (Application No CDSCO/R/T/21/00900 filed on 28 October 2021).
73. Thakur and Reddy (n 67).

74. 'Medicine: Dangerous Drug' [1941] *Time* <http://content.time.com/time/subscriber/article/0,33009,765439,00.html> accessed 17 March 2022; Swann (n 49).
75. Walt Bogdanich and Jake Hooker, 'From China to Panama, a Trail of Poisoned Medicine' *The New York Times* (6 May 2007) <https://www.nytimes.com/2007/05/06/world/americas/06poison.html> accessed 17 March 2022.
76. 21 US Code § 351 (Adulterated drugs and devices).
77. Shri Dharanidhar Basumatari to the Minister of Health and Family Welfare, Rajya Sabha Deb 2 May 1989, Question No 737.
78. Government of India, Ministry of Health & Family Welfare, GSR 431(E)(Gazette of India Extraordinary, Part II—s 3(i), 30 June, 2005) (publishing Drugs and Cosmetics (5th Amendment) Rules, 2005).
79. Chittabratta Mazumdar and Dipankar Mukherjee on the 'Revision of Schedule M of Drugs and Cosmetics Act', Rajya Sabha Debate 10 December 2004, Question No 874.
80. Sushmi Dey, 'If I follow US Standards, I will have to shut almost all drug facilities: G.N. Singh", *Business Standard*, (30 January 2004) *available at* https://www.business-standard.com/article/economy-policy/if-i-follow-us-standards-i-will-have-to-shut-almost-all-drug-facilities-g-n-singh-114013000034_1.html.
81. K.L. Sharma, *Healing the Pharmacy of the World: An Inside Story of Medical Products Manufacturing and Regulation in India* (Notion Press 2021) 104.
82. Katherine Eban, *Bottle of Lies: The Inside Story of the Generic Drug Boom* (HarperCollins 2020).
83. PTI, 'Dr Reddy's Gets a Breather after USFDA Gives More Time to Respond to Warning Letter-Business News' *Firstpost* (26 November 2015) <https://www.firstpost.com/business/dr-reddys-gets-a-breather-after-usfda-gives-more-time-to-respond-to-warning-letter-2522724.html> accessed 17 March 2022.
84. Eban (n 82) 361, 366–367 & 324.
85. Sharma (n 81) 104.
86. Reply to RTI application dated 26 May 2022, Karnataka Drug Control Department (Application No DCD/RTI/114/2021-2022 dated 26 May, 2022).
87. Inspection Report No. DCD/MFG/SR-318/2012-13 by the Drugs Control Department, Government of Karnataka dated 17 November 2018.
88. Inspection Report No. DCD/MFG/SR-506/17-18 by the Drugs Control Department, Government of Karnataka dated 26 March 2019.

89. Inspection Report No. DCD/MFG/SR-1082/16-17 by the Drugs Control Department, Government of Karnataka dated 26 July 2021.
90. Inspection Report No. DCD/MFG/SR-124/13-14 by the Drugs Control Department, Government of Karnataka dated 16 January 2016.
91. Inspection Report No. DCD/MFG/SR-499/11-12 by the Drugs Control Department, Government of Karnataka dated 16 November 2016.
92. Inspection Report No. DCD/MFG/SR-318/2012-13 by the Drugs Control Department, Government of Karnataka dated 19 May 2016.
93. Inspection Report No. DCD/SR-764/MFG/2012-13 by the Drugs Control Department, Government of Karnataka dated 7 April 2016.
94. Inspection Report (n. 90).
95. Ibid.
96. Inspection Report (n 93).
97. Ibid.
98. Inspection Report (n 92).
99. Ibid.
100. Inspection Report No. DCD/MFG/SR-657/2012-13 by the Drugs Control Department, Government of Karnataka dated 14 November 2016.
101. Inspection Report (n 94).
102. Ibid.
103. Inspection Report (n 93).
104. Ibid.
105. Ibid.
106. Ibid.
107. Ibid.
108. Inspection Report (n 95).
109. Ibid.
110. Inspection Report (n 94).
111. Ibid.
112. Ibid.
113. Inspection Report (n 91).
114. Inspection Report (n 101).
115. Inspection Report (n 95).
116. The Drugs and Cosmetics Act 1940, s 27(d).

CHAPTER FIVE

New Drugs and "The Persistent Insolence of the CDSCO..."[1]

One of the landmark events in the history of Indian drug regulation is a report from the Department Related Parliamentary Standing Committee on Health and Family Welfare that was tabled before Parliament on 8 May 2012. This report, which was titled rather drably as the "Fifty-Ninth Report on The Functioning of the Central Drugs Standards Control Organisation (CDSCO)" contained one of the most scathing indictments of India's national drug regulator—the CDSCO—and the Drug Controller General of India (DCGI) who heads the CDSCO. The report marked the first ever independent scrutiny of the functioning of India's drug regulator and it was clear from a reading of the report that the CDSCO failed on all counts.

While most parliamentary reports are usually written in bland bureaucratese, this particular report was punctuated with words such as "persistent insolence", "deep concern", "disappointment", "skewed priorities and perceptions" and "collusive nexus" to describe the conduct of the CDSCO. The report contained a laundry list of sins committed by the CDSCO, including misplacing crucial files, irregular approvals, evidence of collusion between doctors and pharmaceutical companies and a lack of transparency in the regulator's functioning.

The most startling allegations in the report pertained to the manner in which the DCGI approved "new drugs" despite the lack of any supporting evidence of safety and efficacy from rigorous clinical trials demonstrating their safety or efficacy. As a result, all types of "new drugs", which never received approval in the better regulated markets in developed countries were available for sale in India. These approvals by the DCGI included the approval of an antihistamine (anti-allergen) as an appetite stimulant for children, a breast cancer drug approved for infertility treatment in women and two fixed dose combinations that were not approved in most developed countries, including in its country of origin.

In the world of drug regulation, the task of verifying the safety and efficacy of a drug is considered to be one of the most sacrosanct public duties of the drug regulator. Individual doctors or hospitals lack the time and resources to verify the claims made by pharmaceutical companies about the safety and efficacy of their drugs. This is where drug regulators, financed by public money, step in to lay down the rules of the game and ensure that the pharmaceutical companies play by these rules. Historically, the first challenge in this context was to decide the rules of the game to prove safety and efficacy in a scientifically rigorous manner. This has proved to be a tricky issue not just because of resistance from the pharmaceutical industry but also from patient groups who want faster and quicker access to drugs. The second challenge lies in enforcing these rules in a transparent and efficient manner so as to build public confidence in both the drugs approved and the regulator itself. Confidence in the regulator is precious; it is earned by consistently enforcing regulations in a transparent manner and protecting public health over decades. Drugs are often approved based on a limited set of clinical and safety data collected in controlled conditions; it is the trust in the regulator that inspires confidence both among the medical community and patients to take new drugs that are approved based on a limited data set. When a new drug enters the market, it most often encounters real-world conditions that were never evaluated in the clinical trial. Monitoring the usage of the new drug, its adverse events in the population at large, the process by which commercial supplies are manufactured, all go to building the credibility of the drug regulator step by step over decades to a point where those who do this consistently and faithfully are held as a gold standard in the industry. India has gone from not having any rules for several decades, to creating rules which were never applied properly by the regulator that functioned in an opaque manner. In order to understand the scale of the incompetence of the Indian system, it will help if we understand the American system as a useful reference point, especially the manner in which it evolved to become the gold standard of the world.

The gold standard for approving new drugs

The original gold standard for drug approvals is the system put in place in 1962, by the Kefauver-Harris Amendments to the Federal Food, Drugs and Cosmetic Act in the United States, post the thalidomide tragedy. The Senate Committee headed by Kefauver that had conducted an inquiry into the functioning of the American pharmaceutical industry in the years prior to the enactment of this law, had heard repeated complaints from doctors that "detail-men" from pharmaceutical industry, who were selling them drugs, often made greatly exaggerated claims of the efficacy of their drugs and that there was no way for doctors themselves to verify these claims. A simple strategy used in the pre-1962 era to validate the efficacy of a new drug was to publish case-studies based on how new drugs were perceived to act on individual patients. The case-study would then be published in medical journals and more often than not be used as a marketing tool by pharmaceutical companies in order to promote the drug. From a scientific view point, such individual case studies were akin to anecdotal evidence and were plagued by problems ranging from "bias" of the investigators to the "placebo effect" to "statistical insignificance" of the test group. The system, however, worked well for pharmaceutical companies as there was little scientific accountability and they could get away with making exaggerated claims about their new drugs.[2]

It was thus not surprising when more than one doctor had recommended to the Senate sub-committee that a government body like the USFDA or the National Insitute of Health (NIH) be vested with the responsibility to vet the claims of the pharmaceutical industry.[3] Eventually, that is exactly what the US Congress did when it enacted the Kefauver-Harris Act in 1962.

This law set a global benchmark for approving new drugs. For the first time ever, the law required pharmaceutical companies to provide "substantial evidence" that a new drug would have the therapeutic effect advertized on the proposed labelling of the drug.[4] Further, "substantial evidence" was defined in the law as "adequate and well-controlled investigations, including clinical investigations, by experts qualified by scientific training and experience to evaluate the effectiveness of the drug".[5] The power to decide the requirements of an "adequate and well-controlled investigation" was delegated to the USFDA.

The original regulations drafted by the USFDA back in 1965 required all new drugs to go through a three-phase clinical trial process after the investigational drug completed basic in-vitro (in the laboratory) and animal testing. Phase I required testing the new drug on only healthy humans to determine toxicity, metabolism, absorption, elimination, safe dosage range etc. The aim was to determine the dose response in healthy volunteers especially from a safety perspective, which could be used to assess the dosage for testing on actual patients in the next phase. Phase II trials were meant to test efficacy of the new drug on a small number of human patients suffering from the disease that is the target of the new drug. Finally, if the new drug demonstrated promising results in the Phase II trial, the innovator could conduct Phase III trials on a larger number of patients to generate statistically significant safety and efficacy data for the drug. The investigators conducting the study were expected to develop protocols for the Phase III study with the aim of producing "well-controlled clinical data". The regulations left enough flexibility for academia and industry to design their own controls for each trial, subject to the regulator's approval.[6]

Over the years, the research methodology that eventually came to be trusted by both academia and regulators was the double-blind randomized clinical trial (RCT). The British Medical Research Council conducted the first double-blind randomized comparative clinical trial in 1948 to test the effectiveness of the newly discovered antibiotic streptomycin on tuberculosis.[7] This trial brought together, for the first time, the following three important scientific methodologies in the context of clinical trials.

The first was the idea of "comparator trials". Comparator trials have been used by scientists since the 18th century when James Lind divided 12 sick sailors on HMS Salisbury, who were diagnosed with scurvy, into two groups and gave citrus fruits like oranges and lemons to one of these two groups. When only the group that received the oranges and lemons (the treatment group) recovered from scurvy, Lind had proof that citrus fruits could prevent scurvy.[8] In picking a therapy to compare the new drug with, it is up to investigators conducting the clinical trial to either pick the existing standard of care, or alternatively, a "placebo".

The second methodological innovation was the process of

"randomization" of patients between the control group and the treatment group. Simply put, the volunteer patients for the clinical trial would be randomly assigned to the control group and the treatment group by persons other than those who were responsible for conducting the clinical trial without consideration of their individual symptoms. The idea of randomization in experiments has existed since the 1920s and was meant to avoid not just subconscious "bias" on part of the treating doctors but also ensure that patients have an equal chance of getting the treatment in question.[9]

The third methodological innovation was the process of "double blinding" wherein neither the doctors conducting the trial nor the patients would be informed about the identity of the patients in the control group and the treatment group. This was meant to guard against both the biases of the investigating doctors and the "placebo effect".

The placebo effect, also known as the "psychic influence", manifests when patients report feeling better after being administered therapy or medicines that in reality have no curative effects. Doctors have for many centuries given their patients "sham" medicines, also known as placebos, just to please rather than benefit the patient.[10] In 1801, John Haygarth demonstrated the importance of placebos while trying to establish whether metallic rods could relieve symptoms through their electro-magnetic influence. The control group in this case were administered regular wooden rods rather than metallic rods and yet reported feeling better post the "treatment" causing Haygarth to remark about "the wonderful and powerful influence of the passions of the mind upon the state and disorder of the body".[11] "Blinding" the patient to whether they were in the control group or the treatment group would reduce the possibility of the placebo effect. Similarly, it was important to "blind" even investigating doctors from the identity of patients in the treatment and control groups, so as to prevent their own biases from interfering with their recording of the study's clinical observations. Hence the phrase "double blind". The patients in both groups would be typically "unblinded" only after the trial was completed in order to analyze the results of the treatment group against that of the control group, which received either a placebo or the prevailing "standard of care".[12] If patients in the treatment group receiving the new drug demonstrated better treatment outcomes than those in the control group, the researchers would have concrete proof that the new drug was more beneficial than the existing treatment.

After the first double blind RCT by the British Medical Research Council, RCTs gained increasing legitimacy amongst scientific and government institutions such as the influential NIH in the United States. The endorsement of RCTs by the scientific community as a reliable method to produce medical knowledge about the efficacy of new drugs is viewed by many as an attempt by the medical community to hold pharmaceutical companies to account for the highly exaggerated claims made by their salespersons to doctors. The pharmaceutical industry itself was not an enthusiastic supporter of the idea of RCTs because it greatly increased the costs and risks of bringing a new drug to the market.[13]

By the 1980s, RCTs came to be known as the "gold standard" for generating quality clinical evidence required for approvals from regulators. The USFDA amended its existing regulations in 1985 to incorporate more elements of RCTs into its existing framework.[14] For example, the amendments in 1985 specifically mentioned the kind of control groups that should be used and that patients should ideally be assigned to groups in a manner that reduces bias etc. Simply put, the research methodologies being followed by universities and scientists had gone ahead of what was required by the law and the USFDA was borrowing from the best practices in science to update its own regulations. Once these regulations were amended, pharmaceutical companies had no choice but to fall in line.

Incorporating rigorous scientific standards into the law was only one component of the new American approach to evaluating the efficacy of new drugs. There are three other important components to this framework.

The first component was the creation of a well-staffed, inter-disciplinary bureaucracy of scientists and administrators, headed by a public health professional, usually a medical doctor. As of 2020, the USFDA employed approximately 7,000 personnel in the Centre for Drug Evaluation and Research (CDER) as well as the Centre for Biologics Evaluation and Research (CBER), whose sole responsibility is to vet applications for marketing of new drugs.[15] Within CDER, there are different divisions which evaluate each new drug application from the perspective of chemistry, pharmacology, microbiology, clinical pharmacology, as well as a statistical review. The American approach encourages a multi-disciplinary approach to evaluating a new drug by professionals in each one of these fields.

The second important component was a participatory framework which provides both the medical profession and the general population a chance to participate in the approval of new drugs. The USFDA creates "advisory committees" consisting of independent scientists and doctors as well as consumer and industry representatives to provide the agency with outside opinions on each new drug application. In addition, the members of the general public can provide their inputs at public hearings or through written comments to the agency.[16]

The third important component of this regulatory framework was a legal guarantee of transparency which was circumscribed to an extent by trade secret considerations. The scientific evaluations of new drug applications by the CBER and CDER are made publicly available subject to certain redactions to protect proprietary information. Similarly, deliberations of the committees and public hearings are transcribed and made publicly available subject to redactions to protect proprietary information.

The approval process for new drugs at the USFDA was not always so participatory or transparent. A Review Panel on New Drug Regulation which had been setup by the United States Government in 1975 had this to say about the opacity of the entire process in its final report which was published in 1977:

> The present system of new drug regulation is essentially closed to public review and participation and relies heavily on exclusive and informal communications between the FDA and its regulates. The system's lack of openness stems primarily from FDA's trade secrets policy which prohibits the disclosure of most scientific data submitted to the agency in support of drug applications. This policy closes day-to-day decision making to outside participation and prevents the agency from releasing to the public the data which underlie its decision...The Panel urges Congress to amend the Federal Food, Drug and Cosmetic Act to provide that scientific data about new drugs belong in the public domain and should not be considered trade secrets.[17]

The scenario painted in the 1977 report was partly reformed by the enactment of the Drug Regulation Reform Act 1978 which made the approval process more participatory by allowing for experts and citizens to be heard during the approval process.[18] Subsequent laws like the Food and Drug Administration Amendments Act 2007 encouraged even more transparency. Despite these reforms, crucial safety and efficacy data submitted by pharmaceutical companies to the USFDA remains confidential and shielded from disclosure. American academics, doctors, and journalists continue to demand more transparency regarding clinical data through litigation and other advocacy measures.[19] Regardless of these drawbacks the approval process for "new drugs", the USFDA continues to be the "gold standard" around the world because of its scientific rigour and transparency. It is the benchmark against which most countries peg their own drug regulatory system.

The struggle to introduce safety and efficacy requirement for "new drugs" in India

While the thalidomide tragedy catalyzed regulatory reform across developed countries during the 1960s, Indian law saw little reform during the same period.

The only provision that existed in Indian law at the time to regulate the import of "new drugs" was Rule 30A of the Drugs and Cosmetics Rules 1945. This rule, which was inserted into Indian law in 1952, required the submission of all documentary evidence related to standards of quality, purity, and strength of the drug along with "such other information as may be required by the licensing authority including the results of therapeutic trials carried out with it".[20] An identical requirement was extended to even domestically manufactured "new drugs" in 1961, through Rule 69B.[21]

In both instances, the law was silent on whether these "new drugs" necessarily had to be "safe" and "effective" in order to be approved for sale in India. In other words, the law outlined the documentary requirements but not the clinical standards required to approve "new drugs". Hence there was nobody in government actually verifying the therapeutic claims being made by manufacturers of new drugs before they were introduced in the market.

Due to the lax regulatory requirements, all kinds of dangerous drugs not approved elsewhere in developed markets were being sold in India with little evidence of safety or efficacy. By the late 1970s, it became clear that India had a problem due to the sale of dangerous or irrational drugs. The nature of the problem was two-fold.

The *first* was the continued sale of dangerous drugs that had been prohibited in other countries. An illustrative example is Amidopyrine which was first synthesized in the late 1890s by German scientists and sold widely as an anti-fever medicine until countries like Australia and the United States banned it in 1964 and 1977 respectively because it causes agranulocytosis, a life-threatening blood disorder in many patients.[22] The Indian medical community had flagged this drug in medical journals as early as 1955 but the Government of India had not taken any action in this regard.[23]

The *second* problem, which continues till date, is the sale of multiple fixed dose combinations (FDCs) in India. These drugs are usually combinations of two or more drugs into one pill or syrup. The purpose of FDCs is to improve compliance of patients who have to take multiple drugs for a single, or similar ailments. For example, patients diagnosed with HIV or tuberculosis are required to take many different drugs every day. Patients are more likely to take one pill on time, rather than two or three different pills. In these circumstances, FDCs can improve compliance which in turn can significantly improve treatment outcomes.[24] The problem in India is that pharmaceutical companies started marketing all kinds of irrational (meaning the combination of drugs does not make clinical sense) FDCs lacking in any therapeutic rationale or clinical evidence. This was possible because the country lacked regulations that required demonstration of safety and efficacy of new drugs, including FDCs, prior to their marketing. For example, a combination of vitamins with anti-diarrheals or the combination of vitamins with anti-inflammatory agents and tranquilizers is "irrational" and makes little sense, yet these were combinations actually sold in India. Apart from the concern about the lack of any therapeutic rationale, the other problem with combining different drugs into a FDC is that these drugs may interact adversely with each other or neutralize each other, thereby negating any therapeutic effectiveness or worse, lead to serious adverse events. Since at the time there was no legal mandate to evaluate these combinations under clinically controlled conditions, it was largely up to the creative instincts of the pharmaceutical industry on how these FDCs were marketed and prescribed.

One of the primary reasons for the presence of numerous FDCs in India is that these drugs are a convenient tactic to avoid price regulation under the Drug Price Control Order (DPCO).[25] Since the DPCO historically applied only to single ingredient drugs and not FDCs, it is possible that the Indian pharmaceutical industry turned to creating FDCs in order to evade the price control dragnet. The other possible reason for the tsunami of FDCs in India is that they are used as a marketing tactic similar to the earlier practice of the pharmaceutical industry in the United States.[26] Since there are only a limited range of approved new drugs in each therapeutic class, pharmaceutical companies can compete over price only to a certain extent. The other way to distinguish themselves from competition is through innovation and creating new products. Since most Indian pharmaceutical companies lack the R&D skills to create new (chemical or biological) molecules, it is possible that they attempted to innovate by creating new FDCs of existing drugs to distinguish themselves from their competitors and thereby command a higher price.

Both the issues identified above—the continued sale of drugs with dangerous and unknown side-effects as well as the tsunami of FDCs in the Indian market—raised questions about the efficacy of India's drug regulatory framework. The Indian Government was aware of some of these issues as far back as the late 70s after one of its expert committees, the

Hathi Committee (also known as The Committee on Drugs and Pharmaceutical Industry) pointed out in its report in 1975, that "according to medical opinion, in a large number of cases the therapeutic usefulness of particular drug combinations" was "doubtful".[27] In a statement laying the new drug policy before Parliament in 1978, the Minister from the government commanded the drug regulator to "immediately go into the various drug combinations and take prompt measures to eliminate irrational drug combinations or use of ingredients far in excess of what is required".[28]

In the same year, at the meeting of the DCC, which has amongst its members representatives from all the state drug controllers, it was noted that the government was coming under criticism for its failure to properly regulate the entry of new drugs into the Indian market. The minutes of its meeting held in 1978, made the following observation:

> There is a persistent criticism that there is plethora of drug preparations being marketed in the country, some of which have doubtful therapeutic value and in some cases positively harmful. Although there is a provision permitting the Licensing Authority to screen formulations from the angle of therapeutic rationale, yet sufficient use of provisions was not being made and all kinds of drug formulations were being licensed...The Chairman said that it is the responsibility of all concerned to see that irrational combinations are not allowed to be marketed.[29]

In an ideal world, the continued sale in India of drugs with dangerous side-effects like Amidopyrine as well as the presence of hundreds of irrational FDCs should have provoked the Government of India to move swiftly to prohibit these drugs from being sold. Further, the Government should have revamped the entire procedure to vet the safety and efficacy of new drugs before any manufacturing or import licences were granted for new drugs. Surprisingly, the government concentrated only on prohibiting harmful drugs from the market, without putting in place a rigorous clinical trial framework to assess the safety and efficacy of new drugs. This included the cancellation of import licence for drugs like Amidopyrine[30] and the issuance of orders banning FDCs and other harmful drugs under Section 26A, which was a provision that had been inserted into the law in 1982 by Parliament in order to provide the Ministry of Health with the power to prohibit the manufacture and sale of existing drugs.[31]

It would take until 1986 for the Government of India to candidly admit to a problem in regulating the approval of new drugs in India, after having faced a barrage of parliamentary questions over the past years. In pertinent part, the Drugs Policy, 1986, made the following admissions and recommendations:

> The present institutional and statutory arrangements for enforcing quality control for registration of new formulations, for monitoring adverse reactions and for dissemination of unbiased information about the safety and efficacy of products marketed in the country are far from being adequate.
>
> In order to establish the safety and efficacy of the new drugs proposed to be introduced detailed information has to be furnished. This information amongst others, should include toxicity data on animals, pharmacological studies and results of clinical trials in Indian conditions, which may extend over several years.[32]

Further, the new Drug Policy cautioned that new formulations of already approved drugs "would not be allowed to be manufactured unless their therapeutic efficacy and rationality are adequately tested and proved".[33]

Two years later, in 1988, the Government of India moved to implement the promises announced in the Drugs Policy 1986 through the route of delegated legislation; i.e., instead of moving legislation in Parliament to amend the Drugs and

Cosmetics Act 1940, it used its executive powers to enact the Drugs and Cosmetics (Eighth Amendment) Rules 1988.[34] These amendments replaced the existing Rule 30A which defined "new drugs", with a new definition that included for the first time in Indian history, a requirement for the new drug to be "effective and safe for the proposed claims".[35]

In order to be approved under the new rules, an application for a new drug would now have to be complemented with a lengthy list of clinical trial data collected through rigorous three phased clinical trials, much like the requirements under American law that was referenced earlier in this chapter.[36] These amendments also introduced a legal framework for regulating clinical trials in India.[37] Further, the approval of all "new drugs" (which now included FDCs) was centralized with the DCGI for the first four years of the drug's availability in India, after which the drug controllers operating under the state governments could directly issue manufacturing licences for the manufacture of those drugs.[38] This regulatory architecture has remained largely untouched save for a few form changing amendments in 2005 and 2019. Surprisingly, this new regulatory framework was entirely silent on any kind of transitory framework for drugs already on the market.

Despite the amendments in 1988, creating on paper a regulatory standard for "new drug" approvals that was similar to the system followed in the United States, in practice, the new system proved to be a spectacular failure. This was obvious from the fact that the Ministry of Health continued issuing hundreds of orders under Section 26A for several decades after 1988, banning a number of drugs, especially FDCs. In one instance, in 2007, the Government of India banned 294 FDCs in one go, only for those orders to be stayed by a court of law where the matter simply lingered on for years together.[39] In another instance, in 2018 the Ministry of Health banned another 328 FDCs.[40] At no point did the government release any report on how these FDCs entered the market in the first place; but going by its explanation in Parliament, state drug controllers were granting manufacturing licences for these FDCs despite lacking the authority to do so.

Equally worrying was the fact that some Indian doctors continued to complain about the approval of dubious new drugs by the DCGI which had not been approved in developed countries.[41] The lurking suspicion in many quarters was that pharmaceutical companies were exploiting poor regulation in markets like India to sell drugs to unsuspecting patients which they knew would not pass regulatory scrutiny in the developed countries that had robust regulatory structures. The worst, however, was yet to be exposed.

Parliamentary wrath exposes the new drug approval process

The full extent of the rot in the approval process of "new drugs" within the CDSCO became evident only in the year 2012, when the Parliamentary Standing Committee on Health and Family Welfare, consisting of 31 Members of Parliament drawn from both the Lok Sabha and Rajya Sabha, tabled before Parliament a stunning investigation into the functioning of the CDSCO. This report remains till date one of the most scathing and astonishing official reports on the abject failure of India's drug regulatory structure.[42]

One of the focus areas of the parliamentary committee in its 59th report was the process by which the CDSCO and its head—the DCGI—were approving new drugs. Since parliamentary committees can summon records from the government, the committee was able to scrutinize records that have never been made public by the CDSCO. The exception of course were cases where the files went "missing", which is regrettably a frequent occurrence at the CDSCO's office.[43]

The drug approval files that were accessed by the parliamentary committee revealed a worrying state of affairs.

Of the 39 drugs scrutinized by the committee, 13 did not have permission for sale in the better-regulated markets of developed countries. Other drugs were approved without any Phase III clinical trial data (where the efficacy of the drug is established) or without any consultation with experts in the field. In many cases, the CDSCO was faulted with an over-reliance on a small number of Delhi-based experts for consultation on "new drug" approvals.[44]

A closer examination of the manner in which these "new drugs" were approved reveals the jarring realities about the manner in which the drug approval process works in India. In particular, we selected and tracked in detail four sets of approvals that had been red-flagged by the parliamentary committee based on its investigation. These following case-studies reveal the extent of the "rot" within the CDSCO:

1. Buclizine

Buclizine was a drug developed by a Belgian company called UCB Pharma and has since been marketed in India by companies such as Mankind Pharma. Originally approved in India as an anti-histamine on 3 August 1982 to treat allergies, Buclizine was later approved in 2006 by the DCGI for an additional indication, namely, as an appetite stimulant for children.[45] Apparently, the marketing literature accompanying the drug claimed that evidence from three clinical trials supported the claim that the drug was effective as an appetite stimulant.

These claims have been met with a lot of scepticism by the Indian medical community. Writing in the *Indian Journal of Pharmacology,* an Indian doctor questioned whether the lack of appetite was even a condition that could be "cured". He also questioned the methodology of the three clinical trials cited by the manufacturer, criticizing them for being underpowered and poorly designed.[46] The same doctor also explained how a literature survey of studies regarding Buclizine failed to identify any convincing literature justifying the use of Buclizine as an appetite stimulant. The relevant extract from his study is reproduced below:

> We did an unbiased literature search to check if buclizine is really indicated for this purpose. A Pubmed search revealed no published articles on buclizine and weight gain in the last 40 years, and only a very few before 1970, mostly untraceable non-English articles. None of the standard textbooks of Pharmacology mentioned that this drug is indicated for appetite stimulation. We concluded that there is no convincing literature regarding the use of this drug.[47]

So, on what basis did the DCGI approve the sale of the drug as an appetite stimulant for children? During the course of its investigation, the parliamentary committee sent a questionnaire to the Ministry of Health, which oversees the CDSCO, asking it to respond to their questions about these approvals. On receiving the replies from the Ministry, the parliamentary committee accused the Ministry of giving "incorrect and misleading information" about the regulatory status of the drug in other jurisdictions. The committee also levelled the serious allegation that the Ministry "went out of the way to volunteer incorrect information".[48] Further the committee alleged that the company's own "core data sheet" had stated that it lacked clinical studies and scientific data to market the drug as an appetite stimulant.[49] Each allegation levelled by the parliamentary committee against the CDSCO was stunning.

The parliamentary committee, concluded its examination of the Buclizine approval with the following words:

> ...responsibility needs to be fixed for unlawfully approving Buclizine, a drug of hardly any consequence to public health in India, more so since it is being administered to babies/ children. At the same time the approval granted should be reviewed in the light of latest scientific evidence, regulatory status in developed countries, particularly in Belgium, the country of its origin.[50]

2. Letrozole

Another drug investigated by the parliamentary committee was Letrozole, which was originally developed by Novartis as a hormonal treatment for post-menopausal breast cancer patients and as pointed out by the parliamentary committee, it was contraindicated for women of reproductive age i.e., it could not be prescribed to women of reproductive age because of concerns of embryo-toxicity. These concerns were based on observations in animal studies. The drug received marketing approval in 1998 in India for breast cancer patients, especially post-menopausal women.[51]

A few years later, in 2003, there were reports in the Monthly Index of Medical Specialities India (MIMS), edited by Dr Chander Gulati of Letrozole being marketed "off-label" by Sun Pharmaceuticals in India to gynaecologists as a fertility treatment for women i.e., marketing a drug for indications that have not been approved by the regulator.[52] The rationale for marketing it as a fertility treatment was based on the knowledge that Letrozole was known to reduce oestrogen levels. Theoretically speaking, this could increase chances of ovulation. However, in 2003, there was no clinical data to substantiate this hypothesis. More worryingly, the labelling that Novartis had submitted to the USFDA for approval for this drug clearly warned that based on data from animal studies, the drug maybe embryotoxic and fetotoxic (toxic to the foetus).[53] In this backdrop, it was scandalous for any company to be marketing Letrozole as a fertility treatment.

The controversy in 2003 concluded with Sun Pharmaceutical putting out a public statement asserting, "We have stopped giving papers and abstracts related to the use of this drug in infertility to the members of the medical fraternity."[54]

Post that controversy, Sun Pharmaceuticals applied for, and was granted permission to carry out Phase III clinical trials with Letrozole to validate the claim of "induction of ovulation in anovlatory infertility". As explained earlier, Phase III clinical trials are typically large scale double-blind, RCTs carried out on hundreds and sometimes thousands of patients in order to reduce bias and ensure statistically significant benefit-risk information. The clinical trial sponsored by Sun Pharmaceuticals was reportedly conducted on 55 patients wherein Letrozole was compared with another commonly used drug for infertility treatment—Clomiphene Citrate (CC). It is unusual to see a Phase III clinical trial on just 55 patients and we tried to ascertain the reason for this small sample size but were unable to locate any "peer reviewed" publication where Sun Pharmaceuticals published the results of their study. Apparently, this trial sponsored by Sun Pharmaceuticals demonstrated both drugs as being equally effective and safe.[55] As a result, the DCGI granted it approval in 2007 to market Letrozole for infertility treatment based on the clinical trial data submitted to it, recommendations of the experts, and additional clinical literature published in journals.[56]

Once again, this approval ran into controversy for two reasons. The first being a Canadian study based on a retrospective analysis of the medical literature which concluded that babies born from mothers treated with Letrozole were more likely to experience "loco motor malformations and cardiac anomalies".[57] The second reason was the fact that Novartis, which had developed the drug, issued a letter to Canadian doctors informing them that the drug was not approved as a fertility treatment.[58]

The DCGI's decision to approve Letrozole as treatment for infertility received flak across the board, including in Parliament after which the Ministry of Health issued an order under Section 26A of the Drugs and Cosmetics Act 1940 on October 12 2011, prohibiting the use of Letrozole as treatment for infertility.[59] The ban order specifically stated "... the Central Government is satisfied that the use of the drug Letrozole for induction of ovulation in anovulatory infertility is likely to involve risk to human beings and whereas safer alternatives to the said drugs are available".[60]

Although the drug had been banned in 2011, before the parliamentary committee began its work on the 59th report, the committee reserved some biting comments for the manner in which the DCGI granted approval to the drug, including the failure to insist that Sun Pharmaceuticals, the sponsor, submit the mandatory post-marketing surveillance reports. In no uncertain terms, the parliamentary committee made the following observations with regard to the approval given to Letrozole for its use as a fertility treatment:

> Clearly there was a serious lapse on the part of CDSCO. In the wake of media outcry, in a diversionary move, the DCGI instead of investigating the allegations of regulatory lapse and taking corrective measures referred the matter to clinical experts, DTAB etc. on the restricted issue of safety and efficacy. DCGI is expected to take action against those CDSCO functionaries who colluded with private interests and got the drug approved in violation of laws.[61]
>
> The Committee takes special note of this case of gross violation of the laws of the land by the CDSCO. First, in approving the drug for use in case of female infertility and thereafter, in exhibiting overt resistance in taking timely corrective steps despite very strong reasons favouring immediate suspension of use of letrozole for the said indication. Belatedly, the drug has been banned for use in female infertility.[62]

3. Approval of dubious Fixed Dose Combinations (FDCs)

As discussed earlier, the presence of numerous FDCs in India has been a problematic issue in the country since at least the mid-70s. The standard response of the Ministry of Health since the year 1983, when it issued the first order under Section 26A banning FDCs, has been to routinely issue orders under Section 26A prohibiting certain FDCs rather than get to the root of the issue: namely, how do these FDCs get to the market in the first place? The parliamentary investigation examined the issue at two levels.

First, the committee examined files of two specific FDCs approved by the DCGI. In the case of the first FDC of Aceclofenac and Drotaverine approved by the DCGI, the committee noted that the combination was not approved in any of the well-regulated markets in North America, Europe, or Australia.[63] While Aceclofenac is a nonsteroidal, anti-inflammatory drug (NSAID), generally used for the treatment of pain and inflammation, Drotaverine is an "antispasmodic" drug. Neither drug was approved in lucrative and well-regulated markets such as the United States. The committee during its investigation discovered that the six "expert opinions" provided by Themis Medicare to justify its application for the sale of the drug in India were identical to each other despite the fact that the doctors who signed the opinions were in six different parts of the country, from Chandigarh to Hyderabad. The committee alleged that the expert opinions were basically written by the pharmaceutical company that applied for the approval and merely signed by the doctors in question without any study of the clinical evidence.[64]

In the case of a second FDC, consisting of Flupenthixol and Melitracen that was initially marketed by Lundbeck, a Danish company, the committee again made a series of worrying allegations. It first stated that "the Ministry failed to provide any documents and information on the regulatory process that led to its approval (such as import permission, mandatory clinical trials etc.)".[65] The committee also alleged that this FDC was not approved for sale in the better-regulated markets in the West, including in Denmark, the home country of the drug's manufacturer and that the drug was being sold primarily in poorly regulated markets.[66] A third allegation by the committee claimed that the product-insert for the drug included indications other than those for which the drug had been officially approved by the DCGI. Apparently, the drug was officially approved for the following indications: (i) Psychogenic depression, (ii) Depressive neuroses, (iii) Masked depression, and (iv) Psychosomatic affections, but its package insert promoted the drugs for two unapproved indications: "Menopausal depression" and "Dysphoria and depression in alcoholics and drug addicts".[67] In most developed countries, it is a criminal offence to market a drug for indications that are not approved by the drug regulator. In these countries, the product label and the package inserts have to be approved by the drug regulator. In India too, misbranding is a criminal offence, although it is an offence that is rarely prosecuted.

(The company has refuted most of these allegations in an advertisement published in the newspapers and even sued Dr Chander Gulati for criminal defamation before a court in Bangalore.[68] Eventually, the Ministry of Health banned the drug on two occasions under Section 26A except on both occasions the Karnataka High Court set aside the ban on procedural grounds.)

After scrutinizing the manner in which the DCGI was approving FDCs, the committee turned its sights to the various state drug controllers who were indiscriminately issuing manufacturing licences for FDCs despite the fact that they lacked the authority to do so under the law. In pertinent part, the committee states in its report the following:

> Unfortunately some State Drug Authorities have issued manufacturing licenses for a very large number of FDCs without prior clearance from CDSCO. This is in violation of rules though till May 2002, there was some ambiguity on powers of the State Drug Authorities in this respect. However the end result is that many FDCs in the market have not been tested for efficacy and safety. This can put patients at risk.[69]

As per the law, state drug controllers can grant manufacturing licences for any "new drugs", including FDCs, only after the DCGI has approved the "new drug" based on clinical trial data.[70] Many state drug regulators appeared to be ignoring this requirement and were regularly issuing licences for new FDCs not already approved by the DCGI. This complete disobedience of the law by state drug controllers has continued unhindered despite the amendments of 1988 when the Drugs and Cosmetics Rules 1945 were amended to centralize all powers to regulate new drugs, including FDCs, with the DCGI.

The aftermath of the 59th report of the Parliamentary Standing Committee

The tabling of the 59th report before Parliament, in May 2012, sent shockwaves through the Indian pharmaceutical industry and medical community. Never before had a parliamentary committee in India conducted such an in-depth investigation into the functioning of India's drug regulatory system and revealed so many of its darkest secrets to the world. Apart from receiving extensive coverage in the press, the committee's findings attracted a lot of attention from the international academic community with a number of foreign academics publishing studies on various problems with the drug regulatory framework in India, with a special focus on the flood of irrational FDCs in India and its consequences for global public health, especially on the rise of antibiotic resistant bacteria.[71] One study published in the *Lancet* in 2014 specifically called upon the Government of India to enact a new drug regulatory law to replace the Drugs and Cosmetics Act 1940.[72]

The fact that the parliamentary report got extensive coverage in the press meant that the government of the day was under pressure to demonstrate that it was taking some steps to overhaul the drug regulatory mechanism in India, especially the proliferation of FDCs and the process by which new drugs were being approved by the CDSCO. The immediate response was typically bureaucratic. A number of committees were setup to examine different issues, many of which turned in reports of varying quality, most of which were ignored by the Ministry of Health. The other response was draft legislation that pushed for greater centralization of drug regulation but that legislative effort lost steam quickly.[73]

On the issue of FDCs, the government did take action, some of which was rather unconventional. For example, in a bid to crack down on the clearly illegal approvals of FDCs at the level of drug controllers located in states and union territories, the Central Bureau of Investigation (CBI) was roped in to file criminal cases under the Prevention of Corruption Act 1988, against some bureaucrats in the Puducherry drug controller's office and at least five pharmaceutical companies. The government's allegation in these cases was that the pharmaceutical companies and the bureaucrats in question had entered into a conspiracy to deprive the Government of India of revenue by seeking and getting regulatory approval from the state drug controllers in Puducherry when the law was clear that the power to grant regulatory approval for FDCs was vested in the DCGI.[74] The "loss of revenue" is likely a reference to the application fee that would have otherwise been payable to the DCGI. Whether this strategy results in convictions is yet to be seen. It is also highly unlikely that such a similar strategy used in a Union Territory can be used against state drug controllers because the CBI does not have the jurisdiction to proceed against state drug controllers. A more viable strategy would be to prosecute the pharmaceutical companies that sold their FDCs on the basis of licences from state drug controllers for violation of Section 18(c) of the Drugs and Cosmetics Act 1940 on the grounds that they were selling drugs without the required licenses. However, as far as we are aware, no such criminal action was initiated by the CDSCO.

Separate and apart from the corruption cases, the Ministry of Health also issued orders under Section 26A banning 344 FDCs in 2016.[75] These orders under Section 26A prompted massive litigation leading all the way to the Supreme Court which set aside the ban in a strange order and asked the government to hear the complaints of the pharmaceutical companies before banning the FDCs.[76] The order of the court was based on a flawed understanding of the law because judicial precedent on the issue is clear that ban orders under Section 26A are akin to "legislative action" and as such the government is not obliged to hear each and every pharmaceutical company manufacturing the drug that is to be banned.[77] Nevertheless, two years later, the process was completed when after holding the hearings mandated by the Supreme Court, the Health Ministry issued orders under Section 26A banning 328 FDCs in 2018 and another 80 FDCs in 2019.[78] It is important to remember that this problem of irrational FDCs existed in the Indian market since the 70s and the first ban orders under Section 26A were issued in 1983. Yet, as of 2018, the government was still trying to weed out FDCs from the market rather than stopping the introduction of these FDCs into the Indian market in the first place. Only criminal prosecutions of pharmaceutical companies for violation of Section 18(c) will end this practice of pharmaceutical companies selling FDCs on the basis of licences from the state drug controllers.

An investigation, a brazen coverup, and bureaucratic impunity

Given the Parliamentary Committee's scathing indictment of the CDSCO on the issue of drug approvals, one would have expected a swift inquiry from the government so that it could pin accountability on the officers responsible for taking some of these disastrous decisions.

Since there was little reporting in the press on steps taken by the Ministry of Health to fix responsibility on officials responsible for these drug approvals, we filed a series of RTI applications asking the government for records of the action that it had taken to fix accountability on officers involved in the granting of these irregular approvals. This was an arduous process that involved drafting precise queries to be filed with the Ministry and then sifting through a ton of information that the Ministry of Health provided us in response to our request for information. Thanks to an eagle-eyed research assistant, we discovered that the Ministry of Health had informed Parliament that the DCGI had setup a four-member expert committee under Dr Tribhuban Mohan Mohapatra to investigate the suspicious drug approvals identified in the parliamentary report. Some more research led us to discover on the internet a poorly scanned order by the DCGI from 2013 constituting an inquiry committee under the chairmanship of Dr Mohapatra with a specific mandate to examine the manner in which the above-mentioned drugs in question were approved.[79]

Equipped with this new information, we filed two more requests for information under the RTI Act with the Ministry of Health and the CDSCO in May 2018 asking both authorities for a final copy of the inquiry committee's report. The replies that we received were stunning! The CDSCO informed us that the committee report was "not readily available"[80] and that it was transferring our application to the Ministry of Health, which in turn informed us it had "checked all its records" and it was able to confirm that the information sought by us was "not available" with it.[81] The report of the Mohapatra committee had apparently disappeared into thin air. The RTI Act 2005 provides for a departmental appeal, which also failed to turn up any results, after which, we filed an appeal before the Central Information Commission (CIC).

Thanks to the CIC's huge backlog, it took us almost two years to get a hearing. Our appeal finally came up for a hearing on May 12 2020 during the first lockdown of the COVID-19 pandemic. The hearing was to take place via "WhatsApp" since the pandemic made it difficult to travel to the CIC's office in New Delhi. Approximately 15 hours prior to the hearing scheduled before the CIC, we received an email from the CDSCO late in the night, informing us that they had procured a copy of the report from Dr Mohapatra himself and were providing a copy of the same to us![82] The CDSCO could have done this back in 2018 when we first asked it for the report but chose to keep the matter pending for almost two years before trying to procure the report from Dr Mohapatra. Even this version of the report was not signed by its authors and the annexures to the report, which were copies of the drug approval files (and contained the names of the relevant bureaucrats), were missing.

The CDSCO's conduct was brought to the CIC's attention the next day during the hearing which resulted in the CIC expressing "serious concern" about the record-keeping procedures at the CDSCO. The commission also ordered the CDSCO to digitize its records as soon as possible.[83] Even after the CIC ordered the DCGI to provide us with a copy of the annexures to the report, the DCGI failed to do so, necessitating another lawsuit before the Delhi High Court.[84] After almost two years of delays and diversions before the court, the government conceded in court that it had lost half the annexures (which were the most incriminating records that could be used in criminal proceedings).

The reason the CDSCO and the Ministry of Health "misplaced" the Mohapatra committee report for seven long years was evident from a reading of the report. The report had named and accused three former DCGIs for their dubious role in approving some of the drugs identified by the parliamentary committee. It also painted a picture of utter callousness within the DCGI's office while it reviewed applications for new drugs. Take for example the approval of Buclizine as an appetite stimulant in 2006. It was initially approved only as an anti-histamine, although as noted by the Mohapatra committee "the document relating to the first approval is not available".[85] With regard to the additional approval as an appetite stimulant, the Mohapatra committee noted a litany of problems with the drug's approval, including the fact that the published trial reports focussed on "body weight gain" and not on appetite stimulation leading to better intake of food which in turn would result in gain of body weight. Additionally, the committee noted that the standard practice of requiring the status of regulatory approvals in other jurisdictions was also allegedly ignored by the DCGI while processing this application. As per the committee, when warning bells were reportedly rung within the DCGI's office in 2007 by a joint drug controller who informed the DCGI in writing that the drug had faced adverse regulatory action in the United States, the DCGI simply ignored the issue.[86]

A deeper examination of the underlying science and the regulatory status in other countries would have clearly led any reasonable person to deny approval to market this drug as an appetite stimulant. The Mohapatra committee concluded as follows with regard to the approval of Buclizine as an appetite stimulant[87]:

> The order of the DCGI ignoring the statutory requirements under Schedule Y and the valid note of the JDC, the committee finds, was arbitrary, whimsical and inconsistent with the provisions of law that required consideration of legal status in other countries.

and that:

> From the facts available in the file, the Committee finds that the DCGI was solely responsible for the irregular approval of the drug.

If this report had been made public in 2013, it would have immediately paved the way for prohibiting the use of Buclizine as an appetite stimulant. Instead, the fate of this drug bounced around different sub-committees setup by the DTAB until one of us, Dinesh Thakur, sued the Ministry of Health and DCGI in 2018 demanding the government take a decision on the continued sale of Buclizine.[88] In less than a week of the Delhi High Court issuing notice to the government asking it to respond to our petition, the Ministry of Health issued an order under Section 26A prohibiting the sale of Buclizine as an appetite stimulant (its approval as an anti-histamine has not been disturbed).[89]

The second drug scrutinized by the Mohapatra committee was the FDC of Aceclofenac and Drotaverine which was also red-flagged by the parliamentary committee. The Mohapatra committee's report stated that the company seeking approval was asked for clinical trial data of the FDC as well as pharmacodynamic and pharmacokinetic evaluation. Additionally, the manufacturer was asked to produce the opinions of the nine experts with regard to this FDC.[90] This was rather unusual because in most countries it is usually the regulator's job to seek expert opinions on whether to approve a new drug but apparently, at that time, the DCGI asked the applicant companies to submit expert opinions. It was thus not surprising when eight of the nine experts gave the company identical recommendations in favour of the new combination. The Mohapatra committee goes on to make the stunning allegation that this FDC was approved despite the company failing to provide any clinical trial data to support the efficacy of the drug. Once again, if the Mohapatra committee report had been made public in 2013, the Ministry of Health would have been compelled to prohibit the sale of this particular FDC. Instead, after one of us sued the Ministry of Health before the Delhi High Court asking it to take a decision to ban this drug, the government replied stating that Themis Medicare, on March 14 2019, had "surrendered" the "permission" granted to it to market the drug.[91] No other details were provided by the government. The same FDC however continues to be sold by other pharmaceutical companies since the government has not yet prohibited the marketing of this drug.

With regard to the approval of the third drug—Letrozole—as a fertility treatment, the Mohapatra committee made the stunning discovery that the DCGI completely ignored the recommendation of a joint drug controller to ask Sun Pharmaceuticals for animal toxicity data before approving its application for human clinical trials. This was important because Novartis, which had invented the drug, had warned against the use of the drug as a fertility treatment, based on the results of animal studies.[92] As with the other cases, the Mohapatra committee notes that the DCGI ignored the recommendations of the junior officer without providing any reasons in writing and simply referred the clinical trial protocol to handpicked experts for their opinion. Similarly, with regard to the requirement imposed by the DCGI for providing post-marketing surveillance (PMS) reports on the use of Letrozole on the general population, the Mohapatra committee notes that there was a complete and total failure within the CDSCO to insist on the collection of PMS data by pharmaceutical companies and submission of the same to the CDSCO.[93]

It is worth noting that the committee concluded that "... there was no proper system in place to deal with matters pertaining to approval of New Drugs." In particular, the committee pointed out that "the exercise of the discretionary power by the DCGI without stating any reason is totally irregular and undesirable". It found the practice of the DCGI simply ignoring written objections by joint drug controllers and other staff, without stating any reasons, to be a "serious misuse/

abuse of power on the part of the DCGI". The committee also concluded that "commercial needs of the industry" were given "more focus than the regulatory norms". Even something as basic as record keeping and archiving of files by the CDSCO was found to be wanting by the Mohapatra committee report.[94]

If these recommendations of the Mohapatra committee had been implemented by the Ministry of Health, the system may have become more transparent and streamlined. However, since the Ministry of Health and the CDSCO "misplaced" this report for more than seven years, there was no opportunity for policymakers to consider its recommendations. As a result, when the Ministry of Health introduced a new set of New Drugs and Clinical Trial Rules in 2019, it did not have an opportunity to learn from the recommendations of the Mohapatra committee's report. The new rules introduced in 2019 thus represent a continuance of the old status-quo.

The only seemingly substantive change brought about after the scathing observations of the 59th report was the creation of "Subject Expert Committees" (SEC) consisting of external medical experts to scrutinize applications for drug approvals and provide non-binding recommendations to the DCGI. This is largely a superficial reform measure. The problem with the functioning of the SECs is that the sum total of its deliberations is summarized into approximately 100 to 250 words, without any details being provided to citizens on which member dissented or agreed on approving the drug. In fact, on most occasions, the names of the SEC members are not even mentioned in the minutes, reducing transparency and accountability and robbing ordinary citizens the opportunity of checking whether the members in question suffer from any conflict of interest. Moreover, the committee's deliberations are itself not open to the public. Neither is the public provided with an opportunity to contribute to the process. In comparison to most other countries, the processes followed by the CDSCO while approving a new drug continues to be shrouded in secrecy and unaccountability. Simply put, nothing has really changed. Perhaps, if the Mohapatra committee report had been disclosed as soon as it was completed, instead of during the pandemic, it would have generated enough public pressure to bring about substantial reform.

The pandemic stress test

The year after the New Drugs and Clinical Trials Rules 2019 came into effect, the COVID-19 pandemic swept the world. The pharmaceutical industry responded to the pandemic by investing in the creation of new vaccines as well as in the creation of new drugs and repurposing existing treatments to treat COVID-19 patients. Across the world, the pandemic was the ultimate stress test for drug regulators because most of them were under immense political pressure to approve new treatments for COVID-19 regardless of whether viable clinical evidence substantiated their therapeutic efficacy. Not all drug regulators could withstand this stress test. Even the much-vaunted USFDA granted a very contentious Emergency Use Authorization (EUA) for the use of Hydroxychloroquine (HCQ) to treat COVID-19 on the basis of an open-label non-randomized French study on 36 patients, after American President Donald Trump began advocating for HCQ's benefits. Eventually, this EUA was revoked after more rigorous RCTs demonstrated that HCQ had no therapeutic effect on patients affected by Covid-19.[95]

The DCGI's streak of approvals during this same time period was far more controversial.

The first problem was that the DCGI began granting drug approvals in various "modes" that did not find any mention in the New Drugs and Clinical Trial Rules 2019 and way before the completion of Phase III clinical trials.

For example, the DCGI announced that it was granting "Restricted Emergency Use Authorization" to three drugs—Favipiravir, Itolizumab, and Virafin despite the fact that the phrase "Restricted Emergency Use Authorization" does not find any mention in the New Drugs and Clinical Trial Rules 2019.[96] We filed applications under the RTI Act 2005 asking the CDSCO to tell us under which provision of the law it was granting "Restricted Emergency Use Authorization". The CDSCO was unable to give a straight answer on how exactly it was circumventing the legal requirement in Indian law that a new drug necessarily complete a three-phased clinical trial to substantiate its safety and efficacy. In its reply, the CDSCO pointed us to a chapter rather than a specific rule in the law. Its reply is reproduced below:

> Details of regulatory requirements and guidelines for permission to Import and / or Manufacture of new drugs for sale are specified in Chapter X and Second Schedule of the New Drugs and Clinical Trials Rules, 2019.[97]

Neither the chapter nor schedule mentioned in the CDSCO's reply contain the phrase "restricted emergency use authorization"! Simply put, there was no legal basis for these approvals without adequate Phase III clinical trial data. It also quickly became obvious that even the pharmaceutical industry had no clue about the happenings in the DCGI office. For example, after one of us wrote an opinion editorial in a national newspaper criticizing the use of the phrase "Restricted Emergency Use Authorization" by the DCGI while approving Itolizumab (developed by Biocon), the head of regulatory affairs from Biocon wrote a response piece in the same paper defending the manner in which the DCGI approved the drug and claiming that the approval was granted under Section 26B of the Drugs and Cosmetics Act 1940.[98] That response piece by Biocon's head of regulatory affairs, ended with the following conclusion that was dripping with self-righteous indignation:

> In light of the facts provided, we can confidently state that the claims made by the author are factually inaccurate. Claims without evidence constitute a great disservice to the public. The drug regulator acted in public interest to serve an unmet medical need based on science and evidence in a transparent manner.

While Section 26B does give special powers to the Central Government during an epidemic, it also requires all decisions taken under this provision to be published in the *Gazette of India*. When we searched the *Gazette of India,* we could not find any such notifications approving Itolizumab under Section 26B. Subsequently, we filed an application under the RTI Act with the CDSCO asking it whether Biocon's drug was approved under Section 26B. The CDSCO specifically rebutted the claim that Itolizumab was approved under Section 26B of the Drugs and Cosmetics Act 1940.[99] In other words, even the head of regulatory affairs of a major pharmaceutical company was unaware of the legal provisions under which the DCGI was granting questionable approvals to new drugs during the pandemic! (It is a different matter that in 2022, senior officials in Biocon and the CDSCO were arrested on charges of corruption over certain drug approvals.)

We then had to speculate that the DCGI was actually granting "accelerated approvals" which is a regulatory pathway recognized in the New Drugs and Clinical Trial Rules 2019 for drugs treating conditions/diseases lacking adequate treatments. Under this pathway, these drugs could be approved after conclusion of Phase II trials, provided that Phase II clinical trials demonstrate "remarkable efficacy".[100] None of the aforementioned drugs met this milestone. This became evident when the government's own National COVID-19 Taskforce consisting of experts from elite Indian medical institutions like AIIMs and ICMR, did not recommend the inclusion of Favipiravir, Itolizumab, and Virafin in the national COVID-19 treatment guidelines that were being updated periodically to guide doctors in making treatment decisions for patients infected with COVID-19.[101] The decision of this taskforce not to include these drugs in the treatment protocol was never publicly explained but was most likely because of the fact that the clinical trials conducted for these drugs had come under heavy criticism for being underpowered or poorly designed.[102] Notwithstanding the non-inclusion of these drugs in the treatment guidelines laid down by the government's COVID-19 taskforce, the fact that the DCGI had approved them was sufficient for people to hanker after these drugs leading to some of these companies raking in a fortune. For example, the Indian pharmaceutical companies selling Favipiravir, led by Glenmark Pharmaceuticals, earned a stunning ₹762 crores from the sale of Favipiravir making it the top selling drug in India during the pandemic.[103] In many cases, municipal corporations and state governments were placing huge orders for Favipiravir.[104] This transfer of wealth from the middle and working classes to the pharmaceutical industry was facilitated by the DCGI through its opaque regulatory process.

The questionable approvals did not stop with just new drugs. There was plenty of controversy regarding the DCGI's approval of vaccines. For example, when DCGI approved Covaxin, the vaccine developed by Bharat Biotech with support from ICMR to combat Covid-19, it announced that it was granting the vaccine "restricted emergency use authorization" under "clinical trial mode" despite the company not having completed its Phase III trials.[105] Separate from the scandal of approving a vaccine before the conclusion of Phase III trials was the fact that the phrase "clinical trial mode" did not find any mention in the New Drugs and Clinical Trial Rules 2019!

The use of such random legal terminology that does not find mention in the official law and the refusal of the DCGI to identify the provision of law under which such approvals were granted represented a new pinnacle of arbitrariness in the functioning of the DCGI.

The second set of problems with the DCGI's approvals during the pandemic was the lack of transparency. The only information available to the public was a tightly condensed summary of the minutes of the SECs. These minutes barely run into 250 words and were completely inadequate to understand all the complexities of the approval process. Even something as simple as membership of this committee was not made public despite repeated demands by the public health community.[106] It took a parliamentary question by an MP from the opposition to force the government to reveal the membership of the SEC to the public.[107] In an ideal world, the DCGI would transcribe verbatim the discussions of the committee and publish the same or alternatively, like some other regulators, live-stream discussions of the SEC to the public on the internet. In addition, the DCGI should have released all of its own records pertaining to the approval of these medicines so that the medical community could understand the basis of its approval. Unfortunately, the New Drugs and Clinical Trial Rules 2019 does not require the release of such records, although there is a strong case to argue that Section 4 of the RTI Act 2005 mandates the proactive disclosure of such records by the DCGI.

The only silver lining of the COVID-19 related controversies over new drug approvals in India is the fact that many of the controversial approvals granted during the pandemic were meticulously documented by Indian science journalists and doctors. Never before has the DCGI and the pharmaceutical industry faced such scrutiny in India. It certainly helped that both the journalists and doctors had an easy reference point in the actions of foreign regulators in the United States and Europe while approving new drugs during the pandemic.

The absence of evidence-based medicine in India

In our opinion, the heart of the problem in India with the wide availability and sale of dubious drugs of doubtful safety and efficacy is not just an indifferent regulator but also the lack of widespread understanding within the Indian medical community of the basics of "evidence-based medicine". The foremost principle of evidence-based medicine is to insist on the production of high-quality evidence to substantiate the safety and efficacy of a new drug, rather than depending merely on "intuition or unsystematic clinical experience" as the basis of treatment decisions.[108] In the hierarchy of knowledge recognized by evidence-based medicine, data generated through randomized double blind clinical trials is placed on a higher pedestal; much above anecdotal evidence generated through individual case studies. Individual Indian doctors have been making an effort to spread the principles of evidence-based medicine, but an institutional push appears to be lacking. As reported by one Indian practitioner of evidence-based medicine at an elite Indian medical institution, attempts to integrate evidence-based medicine into the curriculum at medical schools has not met with much success.[109]

One possible reason for the lack of awareness of the principles of evidence-based medicine is that most Indian doctors actually have very little exposure to rigorous clinical research. Until 2005, it was rather difficult to conduct clinical trials in India, meaning that doctors and medical students in India never participated in or led clinical trials. This is because in 1988, when the Drugs and Cosmetics Rules 1945 first created a regulatory framework for clinical trials, there was a rule requiring clinical trials in India to always be one step behind clinical trials being conducted elsewhere in the world. This is to say that a Phase II clinical trial for a new drug could be conducted in India only if Phase III trials had begun elsewhere in the world for the same new drug. From a research perspective, it made no sense to be conducting a Phase II trial in India, if Phase III trials are taking place elsewhere in the world, unless it is for a different indication. It is possible that this regulatory structure was created with an intent to dissuade pharmaceutical companies from conducting clinical trials in India because of fears of exploitation of the Indian population by powerful pharmaceutical companies. This position in the law changed in 2005 when the Government of India, upon the recommendations of the Mashelkar committee in 2003, amended the law to "harness [the] country's potential to participate in global multi-centric clinical trials".[110] This recommendation was based on an earlier expert report by another committee headed by Mashelkar in 1999 on how to foster pharmaceutical research and development in India.[111] These committees had identified "clinical research as an area with immense growth potential".[112]

Once the law was changed in 2005 to make it easier to conduct clinical trials in India, the nascent clinical research establishment in India was rocked by a series of scandals over data integrity, informed consent, and even some deaths of volunteers.[113] These scandals, which were inevitable due to the lack of any credible regulatory mechanism to ensure the conduct of ethical clinical trials, eventually led to the Supreme Court imposing a temporary ban on clinical trials in India unless the Secretary of Health approved each and every clinical trial.[114] Ultimately, the government did create a new framework under the New Drugs And Clinical Trial Rules 2019 to regulate clinical trials. Like many other Indian laws, it borrows extensively from the American system of self-regulation without the accompanying stress on transparency or accountability. We do not expect these rules to make any long-term difference.

Perhaps due to these reasons listed above, coupled with the lack of a culture of clinical research, an understanding of evidence-based medicine has not spread amongst the medical community in India because of which it continues to prescribe in large quantities dubious drugs approved by the CDSCO with barely any clinical evidence. This ends up creating a market for new drugs that pharmaceutical companies are unable to market in developed countries.

Further, as is evident from the functioning of the new SECs during the pandemic, many of the so called "experts" on these committees who were independent doctors clearly lacked an understanding of the basic principles of "evidence-based medicine". This problem cannot be resolved only through legal reform. Any sustained long-term reform will depend on overhauling the curriculum taught at medical schools, to ensure that every graduating doctor has a rigorous understanding of evidence-based medicine.

The future of reform of the new drug approval process—transparency, transparency, transparency

The only short-term solution to combat the arbitrariness with which the DCGI approves new drugs for the Indian population is to insist on transparency at every level of the drug approval process. Bureaucrats who are aware that their decisions are going to be publicly accessible are more likely to behave themselves and follow the law. This is the reason that sunshine laws aimed at more transparency are considered to be the best "disinfectant". Such transparency measures also make it easier for doctors, journalists, and academics to track the functioning of the institutions responsible for drug approvals. The situation today is such that the average Indian has to really fight with the bureaucracy in order to get access to even basic information related to drug approvals. Despite multiple requests that we have made to access the approval dossiers of some of the controversial drugs discussed in the chapter, we were never given access. Contrast our experience to the information made public by the American or European drug regulators. The USFDA publishes on its website different reviews of new drug applications which includes a medical review, chemistry review, pharmacology review, statistical review, microbiology review, and a clinical pharmacology biopharmaceutics review. Detailed notes on approvals of the proprietary name, the labelling, and all communications between the USFDA and the pharmaceutical company are also made publicly available. Similarly, the European Medical Agency (EMA) makes available a detailed European Public Assessment Report (EPAR) explaining all the scientific reasons underlying its decision to approve a new drug. In contrast, the CDSCO makes available barely 250 words worth of information, summarizing the recommendation of the subject expert committees. There appears to be little to no understanding within the Ministry of Health on the importance of transparency, or for that matter, the fact that Section 4 of the RTI Act 2005 actually requires all government offices to proactively publish their records online.

It of course helps the government that not many people in civil society or Parliament are asking it to make transparency the cornerstone of future reform. Given our experience while researching for this book, we are well aware of just how difficult it is to access such information, which is why we have taken steps to demand more transparency from the DCGI. During the COVID-19 pandemic, we convinced a group of transparency activists and doctors to petition the Ministry of Health asking for more transparency in the functioning of the DCGI, especially while new drugs were being approved.[115] As usual, the Ministry did not even bother acknowledging receipt of the petition. We have since moved court where the matter remains pending. Hopefully, more doctors and citizens will make similar demands, creating pressure on the Ministry of Health to publish all records pertaining to drug approvals. Once information is available for public scrutiny, we expect the quality of drug approvals to improve incrementally until it reaches the standards followed in developed countries.

Notes

1. Department Related Parliamentary Standing Committee on Health and Family Welfare, *The Functioning of The Central Drugs Standard Control Organisation (CDCSO)* (59th Report) (RS 2012) para 7.51.
2. Laura E. Bothwell and others, 'Assessing the Gold Standard—Lessons from the History of RCTs' (2016) 374 *New England Journal of Medicine*, 2175.
3. United States Senate (Sub-committee on Antitrust and Monopoly), *Study of Administered Prices in the Drug Industry* (Rep No 448, 1961) 156.
4. Jeremy A Greene and Scott H Podolsky, 'Reform, Regulation, and Pharmaceuticals—The Kefauver–Harris Amendments at 50' (2012) 367 *New England Journal of Medicine*, 1481.
5. Public Law 87–871, 1962, s 505(d) (21 U.S.C. 355 (d)).
6. New Drugs, 21 CFR § 130.3 (1965).
7. P D'Arcy Hart, 'A Change in Scientific Approach: From Alternation to Randomised Allocation in Clinical Trials in the 1940s' (1999) 319 *BMJ*, 572.
8. Graham Sutton, 'Putrid Gums and "Dead Men's Cloaths": James Lind Aboard the Salisbury' (2003) 96 *Journal of the Royal Society of Medicine*, 605.
9. Peter Armitage, 'Fisher, Bradford Hill, and Randomization' (2003) 32 *International Journal of Epidemiology*, 925.
10. AJ de Craen and others, 'Placebos and Placebo Effects in Medicine: Historical Overview.' (1999) 92 *Journal of the Royal Society of Medicine*, 511.
11. ibid.
12. Ted J Kaptchuk, 'Intentional Ignorance: A History of Blind Assessment and Placebo Controls in Medicine' (1998) 72 *Bulletin of the History of Medicine*, 389.
13. Bothwell (n 2).
14. David S Jones and Scott H Podolsky, 'The History and Fate of the Gold Standard' (2015) 385 *Lancet*, 1502; 21 CFR § 314.126.

15. US Food and Drug Administration, 'Detail of full-time Equivalents (FY 2020)' (2020).
16. Office of the Commissioner, 'Learn About FDA Advisory Committees' [2020] FDA <https://www.fda.gov/patients/about-office-patient-affairs/learn-about-fda-advisory-committees> accessed 14 July 2021.
17. United States (ed), *Review Panel on New Drug Regulation: Final Report* (Department of Health, Education, and Welfare, Review Panel on New Drug Regulation 1977) 2–3.
18. N Dorsen and JM Miller, 'The Drug Regulation Process and the Challenge of Regulatory Reform' (1979) 91 *Annals of Internal Medicine*, 908, 911.
19. Christopher Morten and Amy Kapczynski, 'The Big Data Regulator, Rebooted: Why and How the FDA Can and Should Disclose Confidential Data on Prescription Drugs and Vaccines' (2021) 109 *California Law Review*, 493. 'UPDATE 1-GSK Promises to Publish Detailed Drug Trial Data' *Reuters* (5 February 2013) <https://www.reuters.com/article/gsk-data-idUSL5N0B5CV920130205> accessed 14 July 2021; 'Unreported Clinical Trial Results: Lost Opportunities for FDA, NIH' *STAT*, (13 April 2020) <https://www.statnews.com/2020/04/13/lost-opportunities-clinical-trial-results-unreported-lost-opportunities/>accessed 14 July 2021.
20. Government of India, Ministry of Health, *SRO 694* (*Gazette of India Weekly*, Part II—s 3, 14 April 1952) published on 19 April 1952.
21. Drugs Third (Amendment) Rules 1961; Government of India, Ministry of Health, *SO 1449* (*Gazette of India Weekly*, Part II—s 3, 13 June 1961) published on 24 June 1961.
22. TY Chan and AW Chan, 'Aminopyrine-Induced Blood Dyscrasias—Still a Problem in Many Parts of the World' (1996) 5 *Pharmacoepidemiology and Drug Safety*, 215.
23. RM Kapadia and AD Desai, 'Amidopyrine (Dipyrone) and Its Toxicity' (1955) 43 *The Indian Journal of Medical Research*, 297.
24. 'Guidelines for Registration of Fixed-Dose Combination Medicinal Products' (World Health Organization 2005) WHO Technical Report Series 929.
25. 'What Are FDC Drugs and Why Has the Govt Decided to Ban Them?' *Business Today* (13 September 2018) <https://www.businesstoday.in/industry/pharma/story/what-are-fdc-drugs-and-why-has-the-govt-decided-to-ban-them-110595-2018-09-13> accessed 18 July 2021; Gauri Kamath, 'Lessons We Must Learn From The Fixed-Dose Combinations Fiasco' *Moneycontrol* (17 September 2018)

<https://www.moneycontrol.com/news/opinion/opinion-lessons-we-must-learn-from-the-fixed-dose-combinations-fiasco-2956901.html> accessed 18 July 2021; Sakthivel Selvaraj, 'Another Bitter Pill for Patients' *The Hindu* (14 July 2013) <https://www.thehindu.com/opinion/op-ed/another-bitter-pill-for-patients/article4912747.ece> accessed 17 July 2021.

26. William Rosen, *Miracle Cure: The Creation of Antibiotics and the Birth of Modern Medicine* (Penguin 2017) 272.
27. Government of India, Ministry of Petroleum & Chemicals, *Report of The Committee on Drugs and Pharmaceutical Industry (Hathi Committee Report)* (1975) 174.
28. Government of India, *Drug Policy, 1978* (1978) para 101.
29. Drugs Consultative Committee (DCC), '*Minutes of the 20TH Meeting of The Drugs Consultative Committee Held at New Delhi on the 4th & 5th July, 1978*' (1978) 37, para 3 <https://cdsco.gov.in/opencms/opencms/system/modules/CDSCO.WEB/elements/common_download.jsp?num_id_pk=ODUz> accessed 17 July 2021.
30. Question raised by Shri Suresh Kalmadi and Shri Arvind Kulkarni, Lok Sabha Debate, 30 April 1982, Question No 478, 122.
31. Government of India, Ministry of Health and Family Welfare, *GSR 578(E)* (*Gazette of India Extraordinary*, Part II—s 3(i), 23 July 1983).
32. Government of India, *Drug Policy, 1986: Measures for Rationalisation, Quality Control and Growth of Drugs & Pharmaceutical Industry In India* (1986).
33. ibid.
34. Government of India, Ministry of Health and Family Welfare, *GSR 944(E)* (*Gazette of India Extraordinary*, Part II—s 3(i), 21 September 1988) 10.
35. Rule 122E (c) contained the new definition of "new drugs". A group of international academics have been critical of the use of the word "effective" as opposed to "efficacy" (which is the preferred international standard) in this new definition of "new drug". In pertinent part, they state "The Cochrane Collaboration defines efficacy as the "extent to which an intervention produces a beneficial result under ideal conditions", and effectiveness as the "extent to which a specific intervention, when used under ordinary circumstances, does what it is intended to do". In requiring new drugs to be "effective for use" since 2001, India's rules have imposed a high standard that should not be confused with "efficacy" which applies in ideal clinical conditions and is generally determined in trials done in tightly defined

populations." *See* Peter Roderick and others, 'India Should Introduce a New Drugs Act' (2014) 383 *The Lancet*, 203.
36. This criterion was laid down in the new Rule 122A, Rule 122B, Rule 122C, and Rule 122D.
37. This framework was laid down in the new Schedule Y to the Drugs and Cosmetics Rules 1945.
38. All applications for new drugs had to be approved by the licencing authority appointed by the Government of India under Rule 21 of the Drugs and Cosmetics Rules 1945.
39. Noemie Bisserbe and Khomba Singh, 'DCGI Likely to Invoke Special Provisions to Ban 294 Drugs' *The Economic Times* (21 November 2007) <https://economictimes.indiatimes.com/industry/healthcare/biotech/pharmaceuticals/dcgi-likely-to-invoke-special-provisions-to-ban-294-drugs/articleshow/2557395.cms?from=mdr> accessed 18 July 2021.
40. Prabha Raghavan and Divya Rajagopal, 'Government Prohibits 328 Fixed Dose Combinations' *The Economic Times* (13 September 2018) <https://economictimes.indiatimes.com/industry/healthcare/biotech/healthcare/government-prohibits-328-fixed-dose-combinations/articleshow/65787565.cms> accessed 1 May 2022.
41. These allegations were documented in detail in the 59th report of the Department Related Parliamentary Standing Committee on Health and Family Welfare: *The Functioning of The Central Drugs Standard Control Organisation (CDCSO)* (n 1).
42. ibid.
43. ibid para 7.12.
44. ibid para 7.14.
45. New Drugs Approved by CDSCO, *Buclizine HCl tablet (25mg) & Syrup 6mg/5ml* (Sr No 3277, 28 June 2006) <https://cdscoonline.gov.in/CDSCO/Drugs> accessed 3 August 2021.
46. Thirunavukkarasu Arun Babu, 'Buclizine Is Back Again! This Time as a Pediatric Appetite Stimulant' (2011) 43 *Indian Journal of Pharmacology*, 219.
47. ibid.
48. *The Functioning of The Central Drugs Standard Control Organization (CDCSO)* (n 1) para 7.39.
49. ibid.
50. ibid para 7.41.
51. New Drugs Approved by CDSCO, *Letrozole tabs* (Sr No 2121, 12 March 1998) <https://cdscoonline.gov.in/CDSCO/Drugs> accessed 3 August 2021.

52. Ganapati Mudur, 'Doctors in India Prescribe Unapproved Fertility Drug' (2003) 327 *BMJ*, 768.
53. Novartis Pharmaceutical Corporation, 'Prescribing Information for FEMARA (letrozole tablets) 2.5 mg Tablets' (2001) <https://www.accessdata.fda.gov/drugsatfda_docs/label/2001/20726S006LBL.PDF> accessed 4 August 2021.
54. Khabir Ahmad, 'Indian Drug Firm Accused of Illegal Marketing of Letrozole' (2003) 4 *The Lancet Oncology*, 647.
55. *The Functioning of The Central Drugs Standard Control Organisation (CDCSO)* (n 1) para 7.42.
56. Minutes of the meeting of an expert group to review marketing of Letrozole for induction of ovulation in anovulatory infertility in the country held on 22 February 2011 in the Committee Room, Resource Centre, DGHS Office, Nirman Bhawan, New Delhi—110011 (On file with authors).
57. Drugs Technical Advisory Board (DTAB), '*MINUTES OF THE 59th MEETING OF DRUGS TECHNICAL ADVISORY BOARD HELD ON 24TH JUNE, 2011 IN THE COMMITTEE ROOM, FDA BHAVAN, KOTLA ROAD, NEW DELHI—110002*' (2011) Agenda No 3 <https://cdsco.gov.in/opencms/opencms/system/modules/CDSCO.WEB/elements/common_download.jsp?num_id_pk=NzU5> accessed 4 August 2021.
58. ibid.
59. Government of India, Ministry of Health and Family Welfare, *GSR 752(E)* (*Gazette of India Extraordinary*, Part II—s 3(i), 12 October 2011).
60. ibid.
61. *The Functioning of The Central Drugs Standard Control Organisation (CDCSO)* (n 1) para 7.42.
62. ibid para 7.43.
63. ibid para 7.32.
64. ibid para 7.34.
65. ibid para 7.44.
66. ibid para 7.45-7.46.
67. ibid para 7.44.
68. *M/S Lundbeck India Private Limited vs Dr Chandra M Gulhati* Criminal Petition No 4683/2011 before the Karnataka HC (26 July 2012) <https://indiankanoon.org/doc/183428285/> last accessed 2 May 2022.
69. *The Functioning of The Central Drugs Standard Control Organisation (CDCSO)* (n 1) para 9.2.

70. The Drugs and Cosmetics Rules 1945, Rule 122E (These approvals are now regulated under the New Drugs and Clinical Trial Rules 2019).
71. Patricia McGettigan et. al., 'Use of Fixed Dose Combination (FDC) Drugs in India: Central Regulatory Approval and Sales of FDCs Containing Non-Steroidal Anti-Inflammatory Drugs (NSAIDs), Metformin, or Psychotropic Drugs' (2015) 12 *PLOS Medicine* e1001826; Akram Ahmad, Muhammad Umair Khan and Rajesh Balkrishnan, 'Fixed-Dose Combination Antibiotics in India: Global Perspectives' (2016) 4 *The Lancet Global Health*, 521; Valerie Evans et. al., 'Adequacy of Clinical Trial Evidence of Metformin Fixed-Dose Combinations for the Treatment of Type 2 Diabetes Mellitus in India' (2018) 3 *BMJ Global Health*, 000263; Virendra S Ligade, et. al., 'Fixed Dose Combinations of Anti-Tubercular, Antimalarial and Antiretroviral Medicines on the Indian Market: Critical Analysis of Ubiquity, Sales and Regulatory Status' (2019) 24(2) *Tropical Medicine & International Health*, 238; Patricia McGettigan and others, 'Threats to Global Antimicrobial Resistance Control: Centrally Approved and Unapproved Antibiotic Formulations Sold in India' (2019) 85 *British Journal of Clinical Pharmacology*, 59.
72. Roderick (n 35).
73. The Drugs and Cosmetics (Amendment) Bill 2013 (Bill No LVIII of 2013).
74. *Accent Pharma vs C.B.I.* 2017 SCC OnLine Mad 29306 (23 November 2017) <https://indiankanoon.org/doc/34295868/> accessed 4 August 2021; *Daeiou Pharmaceuticals Private Limited v. Inspector of Police* 2017 SCC OnLine Mad 28775 (21 December 2017) <https://indiankanoon.org/doc/30673189/> accessed 4 August 2021; *P. Kalavathy v State* Crl. R.C. No. 624–627 of 2018 before the High Court of Madras (31 July 2018) <https://indiankanoon.org/doc/86714795/> accessed 4 August 2021.
75. Press Trust of India, 'Health Ministry Bans 344 Fixed Dose Combination Drugs', *Business Standard India* (14 March 2016) <https://www.business-standard.com/article/pti-stories/health-ministry-bans-344-fixed-dose-combination-drugs-116031400523_1.html> accessed 4 August 2021; List of 344 FDCs that were banned: National Health Portal, 'Complete list of 344 drugs banned by the Ministry of Health Family welfare' (15 March 2016) <https://www.nhp.gov.in/Complete-list-of-344-drugs-banned-by-the-Ministry-of-Health-Family-welfare_pg> accessed 4 August 2021.

76. *Union Of India vs Pfizer Limited* Civil Appeal No. 22972 of 2017 (15 December 2017) <https://indiankanoon.org/doc/179615704/> accessed 4 August 2021.
77. Dinesh Thakur and Prashant Reddy, 'Why the Indian Supreme Court's Judgment on Combination Drugs Sends Wrong Signals' (*Scroll*, 29 December 2017) <https://scroll.in/pulse/863078/why-the-indian-supreme-courts-judgment-on-combination-drugs-sends-wrong-signals> accessed 1 October 2021.
78. Teena Thacker, 'Govt Prohibits Manufacture, Supply, Sale of 328 FDC Drugs', *Mint* (12 September 2018) <https://www.livemint.com/Politics/6aT2TnCIpzTEO7ZG7cYAkJ/Govt-prohibits-manufacture-supply-sale-of-328-FDC-drugs.html> accessed 4 August 2021; Teena Thacker, 'Government Likely to Ban over 150 Fixed Dose Combination Drugs', *Hindustan Times* (8 April 2019) <https://www.hindustantimes.com/health/government-likely-to-ban-over-150-fixed-dose-combination-drugs/story-SvFS67DGMClNGHgyAwNPNK.html> accessed 4 August 2021; PTI, 'Health Ministry Bans 80 More Fixed-Dose Combination Drugs', *The Times of India* (17 January 2019) <https://timesofindia.indiatimes.com/india/health-ministry-bans-80-more-fixed-dose-combination-drugs/articleshow/67577493.cms> accessed 4 August 2021.
79. DCGI Dr GN Singh ordering the "Constitution of a Committee to review the procedure and practices followed by CDSCO for granting marketing approval and clinical trials on certain drugs" (Order no DCG(I) Misc/2013-18, 26 March 2013).
80. Reply to RTI application dated 31 May 2018, Office of the DCGI (Application No CDSCO/R/2018/50052, 7 May 2018).
81. Reply to transferred RTI application dated 21 June 2018, Drug Regulation Branch, Ministry of Health (Application No MOHFW/R/2018/51457, 6 June 2018).
82. Email from the RTI Cell of the CDSCO to one of the authors (11 May 2020 at 9:28 PM).
83. *Prashant Reddy vs Ministry of Health and Family Welfare* Second Appeal No CIC/MH&FW/A/2018/159460-BJ (26 May 2020) <https://indiankanoon.org/doc/115080764/> accessed 5 August 2021.
84. *Prashant Reddy T vs Drug Controller General of India* W.P. No. 7213 of 2020 before the High Court of Delhi.
85. TM Mohapatra et. al, *Report of the Committee Constituted to Review the Procedures and Practices followed by CDSCO for granting approval and clinical trials on certain drugs (Mohapatra Committee Report)* (2013) para 5.2.

86. ibid.
87. ibid.
88. *Dinesh Thakur vs Union of India* W.P.(C) 11107/2018.
89. Government of India, Ministry of Health and Family Welfare, *SO 6161(E)* (*Gazette of India Extraordinary*, Part II—s 3(ii), 13 December 2018).
90. *Mohapatra Committee Report* (n 85) para 5.1.
91. Counter-affidavit dated 24 April 2019 filed by the Ministry of Health and DCGI in LPA No 687 of 2018 filed before the High Court of Delhi at New Delhi (On file with authors).
92. *Mohapatra Committee Report* (n 85) para 5.3.
93. ibid.
94. *Mohapatra Committee Report* (n 85) para 6–7. (The ban on use of Letrozole as an infertility treatment was reversed in 2017 by the Ministry of Health after ICMR conducted a "systematic review and meta-analysis" of studies on the use of Letrozole as a fertility treatment. Novartis, which is the company that developed Letrozole as a treatment for breast cancer continues to include a warning on its USFDA approved labelling/package insert that the drug could potentially cause "embryo-fetal toxicity". However, two relatively large US NIH sponsored comparator clinical trials on the efficacy of Letrozole as an infertility treatment in 2014 threw up contradictory results. One study reported that Letrozole was effective as a fertility treatment, while the other reported that it was ineffective compared to the existing treatment. Neither found embryo-fetal toxicity to be an issue. The citations of the study are as follows: Richard S Legro and others, 'Letrozole versus Clomiphene for Infertility in the Polycystic Ovary Syndrome' (2014) 371 *The New England Journal of Medicine*, 119; Michael P Diamond and others, 'Letrozole, Gonadotropin, or Clomiphene for Unexplained Infertility' (2015) 373 *The New England Journal of Medicine*, 1230. The ICMR study itself was not made available to us under the RTI Act on the grounds that it was in the process of being submitted for publication. Reply to RTI appeal dated 28 September 2021, ICMR (Appeal No. INCMR/A/E/21/00193, 29 October, 2021) This, despite us asking for a copy of the study in 2021, more than four years after it became the basis of the Ministry's decision to reverse the ban on Letrozole.)
95. The United States Food and Drug Administration (FDA), 'Coronavirus (COVID-19) Update: FDA Revokes Emergency Use Authorization for Chloroquine and Hydroxychloroquine' (15 June 2020) <https://

www.fda.gov/news-events/press-announcements/coronavirus-covid-19-update-fda-revokes-emergency-use-authorization-chloroquine-and> accessed 5 August 2021.

96. Drug Controller General of India (DCGI), 'Notice: Approval of Favipiravir Tablets to Glenmark Pharmaceuticals and Remdesivir Injection to Cipla Ltd, Hetero Drugs and Mylan Labs' (2 July 2020) <https://cdsco.gov.in/opencms/resources/UploadCDSCOWeb/2018/UploadPublic_NoticesFiles/faviNOTICE.pdf> accessed 5 August 2021; Press Information Bureau, Government of India, 'DCGI Gives Nod for Restricted Emergency Use to Itolizumab for Moderate to Severe COVID-19 Patients' (11 July 2020) <https://pib.gov.in/pib.gov.in/Pressreleaseshare.aspx?PRID=1637926> accessed 5 August 2021; Staff Writer, 'Covid Treatment: Zydus Gets Emergency Use Approval for Virafin' *Mint* (23 April 2021) <https://www.livemint.com/companies/news/covid-treatment-zydus-gets-emergency-use-approval-for-use-of-virafin-11619169889774.html> accessed 5 August 2021.

97. Reply to RTI application dated 21 October 2020, Central Drugs Standard Control Organisation (Application No CDSCO/R/E/20/00315, 6 September 2020).

98. Dinesh Thakur, 'An Opaque Model of Drug Approval in India' *The Telegraph* (27 July 2020) <https://www.telegraphindia.com/opinion/covid-19-drugs-controller-general-of-india-approval-of-drugs/cid/1787447> accessed 1 October 2021; Sundar Ramanan, 'The Fact of the Matter' *The Telegraph* (28 July 2020) <https://www.telegraphindia.com/opinion/the-fact-of-the-matter-biocons-response-to-questions/cid/1787569> accessed 1 October 2021.

99. Reply to RTI Application dated 4 September 2020, CDSCO (Application No CDSCO/R/E/20/00275, 2 August 2020).

100. The New Drugs & Clinical Trial Rules 2019, Second Schedule.

101. AIIMS/ICMR-COVID-19 National Task Force/Joint Monitoring Group, Ministry of Health and Family Welfare, Government of India, 'CLINICAL GUIDANCE FOR MANAGEMENT OF ADULT COVID-19 PATIENTS' (17 May 2021) <https://www.icmr.gov.in/pdf/covid/techdoc/COVID_Management_Algorithm_17052021.pdf> accessed 5 August 2021.

102. Gayathri Vaidyanathan, 'Scientists Criticize Use of Unproven COVID Drugs in India' (2020) 587 *Nature*, 187; Priyanka Pulla, 'Is Favipiravir Good for COVID-19? Clinical Trial Says No, Press Release Says Yes', *The Wire Science*, (25 November 2020) <https://science.thewire.in/the-sciences/favipiravir-glenmark-open-label-trial-primary-

endpoints-efficacy-cure-times-misleading-press-release/> accessed 5 August 2021; Priyanka Pulla, 'The Worrying Ways in Which Biocon's Itolizumab Trial Was Deeply Flawed', *The Wire Science*, (24 August 2020) <https://science.thewire.in/the-sciences/biocon-itolizumab-phase-ii-clinical-trial-cdsco-simon-two-stage-inconsistencies/> accessed 5 August 2021; Ronak Borana, 'DCGI Approves Virafin for Moderate COVID. Where's the Evidence It Works?' *The Wire Science* (24 April 2021). <https://science.thewire.in/the-sciences/zydus-virafin-pegylated-interferon-alpha-2b-india-dcgi-approve-covid-trial-methods-flaw/> accessed 5 August 2021.

103. Rupali Mukherjee, 'Anti-Covid drug now top-selling pharma brand' *Times of India* (11 May 2021) <https://timesofindia.indiatimes.com/business/india-business/anti-covid-drug-now-top-selling-pharma-brand/articleshow/82540028.cms> accessed 1 October 2021.

104. Prabin Kalita, 'Assam "First State" to Procure Itolizumab for Covid Patients' *The Times of India* (17 July 2020) <https://timesofindia.indiatimes.com/city/guwahati/assam-first-state-to-procure-itolizumab-for-covid-patients/articleshow/77016405.cms> accessed 1 May 2022; Sanjay Jog, 'Coronavirus in Maharashtra: State Govt to Procure Itolizumab to Treat Moderate to Severe Cases' *The Free Press Journal* (12 July 2020) <https://www.freepressjournal.in/mumbai/covid-19-in-maharashtra-government-to-procure-itolizumab-to-treat-moderate-to-severe-cases> accessed 2 May 2022; 'Coronavirus in Mumbai: BMC to Buy 27 Lakh Favipiravir Tablets for Rs 80 per Tablet from Glenmark' *Business Today* (2 July 2020) <https://www.businesstoday.in/latest/economy-politics/story/coronavirus-in-mumbai-bmc-to-buy-27-lakh-favipiravir-tablets-for-rs-80-per-tablet-from-glenmark-262915-2020-07-02> accessed 1 May 2022.

105. Press Information Bureau, Government of India, 'Press Statement by the Drugs Controller General of India (DCGI) on Restricted Emergency approval of COVID-19 virus vaccine' (3 January 2021) <https://www.icmr.gov.in/pdf/press_realease_files/HFW_DCGI_energency_use_authorisation_03012021_2.pdf> accessed 5 August 2021.

106. Shreya Dasgupta, 'India Needs More Transparency in Its COVID-19 Vaccine Trials, Critics Say' *Science | AAAS* 25 November 2020 <https://www.sciencemag.org/news/2020/11/india-needs-more-transparency-its-covid-19-vaccine-trials-critics-say> accessed 5 August 2021.

107. R Prasad, 'Government Releases Names of Vaccine Expert Panel' *The Hindu* (5 April 2021) <https://www.thehindu.com/news/

national/coronavirus-government-releases-names-of-vaccine-expert-panel/article34246372.ece> accessed 5 August 2021.

108. Gordon Guyatt and others, 'Evidence-Based Medicine: A New Approach to Teaching the Practice of Medicine' (1992) 268 *Journal of American Medical Association*, 2420.

109. Kameshwar Prasad, 'Evidence-Based Medicine in India' (2012) 66 *Journal of Clinical Epidemiology*, 6, 8.

110. Government of India, Ministry of Health and Family Welfare, *Report of The Expert Committee on a Comprehensive Examination of Drug Regulatory Issues, including the problem of Spurious Drugs (Mashelkar Committee Report)* (No Z.28015/112/2002-D/DMS&PFA, 2003) 30.

111. Government of India, *Pharmaceutical Research & Development Committee Report* (1999); Amit Sengupta, 'Globalization and Corruption in the Health Sector' in Samiran Nundy, Keshav Desiraju and Sanjay Nagral (eds), *Healers or Predators? Healthcare Corruption in India* (OUP 2018).

112. *Mashelkar Committee Report* (n 110) 66.

113. TNN, 'Clinical Trials: DCGI Faults 9 More CROs' *The Times of India* (20 July 2011) <https://timesofindia.indiatimes.com/city/hyderabad/clinical-trials-dcgi-faults-9-more-cros/articleshow/9290503.cms> accessed 5 August 2021; M Suchitra, 'Lured, Used and Discarded' *DownToEarth* (31 July 2011) <https://www.downtoearth.org.in/news/lured-used-and-discarded-33700> accessed 5 August 2021; Priyanka Pulla, 'Lured by Blood Money: Serial Volunteers Set a Disturbing Trend' *The Hindu* (30 December 2017) <https://www.thehindu.com/opinion/op-ed/lured-by-blood-money-clinical-trials/article22328296.ece> accessed 5 August 2021.

114. Sanjeet Bagcchi, 'Indian Supreme Court Halts Approval of New Clinical Trials until Regulatory Framework Is Set Up' (2013) 347 *BMJ*, f5996.

115. Prabha Raghavan, 'Health Minister Petitioned: Medical Professionals Seek Transparency in Pharma Regulations' *The Indian Express* (7 August 2020) <https://indianexpress.com/article/india/health-minister-petitioned-medical-professionals-seek-transparency-in-pharma-regulations-6543378/> accessed 5 August 2021.

CHAPTER SIX

Can "Made in India" Generic Medicine Be Trusted?

On 17th April 2017, while inaugurating a hospital at Surat, Prime Minister Narendra Modi announced that his government was planning to introduce a law that would require doctors to mandatorily prescribe medicines according to their generic names.[1] To illustrate with an example, if the proposed law was enacted, doctors would be required to write Paracetamol on the prescription instead of Crocin® (which is a brand name owned by one specific company) every time they want to prescribe acetaminophen (the chemical name of paracetamol) for a patient.

The supposed objective of Modi's proposed policy was to break the alleged "pharma-doctor" nexus wherein doctors receive kickbacks from pharmaceutical companies for prescribing their brands.[2] There is anecdotal evidence to support the allegation of a collusive nexus between some Indian doctors and pharmaceutical companies.[3] Modi had made similar allegations against Indian doctors on different occasions leading to protests by Indian doctors.[4] His proposed policy was based on the assumption that the pharmacist filling a prescription containing only the generic name will pick the lowest priced brand of the drug available in the store so as to ensure the maximum cost saving for the patient. Of course, pharmacists can have their own incentives to sell the more expensive brand, unless they are legally required to provide the most affordable generic version of the drug.

For its part, the Indian medical profession had legitimate reasons to oppose Modi's proposed policy; this opposition had little to do with kickbacks being received from the industry and a lot more to do with the functioning of the Indian state's drug regulatory framework. Quite a few Indian doctors have complained in journals and other writings about a lack of faith in India's drug regulatory framework.[5] Based on their own experience with treatment outcomes, Indian doctors are aware that many formulations of Indian generic medicines do not have the expected therapeutic effect on their patients. These doctors have figured out, through "trial and error", specific brands of generic medicine that have the expected therapeutic effect and prescribe only those to their patients. This anecdotal evidence from individual doctors is also reflected in market pricing of generic drugs in India, where different brands of the same generic drug command different prices, with the price differentials in some cases being anywhere between 100% to 200%. For example, a study in 2005 noted that the brand of Ciprofloxacin owned by one company was being sold at a price that was 194% higher than the cheapest substitute in the market. Similarly, the most expensive brand of Nimesulide was 150% higher than the cheapest brand on the market.[6] These price differences between different brands of generics continue to persist in the Indian market even today.

From a theoretical viewpoint, a significant difference in price between different brands of generic drugs makes little sense because these different brands are supposed to contain the same active ingredient and are therefore the same product with the same therapeutic properties. Generic drugs are not like different brands of toothpaste or soap where companies justify price differences based on claims that their product is superior to the other brands. Generic drugs with the same ingredients, once approved by the regulators, are supposed to be exact copies of each other and therefore have an identical therapeutic effect on patients. Rationally acting patients and doctors should therefore buy or prescribe the more affordable formulation, forcing the more expensive version of the generic drug to reduce their price in order to continue competing in the market. But this did not happen in the Indian market for many reasons. One such reason offered by economists is that consumers of drugs as well as doctors do not perceive all generic formulations to be of the same quality and hence interchangeable with each other or with the innovator brand.[7] Hence, pharmaceutical companies that were presumed to be more "trustworthy" could charge a premium for the trust reposed by patients and doctors in their products. These "perceptions" of Indian doctors have been moulded by their clinical experience wherein they have observed different brands of generic medicines have varying therapeutic effects on their patients. The reason they have seen such varying patterns is because Indian law, unlike the law in many countries, does not guarantee that generic drugs are in fact therapeutically equivalent to each other or the innovator brand. The pricing structure for generic drugs in India is in reality a terrible indictment of India's regulatory framework for drugs.

As we will demonstrate through the course of this chapter, the Ministry of Health slumbered while the rest of the world, especially the Americans, worked hard at creating a rigorous scientific and legal framework that would instill confidence in both doctors and patients that all generics approved by the USFDA would in fact be therapeutically equivalent to the innovator drug. Understanding these challenges and the gradual evolution of the regulatory framework of generics across the world is important in order to understand the resistance of Indian doctors to mandatory generic substitution of drugs in India. An excellent starting point to this discussion is the evolution of American regulatory law on approval of generics.

The birth and science behind the rise of generic medicines in the United States

The first half of the 20th century gave rise to a number of pharmaceutical giants like Pfizer, Merck, Eli Lilly, GlaxoSmithKline, Parker Davis, Schering etc. This tremendous growth of the pharmaceutical industry was fueled by greater public and private investment into scientific research that led to marvelous new medical discoveries especially in the field of antibiotics. This period also saw many countries amend their patent laws to protect these pharmaceutical inventions. Since patent terms were mostly limited to 14 years in that era, many of the patents for the breakthrough discoveries in the 40s and 50s were set to expire in the 50s and 60s thereby opening the door for other companies to manufacture generic copies of the same drug. The entry of multiple generic drugs after the expiry of a patent monopoly had the potential to drive down prices by increasing competition. The possibility of hefty price erosion in the pharmaceutical sector was largely welcomed in the 50s by American lawmakers who were shocked by the profit margins of the pharmaceutical industry, especially in contrast with other industries selling essential commodities to the general population.[8]

The innovator pharmaceutical industry in the United States, whose patents had guaranteed them a monopoly so far, was not as enthusiastic in welcoming competition. As documented in detail by Jeremy A. Greene in his extensively researched book on the history of the generic drug industry—*Generic: The Unbranding of Modern Medicine*—the innovator drug industry adopted several "dirty tricks" to slow down the entry and acceptance of generic drugs in the United States. This bag of "dirty tricks" included opposition to simpler generic names for all drugs. At that time, the pharmaceutical companies that invented the drug also designated its final generic name and very often the innovator company would choose exceptionally complicated generic names, while their own brand names would be simple and already popular with the medical community because of the years of patent monopoly enjoyed by their product.[9] The American Congress responded to this problem by creating a government body called the United States Adopted Names (USAN) committee to decide generic names.[10]

Separate and apart from the issue of generic names, the innovator pharmaceutical industry has been accused by historians like Greene of painting generic medicines as being manufactured in dirty and unsafe facilities that could compromise the therapeutic efficacy of these drugs.[11] As per this account, the advocacy campaign by the innovator industry made a conscious effort to equate generic drugs to adulterated drugs in the mind of the common man.[12] While there were instances of the USFDA discovering some of the new generic pharmaceutical companies manufacturing drugs in filthy conditions, a generalization of the entire new generic industry as untrustworthy was certainly unwarranted.[13]

"Dirty tricks" aside, there was also serious scientific uncertainty regarding the manner in which regulators would approve generic versions of innovator drugs once the patents expired. Starting in 1962, after the enactment of the Kefauver-Harris amendments, innovator companies in the United States had to demonstrate safety and efficacy of their new drugs through a system of rigorous clinical trials on patients. These trials were both expensive and risky. Even though the generic drug would have the same "active ingredient" as the innovator drug, most generic drugs would use different binders, stabilizers, disintegrating agents, tasting agents, and would be compressed by different tablet punching machines.[14] For extended-release formulations, which release the drug over a longer period of time in the gut of the human body, the use of different excipients by the innovator and generic manufacturers could significantly influence the timing and the rate at which the drug is released. Each of these factors had the potential to influence the manner in which the generic drug dissolved in the blood stream of patients. Any variations in the way the drug was formulated or in the use of different excipients or compression/milling using a tablet punching machine could affect the rate at which the drug dissolves and is absorbed by the bloodstream of a patient. Depending on the drug in question, this difference in absorption rates can have a material effect on treatment outcomes in patients. If a drug fails to dissolve at the same rate as the innovator drug, it may lead to a differing amount of the drug reaching the site of action in the human body, thereby impeding the expected therapeutic effect of the medication. A lower amount of drug dissolving in the bloodstream may not be adequate to generate a proper dose response, which is instrumental to the therapeutic outcome. Alternately, if too much of the drug dissolved into the bloodstream too quickly, it could be potentially toxic for the patient (a phenomenon called drug-dumping).

One possible regulatory solution to guarantee the efficacy of generic drugs was to put these generic formulations through the same set of clinical trials that the innovator drug was subjected to, in order to generate the required efficacy data. This solution was however both unethical and expensive. The use of placebos during such clinical trials entails depriving one set of patients the best available treatment that has already been scientifically validated by the innovator's clinical trials and is therefore unethical. From a cost perspective, the repetition of clinical trials would be quite expensive, thereby increasing the costs of generic medicine to patients. As a result, repetition of clinical trials for generic formulations did not make any sense if the objective was to introduce competition and drive down prices of generic medicine.

Instead, focus shifted towards the working hypothesis that chemical equivalence between the innovator drug and generic drugs could be established in the laboratory through standard pharmacopeial methods laid down in pharmacopeias (these are official compilations prescribing testing methods to establish the quality of a drug). The tests generally prescribed at the time by a pharmacopeia to test a drug included assay, identification, weight variation, content uniformity, purity, and disintegration. These tests could be carried out in the laboratory at a relatively low cost, especially when compared to the prospect of repeating clinical trials for generic formulations.[15]

This hypothesis came into question in the 60s when scientists began testing the extent to which generic medicines manufactured by different companies were being absorbed by the human body. These tests were conducted by examining blood or urine samples from volunteers who consumed the generic medicines in question. By testing the amount of the drug available in these blood or urine samples, scientists could calculate the extent to which these drugs were being absorbed into the blood stream and otherwise metabolized in the body. This is called the bioavailability of the drug in the human body. These experiments demonstrated that despite the pharmacopeial equivalence of these drugs when tested in the lab, there was a significant variability in the rate at which these drugs were being absorbed into the bloodstream of human volunteers. These experiments led to an entirely new area of research called biopharmaceutics which can be further divided into pharmacodynamics studies (PD) and pharmacokinetics studies (PK).[16]

Canadian researchers J.A. Campbell and D.G. Chapman who worked at the Canadian Food and Drug Laboratories in Ottawa in the 60s were pioneers in this area of research. In one of their first experiments, when Chapman compared eight different versions of shellac-coated Amphetamine, all manufactured by different companies, it was discovered that the amount of drug excreted in the urine of volunteers varied widely. From the urine tests, it was determined that one tablet delivered only 5 mg, while another delivered the full 15mg at once.[17] This was likely because the shellac coatings used for extended-release formulations were disintegrating at different times that were not uniform. From a clinical viewpoint, this could be deeply problematic as it would adversely affect treatment outcomes.

In a different set of experiments, a pharmacologist, John H. Wagner tested time-release capsules and enteric-coated tablets containing a radiopaque contrast agent on dogs trained to lay still on X-ray tables. The aim was to assess the speed at which the drug was being released in the digestive tract of the dogs. This experiment demonstrated that the supposedly identical pills were being released at varying time periods. This meant that although the drugs demonstrated chemical equivalence in the laboratory when tested through standard pharmacopeial techniques, the bioavailability of the drug in the dogs was not equivalent to the innovator drug.[18]

These studies raised questions about whether "in-vitro" testing i.e., testing in the laboratory, using standard pharmacopeial methods could actually replace "in-vivo" testing i.e., on human volunteers, in order to establish the bioequivalence of the generic with the innovator drug.

This issue of bioequivalence between the innovator drug and generic drugs became an actual regulatory concern in 1967 when Parke Davis's Chloromycetin went off patent. The powerful antibiotic was a major revenue earner for the company and it stood to lose significant revenues with the entry of generic copies of the drug. Due to a series of events involving poorly dissolving generic Chloromycetin, the USFDA decided to test various generic versions of Chloromycetin on human volunteers to examine the bioavailability of the generic versions. Those tests revealed that generic versions of the drugs were being absorbed into the blood at widely varying rates. As a result, the USFDA suspended permission for all generic versions of Chloromycetin until it could work out a revised protocol to grant approval for generic medicines.[19] Similar problems were discovered with different brands of Tetracycline and Oxytetracycline, which failed to demonstrate bioequivalence despite showing equivalence in the laboratory when subjected to standard pharmacopeial tests.[20] There was now enough evidence that equivalence as established through pharmacopeial tests in the laboratory did not always guarantee bioequivalence in the human body and hence therapeutic equivalence could not be guaranteed with only in-vitro testing.

The obvious solution to this problem was to test the drugs on human volunteers (not patients but healthy volunteers) in order to generate bioavailability data i.e., the rate of absorption of the drug into the bloodstream of human volunteers. This is measured by testing the blood and urine of the volunteers at different time intervals to compute the dissolution profile of the generic formulation in the human body over a time period. As long as the dissolution curve plotted on a graph is same or substantially similar to that of the innovator drug, the generic formulation can be presumed to be bioequivalent to the innovator drug. The scope for acceptable differences in the dissolution profiles reduces greatly in the case of "narrow therapeutic index" (NTI) drugs where even a small change in dosage may have a significantly large therapeutic effect on the patient. But for broad therapeutic index drugs, for example, standard antibiotics, once bioequivalence was established between the innovator and its generic formulation, doctors and pharmacists could safely substitute the innovator drug with the generic formulation as it was presumed that both versions would guarantee the same therapeutic effect. The problem, however, with mandating bioequivalence testing through in-vivo methods, was that it was more expensive than using in-vitro methods in the lab, although it was way cheaper than full-fledged clinical trials involving patients.

The fact that this debate took place at a time when there was increasing political pressure in the United States to adopt more affordable generic drugs in order to contain healthcare costs meant that a lot of different stakeholders were working towards varying goals. The US Congress wanted to reduce public funds that were spent on the purchase of drugs for publicly funded programs and was actively pressuring state governments to adopt "generic substitution" policies. These substitution policies would allow pharmacists to replace the innovator brand with a more affordable generic version. At the same time, the innovator pharmaceutical industry wanted to make it more complicated for the fledgling generic industry to enter the market and compete. The American Medical Association (AMA), which was the most influential association of medical doctors in the United States, was against the political class stripping doctors of their power to prescribe brands that they felt were most effective.[21] Another dimension to this debate was the struggle between the United States Pharmacopeia (USP) and the USFDA over the efficacy of the former's pharmacopeial standards. The USP, which was a non-governmental entity, had control over the most important standard-setting measures in the form of the pharmacopeia. The fact that the USFDA was putting in place its own regulations to deal with the shortcomings of the pharmacopeia tilted the balance of power in favour of the regulator.[22]

Given the burning importance of creating a simple regulatory pathway for generics and the financial implications of such a policy for public funds and private profits, a number of expert committees were setup in the United States to study the issue of bioequivalence from a regulatory perspective.[23] These included a taskforce of the Health, Education and

Welfare Department of the US Government and another committee by the Office of Technology Assessment under the US Congress.[24] These committees agreed to the fact that using pharmacopeial methods to establish chemical equivalence did not always guarantee bioequivalence of generics and that many drugs would have to be tested on human volunteers in order to generate proof of their bioequivalence to the innovator drugs.[25] There was, however, a disagreement on whether in-vivo bioequivalence testing should be made compulsory for all generics as a default rule or for only those drugs with known dissolution issues.

In 1977, the USFDA published regulations to make in-vivo bioequivalence testing on human volunteers the default rule for all generic medicine, save for some exceptions.[26] For example, ointments, injections etc., were excluded from the requirement of bioequivalence testing. The onus was now on the pharmaceutical company manufacturing generics drugs to request for a waiver from the requirement of conducting in-vivo bioequivalence testing. For those drugs where in-vivo bioequivalence studies were required to be conducted, the generic drug formulation was to be evaluated on a small number of healthy volunteers and as long as the dissolution profile of the generic formulation was in the range of 75% to 125% of the innovator's dissolution profile, it would be deemed bioequivalent to the innovator drug. The USFDA also published a list of drugs for which in-vitro data would suffice.[27] These bioequivalence standards that evolved within the USFDA gradually proliferated around the world into other jurisdictions.[28] To guarantee better dissemination of information about approved generics, the USFDA also began the process of publishing the "Orange Book" which listed all the bioequivalent generics for every "new drug" that had been approved by the USFDA.

This new regulatory structure put in place by the USFDA,

guaranteeing the therapeutic equivalence of generics with the innovator drug, cleared the deck for many American states to pass new laws allowing or mandating pharmacists to substitute innovator drugs with generic formulations thereby lowering healthcare costs across the United States.[29]

This regulatory concept of "bioequivalence" also became one of the central tenets of the Drug Price Competition and Patent Term Restoration Act 1984, better known as the Hatch-Waxman Act. A study on the effect of the Hatch-Waxman Act on drug prices revealed that the prices of generics reduced by 51% to 80% over a period of five years after the entry of generics was permitted.[30] These price reductions highlight the importance of having credible regulatory pathways for generic drugs to enter the market.

The lethargic Indian approach to mandatory in-vivo bioequivalence studies

Indian regulatory authorities were made aware of many of the above problems regarding varying bioavailability as early as in 1972 when the DCC, which has as its members representatives of all the state drug controllers and the DCGI, circulated amongst its members a WHO paper at its 15th meeting held on 9 and 10 March 1972. The WHO paper questioned the reliability of depending upon pharmacopeial dissolution methods used in laboratories to predict the actual rate of drugs being absorbed in the human body.

The WHO paper struck a warning note in the very first paragraph which is reproduced below:

> During the last few years reports have appeared in the literature concerning drugs which either have not given the expected clinical results or which have caused unexpected toxic reactions. This has been more noticeable in patients who have been stabilized on drug for a period of time and, after taking—a new batch or brand, have experienced a change in

> the clinical effectiveness of their medication. A suspected cause of malabsorption or enhanced absorption is the variation of release characteristics of the final product.

The paper also warned how changing brands during the course of treatment could affect treatment outcomes:

> The decision as to which drugs (and dosage forms) require dissolution tests depends upon a number of factors. It has been shown that changes in formulation may produce clinical hazards, e.g. increased toxicity of phenytoin with change of excipient; ineffective control of blood sugar with some brands of tolbutamide. The number of drugs and formulations where a dissolution test should be included is probably not great. Where a patient is being treated for a chronic illness or requiring continuous replacement therapy, a change in formulation between batches or brands may result in lack of clinical efficacy or in an increase in toxicity. Such drugs may include. (i) Oral anti-inflammatory steroids (Prednisone; prednisolone); (ii) Oral antidiabetic agents (Tolbutamide); (iii) Oral anti-epileptic agents (Phenytoin); (iv) Digoxin tablets; (v) "Insoluble" intestinal antiseptics (iodochlorhydroxyquinolines, nitrofurantoin); (vi) Oral anticoagulant drugs (dicoumarol, Phenindione); (vii) possible some oral diuretics (hydrochlorthiazide).[31]

The WHO paper ended with a recommendation for greater international coordination to study the correlation between dissolution tests and "physiological availability" of drugs. Given the serious revelations in that paper, one would have expected the DCC and the Ministry of Health to sincerely consider reforming existing regulations in India. Yet, no action was taken.

In 1975, the Hathi Committee Report on Drugs and Pharmaceutical Industry, which was commissioned by the Government of India to study the pharmaceutical industry, made a fleeting reference to the WHO paper while flagging the issue of bioavailability of different brands of drugs. The committee made the following pertinent observation on the importance of bioequivalence studies, without exactly laying down any specific standards to be followed in the future:

> It is often argued that bioavailability is an important factor in the efficiency of a drug. The W.H.O. Technical Series Report on bioavailability has highlighted different facets of this problem, particularly, the fact that as yet there are no established and accepted methods for evaluation of bioavailability of different brands of drugs. A drug manufactured by a firm, may differ from batch to batch in its bioavailability. Bioavailability is particularly important in the case of oral preparations and that too with respect to only a very few drugs. It cannot be denied, that in case of drugs like digoxin, phenytoin etc. bioavailability is important, but this has nothing to do with brand or generic names. The Drug Control authorities will have to exercise effective control over the standards of such drugs which will need bioavailability studies as per recommendations of the W.H.O., whether these drugs are introduced under generic or brand names.[32]

The fact that the Ministry of Health took no action to tackle this pressing issue should not surprise anybody. What is astonishing however is that in 1981, the Ministry of Health selectively enforced a recommendation made by the Hathi Committee to abolish the use of trade names for select generic drugs, without paying any heed to the recommendations pertaining to the issue of varying bioavailability amongst generic drugs. Issued on 17 January 1981, this notification of the Ministry of Health amended the Drugs and Cosmetics Rules 1945 to prohibit the use of any brand names on the packaging of the following drugs: Analgin, Aspirin, Chlorpromazine and its salts, Ferrous Sulphate, Piperazine and its salts. The same set of amendments also declared that all future drugs licenced for manufacture or imported into India could no longer feature the trade name on the labelling of the drug.[33] This was an astonishingly radical policy since it effectively banned brand names for all these drugs, thereby making it impossible for pharmaceutical companies to market or advertize their own specific brands. The Hathi committee had recommended this move as part of its effort to lower drug costs and to encourage greater use of the more affordable generic drugs; but it was also careful to explain how other quality control measures, including the issue of bioavailability had to be addressed before taking the aforementioned steps.[34] The government selectively chose to enforce only the recommendation to abolish trade names without taking action on any of the committee's other recommendations to address issues related to bioavailability.

This decision to do away with trade names for most drugs was challenged by pharmaceutical companies like Pfizer, Hoescht, Cyanamid India Ltd, and Cosme Farma Laboratories before the Delhi High Court on a number of grounds. The High Court ultimately struck down the policy as unconstitutional after the government was unable to present a coherent defense of its policy.[35] One of the factors that contributed to the court's decision was "bioequivalence". The court's reasoning on the issue is reproduced as follows:

> Similarly, we cannot accept the contention that there would be no difference in formulations made by different formulators out of the same bulk drug. High-powered advertisement techniques apart, it is common knowledge and is well supported by medical opinion that two different patients may react differently on taking the same drug. Obviously, this is because of the difference in what the petitioners call the bio-availability, i.e. therapeutic impact. Respondent No. 4's contention in support of what has been said by first three respondents that there is no particular difference in therapeutic impact of various formulations manufactured from the same bulk drug cannot be accepted. We are inclined to agree with

> what the petitioners say because that is not only based on reason but also on experience.[36]

Even after this loss before the courts, the government did not take steps to tackle the issue of bioequivalence for another two decades despite members of Parliament prodding it to take some action. Even as late as the year 1986, when parliamentarians raised the issue of bioequivalence testing and its impact on efficacy of medicine in both chambers of Parliament during Question Hour, the government was mostly indifferent.

In the Rajya Sabha, an MP by the name Raique Alam asked the Government of India, during Question Hour on 5 November 1986, whether the government proposed to make bioequivalence testing compulsory in order to guarantee the effectiveness of medicine sold in India. The question and the government's response are reproduced below:

> 248. Shri Raique Alam: Will the Minister of Health and Family Welfare be pleased to state:
>
> (a) whether it is a fact that a number of medicines being marketed have not proved to be effective;
>
> (b) the names of the medicines for which bio-equivalence tests were conducted during last three years by Government laboratories;
>
> (c) what was the percentage of efficacy in each product which was tested;
>
> (d) whether government proposes to make bio-equivalence test compulsory for effective medicines; and
>
> (e) if so, by when?
>
> The Minister of State in the Department of Health in the Ministry of Health and Family Welfare (Kumari Saroj Khaparde):
>
> (a) The Government have not received any published report regarding any medicine being marketed which has not proved effective.

> (b) and (c) Bioequivalence test is not a pharmacopeial requirement in the country and as such no data in this regard are available from Government laboratories';
>
> (d) and (e) There is no immediate proposal to make bioequivalence test compulsory.[37]

Two weeks later, in the Lok Sabha, an MP by the name Kumari Pushpa Devi asked a similar question. The question and the government's response are reproduced below:

> Q.2655 Kumari Pushpa Devi: Will the Minister of Health and Family Welfare be pleased to state:
>
> (a) The names of the medicines for which bioequivalence tests were conducted during the last three years; and
>
> (b) The efficacy percentage in each case?
>
> The Minister of State in the Ministry of Health and Family Welfare (Kumari Saroj Khaparde): (a) and (b) Bio-equivalence tests are not pharmacopeial requirements in the country and as such no data in this regard are available from Government laboratories.[38]

By any standard, answers to both the questions provided by the government on the floor of Parliament were astonishingly cavalier, especially when viewed in the context of the heated debates in the United States since 1968 on the failure of in-vitro pharmacopeial methods to guarantee bioequivalence with the same certainty as in-vivo tests. The two MPs who posed the questions on bioequivalence to the government appeared to have a better understanding of regulatory sciences than the entire Ministry of Health of the Government of India. The requirement of bioavailability/bioequivalence studies as precondition for manufacturing approval of generics finally made its debut in Indian law only in 2001[39] but even then, it did not apply retrospectively for generic drugs already approved and more worryingly, was limited to only generic drugs approved by the DCGI for an initial four-year period while the drug maintained a "new drug" status under Indian law. After the expiry of the arbitrary four-year period, applications to manufacture generic copies of the erstwhile "new drug" were required to be filed with state drug controllers rather than the DCGI. To illustrate this with the help of an example, if new drug "Formula X" got approved in 2001 by the DCGI and presuming it was not under patent protection, all companies seeking permission to manufacture generic versions of "Formula X" till 2005 would have to seek approval from the DCGI. Thereafter, any company seeking approval to manufacture their generic version had to simply approach the state drug controller for a licence to manufacture a generic version of "Formula X" in India. The requirement to submit bioavailability/bioequivalence data, inserted into the law in 2001, was limited to only applications filed with the DCGI while the drug maintained its "new drug" status. Therefore, if a new pharmaceutical company wanted to manufacture "Formula X" after 2005, it could apply to the state drug controller without conducting/providing any proof of bioequivalence testing!

There is no scientific rationale for this bizarre distinction where new manufacturers of generic drugs entering the market after the expiry of the four-year period did not have to establish the bioequivalence of their formulations with the innovator drug. The only possible explanation for this bizarre distinction in regulatory standards is that the powerful domestic pharmaceutical industry had leaned on the government in order to avoid paying for more expensive in-vivo bioequivalence testing on human volunteers in order to reduce costs and also reduce the probability of their applications being rejected due to their inability to formulate bioequivalent formulations.

In 2013, after the scathing 59th report of the Parliamentary Standing Committee on Health, the government setup an expert committee under Professor Ranjit Roy Chaudhury to "formulate policy and guidelines for approval of new drugs, clinical trials and banning of drugs". While remaining silent on the absurdity of the four-year cut-off for bioequivalence testing, the Ranjit Roy Chaudhury Committee did make a recommendation that all generic drugs (regardless of whether they were in the "new drug" status) being manufactured in India be subject to mandatory bioequivalence testing on human volunteers.[40] Thankfully its recommendations were taken seriously by the Ministry of Health and it began a process of deliberations on the issue of making bioequivalence testing mandatory.

When the above recommendations were deliberated upon in 2014 by the DCC, which has representatives of all state drug controllers, the recommendation made by the Ranjit Roy Chaudhury Committee was opposed on the most ridiculous grounds! The relevant extract of the Minutes is reproduced as follows:

> The recommendations of the Prof Ranjit Roy Chaudhury Committee in respect of Bioavailability or Bioequivalence (BA/BE) studies conducted in India were deliberated in detail. The members were of the view that BA/BE studies in respect of drugs manufactured in the country shall be insisted whenever there are issues relating to patient safety and variable bioavailability. As the infrastructure for conduct of such studies is not uniformly available in the country it cannot be implemented as a rule.[41]

As evident from the minutes above, the DCC's opposition was not based on any scientific disagreement on the importance of bioequivalence testing to public health in India, but rather on the grounds that "infrastructure" for conducting bioequivalence studies was "not uniformly available" across the country. This was a rather surprising assertion since by 2014 many foreign pharmaceutical companies were outsourcing their bioequivalence studies to Indian clinical research organizations. As usual, the DCC never provided any empirical evidence to back its claim regarding the "shortage of infrastructure". Even presuming a shortage did exist, the appropriate step would be to create a staggered deadline for making BE studies mandatory, so that necessary investments could be made in creating BE study centres.

The fact that the DCC so blatantly placed the interests of the pharmaceutical companies over and above the public health requirements of the people of India is worrying and perhaps reflective of the cozy relationships between the pharmaceutical industry and state drug controllers.

The issue of mandatory bioequivalence testing for all generic drugs was revived in 2016, coincidentally after we submitted a report to the Ministry of Health pointing out the absurdity of requiring bioequivalence testing for only generics in the "new drug" phase and not for those entering the market after the "four year" period.[42] A few weeks after the submission of our report, the issue was taken up by the DTAB at its 72nd meeting held in June 2016. Unlike the DCC, the DTAB, which is staffed by experts from different government institutions, recommended to the government that bioequivalence testing be made mandatory for all Indian generic medicine subject to the Biopharmaceutical Classification System (BCS).[43]

The BCS, which was developed by scientists working for the USFDA's Division of Biopharmaceutics, is basically a framework that helps determine which generic drugs are required to go through in-vivo bioequivalence testing on humans as opposed to in-vitro testing in the laboratories (and therefore considerably cheaper).[44] The BCS classified all formulations into four categories as explained on the opposite page.

Class	*Solubility*	*Permeability*
Class I	High	High
Class II	Low	High
Class III	High	Low
Class IV	Low	Low

The classification of drugs on the basis of solubility and permeability was due to the fact that these two factors contribute the most to the bioavailability of a formulation in the human body. "Availability" of the drug, i.e., its concentration in the blood stream post ingestion, is largely determined by how effectively the formulation dissolves in the stomach-acid (for oral formulations) and its ability to permeate through the intestinal tissue. The higher the solubility and permeability, the easier it is for the drug to enter the bloodstream. Drugs with high solubility are typically easier to test through in-vitro methods and hence it has been argued that these drugs be given a waiver from being evaluated through in-vivo bioequivalence testing.

The BCS system was then used by the USFDA to evolve guidelines on biowaivers; i.e., if a formulation fell within Class I or Class III, where it demonstrated high solubility, the manufacturer could apply for a waiver from in-vivo bioequivalence studies and instead produce only in-vitro data i.e., data collected through laboratory tests.[45] The concept of biowaivers was meant to reduce the costs for formulating generic drugs to enter the market since in-vivo bioequivalence studies on humans are more expensive than in-vitro testing conducted in laboratories. As per one published study, which attempted to classify the top 200 selling drugs in the United States, EU, and Japan, according to the BCS methodology, it was found that more than 55% fell within Class I and Class III, meaning that they qualified for biowaiver.[46] An earlier study by the same authors found a similar percentage of drugs on the WHO's Essential Drug List qualifying for biowaivers.[47]

Granting biowaivers could certainly open the door to a more affordable regulatory pathway but the science around biowaivers and the development of in-vitro testing methods is still evolving. As a result, most international regulators that allow for biowaivers do so on a case-by-case basis for the applications made for each formulation by the company in question. Recall that generic drug formulations may use excipients—fillers, binders, flavouring agents etc., which may be different from each other and therefore have a determinant impact on the bioavailability of the formulation. Therefore, it is not possible to assign de-facto classification to each generic drug formulation without assessing the impact of such excipients on dissolution. The process of classifying all formulations into the four categories is an ongoing process. Until that process is complete, most regulators will allow for waivers only on a case-by-case basis. As a result, the biowaiver pathway is not invoked very frequently by the generic pharmaceutical industry in most countries.[48]

The DTAB in its deliberations appears to have missed out entirely on this fact that all regulators use the concept of biowaivers on a case-by-case basis. Instead, the DTAB recommended mandatory bioequivalence studies only for drugs in Category II and IV, thereby implying blanket biowaivers for all drugs in Category I and III.

By 3 April 2017, the Ministry of Health notified the Drugs and Cosmetics (Ninth Amendment) Rules 2017 making bioequivalence testing compulsory on the lines suggested by the DTAB i.e., drugs in Category II and IV of the BCS would have to go through bioequivalence studies while drugs in Category I and III of the BCS would classify for biowaivers and would not be required to be evaluated through bioequivalence studies.[49] The incorporation of the BCS into Indian law and the blanket exemption for drugs in Category I and III was problematic for many reasons. To begin with, the amendments do not provide a legal definition of the phrases "highly soluble" or "highly permeable" or define the parameters for each of the categories in the BCS system. Most problematically though, Indian law does not classify all known drugs in these four categories of the BCS.

Given this ambiguity in the Drugs and Cosmetics Rules 1945, it is not clear how the 28 state drug controllers and nine drug controllers in the union territories who grant approvals for manufacturing generic drugs are going to interpret the requirements of the BCS system in a uniform and consistent manner across the country. To make matters worse, the DTAB and Ministry of Health missed the fact that regulators like the USFDA, which developed the BCS, prohibit biowaivers for drugs with a NTI. These are drugs where even a small dosage variation can have significant variations in therapeutic outcomes. Given this variability, these drug formulations are always subject to in-vivo bioequivalence studies in the United States. The Indian regulations are entirely silent on whether drugs with a NTI can get approved through the route of biowaivers.

Equally concerning is the silence of the government on DTAB's recommendation that all existing generic drugs (approved prior to the 2017 bioequivalence regulations) go through the bioequivalence testing protocols within three years.[50] This was an essential and excellent recommendation by the DTAB to guarantee that all Indian generics approved prior to 2017 were in fact therapeutically equivalent to the innovator drugs. Unfortunately, this recommendation has not been enforced by the Ministry of Health via the Drugs and Cosmetics (Ninth Amendment) Rules 2017 which made bioequivalence testing mandatory for all future approvals in Class II and IV. We have no idea why the Ministry chose to ignore this recommendation but it is very likely that the generic pharmaceutical industry lobbied the Ministry to ignore it. It is no secret that the Indian generic pharmaceutical industry is not in favour of mandatory in-vivo bioequivalence testing. In fact, the generic drug industry has reportedly lobbied the Ministry of Health to do away with this requirement for drugs that are being exported to other countries.[51] It would be clearly unethical for India to exempt exports from such a requirement.

Many of the issues described above, including the poor drafting of the 2017 amendments that brought in the BCS and biowaiver system, were clearly identified in a petition that one of us, Dinesh Thakur, sent to the Ministry of Health in June 2020.[52] As usual, the Ministry did not even bother acknowledging receipt of the petition, much less implement the recommendations contained in it.

We will never know the true human cost of not having put in place a well-designed bioequivalence framework since 1968 when there was clear evidence that in-vitro testing techniques were inferior to in-vivo testing for a number of generic medicines. Suffice it to say that the lack of mandatory bioequivalence testing has resulted in the approvals of hundreds if not thousands of brands of generics in India and it is very likely that many of these brands have adversely affected the lives of patients, whether Indian or foreign, who consumed these “Made in India” medicines.

The large-scale data fabrication of bioequivalence data by Indian CRO for export markets

Although Indian law did not require bioequivalence testing till a few years ago, most of the developed countries in the West, which are the chief export markets for the biggest Indian pharmaceutical companies, have always required bioequivalence testing for any generic drug being sold in their markets. It is a general practice for most Indian pharmaceutical companies exporting drugs to the West to outsource bioequivalence studies to external clinical research organisations (CROs) in order to generate data required to acquire approvals from American and European regulators to sell their generic medicine in those markets.

In order to conduct these bioequivalence tests, CROs recruit healthy volunteers on whom the generic drug is administered so as to generate data on its dissolution profile in human bodies. This data is generated by measuring the blood and urine of volunteers at specified intervals in order to measure the rate at which the drug is being metabolized by the human body. In order to establish bioequivalence to the innovator's drug, the generic drug formulation will have to demonstrate a rate of dissolution equal or similar to that of the innovator's drug. This is measured by the area under a graph which plots the rate of dissolution against a time period. Once the data is generated by the CRO, it is submitted to the foreign regulators as a part of the regulatory process to seek approval for the sale of generic formulation in each country's markets.

However, if the generic formulation of the innovator drug fails to demonstrate bioequivalence with the innovator drug during the course of a bioequivalence study, the pharmaceutical company manufacturing the generic copy could face delays in launching its product in the market because it would necessarily have to go back to the drawing board and improve its formulation and then go through a second round of bioequivalence tests. All of this takes time and in a hyper-competitive market, these delays could cause millions of dollars in potential losses. In some countries like the United States, which has a unique regulatory mechanism under the Hatch Waxman Act, launching the first generic formulation can result in a windfall gain of millions of dollars for a period of six months.

Given these financial implications, there is a huge incentive for generic pharmaceutical companies to collude with CROs in cases where the generic formulation has failed to complete the bioequivalence study successfully and fabricate the results to demonstrate bioequivalence data. The simpler scam is to pass off the innovator's drug as the generic drug i.e., instead of providing its own generic formulation to the CRO, the manufacturer of the generic drug seeking approval will misrepresent the innovator drug as its own generic drug to the CRO. This will virtually ensure a finding of bioequivalence in favour of the generic drug without having to necessarily collude with the management of the CRO. For example, in 1989, Bolar Pharmaceuticals, one of the pioneers in the American generic pharmaceutical industry, was caught red-handed for passing off to a CRO an innovator drug as its own generic formulation for the purposes of a bioequivalence study.[53] Less than two decades later, a pioneer of the Indian generics pharmaceutical industry—Ranbaxy Laboratories—was suspected of indulging in similar fraud.[54]

The genesis of the Ranbaxy scandal was at a Hyderabad-based CRO, Vimta Labs, which had been contracted by Ranbaxy to generate the required bioequivalence data for a number of its generic AIDS drugs. An inspection was conducted by the WHO on behalf of the South African government which was buying anti-retroviral drugs from Indian generic manufacturers. A French inspector by the name Olivier LeBlaye, who led one of the inspections on Vimta Labs in 2003 on behalf of WHO, questioned the integrity of the bioequivalence and other data generated by the CRO for Ranbaxy's drugs.[55] That one inspection opened the can of worms for Ranbaxy, culminating in its guilty plea in 2013.

In the years that followed the guilty plea by Ranbaxy, regulators around the world began focusing their attention not just on manufacturing facilities owned by Indian pharmaceutical companies but also Indian CROs. The object of such inspections was to examine whether the CROs were adhering to Good Clinical/Laboratory Practices (GCP/GLP) while conducting bioequivalence testing on behalf of generic pharmaceutical companies. GCPs and GLPs are designed to create a system of documentation that can be inspected in order to assess the data-integrity of the bioequivalence study. Typically, these GCP/GLP practices require the use of software and equipment that creates an audit trail making it difficult for the staff at CROs to engage in retrospective manipulation of data.

Typically, CROs may fabricate data for one of two reasons. The first is if the generic drug fails the bioequivalence test; in which case the client-generic company may pressure the CRO to manipulate records to demonstrate bioequivalence so as to not delay launch plans for the generic drug. The second reason for manipulation may just be poorly trained staff who cut corners without any pressure from the client-generic pharmaceutical company. Since proof of outright fraud is usually difficult to collect, unless a whistleblower can provide such information, in most of these cases evidence of a pattern of poor documentation practices at a CRO can lead to a presumption of poor data-integrity practices at the CRO. Foreign regulators can be unforgiving of data-integrity issues because there is no way for regulators to verify the bioavailability of a drug through conventional laboratory techniques and no regulator is going to replicate bioequivalence studies on actual human volunteers, due to the cost and resources involved. This is why any discrepancies with regard to data integrity are severely punished by regulators.

During the course of the last six years, at least seven Indian CROs have been accused of significant failures to adhere to GCP/GLPs by American and European regulators. The seven CROs in question were Alkem Laboratories Ltd[56], Semler

Research Centre Pvt Ltd[57], Quest Life Sciences Pvt Ltd[58], GVK BioSciences Pvt Ltd[59], Micro Therapeutic Research Pvt Ltd[60], Panexcell Clinical Lab Pvt Ltd[61], and Synchron Research Services Pvt Ltd.[62]

It is interesting to note that in each of these cases, multiple foreign regulators investigated the aforementioned Indian CROs across the span of a decade. While Semler and Synchron had been investigated by the USFDA, Quest Life Sciences had been investigated first by British, Spanish, and German regulators[63] followed by representatives of WHO. GVK Biosciences had been investigated by the French regulator and Micro Therapeutic Research had been jointly investigated by Austrian and Dutch regulators. Panexcell was investigated by Austrian, German, and American regulators at different times and accused of irregularities by all three regulators.

A recurring allegation during the inspections of Quest Life Sciences, GVK Biosciences, and others was the suspected fabrication of electro cardiogram (ECG) data. It is generally standard practice to record ECG data as part of a bioequivalence study in order to monitor the health of the volunteers. Monitoring the health of volunteers is particularly important in the Indian context because it has been well documented that many volunteers sign up for multiple bioequivalence studies and clinical trials at the same time because of the financial incentives offered by CROs for participating in these trials.[64] This is dangerous for the volunteers. There is at least one reported instance of a volunteer dying during a bioequivalence study, allegedly, at GVK Biosciences.[65] Rather than actually monitoring the health of these volunteers, a persistent problem with Indian CROs is the tendency of their staff to fabricate ECG data by recording the names of different volunteers against the ECG of a single patient. Such fabrication likely takes place in order to save time and effort but at the cost of safety of the volunteers. Fabricated ECGs reflect very poorly on CROs because it demonstrates a cavalier approach toward both the safety of volunteers and standard operating procedures laid down in the law, raising doubts about the rigour with which the rest of the data has been recorded.

A second problem with the Indian CROs has been the failure of staff to maintain records accurately. This is a problem across the entire CRO sector in India. An illustrative example of poor documentation practices from the "Notice of Concern" issued by the WHO after inspecting Quest Life Sciences is as follows:

> As inspectors entered the bioanalytical laboratory, laboratory staff members were seen in the process of completing records, some of them back-dated. An apparent attempt was made to hide documents from inspectors.[66]

Similarly, the European Medicines Agency (EMA), while announcing action against Micro Therapeutics Research Labs revealed that inspections by Austrian and Dutch regulators "identified several concerns at the company's sites regarding misrepresentation of study data and deficiencies in documentation and data handling".[67] As per the EMA, the problems with handling data included "...the practice to generate source data retrospectively, documentation of incorrect information, overwriting and changing raw data without ensuring the readability of the initial entry and the practice to apply implausible changes without giving a sound justification."[68]

This issue of poor documentation and back-dating of records is endemic to the Indian pharmaceutical industry, including at manufacturing facilities, and reflects a culture of poor training and poor compliance across the board.

A third problem identified with Indian CROs has been the fabrication of the final results of the bioequivalence studies i.e., the drug likely failed the bioequivalence testing but the results were manipulated in order to enable the client pharmaceutical corporations to obtain regulatory approval. Finding evidence of such fabrication without information from whistleblowers is very difficult. In the case of the USFDA's inspection of Semler Research Centre, the American inspectors claimed to have found a spreadsheet on one of the computers documenting in detail data manipulation in some of the older bioequivalence studies. Semler Research Centre of course denied the allegation levelled against it, claiming that a former rogue employee who had left to work for a competitor had covertly placed the spreadsheet on its computer server to undercut the CRO's business.[69]

A similar allegation was made by a whistleblower against GVK Biosciences accusing it of replacing the dissolution profiles of 14 volunteers participating in a bioequivalence study for a generic drug in order to make it look like the generic formulation was indeed bioequivalent to the innovator drug. The trial was being conducted for a major Indian pharmaceutical company that was looking to launch its generic drug in the United States. The French regulator found the accusations made by the whistleblower to be credible.[70] Although the USFDA, which was the recipient of the data, did not take any public action against the Indian company in question, it is worthwhile to note that the company withdrew its marketing application for the generic drug flagged by the whistleblower from the American regulator.

Similarly, both Panexcell and Synchron were accused by the USFDA of submitting "falsified study data" thereby raising doubts about the bioavailability data generated at the firms.[71]

The nature of these regulatory actions is such that the regulator conducts the inquiry and provides an opportunity to the company to respond before deciding to take action. There is no trial or jury in such cases and the punishments can vary depending on the issues discovered during inspections.

These alleged infractions by Indian CROs were punished by foreign regulators in different ways. In many of these cases, regulators announced the cancellation of all drug approvals granted on the basis of studies at the CRO found to be in violation of GCPs. This hurts the pharmaceutical companies that have engaged these CROs to generate regulatory data for their drugs.

After the French investigation into GVK Biosciences, the EMA on July 15 2015 cancelled the approval of 700 drugs whose manufacturers had relied on GVK Biosciences for generating data that was submitted to various European regulators.[72] Two years later, the EMA suspended 300 drug approvals because these approvals were based on unreliable data from Micro Therapeutics.[73] Similarly in 2016, the USFDA cancelled approvals secured on the basis of studies at Semler.[74] In July 2020, the EMA recommended the cancellation of marketing authorizations of all generic medicine that were approved on the basis of bioequivalence studies at Panexcell.[75] The USFDA in September 2021 announced the cancellation of all drug authorizations based on data generated at Synchron Research Services and Panexcell Clinical Lab because of data-integrity issues.[76]

These cancellations affected not just Indian pharmaceutical companies but also a significant number of American and European pharmaceutical companies who were outsourcing their bioequivalence studies to Indian CROs because of the lower costs of such studies in India. Apart from scorching the reputation of these CROs in the eyes of their clientele, cancellation of drug approvals by foreign regulators also triggers contractual litigation between the CROs and their customers who can now legitimately sue for damages suffered due to the cancellations.

In some cases, CROs like Semler Research Centre tried suing the USFDA before a federal court in the United States demanding damages for the loss of business it suffered as a result of the USFDA's public announcement. The case was eventually dismissed in 2019.[77]

The most controversial fallout of an Indian CRO scandal was in the GVK Bio case. After the European regulator ended up cancelling the approval of approximately 700 generic drugs of various Indian and foreign pharmaceutical companies because of suspect data from GVK Biosciences, the matter quickly escalated with the Indian Government getting involved and threatening to sue the EU before the World Trade Organization (WTO).[78] The basis of such action before the WTO was never clear, especially since regulatory issues are not covered by the WTO Agreement. The Indian government also called off ongoing free trade talks with the EU in retaliation to the action taken against GVK Biosciences.[79] Some senior officials from the Indian Government including the then incumbent DCGI, G.N. Singh, made some truly bizarre statements on the controversy. He stated in pertinent part, "One must understand that there is a bigger game being played out here. I have repeatedly stated that multinational pharmaceutical companies constantly use incidents like this to bring disrepute to Indian generic drug makers."[80] The DCGI never produced any evidence to indicate that multinational pharmaceutical companies were behind the EMA's moves. In fact, many multinational pharmaceutical companies suffered from the cancellations because they too had got their drugs tested at GVK Biosciences. The Europeans did not blink in this stand-off. The Indian government never did sue the EU before the WTO and eventually restarted trade talks.[81]

Many years later in 2021, after much wrangling, obfuscation, and an appeal under the RTI Act, the CDSCO finally gave us a copy of the report of the investigating committee set up by the DCGI to investigate GVK Biosciences. The report was barely two pages long. The only relevant observation in the report was as follows:

> The committee also reviewed the ECGs mentioned in the recent ANSM report and found some to be very similar between different subjects raising the doubt of duplication. However this did not affect, in any way, the safety and well being of the subjects nor did it affect the determination of bioequivalence, which was the main objective of the studies, as already acknowledged by the ANSM.[82]

Obviously, the committee appears to have found some merit in the allegations made by the French regulator about fabrication of ECG reports, but then, rather bizarrely concludes that such fabrication would not affect the safety of the subjects. This was a bizarre conclusion because if the ECG reports were in fact being fabricated, it meant that the health of volunteers was not being monitored as per the approved study protocols. If the health of the volunteers was not being monitored and the approved study protocols were not being followed, how could anybody assume that the rest of the study data had not been tampered with? The CDSCO's report is silent on this issue.

We also filed requests under the RTI Act 2005 with the CDSCO, asking them specific questions in relation to some of the CRO scandals in India. At the first level, the Public Information Officer often refused to give us any information by invoking exceptions under Section 8 of the RTI Act 2005. The only information we received at this level was that Quest Life Sciences was investigated by the CDSCO and its licence to conduct bioequivalence studies was suspended for a grand total of 15 days! Further information was denied by invoking specific exemptions in the RTI Act 2005 that prohibit the sharing of information that may impede an investigation.[83] When we filed an appeal before a senior officer at the CDSCO, we were given a list of remedial action taken by Quest Life Sciences but were not told of any action taken by the CDSCO against Quest Life Sciences. We followed up with another request for information under the RTI Act 2005, more than four years later in 2021, asking the DCGI's office whether it had completed its investigation into Quest Life Sciences and if so, to provide us with a copy of the report. We received a one-line reply stating that the information sought could not be provided because of the exemptions in Section 8(1)(e) and (h) of the RTI Act 2005 i.e., it would impede an ongoing investigation as well as be in violation of the fiduciary duty owed by the DCGI to Quest Life Sciences.[84] Apart from the surprising fact that the investigation continued for more than four years without an outcome, there is also the fact that the DCGI as a regulator actually does not owe a fiduciary duty to these companies.

Even with regard to a publicly announced probe into nine CROs by the CDSCO in the year 2011, after reports of various malpractices and at least one death at one of these CROs, the CDSCO refused to provide us with any information on the outcome of the probe merely stating that a show-cause notice had been served on two of the CROs and that information about an ongoing investigation could not be shared under the RTI Act 2005.[85] This, despite the fact that our request for information had been filed in 2017, several years after the scandal was reported in the press in 2011.[86] The fact that the investigation was not completed six years later is telling of the regulator's lackadaisical attitude towards this crisis at Indian CROs; but the story does not end over there. We filed another request for information under the RTI Act 2005 in October 2021, asking for a copy of the final investigation report. This time, the CDSCO claimed it did not have any information with respect to the said investigation. An appeal to the departmental appellate authority resulted in a similar answer.[87]

Some of the other replies received were even more bizarre. For example, when we asked the CDSCO for a copy of its inspection report into Semler Research, we were told that while it had been informed of the USFDA investigation and that it had proposed its own investigation, "no information with respect to further action is available. Hence no investigation report is available"![88] We were not provided with a reason as to why the proposed investigation never took place.

In the end, the only two reports given to us by the CDSCO under the RTI Act pertained to the investigations conducted into Micro Therapeutics Research Labs and another CRO for which we did not even request any information.[89] Stunningly, the CDSCO redacted the names of the officers who carried out the investigations! From the final reports, it was clear that the CDSCO officials did not really follow up on accusations by foreign regulators against Micro Therapeutics Research Labs. The CDSCO's investigation report did not strike us as rigorous or aimed at unearthing data-integrity issues.

As should be obvious by now, the CDSCO has traditionally done a poor job in regulating CROs. With the enactment of the New Drugs and Clinical Trial Rules 2019, the Ministry of Health has on paper introduced a marginally better legal framework for CROs conducting BA/BE studies. Moreover, since it chose the route of writing its own rules rather than asking Parliament to amend the law, it follows that the Ministry of Health could not provide for any criminal offences meaning that at most it could only cancel the licences of erring CROs. Given the history of scandal and opacity in the regulation of Indian CROs, the only way to build trust in both the industry and the regulator is to insist on a culture of unrelenting transparency. The new rules do little to increase transparency.

The stability question: How "stable" are Indian generic medicines?

Separate and apart from bioequivalence, the other critical problem with Indian generics is the issue of stability testing which in most countries is presumed to be the most basic of quality regulations. That has unfortunately not been the case with Indian law or its pharmaceutical industry. For example, one of the main charges against Ranbaxy by the United States government and its agencies, leading to the historic guilty plea by the company in 2013, was the failure of Ranbaxy to comply with mandatory regulatory requirements in America for "stability testing" of each batch of drugs being shipped to the American market.[90]

There is a reason that the American legal system takes the failure to comply with regulations on stability testing so seriously. A poorly synthesized and formulated drug that is not stable will degrade as it travels through the supply chain. An unstable drug can break down for a number of reasons that include changes in temperature, humidity, and exposure to sunlight. The degradation can also happen due to the type of ingredients used in the drug. This includes the active pharmaceutical ingredient (API), the binder used to increase adhesion of the formulation, additives such as flavouring agents etc. If any of these ingredients degrade, it can either cause impurities in the drug or reduce the therapeutic efficacy of the drug. For example, wax, which is used as a binder, may degrade into oil at high temperatures and this oil can become rancid over time and react with the API to generate chemical substances that may have unintended consequences for patients.

In most instances, patients themselves will not know that a formulation has become unstable unless the degradation manifests itself in the form of visual discolouration of the formulation or emanate some kind of odour. It is therefore imperative that pharmaceutical companies conduct stability testing before they release a batch of their product to the market and continue such testing throughout the lifecycle of the batch until the expiry date. Before batch release, this stability testing is conducted in special chambers by exposing formulations to elements like heat, light, and humidity in an effort to replicate the conditions that shipped consignments may face while travelling through the supply chain. After the batch is subject to these conditions in these special chambers, the samples are subject to regular pharmacopeial testing in the laboratory to check for impurities, the rate of dissolution, an assay test, etc. After batch release, retained samples of each batch are tested through the life-cycle until expiry. If a batch that has been released fails any of this pharmacopeial testing, the manufacturer should publicly announce the recall of the batch from the market. If a batch fails stability testing before it is released in the market, the manufacturer should be required to destroy the batch. In both instances, the manufacturer faces a loss of revenue and at times, a loss of face because of which there is very little incentive for manufacturers to carry out stability testing or announce recalls unless mandated by the law.

In a country like India, with its heat, humidity, and stressed supply chains, it is absolutely vital to mandatorily conduct stability testing before and after batch release to ensure that every formulation shipping out to the market is stable and remains that way for the duration of its expected journey, till it reaches the patient. Shockingly however, India for the longest time simply did not mandate stability testing for all generic drugs being sold in the country. As explained earlier, India essentially has two different regulatory regimes, one for "new drugs", a status which exists for the first four years after the DCGI approves a new drug for the Indian market. Thereafter from the fifth year onward, manufacturers are only required to approach the state drug controllers for manufacturing licences. For unknown reasons, the regulatory data requirements until recently have been different for each of these categories. Thus, while all drugs, even generics, in the "new drugs" phase have been required to submit stability data to the DCGI since 2001[91], there was no requirement for manufacturers seeking manufacturing licences for generic drugs from state drug controllers, after expiry of the four year "new drugs" phase, to submit any stability data. From a regulatory standpoint, it is absurd to treat the same class of drugs to different regulatory requirements. The policy silence on stability testing was particularly worrying because of the safety and efficacy implications for patients.

In 2013, at a meeting of the DCC, the lack of stability testing for all generics entering the market after the four-years mark was identified as a "serious lacuna" by the committee. The following is an extract from the minutes of the DCC meeting discussing the issue of stability testing:

> Since there is no requirement as a condition of license of proving that drugs are stable under recommended conditions of storage for other than Patent & Proprietary Medicine in Drugs & Cosmetics rules it can lead to unstable products being licensed in the country. As it is serious lacuna, it is very important to put it in rules. Therefore, it is proposed that in condition of license (s) to manufacture drugs it shall be clearly written "in rule 71, 71-B in rule 76 etc." that——" The applicant shall, while applying for license to manufacture drugs, furnish to the Licensing Authority evidence and data justifying that the drugs are stable for proposed shelf life under the condition of storage recommended. The data shall be generated as per Appendix IX of Schedule Y.[92]

This recommendation to make stability testing mandatory for all drugs was accepted without much opposition. The relevant extract from the Minutes state the following:

> ...it is necessary that evidence and data of the stability of the drug products proposed to be manufactured by the licensee are required to be submitted to the regulatory authorities so as to ensure the stability of the drug formulations licensed in the country by the State Licensing Authorities.[93]

A few weeks later, this proposal to make stability testing mandatory for all generics, including those securing approval from state drug controllers, was approved even by the DTAB.[94] Despite this bureaucratic consensus in 2013 on making stability testing mandatory for all generic medicine, it would take until 2015 for the Ministry of Health to publish draft stability testing rules in the *Gazette of India* for public comment.[95] Astonishingly, even these draft rules were never converted into law! The reason for this bureaucratic inaction is not known. However, as explained in the minutes of later meetings of the DTAB, the pharmaceutical lobby had complained that such a requirement would affect the small and medium enterprises manufacturing drugs, and increase the cost of drugs. The relevant passage from the DTAB's minutes is extracted below:

> 2.3 The recommendations of the Board had been considered by the Central Government and a draft notification was published vide GSR 68(E) dated 03.02.2015 inviting comments from stakeholders.
>
> 2.4 The comments have been received from various stakeholders. Briefly, the major comments are that it would adversely affect the SMEs and increase the cost of majority of medicines, etc.[96]

This successful opposition from the pharmaceutical industry is revealing of both the influence wielded by the pharmaceutical industry on drug regulation in India as well as the complete indifference of the Indian pharmaceutical industry towards patient safety. In any event, it is likely that this opposition from the industry appears to have been enough to paralyze the decision-making machinery at the Ministry of Health. Industry profits had triumphed over concerns for public health; and not for the first time.

In 2016, we red-flagged this lack of mandatory stability testing in a report that we sent to the Ministry of Health containing recommendations for reform of the drug regulatory framework in India.[97] In the same year, the issue of compulsory stability testing was taken up once again by both DTAB and DCC. The DTAB reiterated its earlier recommendation to make stability testing compulsory.[98] The DCC which specifically stated that "representations" had been received regarding the lack of compulsory stability studies for all generic drugs in India, accepted the importance of stability testing, but did not specifically reiterate its support for the pending amendment to make stability testing compulsory for all generics.[99]

On 2 May 2017, the Ministry of Health once again published another set of draft rules on stability testing, inviting public comments.[100] These rules were, however, very vague. Unlike the draft rules from 2015 which simply extended the existing (albeit inadequate) stability testing requirements for "new drugs" to even those generic drugs approved by state drug controllers, the new draft rules made stability testing mandatory but without prescribing any standards or parameters that were to be met during the course of such testing! For example, it is necessary to state the conditions for which the drug has to be tested as stable. A country like India is classified as a Zone IV country, which means that drugs have to be stable for atmospheric conditions of 30 degree Celsius. Similarly, it is necessary for the law to provide some guidance on the batch strength from which the samples for testing are to be drawn. Most importantly, the law was silent on drug approvals already granted over the last several decades. Nevertheless, a year after the draft rules were published, the Ministry of Health officially notified the Drugs and Cosmetics (Third Amendment) Rules 2018 on 10 April 2018 making stability testing compulsory for all generic medicine manufactured in India.[101]

Even a year after these rules became the law, lobbies representing the small and medium units within the Indian pharmaceutical industry were publicly lobbying for a rollback of the requirement for mandatory submission of stability data for drug approval. One of these lobbyists made the following statement in the press, clearly putting industry profits before drug quality and public health:

> This is indeed a big challenge for existing as well as new manufacturers and becomes a hurdle for implementing the mission "Make in India" to invite new plant, will badly affect the export and unit in the pharmaceutical sector. Because due to this it shall take minimum 8 to 9 months to finish stability test and get product approval of molecules for commercial production for the new as well as existing manufacturing units, a delay which shall put a huge financial burden.[102]

Such comments from the pharmaceutical lobby are truly worrying because it demonstrates little concern for one of the most important quality control tests in the pharmaceutical industry.

Separate from this opposition, we seriously doubt the extent to which these new stability requirements are actually being enforced. As per one media report, a local pharmaceutical lobbying group in the state of Bihar was on a mission to have the state drug controller for Bihar removed because he sought to enforce stability testing requirements under the new amendments. A relevant extract of the news report is reproduced below:

> A pharmaceutical lobby group in Bihar is planning to approach the Central Drugs Standard Control Organisation (CDSCO) requesting the country's drug regulator to seek clarification from the in-charge drugs controller of Bihar for mandating submission of stability testing data along with application for renewal of manufacturing licences for products approved before 1988.
>
> The association of drug manufacturers sent one letter through RTI to the DC asking him to answer what guidelines

> he is following in mandating stability testing report for products approved before 1988. They marked a copy of the letter to the DCGI asking whether the national drug regulator is aware about the unilateral decision taken by Ravindra Sinha while discharging duties of a state drugs controller.
>
> The present drugs controller of our state is spoiling the pharma industry sector in Bihar. He is not supporting the industry, but only destroying it. Government is fully aware of his anti-industry activities. We have apprised of his actions to the health minister and to the health secretary. But somehow he is still continuing on the seat. In one way or other, the government itself is destroying the pharma industry in our state. So, we are approaching the CDSCO to take the issue seriously and recommend the state government for appointing a new drugs controller to support the industry, said one industry leader in anonymity.[103]

One of us, Dinesh Thakur, brought these issues to the notice of the Ministry of Health in two petitions in 2019 and 2020, seeking urgent reform of both the new stability testing rules and also the existing, inadequate stability testing requirements in Annexure IX. In those same petitions, we had requested the government to consider setting up an expert committee to study the issues raised by us so that a scientifically sound policy could be put in place to guide state drug controllers.[104] The Ministry has not even acknowledged our petitions; much less provide substantive replies.

Even presuming the Ministry of Health does take corrective action on the policy front, we are doubtful of the extent to which Indian pharmaceutical companies will actually conduct mandatory stability testing and whether the Indian regulators, especially state drug controllers, have the capacity to conduct rigorous inspections like American and European regulators to ensure data is not being fabricated. Our concern is based on the slew of allegations made by foreign regulators accusing Indian pharmaceutical companies of regularly fabricating stability data for drugs being exported to their jurisdictions. The Indian pharmaceutical industry has a high incentive to fabricate stability test reports because a batch that fails stability testing will have to be destroyed. This means lost revenues, and depending on the size of the batch, such financial loss can be massive, especially if it triggers other contractual violations.

The future of generics in India—an interim labelling requirement for bioequivalent and stability-tested drugs

Prime Minister Modi never went through with his promise of enacting a law to force doctors to prescribe drugs only by their generic names. The question however remains as to whether the Indian state and its regulators can guarantee to the medical profession and patient community, that generic drugs manufactured in India are therapeutically equivalent and interchangeable with the innovator drug. We think not.

This is not because we doubt the science of similarity between generics and innovator drugs. We absolutely believe that it is possible for most generics to be bioequivalent to their innovator counterpart. Our concern rather is with the shoddily drafted regulations, the poorly equipped regulators and the overwhelming political might of the pharmaceutical industry that has already delayed implementation of these essential regulations for way too long. We need to ask ourselves as to why bioequivalence testing was made mandatory in India for all generic drugs only in the year 2017 when the United States had made it compulsory as early as 1977. We need to ask similar questions on why stability testing was made mandatory for all generics in India only in the year 2018 when the rest of the world has mandated such testing since the birth of the modern pharmaceutical industry. Why was such a crucial quality-control measure delayed for so long, especially in a country like India with its climate and challenging supply chain?

One possible answer to the above questions is the fact that the Ministry of Health, which is responsible for formulating safety and quality standards under the Drugs and Cosmetics Act 1940, simply lacks the expertise and "capacity" to make the necessary regulations. This would not be surprising, since it is well documented that the Indian Government lacks "state capacity" in several areas of governance. In fact, even in cases where it commissions external "experts" to study the issue and provide advice; as we have seen in many instances, the chosen experts deliver reports lacking in the rigour required of policy documents and legal regulations.

The other possible answer to these questions is the simple fact that the Government of India favours the growth of the Indian pharmaceutical industry over the health of its citizens and foreign trade partners because it has been "captured" by the powerful domestic pharmaceutical lobby in the country. Breaking the hold of industry over the government will require political intervention and that is quite difficult despite health being a politically sensitive subject.

Changing the status quo will take consistent and renewed public pressure from doctors and ordinary citizens invested in a regulatory framework that privileges public health over the profits of the pharmaceutical industry. In the meantime, there is the very real problem faced by doctors and patients in identifying the formulations of generic drugs that have been properly tested on quality parameters. It is doubtful if the new bioequivalence and stability regulations introduced over the last few years apply retrospectively, meaning that formulations approved prior to these regulations coming into effect have not been tested for bioequivalence and stability. If 95% of the generic drugs on the Indian market were approved prior to these regulations coming into effect in 2017 and 2018, then it would mean that 95% of the generic drugs in the Indian market have likely not gone through bioequivalence or stability testing. The government currently is showing no indication of enforcing these regulations retrospectively, possibly because of industry pressure. So how then are doctors and patients to identify those generic drugs that have successfully cleared bioequivalence and stability testing?

To help doctors and patients on this count, we propose that the government should introduce a mandatory labelling requirement for all drugs sold in India indicating whether the drug in question has successfully undergone bioequivalence and stability testing. Such a labelling requirement combined with a mandatory requirement to publicly disclose bioequivalence and stability data will give doctors the necessary information to ascertain the trustworthy formulations for themselves. Hopefully, such a labelling requirement will create pressure on the industry to voluntarily adhere to the bioequivalence and stability testing requirements even if the government does not enforce the regulations retrospectively.[105]

Notes

1. Saubhadra Chatterji, 'Modi Says Govt Will Bring Law to Push Doctors to Prescribe Generic Medicines' *Hindustan Times* (17 April 2017) <https://www.hindustantimes.com/india-news/pm-modi-says-govt-will-bring-law-to-push-doctors-to-prescribe-generic-medicines/story-g6kv0LZefi8KG2EcuyiPOP.html> accessed 16 August 2021.
2. Joe C Mathew, 'PM Modi Wants to End the Unholy Doctor-Drug Industry Nexus, but There Are Many Challenges' *Business Today* (20 April 2017) <https://www.businesstoday.in/latest/economy-politics/story/modis-generic-drug-pitch-is-noble-but-at-what-cost-80042-2017-04-20> accessed 16 August 2021.
3. Samiran Nundy, Keshav Desiraju and Sanjay Nagral, *Healers or Predators? Healthcare Corruption in India* (OUP 2018).
4. Jyoti Shelar, 'PM's Comment on Generic Drugs a Bitter Pill for Doctors' *The Hindu* (22 April 2018) <https://www.thehindu.com/news/national/pms-comment-on-generic-drugs-a-bitter-pill-for-doctors/article23638750.ece> accessed 16 August 2021; Himani Chandna, 'PM Modi Warns Pharma Companies Not to Bribe

Doctors with Women, Foreign Trips and Gadgets' *The Print* (13 January 2020) <https://theprint.in/health/pm-modi-warns-pharma-companies-not-to-bribe-doctors-with-women-foreign-trips-and-gadgets/347805/> accessed 16 August 2021.

5. Rhishikesh Thakre and Pralhad Patil, 'Generic Drugs: A Call for Balanced Approach' (2017) 54 *Indian Pediatrics*, 692; Anup Soans, 'Quality, Not Price, Is the Key Issue When Prescribing Generic Drugs in India' *The Wire* (1 May 2017) <https://thewire.in/health/drugs-generics-branded-health> accessed 16 August 2021; Yash Paul, 'Why Should I Not Prescribe Branded Drugs?' (2016) 9 *Indian Journal of Medical Ethics*, 138; Elizabeth Gourd, 'India's Generics-Only Drug Policy Could Put Health at Risk' (2017) 18 *The Lancet Oncology*, E373.
6. Sudip Chaudhuri, *The WTO and India's Pharmaceuticals Industry: Patent Protection, TRIPS, and Developing Countries* (OUP 2005) 246.
7. ibid 247. Other reasons include information asymmetry wherein consumers may not have enough information about different brands.
8. United States Senate (Sub-committee on Antitrust and Monopoly), *Study of Administered Prices in the Drug Industry* (Rep No 448, 1961).
9. Jeremy A Greene, *Generic: The Unbranding of Modern Medicine* (John Hopkins University Press 2014) 37–41.
10. ibid 49.
11. ibid 56.
12. ibid 56–58.
13. ibid 70.
14. ibid 93–94.
15. ibid 96.
16. Jerome Philip Skelly, 'A History of Biopharmaceutics in the Food and Drug Administration 1968–1993' (2009) 12 *The AAPS Journal*, 44.
17. Greene (n 9) 99–100.
18. ibid 100.
19. ibid 111.
20. Skelly (n 16) 46.
21. Daniel Carpenter and Dominique A Tobbell, 'Bioequivalence: The Regulatory Career of a Pharmaceutical Concept' (2011) 85 *Bulletin of the History of Medicine*, 93, 103.
22. ibid 106–107.
23. Skelly (n 16).

24. United States Task Force on Prescription Drugs, *Final Report* (Washington DC: Government Printing Office 1969); United States Task Force on Prescription Drugs, *Report of the Secretary's Review Committee of the Task Force on Prescription Drugs* (Washington DC: Government Printing Office 1969); Drug Bioequivalence Study Panel, *A Report of the Drug Bioequivalence Study Panel to the Office of Technology Assessment* (Congress of the United States 1974); National Research Council, *Drug Efficacy Study: Final Report to the Commissioner of Food and Drugs—Food and Drug Administration* (The National Academies Press 1969).
25. Greene (n 9) 118–120.
26. 'Bioavailability and Bioequivalence Requirements' 21 CFR 117 (1977).
27. Bernard E Cabana, 'Bioavailability/Bioequivalence' (1977) 32 *Food, Drug, Cosmetic Law Journal*, 512, 519.
28. Roger L Nation and Lloyd N Sansom, 'Bioequivalence Requirements for Generic Products' (1994) 62 *Pharmacology and Therapeutics*, 41.
29. Greene (n 9) 137–154.
30. 'Price Declines after Branded Medicines Lose Exclusivity in the U.S.' (IMS Institute for Healthcare Informatics 2016).
31. Dr G.B. Engel, 'The Introduction of a Dissolution Test in Pharmacopoeial Specifications', World Health Organization WHO/PHARM/70.459 as reproduced in Annexure II of the Drugs Consultative Committee (DCC), *'REPORT OF THE 15th MEETING OF THE DRUGS CONSULTATIVE COMMITTEE HELD ON 9th AND 10th March, 1972 AT NEW DELHI'* (1972) 308–312.
32. Government of India, Ministry of Petroleum & Chemicals, *Report of The Committee on Drugs and Pharmaceutical Industry (Hathi Committee Report)* (1975) 254.
33. Government of India, Ministry of Health and Family Welfare, *GSR 27(E)* (Gazette of India Extraordinary, Part II—s 3(i), 17 January 1981)—Drugs and Cosmetics (Amendment) Rules 1981.
34. Hathi Committee (n 32).
35. *Hoechst Pharmaceuticals vs C.V.S. Mani* ILR 1983 Delhi 548 (Delhi HC, 13 August 1982).
36. ibid para 29.
37. Shri Raique Alam to the Minister of Health and Family Welfare, Rajya Sabha Deb 5 November 1986, Question No 248, 124.
38. Kumari Pushpa Devi to the Minister of Health and Family Welfare, Lok Sabha Deb 20 November 1986, Question No 2655, 231.

39. Government of India, Ministry of Health and Family Welfare, *GSR 900(E)* (*Gazette of India Extraordinary*, Part II—s 3(i), 12 December 2001) (inserting Form 44 and Appendix 1A into the Drugs and Cosmetics Rules 1945).
40. Government of India, Ministry of Health and Family Welfare, *Report of the Prof. Ranjit Roy Chaudhury Expert Committee to Formulate Policy and Guidelines for Approval of New Drugs, Clinical Trials and Banning of Drugs* (2013) 5.
41. Drugs Consultative Committee (DCC), *'REPORT OF THE 47th MEETING OF THE DRUGS CONSULTATIVE COMMITTEE HELD ON 30TH AND 31ST JULY, 2014 AT NEW DELHI'* (2014) 9–10. <https://cdsco.gov.in/opencms/opencms/system/modules/CDSCO.WEB/elements/common_download.jsp?num_id_pk=ODA5> accessed 17 August 2021.
42. Dinesh S Thakur and Prashant Reddy T, *A report on fixing India's broken drug regulatory framework* (4 June 2016) (on file with authors).
43. Drugs Technical Advisory Board (DTAB), *'MINUTES OF THE 72ND MEETING OF DRUGS TECHNICAL ADVISORY BOARD HELD ON 27TH JUNE, 2016 AT NIRMAN BHAWAN, NEW DELHI'* (2016) 8–9 <https://cdsco.gov.in/opencms/opencms/system/modules/CDSCO.WEB/elements/common_download.jsp?num_id_pk=Nzcy> accessed 17 August 2021.
44. Vinod P Shah and Gordon L Amidon, 'G.L. Amidon, H. Lennernas, V.P. Shah, and J.R. Crison,' A Theoretical Basis for a Biopharmaceutic Drug Classification: The Correlation of In Vitro Drug Product Dissolution and In Vivo Bioavailability, Pharm Res 12, 413–420, 1995—Backstory of BCS' (2014) 16 *The AAPS Journal*, 894.
45. Office of Pharmaceutical Quality and the Office of Translational Sciences, Center for Drug Evaluation and Research (CDER), 'Waiver of In Vivo Bioavailability and Bioequivalence Studies for Immediate-Release Solid Oral Dosage Forms Based on a Biopharmaceutics Classification System Guidance for Industry' (Food and Drug Administration (USFDA) 2017.
46. Toshihide Takagi and others, 'A Provisional Biopharmaceutical Classification of the Top 200 Oral Drug Products in the United States, Great Britain, Spain, and Japan' (2006) 3 *Molecular Pharmaceutics*, 631.
47. Nehal A Kasim and others, 'Molecular Properties of WHO Essential Drugs and Provisional Biopharmaceutical Classification' (2004) 1 *Molecular Pharmaceutics*, 85; Dinesh Thakur to the Union

Minister for Health, 'Petition to Setup Expert Committee to Amend the Bioequivalence Framework Put in Place by the Drugs & Cosmetics (Ninth Amendment) Rules, 2017' (7 June 2020) <https://casemindia.org/wp-content/uploads/2020/06/BE-Petition.pdf> accessed 16 August 2021.

48. Lorena Barbosa Arrunátegui and others, 'Biopharmaceutics Classification System: Importance and Inclusion in Biowaiver Guidance' (2015) 51 *Brazilian Journal of Pharmaceutical Sciences*, 143 ("Although there was an increase in the number of applications of biowaiver based on BCS, this progress has been tempered by the lack of international harmonization and the reluctance of companies to adhere to the methodology due to fears raised by a possible delay in the registers."); Ines Leni and others, 'Overview of the European Medicines Agency's Experience With Biowaivers in Centralized Applications' (2019) 12 *Clinical and Translational Science*, 490; Barbara M Davit and others, 'BCS Biowaivers: Similarities and Differences Among EMA, FDA, and WHO Requirements' (2016) 18 *The AAPS Journal*, 612.
49. Government of India, Ministry of Health and Family Welfare, *GSR 327(E)* (*Gazette of India Extraordinary*, Part II—s 3(i), 3 April 2017).
50. Drugs Technical Advisory Board (DTAB) (n 43) 9, para 4.7.
51. Shardul Nautiyal, 'Health Ministry Soon to Exempt BA/BE Studies for Drugs Manufactured Solely for Export Purpose' *Pharmabiz* (10 December 2020) <http://www.pharmabiz.com/NewsDetails.aspx?aid=134044&sid=1> accessed 30 September 2021.
52. Dinesh Thakur to the Union Minister for Health, 'Petition to Setup Expert Committee to Amend the Bioequivalence Framework Put in Place by the Drugs & Cosmetics (Ninth Amendment) Rules, 2017' (7 June 2020) <https://casemindia.org/wp-content/uploads/2020/06/BE-Petition.pdf> accessed 16 August 2021.
53. Greene (n 9) 4.
54. Katherine Eban, *Bottle of Lies: The Inside Story of the Generic Drug Boom* (HarperCollins 2020) 127.
55. ibid 63.
56. EJ Lane, 'India's Alkem to Respond to European Data Fraud Probe' *FiercePharma* (17 April 2016) <https://www.fiercepharma.com/pharma-asia/india-s-alkem-to-respond-to-european-data-fraud-probe> accessed 18 August 2021.
57. Zachary Brennan, 'A Rogue CRO Employee, a Suspect Spreadsheet, and Now a $50m Lawsuit Against FDA' (*Regulatory Affairs*

Professionals Society (RAPS), 29 January 2018) <https://www.raps.org/news-and-articles/news-articles/2018/1/a-rogue-cro-employee,-a-suspect-spreadsheet,-and-n> accessed 18 August 2021.

58. Bureau, 'WHO Questions Integrity of Clinical Trials Data of Quest Life Sciences' *Business Line* (24 January 2018) <https://www.thehindubusinessline.com/companies/who-questions-integrity-of-clinical-trials-data-of-quest-life-sciences/article7395881.ece> accessed 18 August 2021.
59. PTI, 'GVK Bio Manipulated Clinical Trials of Generic Drugs: Reports' *The Economic Times* (5 December 2014) <https://economictimes.indiatimes.com/industry/healthcare/biotech/pharmaceuticals/gvk-bio-manipulated-clinical-trials-of-generic-drugs-reports/articleshow/45385764.cms?from=mdr> accessed 18 August 2021.
60. PTI, 'EMA Recommends Suspending 300 Drugs Tested by Indian CRO Firm' *Business Line* (15 January 2018) <https://www.thehindubusinessline.com/companies/ema-recommends-suspending-300-drugs-tested-by-indian-cro-firm/article9601315.ece> accessed 18 August 2021.
61. 'EMA Recommends Suspension of Panexcell-Tested Meds' *thepharmaletter* (28 July 2020) <https://www.thepharmaletter.com/article/ema-recommends-suspension-of-panexcell-tested-meds> accessed 30 September 2021.
62. Press Release, 'Questions and Answers Regarding Data Integrity Violations at Panexcell Clinical Lab and Synchron Research Services', *United States Food & Drug Administration* (16 September 2021) <https://www.fda.gov/drugs/drug-safety-and-availability/questions-and-answers-regarding-data-integrity-violations-panexcell-clinical-lab-and-synchron> accessed 23 September 2021.
63. Zeba Siddiqui, 'Serial Testers and Cursory Checks: India's Flawed Generic Drug Trials Business' *Reuters* (28 December 2016) <https://www.reuters.com/article/us-india-drug-testing-insight-idUSKBN14G1U6> accessed 18 August 2021.
64. Priyanka Pulla, 'Lured by Blood Money: Serial Volunteers Set a Disturbing Trend' *The Hindu* (30 December 2017) <https://www.thehindu.com/opinion/op-ed/lured-by-blood-money-clinical-trials/article22328296.ece> accessed 18 August 2021.
65. 'Man Undergoing Drug Test Dies in Andhra' *The New Indian Express* (7 December 2008) <https://www.newindianexpress.com/states/andhra-pradesh/2008/dec/07/man-undergoing-drug-test-dies-in-andhra-8853.html> accessed 18 August 2021.

66. Letter from Dr Mark McDonald, Coordinator, Pre-qualification Team, World Health Organisation to Dr Sivakumar, Quest Life Sciences Pvt Ltd (No P5-447-3/DM/MM/SC, 30 June 2015).
67. EMA Press Office, 'EMA Recommends Suspension of Medicines Due to Unreliable Studies from Micro Therapeutic Research Labs' *European Medicines Agency* (24 March 2017) <https://www.ema.europa.eu/en/news/ema-recommends-suspension-medicines-due-unreliable-studies-micro-therapeutic-research-labs> accessed 18 August 2021.
68. Committee for Medicinal Products for Human Use (CHMP), 'CHMP Assessment Report' (European Medicines Agency (EMA) 2017) EMA/420215/2017.
69. Brennan (n 57).
70. ANSM, *Final Inspection Report of GVK Biosciences* (Inspection Reference No: GCP-121501-FR, 11 July 2013).
71. Letter from Sean Kassim, Director, Office of Study Integrity and Surveillance, USFDA to Mr Umesh Mishra, CEO of Panexcell Cinical Lab Pvt Ltd at p.3 undated <https://www.fda.gov/media/151569/download> accessed 24 September, 2021; Letter from Sean Kassim, Director, Office of Study Integrity and Surveillance, USFDA to Dr. Shivprakash Rathnam, Managing Director, Synchron Research Services Pvt. Ltd. at p.3. undated < https://www.fda.gov/media/151570/download> accessed 24 September, 2021.
72. Asit Ranjan Mishra and Udgirkar Trushna, 'EU Defends Ban on 700 GVK Biosciences Drugs' *Mint* (8 August 2015) <https://www.livemint.com/Politics/BB5yiv1k6Upq6vB2z385JI/EU-defends-ban-on-700-GVK-Biosciences-drugs.html> accessed 18 August 2021.
73. EMA Press Office (n 67).
74. The United States Food and Drug Administration (USFDA), 'Notification to Pharmaceutical Companies: Clinical and Bioanalytical Studies Conducted by Semler Research Are Unacceptable' (20 April 2016) <https://www.fda.gov/drugs/drug-safety-and-availability/notification-pharmaceutical-companies-clinical-and-bioanalytical-studies-conducted-semler-research> accessed 18 August 2021.
75. EMA Press Office, 'Panexcell Clinical Laboratories: suspension of medicines over flawed studies' *European Medicines Agency* (24 July 2020) < https://www.ema.europa.eu/en/news/panexcell-clinical-laboratories-suspension-medicines-over-flawed-studies> accessed 30 September 2021.
76. The United States Food and Drug Administration (USFDA), 'Notification to Pharmaceutical Companies: Clinical and Bioanalytical

Studies Conducted by Panexcell Clinical Lab or Synchron Research Services are Are Unacceptable' (16 September 2021) <https://www.fda.gov/drugs/drug-safety-and-availability/notification-pharmaceutical-companies-clinical-and-bioanalytical-studies-conducted-panexcell> accessed 30 September 2021.

77. *Semler Research Center Pvt Ltd v United States Food and Drug Administration and Ors* [2018] United States District Court for the Central District of California 2:18-CV-00534.
78. Reuters, 'India May Take WTO Action against EU over Drug Clinical Trials: GVK Bio' *Business Line* (23 January 2018) <https://www.thehindubusinessline.com/companies/india-may-take-wto-action-against-eu-over-drug-clinical-trials-gvk-bio/article7104897.ece> accessed 18 August 2021.
79. Bureau, 'India Defers FTA Talks with EU on Drug Ban Issue' *Business Line* (23 January 2018) <https://www.thehindubusinessline.com/economy/india-defers-fta-talks-with-eu-on-drug-ban-issue/article7503152.ece> accessed 18 August 2021.
80. Vidya Krishnan, 'A Love Story That Cost GVK Its International Reputation' *The Hindu* (8 October 2015) <https://www.thehindu.com/news/national/A-love-story-that-cost-GVK-its-international-reputation/article60296519.ece> accessed 21 April 2022.
81. Amiti Sen, 'India, EU Agree to Re-Start Talks on Free Trade Pact Early next Year' *Business Line* (22 November 2015) <https://www.thehindubusinessline.com/economy/india-eu-agree-to-restart-talks-on-free-trade-pact-early-next-year/article7905816.ece> accessed 21 April 2022.
82. Reply to RTI application dated 7 December 2021, CDSCO (Application No CDSCO/A/E/21/00117, 12 October 2021).
83. Reply to RTI application dated 12 December 2017, CDSCO (Application No DTGHS/R/2017/80446, 8 November 2017).
84. Reply to RTI application dated 21 September 2021, CDSCO (Application No CDSCO/R/E/21/00393, 17 August 2021).
85. Reply to RTI application dated 13 December 2017, CDSCO (Application No DTGHS/R/2017/80448, 8 November 2017); TNN, 'Clinical Trials: DCGI Faults 9 More CROs' *The Times of India* (20 July 2011) <https://timesofindia.indiatimes.com/city/hyderabad/clinical-trials-dcgi-faults-9-more-cros/articleshow/9290503.cms> accessed 21 April 2022.
86. ibid.
87. Reply to RTI application dated 19 December 2021, CDSCO (Application No CDSCO/A/E/21/00118, 12 October 2021).

88. Reply to RTI application dated 7 December 2021, CDSCO (Application No CDSCO/A/E/21/00116, 12 October 2021).
89. ibid.
90. *United States of America vs Ranbaxy USA, Inc* [2013] United States District Court for the District of Maryland 1:13-cr-00238-JFM, 10; *The United States of America ex rel Dinesh S Thakur vs Ranbaxy USA, Inc* [2012] United States District Court for the District of Maryland 1:07-cv-00962-JFM, 19.
91. Government of India, Ministry of Health and Family Welfare, *GSR 900(E)* (*Gazette of India Extraordinary*, Part II—s 3(i), 12 December 2001) (inserting Form 44 and Appendix 1A into the Drugs and Cosmetics Rules 1945).
92. Drugs Consultative Committee (DCC), '*REPORT OF THE 46TH MEETING OF THE DRUGS CONSULTATIVE COMMITTEE HELD ON 12TH AND 13TH NOVEMBER, 2013 AT THE HOTEL METROPOLITAN NEW DELHI-110001*' (2013) 28 <https://cdsco.gov.in/opencms/opencms/system/modules/CDSCO.WEB/elements/common_download.jsp?num_id_pk=ODA4> accessed 21 August 2021.
93. ibid 29.
94. Drugs Technical Advisory Board (DTAB), '*MINUTES OF THE 65TH MEETING OF DRUGS TECHNICAL ADVISORY BOARD HELD ON 25TH NOVEMBER, 2013 IN THE CHAMBER OF DGHS, NIRMAN BHAWAN, NEW DELHI-110002*' (2013) <https://cdsco.gov.in/opencms/opencms/system/modules/CDSCO.WEB/elements/common_download.jsp?num_id_pk=NzY1> accessed 21 August 2021.
95. Government of India, Ministry of Health and Family Welfare, *GSR 68(E)* (*Gazette of India Extraordinary*, Part II—s 3(i), 3 February 2015).
96. Drugs Technical Advisory Board (DTAB), '*MINUTES OF THE 72ND MEETING OF DRUGS TECHNICAL ADVISORY BOARD HELD ON 27TH JUNE, 2016 AT NIRMAN BHAWAN, NEW DELHI*' (2016) 5 <https://cdsco.gov.in/opencms/opencms/system/modules/CDSCO.WEB/elements/common_download.jsp?num_id_pk=Nzcy> accessed 21 August 2021.
97. Thakur and Reddy, (n 42).
98. Drugs Technical Advisory Board (DTAB), *MINUTES OF THE 72ND MEETING* (n 43) 5, 25.
99. Drugs Consultative Committee (DCC), '*REPORT OF 50TH MEETING OF DRUGS CONSULTATIVE COMMITTEE HELD*

ON 04 & 05TH NOVEMBER, 2016 AT NEW DELHI' (2016) 25-27 <https://cdsco.gov.in/opencms/opencms/system/modules/CDSCO.WEB/elements/common_download.jsp?num_id_pk=ODEy> accessed 21 August 2021.

100. Government of India, Ministry of Health and Family Welfare, *GSR 429(E)* (*Gazette of India Extraordinary*, Part II—s 3(i), 2 May 2017).
101. Government of India, Ministry of Health and Family Welfare, *GSR 360(E)* (*Gazette of India Extraordinary*, Part II—s 3(i), 10 April 2018).
102. Laxmi Yadav, 'Pharma SMEs Seek Rollback of Mandatory Submission of Stability Test for Drug Approval' *Pharmabiz* (11 February 2019) <http://pharmabiz.com/ArticleDetails.aspx?aid=114054&sid=1> accessed 21 August 2021.
103. Peethaambaran Kunnathoor, 'Drug Manufacturers in Bihar to Approach DCGI to Complain against State DC for Anti-Industry Policies' *Pharmabiz* (17 April 2019) <http://www.pharmabiz.com/NewsDetails.aspx?aid=115253&sid=1> accessed 21 August 2021.
104. Dinesh Thakur to the Union Minister for Health, 'Petition to setup Expert Committee to amend the framework put in place by the Drugs & Cosmetics (Third Amendment) Rules, 2018 for stability testing of drugs' (7 June 2020) <https://casemindia.org/wp-content/uploads/2020/06/Stability-Petition.pdf> accessed 21 August 2021; Dinesh Thakur to the Union Health Secretary Preeti Sudan, 'Petition regarding stability testing' (25 April 2019) <https://dineshthakur.com/wp-content/uploads/2020/06/Letter-to-Preeti-Sudan_2.pdf> accessed 25 September 2021.
105. Nautiyal (n 51).

CHAPTER SEVEN

The Losing Battle to Regulate Traditional Indian Medicine

At the height of the first wave of the Covid-19 pandemic in India in the year 2020, the Indian media aired a most extraordinary press conference by the yoga-guru-turned-entrepreneur, Baba Ramdev, in his avatar as the founder of Patanjali Ayurved, a company that shot to fame for its herbal, ayurvedic and swadeshi products ranging from toothpaste to ayurvedic "cures". At the press conference, Ramdev proclaimed to the world the discovery of an Ayurvedic remedy, Coronil, that had apparently proved its "effectiveness" in treating Covid-19 during "clinical trials". In the ensuing publicity campaign, Patanjali claimed to the press that Coronil had proven 100% effective during clinical trials conducted at its facilities.[1]

At any other time, for any other disease, Ramdev could have made a similar claim and escaped with minimal scrutiny. However, to make such a claim at the height of a pandemic that was claiming thousands of lives daily, especially when the world's best scientific minds were struggling to find a cure for Covid-19, was pushing the boundaries of credulity of even the otherwise gullible Indian population. Initially, the Government of India and various state governments, which were already dealing with the fallout of the pandemic and its mounting death toll, made feeble attempts to restrain Ramdev from making such outlandish claims, only to settle for him marketing his "cure" as an "immunity booster".[2] In the later days of the pandemic, the Minister of Health and Family Welfare, Harsh Vardhan, appeared alongside Baba Ramdev as the latter released the results of the "clinical trial" of Coronil.[3] The Indian Medical Association and other groups of doctors lashed out at the Minister for endorsing what they described as an "unscientific product".[4] Nevertheless, sales of Coronil were reportedly well in the range of ₹250 crores by early November 2020, just as the first wave of the pandemic began to ebb.[5]

This entire fiasco was the result of policies actively peddled by the Government of India since independence to validate Ayurveda by attempting to mimic the language and techniques of modern medicine without paying heed to the scientific temperament or intellectual rigour that underlies the development of modern medicine. These attempts to establish the viability of traditional medicine, especially Ayurveda, in face of the steady popularity of modern medicine dates back to the time around India's independence from the British when India had to make several important decisions between the traditional and the modern in different areas ranging from the ideological foundations of its Constitution to its economy. More often than not, Indian policymakers tried to balance the demands of various interest groups by retaining elements of the traditional to placate the conservative elements within the society, while also pushing ahead with modernization. In the context of medicine, this struggle between the traditional and modern manifested itself in debates between the practitioners of traditional medicine and modern medicine, which by the time of independence from the British had already taken firm roots in India.

This debate over a "national medicine" for independent India initially appeared to have been settled when the political class, in 1946, categorically endorsed the recommendations of a high-profile committee called the Health Survey and Development Committee, better known as the Bhore Committee after its chairperson—Joseph Bhore. This committee had recommended the adoption of modern scientific medicine without specifically labeling such medicine as "Indian" or "western". Despite being set up by the British-India government, the Bhore Committee's recommendation received the endorsement of the provincial health ministers in 1946 and was set to become the foundational health policy document for independent India.[6]

The implicit refusal of the Bhore committee to endorse traditional medicinal systems like Ayurveda and Unani did not go un-noticed by the proponents of traditional medicine. After a public outcry over this issue, the Government of India set up yet another committee to study indigenous medicine in India and the manner in which Ayurveda and Unani could be bolstered and perhaps combined with modern medicine.[7] Named the "Committee on Indigenous Systems of Medicine", it was headed by Col Sir R.N. Chopra of the IMS. Chopra was a Cambridge-educated pharmacologist who also headed the Drugs Inquiry Committee 1931 that preceded the Drugs and Cosmetics Act 1940. The other members of the committee were three vaids practicing Ayurveda, three hakims practicing Unani, and two other practitioners of modern medicine. The final report of the committee was unabashed in its praise of Ayurveda, which it described as a "Hindu medicine" dating back to the Vedic age of Indian history. Sample the following extract from the "introduction" of the report:

> About the beginning of the Christian era Ayurveda, (or Hindu Medicine), had reached its apogee and had spread far and wide influencing deeply the systems of medicine in Egypt, Greece, Rome and Arabia. The influence of the Hindu Medicine was not confined to ancient and medieval periods alone. Through

> its influence on Greek medicine and through the influence of the Greek on Arabian medicine and of the Arabian on the medicine in Europe, the Ayurvedic system can well claim to be the chief, though remote source, from which the mighty river of Western medicine has had its beginnings.[8]

Separate from these declarations of Ayurveda as "Hindu medicine" and the "chief" source of medical knowledge for the rest of the world, the report also declared Ayurveda to be the only "native to soil"[9] medicinal system in India and attributed the decline of Ayurveda to the invasions by the Mughals who brought in their own medicinal system called Unani which then declined because of British colonialism and its import of western medicine. The following extract from the report makes clear this narrative:

> Ayurveda which is based on the Vedas, was developed systematically more than three thousand years ago, and made great progress both on the preventive and curative side of medicine. When India was subjected to foreign domination Ayurvedic medicine received a setback. The Unani Tibb is not strictly speaking indigenous to India. It came with the Mohammedan rule and gained popularity generally in those areas where Muslims were in the majority and was developed by State support under the Muslim rule. When the British came to India the Western medicine was introduced and came to be adopted as the State system of relief. As a consequence, Ayurveda and Unani Tibb both declined.[10]

Many of the above facts are disputed by modern historians who argue that the Brahmins of Vedic society actively discriminated against healers because the latter were considered to be "impure" given the nature of their profession, especially the requirement to handle bodily fluids like blood or pus. Modern historians claim that these denigrated healers came to join Buddhism, opening the window for some kind of institutionalization of medicine in Buddhist monasteries and it is this consolidated body of medical knowledge that came to be reflected in ancient texts like *Charakasamhita* and *Sushrutasamhita*. This school of thought also points out that the knowledge of medicine found in the vedas is primarily magico-religious (involving prayers and lucky charms) unlike the medicine found in *Charakasamhita* and *Sushrutasamhita* which is mostly "empirical-rational" and only marginally magico-religious.[11]

It is important to pay attention to the manner in which the Committee on Indigenous Systems of Medicine framed the entire issue, especially its unabashed attempt to link specific religions to identified medicinal systems and demarcate the "indigenous" medicinal systems from the "foreign" medicinal systems. Classification of Ayurveda as the Hindu medicine and hence its characterization as truly "indigenous" medicine was a crude attempt by the Committee to appeal to the baser political instincts of Hindus by making them view the issue through the communal lens of "Hindu-Muslim" politics that had set the country on fire in the 40s. Rather than cultivate the idea that the evolution or decline of medicinal systems could be linked to any number of cultural, sociological and scientific factors, the report preferred to fall back on the politics of religion; and if anything, was a dog-whistle to the politics of Hindu nationalism that insisted on viewing India as a Hindu country.

The more damaging aspect of this Committee's report was its demand to integrate what it defined as "Indian medicine" with "Western medicine". In its words:

> We believe that, while Indian medicine can take much of practical value from the Western medicine, the latter can also learn much from the philosophic background of Indian system, its comprehensiveness, the importance it attaches to the soil factor and dietary. Its generalisation of principles and the knowledge of truth gained by the use of supra-sensory perception.

> Opinion in favour of integration leading to synthesis has been expressed by exponents of Western end Indian medicine and by the prominent members of the lay public and we are of opinion that immediate steps should be taken in this direction.
>
> The first step to be taken in this regard will be the integration of courses of studies by arranging the curricula in such a way that whatever is weak in the one system is supplemented and strengthened by the strong points of the other system or systems.[12]

Ignoring for a moment the absurdity of relying on "supra-sensory perception" for medical treatment, it is necessary to point out that medicine, like most science and unlike most politics, is not open to the kind of compromises sought by the Committee on Indigenous Systems of Medicine. Sound, empirical policy making would require deploying modern scientific knowledge to conclusively test the fundamental theories of traditional medicine be it Ayurveda or Unani, without viewing the issue through the lens of religion or civilizational superiority. This is not all that complicated.

Let us begin with the Tridosha theory of Ayurveda, which is the most important Ayurvedic theory that is supposed to explain the workings of the human body and the cause of disease. The Tridosha theory presumes that three doshas namely Vata, Pitta and Kapha are the three pillars of life. Each dosha is presumed to draw its energy from a combination of five elements, i.e., space, air, water, fire, and earth. While each dosha has all five elements, two elements are supposed to be predominant in each. For example, Pitta is predominantly a combination of fire and water. These doshas are not to be mistaken as organs but rather as a form of "energy" that pervade the body while being concentrated in specific parts of the human body influencing certain aspects of functioning. Ayurveda characterizes each person's body type into one of these three categories of doshas. For example, pitta supposedly governs digestion, absorption, assimilation, nutrition, metabolism, body temperature. As long as pitta is in balance, it supposedly promotes understanding and intelligence. If it is out of balance, pitta supposedly arouses anger hatred, jealously, and inflammatory disorders.[13]

One account published by the Indian National Science Academy explained the workings of doshas in the following words:

> The three doshas work under impact of the environmental factors and consequently undergo fluctuations according to change in time (diurnal, nocturnal and seasonal), age and with relation to food.[14] An imbalance of doshas is considered to be one of the reasons for diseases in the human body, apart from external factors. As per this account, 'Doshas are indispensable factors in the diseases—process. No disease in the body takes place keeping the doshas apart. Doshas are real initiators and intimately related through all stages of the disease.'[15]

This concept of balance in Ayurveda has some similarities to the humoral theory of medicine that underlies Greek medicine, which also forms the basis of Unani. In fact, as pointed out earlier, many Ayurvedic practitioners claim that the humoral theory in Greek medicine was actually inspired by Ayurveda.[16] Like Ayurveda, which postulates the balancing of different energies, the humoral theory of medicine posits that all disease is caused by an imbalance of the four humors found in every human body—blood, phlegm, yellow bile, and black bile. The humors were supposedly linked to elements of nature. Blood was supposedly linked to air, phlegm was linked to water, yellow bile to fire, and black bile to earth.[17] Since a humoral imbalance was presumed to be the cause of disease, treatment options at the time aimed to restore the balance through painful treatments such as bloodletting, purging, sweating etc.

Both the humoral theory of medicine and the Tridosha theory should have lost all credibility after the scientific breakthroughs of the 19th century. These breakthroughs included the "Cell Theory" that identified cells as the basic constituents of life that were key to processing energy and the "Germ Theory" which proved that infectious diseases were caused by germs and microbes that could be transmitted from one person to another.[18] These theoretical breakthroughs combined with knowledge of human anatomy gleaned from dissections of human bodies revolutionized medicine across the world.

While most countries, both developed and developing, have rightly discarded the humoral theory of medicine, the Indian state has been deeply invested in keeping alive Ayurveda and to a much lesser extent, Unani, since the early days after independence in 1947. While further research maybe warranted into the medicinal properties of many herbs and plants listed in Ayurvedic texts, there was really no scientific rationale behind the push for more research into the theories of Ayurveda, such as the Tridosha theory. Yet, this was the demand of the time. In the years that followed the report of the Committee on Indigenous Systems of Medicine in 1948, five other committees set up to study the issue of traditional medicine produced five more reports on a variety of topics like research, training, and practice of traditional medicine.

The first was the *Report of the Committee on Research in Ayurveda* setup by the Government of Bombay, Health and Local Government Department (1950), also known as the Bombay Committee Report. The second was the *Report of the Committee Appointed by the Government of India to Advise them on the Steps to be Taken to Establish a Research Centre in the Indigenous Systems of Medicine and other Cognate Matters* (1951) also known as the Pandit Committee Report. The third was the *Interim Report of the Committee*

Appointed by the Government of India to Study and Report on the Question of Establishing Uniform Standards in Respect of Education and Regulation of Practice of Vaidyas, Hakims and Homeopaths (1956) also called the Dave Committee Report. The fourth was the *Report of the Committee on Ayurveda Research Evaluation* (1958) also known as the Udupa Committee Report. The fifth was the *Report of the Shuddha Ayurvedic Education Committee* (1963).

Each of these committees were setup with the intent of advocating for traditional medicine, especially Ayurveda, and not to objectively evaluate the effectiveness of Ayurveda in treating patients. From a reading of these reports, it is clear that some of these committees were convinced of the superiority of Ayurveda's Tridosha theory over modern medicine as pioneered in the West.

For example, the Vyas Committee which had been setup to draw up a syllabus and curriculum for "pure" Ayurveda (as opposed to the integrative approach suggested by the earlier committees) had this to say about the Tridosha theory while comparing it to modern medicine:

> The Committee after giving considerable thought to the term, 'modern' medicine', 'scientific medicine', 'western medicine's 'allopathy' etc., feels that the application of the former two epithets 'modern' and 'scientific' exclusively to one medical system is unjustifiable and prejudicial to others. Theoretically the tridoshic basis of the human constitution in the Ayurvedic system appears to be more consistent and coherent as a whole than that of the stray and non-coordinated concepts of individual idiosyncracies, susceptibilities, immunities and allergies. From this angle the former may be considered more scientific and modern than the latter, particularly as long as the former concept remains undisproved. As stated earlier, far from effectively disproving the constitutional approach, the western medicine is itself veering round to what may, with good reason, be called a neo-Ayurvedic approach, as revealed

> by the introduction of the terms, ectomorph, endomorph, mesomorph, stress, natural immunities and susceptibilities psychosomatic conditions, etc. The Committee is, therefore, of the opinion that the exclusive reservation of the term 'scientific' for a single system of medicine, howsoever well organised it may be, should always be avoided.[19]

Another example can be found in the following excerpt from the report of the expert committee setup by the Government of Bombay in 1949 which demanded greater research into the Tridosha theory:

> If the Tridosha theory is proved to have a scientific basis, it follows clearly enough that deficiency or excess in any of the Doshas would cause an unbalance, which can return to normality by supplying the deficiency or removing the excess...
>
> It is absolutely essential to devise methods that can indicate the presence or absence of any of these Doshas qualitatively. Accurate diagnosis would further require a quantitative estimation of the same. Blood-examination, in all its aspects, has been suggested by some as one of the methods of elucidating the presence and quality of these Doshas. Patients suffering from well-defined and gross derangements of the Doshas might prove useful subjects of study in the beginning in a Bio-Chemical Laboratory. Should the blood examination not lead to a conclusive result, it cannot discredit the original Tridosha theory but can only show that this approach is unsuitable.[20]

The closing line of the above excerpt demonstrates the absurdity of the entire enterprise wherein the method is presumed to be flawed if it disproves the hypothesis. This goes against every principle of rational science. Sadly, this line of thinking pervades the deliberations of all of these committees whose sole objective seems to be active "promotion" of Ayurveda rather than a critical evaluation of the theory, the methods, and the outcomes resultant from these practices.

Yet, the political pressure appears to have been so great that the Indian state actually began to take seriously demands put forth by the practitioners of traditional Indian medicine. The state support for traditional medicine manifested itself in the enactment of new laws creating legal frameworks, which often imitated existing frameworks for modern medicine without understanding or explaining the difference between both systems of medicine. Hence, the Drugs and Cosmetics Act 1940 was amended in 1963 to officially recognize and regulate both Ayurvedic and Unani medicine. In 1970, a new law called the Indian Medicine Central Council Act was enacted to officially recognize the right of the Ayurvedic and Unani practitioners to practice Indian medicine, except on more than one occasion, these practitioners of Indian medicines have trespassed into the domain of modern medicine by prescribing antibiotics and painkillers instead of confining themselves to prescribing traditional medicine.

Along with these regulatory reforms, the Government of India also created a "research ecosystem" dedicated to traditional medicine and began spending thousands of crores of rupees funding research into these areas. Each of these regulatory moves have seriously endangered public health in India as will be explained in the next few pages.

The faulty regulatory model created for traditional "cures"

Separate and apart from the questionable theories underlying Ayurveda is its vast arsenal of herbs, roots, leaves, and other plant-based concoctions that are supposed to cure various diseases. This again should not be viewed as something exceptional or unique to India. Other ancient civilizations also have a tradition of using herbs and plants to treat various ailments. The ancient Greeks and Chinese are two such examples.[21]

Traditionally, plant-based "cures" in Ayurveda were

delivered to the patient in the form of "pastes" or "extracts" by crushing the plant or its parts. The aim being to extract the "juice" by crushing it or by decoction i.e., boiling the plant or its parts in water to dissolve the chemicals from the plant into water. Viewed through the lens of modern science, ancient practitioners of Ayurveda were basically trying to extract the active ingredient of the plant that had medicinal properties but they lacked the tools or knowledge of chemistry to identify and separate the precise active ingredient that exhibited curative properties. In the context of Ayurveda, while modern science has validated the medicinal properties of certain traditional "cures", such as neem[22], it is still skeptical about another famous traditional remedy—turmeric.[23]

In the modern era, many of these Ayurvedic "cures" have morphed into mass-manufactured tablets, capsules, and syrups that mimic the packaging of modern medicine without having to establish their efficacy and safety through clinical trials. Even presuming that some of these traditional cures like neem have medicinal properties, it is a whole new challenge to mass-manufacture and package them for sale as commodities with a long shelf-life. This requires a degree of skill in modern chemistry since it involves manufacturing a formulation that preserves the properties of the active ingredient over a reasonable period of time.

The issue of regulating these various Ayurvedic "cures" in India came up as early as 1927 when the Council of States (one of the legislative bodies under the Government of India Act 1919), was debating a resolution on the need for a drug regulation law in India.[24] While the focus of that debate was on modern medicine and false advertizing, the issue of Ayurvedic "cures" did come up during the debates. Some members called for a more detailed investigation into the efficacy of traditional medicine using the tools of modern science, while other members had expressed their concern that the new drug regulatory law would be used to throttle the Indian Ayurvedic industry.[25] The fear of the British using this new law to stifle the growth of domestic Indian industry was not new. Other members had expressed similar fears about the British using this law to stymie the growth of the domestic industry specializing in modern medicine. These concerns were not all that surprising since colonialism was largely about economic exploitation of the Indian sub-continent. At the same time, there were also members of the Council of States who were less worried about possible discrimination against traditional medicine and more concerned with the efficacy of traditional medicine, especially Ayurveda which was quite popular in that day and age. These members called for a systematic review of Ayurvedic "cures" in light of the recent breakthroughs in modern science.[26]

The issue of regulating Ayurvedic "cures" was eventually examined by the Drugs Inquiry Committee which was setup by the British rulers of India in 1930, to study the need for a drug regulatory law in India.[27] This Committee highlighted two specific problems when it came to regulating Ayurvedic "cures". The first problem was resistance from the practitioners of Ayurveda. In the words of the committee:

> Some of the indigenous practitioners objected to it on merely sentimental grounds, saying that there is something higher and more vital in their systems which is inscrutable and impenetrable by modern science and which modern chemists cannot analyse and determine.[28]

This characterization of Ayurveda as being "something higher" that cannot be understood by modern science is quite revealing. This shows that many Ayurvedic practitioners of medicine, at that time, viewed their version of indigenous medicine as "magico-religious" rather than an empirical, rational science that could be understood by rational humans.

The second problem, according to the Drugs Inquiry Committee was the fact that the composition for many Ayurvedic "cures" was not known, making it impossible to standardize Ayurvedic remedies for mass consumption. It recommended a scientific study of Ayurvedic "cures" so as to make it possible to standardize such "cures".[29] This recommendation for standardization was in line with the regulatory model proposed for modern medicines, wherein a pharmacopeia would establish uniform standards against which any medicine would be tested, per scientifically accepted techniques in order to determine its quality. This was relatively easy to do with modern medicine given the developments in modern chemistry and biology. The exact ingredients or a serum or an antibiotic could be identified and measured for characteristics such as toxicity, purity, and weight. Such knowledge also made it possible to lay out uniform testing methods. This was not possible with traditional medicine like Ayurveda unless there was complete disclosure of the ingredients that went into these cures, and more importantly, a scientific understanding of the ingredients themselves. In the concluding words of the committee:

> Unless and until these drugs are investigated on scientific lines, control is not feasible. The useful remedies should be separated from the inert and useless by a proper scientific study and the potent drugs should be analysed and standardized before any steps can be taken.[30]

For reasons not clear, the subsequent Drugs and Cosmetics Act 1940 enacted by the Legislative Assembly for British India covered only modern medicine and did not address traditional medicines such as Ayurveda etc. Perhaps this reluctance to cover traditional medicine was in line with the British policy of keeping away from issues deemed to be sensitive to the sentimentalities of the Indian people.

Post-independence from the British, the first serious attempt by the Government of India to regulate the traditional medicines sector, especially Ayurveda, was in 1963 when a Bill—The Drugs and Cosmetics (Amendment) Bill 1963—to amend the Drugs and Cosmetics Act 1940 was introduced in Parliament. Explaining to Parliament the need for regulation of Ayurveda and other traditional medicinal systems like Unani, the Health Minister said that apart from complaints of adulteration of Ayurvedic "cures" that were raised in Parliament and other fora, there was also the fact that the manufacture of these "cures" had shifted hands from traditional vaids and hakims to companies that used mass manufacturing techniques to produce these "cures". Such mass manufacture, according to the Minister, required some form of regulation by the state.[31]

However, the model of regulation proposed by the new legislation did not require investigation and standardization of Ayurvedic and Unani "cures". Rather, the limited focus of the legislation was to ensure that manufacturers of traditional "cures" could manufacture only those "cures" that were listed in the 54 Ayurvedic texts, 28 Siddha texts, and 12 Unani texts, that were mentioned in the proposed "First Schedule" to the Drugs and Cosmetics Act 1940. These texts include the ancient *Charakasamhita* which is presumed to have been first written between 100 BCE and 200 CE and subsequently revised by different practitioners. The problem however is that the First Schedule does not mention any specific version/publisher for each of the traditional texts. Over the centuries, each of these texts could have been revised and translated or mistranslated any number of times. Without specifying an authoritative version of these texts, the regulatory model proposed by this legislation was likely an entirely pointless exercise. Perhaps that was its precise intent; to merely create an illusion of regulation.

The rest of the amending legislation aped the regulatory model for modern medicine. The new regulatory bodies for traditional medicine proposed by this legislation mirrored those for modern medicine under the Drugs and Cosmetics Act 1940 i.e., there would be an Ayurvedic and Unani Drugs Technical Advisory Board to advise the government on technical policy issues related to traditional medicine.[32] Similarly, there would be specific drug inspectors and government analysts for traditional medicine. As with the case for modern medicine, Ayurvedic and Unani "cures" could now be manufactured only in facilities licensed by the government.[33] Labelling and certification requirements were also inserted to protect consumer interests.[34]

The major and very significant difference between the existing regulatory model for modern medicines and the one proposed for traditional "cures" by the legislation in 1964, was that only the former created a system of standardization via a pharmacopeia, which is a publication that contains uniform methods to characterize and test the identity and quality of each drug on the market. Simply put, the pharmacopeia is what ensures that any two pills of paracetamol are the same across the country despite being manufactured by different companies. Since the enactment of the Drugs and Cosmetics Act 1940, any failure of modern medicine to pass the quality tests prescribed under a recognized pharmacopeia could result in the prosecution of the manufacturer for selling NSQ drugs. The law at the time was clear that the British Pharmacopeia or the British Pharmaceutical Codex, amongst others, were legal recognized standards for modern medicine.[35] These standards prescribed by the pharmacopeia were at the heart of the regulatory model for modern medicine.

The regulatory model for traditional medicine sought to ape the regulatory model of modern medicine without copying the foundational concept of standardization through a pharmacopoeia. Without a standardized pharmacopeia, there could be no standardized tests for regulators to test the ingredients of Ayurvedic and Unani "cures". This was a huge lacuna because most traditional "cures", especially Ayurvedic "cures", consist of extracts of plants or leaves or herbs. In their natural form, each plant or leaf or herb will have differences in quality and quantities of the active ingredient, which is why it is important to standardize the active ingredient extracted from these plants or leaves or herbs. This issue becomes more important in an age where production had shifted from individual hakims and vaids preparing remedies on the spot for a specific patient to a system of mass manufacture. Now preservatives, colouring agents, and other excipients such as binders were required to be added to traditional "cures" in order to formulate them as tablets or capsules and store them for a longer time as "commodities" on the shelf of supermarkets and pharmacies. All of this was being done without any understanding of the possible interactions between the traditional cures and these various excipients.

Without standardization of these traditional "cures", there could be no uniformity or consistency in the market and hence no way to test these traditional "cures" for their quality. Simply put, if there were no legally recognized standards, there was no question of selling NSQ Ayurvedic "cures". All these issues had been pointed out by the Drugs Inquiry Committee back in the year 1931, more than 32 years before the present legislation was introduced in Parliament. That Committee pointed out the impossibility of regulating the traditional medicine industry without some level of standardization of traditional medicine itself. To conduct such standardization and bring some much needed order to the hitherto chaotic world of traditional medicine, it would have been necessary to conduct some level of scientific inquiry into traditional medicine, but the political fallout of such an inquiry would have likely been unpalatable for any government.

The other big question, which the legislation of 1963 did not even try to tackle was whether the many "cures" mentioned in traditional Ayurvedic and Unani texts actually had any "therapeutic efficacy"; whether in their natural form or as a formulation. This would have required putting in place a mechanism to rigorously validate all claims made by the manufacturers of traditional medicine, whether Ayurvedic or Unani, through double-blind randomized controlled clinical trials as is done for modern medicine. This was never done; perhaps it was never a priority of any administration to scientifically establish the therapeutic efficacy of these "cures".

Given the lack of any standardization or efficacy requirement, the regulatory model brought in by this new amendment to the Drugs and Cosmetics Act in 1964 was mostly pointless.

Unfortunately, when this legislation to regulate Ayurveda, Unani, and other traditional medicine was debated in Parliament in 1963 and 1964, there was surprisingly little skepticism amongst Members of Parliament about the efficacy of both traditional "cures" and the proposed regulatory model to regulate the traditional medicine industry. The "scientific temperament" encouraged by the late Prime Minister Nehru was mostly missing in the parliamentary debates concerning the issue of regulating traditional medicines like Ayurveda and Unani. The sentiment in Parliament on the issue of traditional medicine, was summarized in the Rajya Sabha by the Deputy Minister of Health, Dr D.S. Raju, in the following words:

> Several hon. Members made out a case for Ayurvedic and Unani medicines. There is no doubt about their scientific aspect. We are all agreed that Ayurvedic and Unani systems are great and ancient sciences. They have stood the test of time. It does not require any proof as to their efficacy. And

> now since independence gradually Ayurvedic and Unani are coming into prominence. More and more patients are seeking their assistance, thousands and thousands.[36]

The Minister appears to have missed the irony of his claim that no "proof" of "efficacy" was required for Ayurveda and Unani, while at the same time maintaining that there can be no doubt about the "scientific aspect" of these systems. What is science, without the requirement of any proof or evidence to substantiate supposedly scientific claims?

Only one MP from the Lok Sabha, Chandrabhan Singh, an elected representative from Bilaspur in the Lok Sabha expressed skepticism about both the efficacy of Ayurvedic medicine and the regulatory model put forth by the government in the Bill. On the point of efficacy, he provided the House with examples of a supposedly potent Ayurvedic drug that turned out to be a dud when examined in a modern scientific laboratory using the tools of modern science.[37]

The "cure" in question was *Makaradhwaja,* a well-known Ayurvedic "cure", that contains mercury and gold, and which at the time was used as a cardio-vascular stimulant by Ayurvedic practitioners. According to Chandrabhan Singh, after the Central Drug Research Institute (CDRI) at Lucknow had tasked a well-known scientist—Dr Ramnath Chopra, a pharmacologist who was educated at Cambridge University and who had headed both the Drugs Inquiry Committee and the Committee on Indigenous Systems of Medicine—the work of studying Makaradhwaja, he came back with a finding declaring it to be inert, much to the "consternation" of all involved.[38]

In other words, once a well-known Ayurvedic "cure" was subject to scientific scrutiny, its credibility collapsed. It is a different story that Makaradhwaja continues to be marketed in India in the 21st century for a range of conditions such as "general weakness" to "anti-aging" as well as an "aphrodisiac".[39]

Equally pertinent were Chandrabhan Singh's astute observations about the faulty regulatory model proposed by the government's legislation. In particular, he pointed out the fallacy of quality testing when there was no pharmacopeia of standardized testing mechanisms for traditional medicine, be it Ayurveda or Unani. He pointed out how for vitamins, hormones, and other products of modern science and medicine, the law clearly required the following of standards regarding strength, quality, and purity as prescribed by institutions like the International Laboratory for Biological Standards etc. However, as correctly pointed out by Chandrabhan Singh, the legislation under discussion did not prescribe any standards for traditional medicine.[40] How then were inspectors meant to guarantee quality of these traditional "cures" in the absence of any standardization? As for the traditional Ayurvedic and Unani texts mentioned in the Schedule to the law, he warned that most of these books, which he classified as "ancient, not so ancient, not so modern and modern", use the same name for different drugs with each prescribing different quantities and qualities.[41]

The third and final observation by Chandrabhan Singh was the lack of laboratories with the equipment and skills to test traditional "cures". He provided the example of an instance where samples of a "Tonic tablet", manufactured by a big Ayurvedic firm were sent to the CDRI, Lucknow, for testing. In its report, CDRI reportedly stated that while the inorganic component had traces of iron and arsenic in it, the organic components could not be identified by the laboratory.[42] He asked the Minister:

> When this is the condition of testing by a world renowned laboratory where will the Government send the samples which they will collect from the various firms for examination and investigation?[43]

Chandrabhan Singh concluded his speech by imploring upon the government to rope in the country's sizeable scientific establishment, including the Indian Council for Medical Research (ICMR) and the All India Institute for Medical Sciences (AIIMS) for a rigorous testing program to test all traditional medicine for their efficacy and to collect scientific information that could be compiled in a separate pharmacopeia.[44] And only after such testing and collection of evidence of "efficacy", did he recommend these traditional "cures" be procured for use across the country.[45]

Unfortunately, the Deputy Health Minister paid only lip service to Chandrabhan Singh's incisive arguments during his closing speech in the Lok Sabha. The Minister kept making repeated references to Ayurveda's alleged "greatness" and how it was the government's duty to revive this supposedly "ancient science". He stated in pertinent part, the following:

> I am at one with the hon. Member who has suggested that Ayurveda is a great science. We agree. There is no dispute about it. It was there some thousands of years ago. But, unfortunately, just as we went down politically and otherwise the system also went under debris. It is our sacred duty now to renovate it and to remove that debris and bring it up to the level of our expectations...But there is no doubt that there is some inherent truth in Ayurveda. Otherwise, it would not have survived for all these thousands of years.[46]

The Minister's statement reflected the popular trope that traditional medicine systems, especially Ayurveda, had suffered only because of "foreign rule" and that it was time to reclaim India's scientific glory by investing in the past, rather than in the science of the future. Simply put, civilizational hubris had blinded most of India's Parliament to the utterly pointless regulatory system being put in place by the proposed legislation as a façade to provide legitimacy to traditional medicine.

The failed attempts to modernize regulation of the traditional medicine industry

As the decades passed, the Government of India tried adopting various strategies to improve regulation for the fast-expanding Ayurvedic industry. Most of these attempts have failed due to the reluctance of Indian policymakers to accept some basic scientific truths.

For example, starting in 1986, the Government of India began publishing an Ayurvedic Pharmacopeia, with each new version containing an expanding number of monographs of Ayurvedic "cures".[47] In 1995, it also took steps to make its Ayurvedic Pharmacopoeia legally binding on the Ayurvedic industry.[48] As explained earlier, pharmacopeias have provided the foundations for regulating the modern pharmaceutical industry by laying down uniform standards that ensure that different formulations (e.g., tablets) containing the same active pharmaceutical ingredient are identical in all material respects regardless of who manufactures them. Pharmacopeias do this by prescribing uniform testing protocols, and the body that produces such pharmacopeia also supplies reference standards to manufacturers and government laboratories to test the purity of the drugs in question.

The Ayurvedic Pharmacopeia, however, is nothing like the pharmacopeias for modern medicine. A modern pharmacopeia prescribes a range of tests that help determine the quality of a drug. These tests include the identity test, the assay test to determine the content of the active ingredient and dissolution test which measures the rate at which the drug dissolves in a solvent. It also prescribes methods to determine if the formulation contains any impurities. Dissolution testing is crucial for testing drugs being sold in the form of tablets because if a tablet fails to dissolve at the prescribed rate, i.e., become bioavailable, its active ingredient will not have the necessary therapeutic effect on the human body.

Despite conceding that many Ayurvedic manufacturers are marketing their "cures" as tablets and capsules, the Ayurvedic Pharmacopeia does not actually prescribe tests for dissolution of tablets or capsules.[49] As a result, most of the Ayurvedic "cures" being sold as tablets and capsules cannot be tested for their ability to dissolve in the blood stream to have therapeutic efficacy. In our opinion, this omission to prescribe dissolution testing was not a mistake but a conscious decision because ensuring uniform dissolution rates for an active ingredient in the form of a tablet or a capsule goes to the heart of advanced skills in chemistry, which most of the Ayurvedic industry does not possess. Prescribing rigorous standards for dissolution will likely have a material adverse effect on a large chunk of the Ayurvedic industry and hence was likely avoided by the Ayurvedic Pharmacopeia.

Instead, the primary focus of the Ayurvedic Pharmacopeia is on identifying and measuring the presence of certain active ingredients for a range of Ayurvedic "cures" using modern scientific tools and methods like thin-layer chromatography, liquid chromotography etc. This pharmacopoeia basically lists a range of plants/herbs, identifying the active ingredient in each herb and describing tests to identify the active ingredient. For example, for Apamarga, which is basically a herb, the monograph in the pharmacopoeia identifies the active ingredient as oleanolic acid. The monograph for Apamarga mentions the techniques to identify oleanolic acid and identifies its therapeutic uses as including piles, pain, disease of abdomen, obesity etc.[50] (The list of indications especially "disease of abdomen" is absurd. The monograph is silent on the source of these claims.) The monograph describes the method to identify oleanolic acid if the herb is sold in the form of a powder, water extract, or hydro-alcoholic extract. There are no tests in the pharmacopoeia for Apamarga sold as capsules or tablets.

More importantly, it should be noted that the Ayurvedic Pharmacopeia references only herbs and cures mentioned in traditional texts and not the "patent and proprietary" Ayurvedic cures which supposedly accounts for the bulk of the Ayurvedic trade in India.

The door to these "patent and proprietary" Ayurvedic cures was opened by a legislative amendment in 1982[51]. Historically, the phrase "patent or proprietary" has been used in drug regulatory law to describe new medicines not included in the pharmacopeia and whose ingredients were protected as trade secrets. One of the early measures of reforms in the 20th century was forcing manufacturers of "patent or proprietary" products to disclose their ingredients. Thanks to an amendment in 1982 to the Drugs and Cosmetics Act, manufacturers of traditional medicinal systems like Ayurveda could use ingredients mentioned in the existing traditional texts to create new formulations that find no mention in the traditional Ayurvedic and Unani texts that were previously recognized by the law of 1964. These new formulations, which for all practical purposes, were new medicines and not traditional medicine, should have been governed by the same framework as modern medicine.

Instead, this new framework created for "patent and proprietary" traditional medicine did not require the new formulations to prove their safety and efficacy as precondition to being sold in the market. This created a most bizarre state of affairs. Simply put, the Government of India was helping dupe its own citizens into believing they were consuming traditional medicines that were discovered thousands of years ago through the genius of their ancestors, while in reality allowing the private industry to dose Indian citizens with untested concoctions not found in any traditional texts.

Many decades later, in the year 2010, a new Rule 158B was inserted into the Drugs and Cosmetics Rules 1945, by the

Ministry of Health. This new rule required all manufacturers of traditional medicine to supply photocopies of published literature about traditional medicine to state regulators, as a pre-condition to manufacture the said medicine. The law was silent on the meaning of "published literature". Did it mean peer-reviewed publications or would any publication in any journal regardless of its quality, suffice? Further, Rule 158B also required manufacturers making new treatment claims for old formulations or manufacturing new "patent or proprietary" medicine to submit proof of "effectiveness" as a precondition for a manufacturing license. This could have been a potentially game-changing regulatory move, except for the fact that the law did not really require the standard double-blind randomized clinical trials that brought so much rigour to modern medicine since the late 1940s. Instead, Rule 158B required "Pilot study as per relevant protocol for Ayurveda, Sidha and Unani drugs". A footnote to this provision adds, "The standard protocol will also include concept of Anupan, Prakriti & Tridosh etc. published by Central Research Councils Ayurveda, Siddha, Unani and other Government/ Research Bodies." Even by the poor standards of drafting of legal and regulatory law within the Indian government, the aforementioned wording of Rule 158B is abysmal since it is lacking in clarity. If the idea was to genuinely generate data about the safety and efficacy of these new, yet traditional medicine, the government should have simply prescribed the same clinical trial standards prescribed for modern medicine; i.e., a double-blind RCT preceded by animal studies to generate some proof of concept. Instead, these rules made bizarre references to vague concepts like Prakriti and Tridosha which are yet to be established as having any scientific validity.

The same Rule 158B also introduced the requirement of safety studies for certain categories of Ayurvedic, Siddha, and Unani cures that contained poisonous substances such as "snake poison", "arsenic", and "mercury"! Yes, you read that right—it is permissible to use "snake poison", "arsenic", and "mercury" as long as "a safety study" establishes that it is okay to do so.

Perhaps due to the poorly drafted Rule 158B and its lack of guidance on the meaning of "pilot study", the Department of Ayush in the year 2013 released "Good Clinical Practice Guidelines" for "Clinical Trials in Ayurveda, Siddha and Unani Medicine".[52] In essence, these guidelines laid down a framework to guarantee scientifically rigorous ethical clinical trials. While these guidelines were a step in the right direction, the government also made it clear that these guidelines were completely "voluntary".[53]

Despite these guidelines, some manufacturers of "patent and proprietary" Ayurvedic, Siddha, and Unani formulations went the route of conducting poorly designed, half-baked clinical trials. From anecdotal evidence, we know that most of these trials were tremendously underpowered i.e., these trials were carried out on very small, statistically insignificant patient populations. Further, these trials also generally lack a comparator product and tend to be open label instead of being double blinded.

Then in 2018, the Ministry of Ayush threw up a new surprise when it issued a circular informing state drug regulators that Rule 158B did not require the conduct of any clinical trials, since the phrase "clinical trial" is not mentioned in the legal provision! According to the Ministry's circular, "experience or evidence of effectiveness of the ASU [Ayurveda, Siddha, Unani] drug based on textual rationale, published literature and pilot study [was] required in support of the claim of indication or use for issue of licence in accordance with the provisions of Rule 158(b)".[54] This circular went against everything contained in the aforementioned guidelines of the Department of Ayush from 2013 which literally had the phrase "clinical trials" in its title while explaining the expectations from Rule 158.[55] And so, the "circus" of law making ended with no requirement upon the Ayurvedic industry to establish the safety and efficacy of their products through rigorous clinical trials. So much for scientific temperament of the Ministry of Ayush!

An attempt to rein in the Ayurvedic industry by regulating its advertisements

The Achilles heel of the Ayurvedic drug industry is its constant need to make tall, almost unbelievable claims in advertisements that it publishes widely across different media. Such advertisements inevitably draw political attention. As far back as 2012, the Parliamentary Standing Committee had flagged misleading advertisements by the Ayush industry as a public health hazard and urged the government to review the working of the Drugs and Magic Remedies (Objectionable Advertisement) Act 1954—the only legislation to regulate drug advertisements.[56] The committee noted in pertinent part, the following:

> 13.6 The Committee was given to understand that a considerable number of AYUSH practitioners are making tall claims of very effective cure and treatment of various ailments, viral/bacterial/fungal infections, AIDS, cancer, Hepatitis etc. The Committee recommends that instead of ignoring such claims, the Department should make all out efforts to verify these claims and find out whether there is any substance therein. In case any of these claims are found to be true, the Department should initiate further research thereon and assist such claimants in developing their line of treatment in public interest.[57]

Over the years, some progress was made on this issue by the government, although there still remained considerable bureaucratic red-tape. While it was the Ministry of Ayush that was being hauled up by the Parliamentary Standing Committee, it was the Ministry of Health, that was actually responsible for amending the Drugs and Magic Remedies (Objectionable Advertisement) Act 1954.[58] When the process of reform had not yet been completed as of 2018, the Parliamentary Standing Committee severely criticized the Ministry of Ayush for its "laidback" approach on the issue of new legislation to curb the menace of misleading Ayush advertisements.[59] Before the publication of that report, the Ministry of Ayush had published a draft amendment aimed at changing the Drugs and Cosmetics Rules 1945 to regulate advertisements put out by the Ayurvedic industry but did not translate it into binding law. When we asked the Ministry of Ayush, via a request for information under the RTI Act in the year 2017, the reason for the delay in notifying into the law the draft amendment that it had published in the *Gazette of India* for feedback, we received the following reply from the Ministry:

> Draft Rule 170 could not be finalized so far owing to a large number of diverse comments from the stakeholders and the proposed amendment in the Drugs & Cosmetics Rules, 1945 has not been notified.[60]

Stripped of its bureaucratese, the above reply hints at the fact that an immense pushback from the very powerful Ayurvedic industry blocked the government's attempt to enact new rules. Nevertheless given the relentless pressure from the Parliamentary Standing Committee, the Ministry pushed through the amendments on 21 December 2018 and finally amended the Drugs and Cosmetics Rules 1945 to impose new restrictions on the advertisements of Ayush products.[61] This included a requirement to submit the advertisements to the Ministry of Ayush for prior approval and a straight out ban on advertisements if they featured certain material.[62] For example, misleading or exaggerated claims about the therapeutic effectiveness of the Ayurvedic product in question or if it featured references or photographs of any government labs or public officials, the advertisement would be rejected.

In less than a month after the rules were notified into law, the constitutionality of the same was challenged before the Delhi High Court by multiple litigants with commercial interests in the Ayush industry.[63] The list of litigants challenging the constitutionality of the rules were not vaids and hakims who had descended from the Himalayas to protect their craft but rather huge pharmaceutical and FMCG companies like Reckitt Benckiser, Perfetti Van Melle India, and Mankind Pharma as well as industry groups such as the Ayurvedic Drug Manufacturers Association (ADMA). These litigants argued, amongst other grounds, that the new rules restricting advertisements were an unconstitutional restriction on their fundamental right to speech. This constitutional challenge has been pending before the Delhi High Court since 15 January 2019, when the court took cognizance of the petition.[64] The industry appears to be unperturbed by these new rules as obvious from breathtakingly audacious advertizing campaigns that have been run in the Indian press in the last few years by some of the biggest Ayurvedic companies in India.[65]

The future of regulating the traditional medicinal industry

As it stands today, the regulatory model created for the traditional medicine industry has no element of standardization, a pharmacopeia that is not really a pharmacopeia and no requirement to establish safety and efficacy through scientifically rigorous and ethical clinical trials. Since Indian regulations regarding traditional medicine have liberally borrowed terminology, rather than scientific method, from modern science, the Ayurvedic industry often uses this very same terminology to give its products the veneer of scientific credibility. We saw this happen time and again during the Covid-19 pandemic.

Reforming this sector is politically challenging because the traditional medicine industry, especially Ayurveda, represents a potent mix of heady Hindu nationalism that revels in ancient India's glory and global capitalism, as obvious from the fact that multinational companies like Reckitt Benckiser, Perfetti Van Melle, and Mankind Pharma are involved in the constitutional challenge against Rule 170. Any attempt to question the safety and efficacy of these Ayurvedic cures can be painted as questioning the glory of India's ancient civilization. In addition, there are politically powerful companies like Baba Ramdev's Patanjali which have made huge investments in this area.

It may still be possible for public health advocates to push back against multinational companies but winning the battle against public sentiment is a bit more complicated when even mainstream political parties indulge in fantasies about Ayurveda's supposedly glorious past. Given this virtual political consensus, it is not surprising that an alarming number of Indians genuinely believe that Ayurveda has the answers for many of their medical problems. While some of this faith is tied to the framing of Ayurveda as an example of India's allegedly glorious Hindu past, there are several who believe in the supposedly herbal and "chemical free" properties of Ayurvedic medicine. Changing this perception in a country where "scientific temper" is fast disappearing is no easy task.

Any measure of reform will require a political class with the courage of conviction to follow the science on Ayurveda and Unani to its logical conclusion. That is unlikely to happen any time soon. As of now, the only viable regulatory option to tackle the Ayurvedic and Unani industry is to simply prohibit the entire industry from making any kind of therapeutic claims. This appears to be the easiest and most politically feasible regulatory model to implement on the ground. To that extent, the Ministry of Ayush has taken the right steps in notifying Rule 170, although there is room to sharpen the law on the point. This would in effect reduce Ayurvedic and Unani products to the status of food or supplements. If there is an Ayurvedic product that demonstrates the potential to "cure" or "treat" a disease or ailment, it should go through the same regulatory pathway as any other "new drug" i.e., a rigorous three-phased double-blinded RCT to establish its safety and efficacy. Imposing such a requirement on all Ayurvedic and Unani products will certainly face immense push back especially from the Ayurvedic industry.

Notes

1. Ravi Prakash Kumar, 'Coronavirus Treatment: Ramdev's Patanjali Launches Coronil Kit for 545' *Mint* (23 June 2020) <https://www.livemint.com/news/india/coronavirus-vaccine-coronil-patanjali-baba-ramdev-press-conference-live-updates-11592893304534.html> accessed 10 September 2021.
2. Shiv Kumar, 'Maharashtra Bans Baba Ramdev's Coronil' *The Tribune* (25 June 2020) <https://www.tribuneindia.com/news/nation/maharashtra-bans-baba-ramdevs-coronil-104365> accessed 10 September 2021; BQ Desk, 'Ayush Ministry Stops Patanjali From Selling, Advertising Purported Covid Medicine' *Bloomberg Quint* (23 June 2020) <https://www.bloombergquint.com/business/ayush-ministry-stops-patanjali-from-advertising-purported-covid-medicine> accessed 10 September 2021; Milan Sharma, 'Ayush Ministry Allows Sale of Patanjali's Coronil as Immunity Booster' *India Today* (1 July 2020) <https://www.indiatoday.in/india/story/ayush-ministry-allows-sale-of-patanjali-s-coronil-as-immunity-booster-1695911-2020-07-01> accessed 10 September 2021.
3. 'Ramdev Launches Covid-19 Medicine Coronil, Harsh Vardhan Attends Event' *Hindustan Times* (19 February 2021) <https://www.hindustantimes.com/videos/news/watch-ramdev-launches-covid-19-medicine-coronil-harsh-vardhan-attends-event-101613737807861.html> accessed 10 September 2021; Dr Jammi Nagaraj Rao, 'By Publicly Endorsing a Commercial Drug, Did the Health Minister Cross a Line?' *The Wire Science* (23 February 2021) <https://science.thewire.in/the-sciences/harsh-vardhan-coronil-endorsement-patanjali-ayurved-pseudoscience-standard-of-behaviour/> accessed 10 September 2021.

4. 'IMA "Shocked" over Patanjali's Claim on Coronil; Demands Explanation from Harsh Vardhan' *The Hindu* (22 February 2021) <https://www.thehindu.com/news/national/ima-shocked-over-patanjalis-claim-on-coronil-demands-explanation-from-harsh-vardhan/article33902720.ece> accessed 10 September 2021.
5. Sanjay Sharma, 'Patanjali Sold 25 Lakh Coronil Kits Worth Rs 250 Crore in 4 Months' *India Today* (2 November 2020) <https://www.indiatoday.in/india/story/patanjali-sold-25-lakh-coronil-kits-worth-rs-250-crore-in-4-months-1737229-2020-11-02> accessed 10 September 2021.
6. Kiran Kumbhar, 'The Cure' *Fifty Two (52)* (30 April 2021) <https://fiftytwo.in/story/the-cure/> accessed 10 September 2021.
7. Government of India, Ministry of Health, *Report of the Committee on Indigenous Systems of Medicine (Chopra Committee Report)* (Vol I, 1948) 6–7.
8. ibid 2.
9. ibid 1.
10. ibid 8.
11. Kiran Kumbhar, 'The Forgotten Buddhist Origins of India's Ayurvedic Medicine' *Medium* (18 March 2021) <https://kikumbhar.medium.com/zysk-chattopadhyaya-history-ayurveda-india-medicine-buddhist-hindu-e85712cc9b52> accessed 10 September 2021; Kenneth G Zysk, *Asceticism and Healing in Ancient India: Medicine in the Buddhist Monastery* (Motilal Banarsidass Publisher 1998); Steven Engler, '"Science" vs. "Religion" in Classical Ayurveda' (2003) 50 *Numen*, 416.
12. *Chopra Committee Report* (n 7) 188.
13. Vasant Dattatray Lad, *Textbook of Ayurveda Vol. 1. Fundamental Principles of Ayurveda*, vol 1 (Ayurvedic Press 2002) 25–30.
14. V J Thakar, 'Basic Concepts of Ayurveda' in Priya Vrat Sharma (ed), *History of Medicine in India (From Antiquity to 1000 A.D)* (Indian National Science Academy, New Delhi 1992) 383.
15. ibid 386.
16. Lad (n 13) 30.
17. William Bynum, *The History of Medicine: A Very Short Introduction* (OUP Oxford 2008) 10–11.
18. ibid 97.
19. Government of India, Ministry of Health, *Report of the Shuddha Ayurvedic Education Committee (Vyas Committee)* (1963) 11.
20. Government of Bombay, Health and Local Government Department, *Report of the Committee on Research in Ayurveda (Bombay Committee Report)* (1950) 12.

21. Biljana Bauer Petrovska, 'Historical Review of Medicinal Plants' Usage' (2012) 6 *Pharmacognosy Reviews*, 1.
22. R Subapriya and S Nagini, 'Medicinal Properties of Neem Leaves: A Review' (2005) 5 *Current Medicinal Chemistry—Anti-Cancer Agents*, 149.
23. Andy Extance, 'Separating Turmeric Fact from Fiction' *Chemistry World* (11 November 2019) <https://www.chemistryworld.com/features/separating-turmeric-fact-from-fiction/4010612.article> accessed 13 September 2021.
24. Council of State Debates 9 March 1927, vol I, 515.
25. ibid 523.
26. ibid 515.
27. Government of India, *Report of The Drugs Enquiry Committee* (1930-31). See Chapter 2 to read more about the conclusions of the Drugs Inquiry Committee Report, 1931.
28. ibid 62, para 158.
29. ibid.
30. ibid 158.
31. Dr D S Raju (Deputy Minister in the Ministry of Health) in the Rajya Sabha (Official Reporter, 28 August 1963) 1837.
32. The Drugs and Cosmetics (Amendment) Act 1964, s 33C.
33. The Drugs and Cosmetics (Amendment) Act 1964, s 33D.
34. The Drugs and Cosmetics (Amendment) Act 1964, s 33N.
35. The Schedule to the Drugs Act 1940.
36. Dr Raju in the Rajya Sabha (n 31) 1891.
37. Chandrabhan Singh during debate on Drugs and Cosmetics (Amendment) Bill, Lok Sabha Debate 5 May 1964, 14330–14334.
38. ibid 14330–31.
39. '*Baidyanath Siddha Makardhwaj Special*' available at Amazon India <https://www.amazon.in/Baidyanath-Siddha-Makardhwaj-Special-Tablets/dp/B07HB9BDQZ> accessed 13 September 2021; 'Makardhwaj—Benefits, Dosage, Side Effects, Ingredients' (*AyurMedInfo*) <https://www.ayurmedinfo.com/2012/06/30/makardhwaj-benefits-dosage-side-effects-ingredients/> accessed 13 September 2021.
40. Singh in the Lok Sabha (n 37) 14329–30.
41. ibid 14330.
42. ibid 14331–32.
43. ibid 14332.
44. ibid 14332.
45. ibid 14333.

46. ibid 14359.
47. Government of India, Ministry of AYUSH, Pharmacopoeia Commission for Indian Medicine & Homoeopathy, 'Ayurveda Pharmacopeial Publication' <https://pcimh.gov.in/show_content.php?lang=1&level=1&ls_id=56&lid=54> accessed 23 September 2021.
48. The Drugs and Cosmetics Rules 1945, Rule 168.
49. Government of India, Ministry of AYUSH, Pharmacopoeia Commission for Indian Medicine & Homoeopathy, *The Ayurvedic Pharmacopoeia of India* (Part I, Vol IX, 2016) xxvii.
50. ibid 1–4.
51. The Drugs and Cosmetics (Amendment) Act 1982.
52. Government of India, Ministry of Health and Family Welfare, Department of AYUSH, *Good Clinical Practice Guidelines for Clinical Trials in Ayurveda, Siddha and Unani Medicine (GCP-ASU)* (March 2013).
53. ibid v.
54. Government of India, Ministry of Ayurveda, Yoga & Naturopathy, Unani, Siddha and Homeopathy (AYUSH), *Government Notification* (No K.11020/03/2017-DCC (AYUSH), 4 July 2018).
55. *See generally, GCP-ASU* (n 52).
56. Department Related Parliamentary Standing Committee on Health and Family Welfare, *DEMANDS FOR GRANTS 2012-13 (DEMAND NO. 47) OF THE DEPARTMENT OF AYUSH (MINISTRY OF HEALTH AND FAMILY WELFARE)* (Fifty-Fifth Report) (RS 2012) para 13.5–13.6.
57. ibid para 13.6.
58. Department Related Parliamentary Standing Committee on Health and Family Welfare, *Action Taken by Government on the Recommendations/Observations contained in the Ninety-Fifth Report on Demands for Grants 2016-17 (Demand No. 5) of the Ministry of AYUSH* (Ninety-Eighth Report) (RS 2016) para 3.23.
59. Department Related Parliamentary Standing Committee on Health and Family Welfare, *Demands for Grants 2018-19 (Demand No. 5) of the Ministry of AYUSH* (One Hundred Eighth Report) (RS 2018) para 3.13.
60. Reply to RTI application dated 14 November 2017 by the Ministry of Ayush (Application No. AYUSH/R/2017/50378 dated 3 October 2017).
61. The Drugs & Cosmetics (Eleventh Amendment) Rules 2018 published in the *Gazette of India* (21 December 2018).
62. The Drugs and Cosmetics Rules 1945, Rule 170.

63. *Reckitt Benckiser India vs Union of India* W.P. (C) 321 of 2019 before the High Court of Delhi (15 January 2019); *Magnet Labs Pvt Ltd vs Union of India* W.P. (C) 502 of 2019 before the High Court of Delhi (18 January 2019); *Mankind Pharma Ltd vs Union of India* W.P. (C) 505 of 2019 before the High Court of Delhi (18 January 2019); *Association of Manufacturers of Ayurvedic Medicine vs Union of India* W.P. (C) 985 of 2019 before the High Court of Delhi (18 January 2019).
64. *Reckitt Benckiser India vs Union of India* W.P.(C) 321 of 2019, C.M. Appl. No. 1529-1530/2019 before the High Court of Delhi (15 January 2019) <http://delhihighcourt.nic.in/dhcqrydisp_o.asp?pn=6336&yr=2019> accessed 23 September 2021.
65. Dinesh Thakur and Prashant Reddy T., 'When Violations Aren't Penalised: The Legality of the Patanjali Advertising Tsunami' *Newslaundry* (12 February 2022) <https://www.newslaundry.com/2022/02/12/when-violations-arent-penalised-the-legality-of-the-patanjali-advertising-tsunami> accessed 2 May 2022.

CHAPTER EIGHT

The Dangers Posed by Traditional Medicine and Its Practitioners to Public Health

The dangers posed to public health in India due to the absence of a credible regulatory framework for traditional medicines are very significant. These dangers emanate from not just the practitioners and manufacturers of traditional medicine but also the Indian state, especially the huge research establishment for traditional medicine that has been funded by the government with public money. There is very little public understanding about the manner in which the publicly funded research ecosystem for traditional Indian medicine in India has played fast and loose with public health.

The threats to public health from private practitioners and manufacturers of traditional medicine, which include the former prescribing modern medicine and the latter often manufacturing products that contain heavy metal or modern medicine like steroids is known quite well in medical circles. However, the manner in which the Indian state has enabled these threats to public health through either complete inaction or woefully poor regulation is rarely discussed in India.

An in-depth discussion of the lethargic, if not negligent, regulatory response of the Indian state to many of these threats posed by traditional medicine and its practitioners will hopefully initiate a public conversation on the need for a decisive regulatory response.

The government-funded search for traditional medicines and its deadly effects on public health

Starting with the first Five Year plan announced in 1951, the Planning Commission of India, which is headed by the Prime Minister of India has been investing in the research of traditional medicine, especially Ayurveda. While disapproving of the policy uncertainty over the role of traditional medicine in the overall health policy of independent India, the Planning Commission called for scientific research to establish the validity of traditional medicine. In its words:

> The controversy with regard to the truth and merits of any particular technique of cure or approach to the problems of health and disease can only be settled on the touchstone of research. Scientifically conducted investigations will, in course of time, decide the value and validity of the different techniques and those which can justify their existence will necessarily become branches of an integrated system of medicine.[1]

Towards this end, the Planning Commission allotted what was then a princely sum of ₹37.5 lakhs for research into traditional medicinal systems. At the time, the Planning Commission urged a "systematic investigation into Indian medical herbs, from the point of view of identification, nomenclature, the area in which they are available and those localities in which individual herbs can be grown to the best advantage".[2]

With every Five Year plan, this allocation for research into traditional Indian medicine increased. The third Five Year plan, announced in 1966 had the Planning Commission allocate a sum of ₹9.8 crores for such research activities involving traditional Indian medicine. It urged for more "research on the fundamental doctrines on Ayurveda, literary research, clinical research, drug research, etc".[3]

This increased funding was accompanied with the creation of new institutions to conduct such research. For example, the Central Council for Ayurvedic Research which was setup as an advisory body by the Ministry of Health in 1962, was reorganized in 1969 by the Government of India under Prime Minister Indira Gandhi, as a separate registered society called the Central Council for Research in Indian Medicine & Homeopathy (CCRIMH). The mandate of this body was to conduct further research into both traditional Indian medicinal systems and homeopathy. In 1978, the CCRIMH was reorganized, when Raj Narain was the Health Minister (famous for successfully challenging Indira Gandhi's election before the Allahabad High Court in 1975 leading to the imposition of the Emergency) under the leadership of Prime Minister Morarji Desai (also famous for drinking his own urine every morning), broke up the CCRIMH into four different councils: The Central Council for Research in Ayurvedic and Siddha (CCRAS), The Central Council for Research in Unani Medicine (CCRUM), the Central Council for Research in Homeopathy (CCRH), and the Central Council for Yoga and Naturopathy (CCRYN). These Central Councils were further reorganized in 2011, with CCRAS being split into two—the Central Council for Research in Ayurvedic Sciences (CCRAS) and the Central Council for Research in Siddha (CCRS).[4]

Apart from these four councils, with the passage of time, the Government of India setup several autonomous research institutes for traditional medicine. These include the National Institute of Ayurveda, the National Institute of Unani, the All India Institute of Ayurveda, the National Institute for Siddha etc. As these research institutions ballooned in number, the administrative machinery overseeing this research establishment also grew. In 1995, Prime Minister P.V. Narasimha Rao announced the creation of a separate department within the Ministry of Health, called the Department of Ayush, to oversee this area of traditional Indian medicine.[5] This meant that the

Department would necessarily get its own Secretary, thereby increasing its profile within the government. In 2014, Prime Minister Narendra Modi went one step ahead and upgraded this department to a full-fledged Ministry, to be headed by an elected Minister.[6]

These upgrades in the administrative status of the Ministry of Ayush reflected the growing political importance of traditional medicine in India. This in turn boosted the financial resources allocated to the "research" and administrative setup under the Ministry of Ayush. For example, the budgets for the five aforementioned councils, setup for research into traditional medicine and homeopathy, almost tripled from ₹262.08 crores in 2011 to ₹663.64 crores in 2021.[7] The total budget allocated to these research councils during the same period was ₹4,619.75 crores. The entire budget of the Ministry of Ayush, inclusive of the autonomous research institutes during this same period and the four councils, was a whopping ₹17,424.51 crores.[8]

The year-wise breakup is as below:

Financial Year	*Budget (In Rupees Crores)*
2011–12	1,088
2012–13	1,178
2013–14	1,259
2014–15	1,272.15
2015–16	1,214
2016–17	1,326.2
2017–18	1,428.65
2018–19	1,626.37
2019–20	1,939.76
2020–21	2,122.08
2021–22	2,970.3

It is not unknown for countries to invest in the research of their traditional medicinal systems in the hopes of finding leads for new drugs. This a perfectly acceptable approach to science since a good share of breakthrough therapies, like quinine for example, has come from plants identified by local communities. Some of these modern-day research projects in certain countries have succeeded in creating new medicine through rigorous science. A great example in this context is the discovery of Artemisinin for treatment of malaria by Chinese scientist Tu Youyou after screening thousands of herbs mentioned in traditional Chinese medicinal texts. The herb from which Tu successfully isolated—*Artemisia annua*—was already known in traditional Chinese medicine for over 2,000 years as a potential cure for malaria. However, Tu was the first to successfully isolate the active ingredient—Artemisinin—from the herb and conduct a series of tests on it validating its use as a successful anti-malarial medicine. Since its commercialization and large-scale availability, Artemisinin has been the most successful anti-malarial therapy since quinine, saving hundreds of thousands, if not millions of patients. For her research, Tu Youyou received the Nobel Prize for Medicine in 2015.[9]

The story of the research conducted by the CCRAS and other research institutions under the Ministry of Ayush, does not have happy endings like Artemisinin. While failures in the scientific world are common across the world and should not be ridiculed, the problem with the public-funded Ayush research establishment is that it has not been scientifically rigorous in establishing the safety and efficacy of some of its inventions before pushing them into the market in a manner that endangers the health of common citizens. To make matters worse, this research establishment has been economical with the truth when advertizing its success stories to either Parliament or the general public. For example, in a publication it released during its 50th anniversary celebration in 2018, it made the following claims:

> The Council has been putting efforts to translate the research findings into practice and make available to the needful at large. In this direction, the technologies of new coded drugs and formulations developed by the Council such as Ayush-64 for Malaria, Ayush-56 for Epilepsy, and Ayush-82 for Diabetes mellitus etc. have been transferred to the Industry through National Research Development Corporation, Department of Scientific and Industrial Research, Ministry of Science & Technology, Government of India.[10]

The Ministry of Ayush has made similar statements in Parliament in response to questions raised by its members. For example, in 2017, a question was raised by a MP in Parliament asking the government for information about the achievements of CCRAS. In a long, ambiguously-worded response, the Minister for Ayush made the following claim:

> Under Drug Development several coded Ayurvedic formulations such as Ayush-56 for epilepsy, Ayush-64 for malaria, Ayush-82 for diabetes, Ayush-SG for Rheumatoid Arthritis and 17 formulations for RCH etc. are developed. Some formulations (Ayush 82, Ayush 64 and Ayush SG) have been gone for commercialization and in near future a series of drug are going to be commercialized...[11]

Ignoring for a moment that in the same sentence, the Ministry claims that the drugs are both under "development" and "developed", we decided to undertake a deep dive into two of the drugs showcased by the Ministry as examples of successful commercialization: Ayush-64 and Ayush-82.

Both drugs have a long history of being touted by the government as success stories from the CCRAS stable. As far back as the late 1980s, in response to Parliamentary questions, the government claimed that Ayush-64 which had been developed by CCRAS was found to be beneficial for the treatment of malaria and that it had been released for commercial exploitation through 15 firms.[12] The government had claimed that in 65–70% of cases during trials, the drug was able to clear the "parasitiemia" within seven days.[13] While the government does not state the basis of its claim, we presume it was based on a study from 1982 conducted by CCRAS in Madras and published in a journal owned by CCRAS.[14] That study, which was a double-blind study, was conducted on a small patient group of 60 patients infected with malaria. The treatment group was given Ayush-64, and the other was given the prevailing standard of care, which was chloroquine and primaquine. Despite only 72.4% of the treatment group getting cured by Ayush-64, against 100% of the control group that received the prevailing standard of care, the authors from CCRAS concluded that Ayush-64 had "good anti-malarial property".[15] This was a strange interpretation because by its own admission, Ayush-64 was not as good as the prevailing standard of care. In any event, given the small size of the trial, it should not have formed the basis of a policy decision to include the drug in treatment guidelines.

In the following years, the government reported buying thousands of Ayush-64 doses. For example, in response to a malaria outbreak in Rajasthan in 1994, the Health Minister informed Parliament that in addition to quinine and chloroquine, the government was also sending 60,000 doses of Ayush-64.[16] A year later, in another discussion in Parliament on malaria, the government informed Parliament that it had ordered 2 crore tablets of Ayush-64.[17]

The problem with repeating such claims in Parliament in the recent past is that in the year 2000, the results of a clinical trial that declared Ayush-64 to be ineffective in treating malaria had been published. This well-designed Phase II clinical trial was conducted by scientists at the Malaria Research Centre, the National Anti-Malaria Programme, and CCRAS with the aim of comparing Ayush-64 to the standard of care, chloroquine. The trial had concluded that Ayush-64 was not as effective a treatment as chloroquine. While all 41 patients who received chloroquine were cured of malaria at day 28, only 23 of the 47 patients who received Ayush-64 were cured at day 28. For even the 23 patients in the Ayush group who were cured, the clearance time was much longer than the group that got chloroquine (3.16 v. 1.5 days). Of the 16 patients in the Ayush-64 group who were considered treatment failures, three had to be transferred to the hospital, where all three responded to chloroquine. The study concluded by saying:

> It is evident from the present study that Ayush-64 does not have specific schizonticidal or gametocytocidal activity... The drug does not appear promising as a primary drug for treatment of malaria in the present dose regimen. In addition to increasing morbidity, slow parasite clearance poses a threat of continuing transmission of the disease.[18]

The above findings which were published in 2000 in a credible, well-known peer-reviewed journal—*Current Science*—should have put an end to the government claiming Ayush-64 as a success story. Yet, as mentioned earlier in this chapter, CCRAS mentioned Ayush-64 as a success story in its promotional literature as late as 2018 and the Minister for Ayush cited Ayush-64 in Parliament in 2017, as a successful example of commercialization of an Ayurvedic "cure", with no mention of the study published in *Current Science* in 2000.

The story with Ayush-64 does not end with the misleading claims in CCRAS's promotional literature and ambiguous answers to parliamentary questions. During the Covid-19 pandemic, the Ministry of Ayush made astonishing claims that Ayush-64 could be used to treat Covid-19. In a memorandum published online, the Ministry made the following claim:

> The recent scientific studies conducted by AYUSH-CSIR research team, provided evidence that usage of the AYUSH-64

> formulation has shown early recovery, shortened duration of hospital stay, and prevention of serious complications when administered along with standard of care. The encouraging outcomes of AYUSH-CSIR collaborative multi-centric studies at reputed medical institutions also shown to help reduce symptoms, disease progression to severe form and duration to become COVID Negative in the management of asymptomatic, mild & moderate cases of Covid 19.[19]

The Ministry of Ayush was so incredibly confident about the drug that it ordered all state drug controllers to allow licenced manufacturers to include "management of asymptomatic, mild to moderate Covid-19" as an additional indication for all manufacturers selling Ayush-64.[20] The Ministry of Ayush then also issued "directions" to the "Ayush fraternity" directing them to prescribe Ayush-64 for "asymptomatic & mild cases as standalone and for the management of mild and moderate Covid-19 infection as an adjunct to standard care".[21] Post these victorious proclamations, ministers of the Government of India started distribution drives to distribute Ayush-64 to the general public.[22]

A few months after the above announcements, an open label trial by AIIMs-Jodhpur, on a small group of patients concluded that "AYUSH 64 has no significant beneficial effect as compared to control group" while also acknowledging that a larger study was required.[23]

When the findings of this study were reported in the press, the Ministry of Ayush lashed out with a furious press release, titled: "Ayush Ministry Strongly Condemns the Tirade Against AYUSH-64 by a Section of Media". The press release contained lines such as this: "The motivated news articles are a classic case of misinterpreting the facts and seeing the glass half empty." And, "These news articles go against the tenet of unbiased reporting. Generalising outcome of a pilot study with limited sample size is wrong."[24] The press release also attempted to provide a not very convincing scientific explanation to justify its faith in Ayush-64 as a treatment of Covid-19. Such bluster from the Ministry of Ayush when challenged on facts is not atypical. As a result, Ayush-64 continued to be doled out across the country as a Covid-19 treatment by the Ayurvedic fraternity.

The story around Ayush-82, another drug developed by CCRAS, is even more startling. The drug was first mentioned in Parliament long ago in 1996, when it was described by a Minister as one of the Ayurvedic drugs undergoing clinical trials to evaluate its potential as a treatment for diabetes. While the outcome of those studies in 1996 is not known, what we do know is that sometime around 2014 or 2015, the CCRAS licenced Ayush-82 to 10 private companies through a government-owned technology licencing company called the National Research Development Corporation (NRDC) for a cumulative sum of ₹1.47 crores.[25] NRDC then further licenced this technology to private companies.

One of the recipients of these licences for Ayush-82 was Kudos Laboratories India Ltd, a company in the business of selling Ayurvedic products. Kudos sold this product under the brand name "IME-9" which stood for "Insulin Management Expert". The original packaging of the drug stated that it was an "Ayurvedic 'cure' for Diabetes" and that it was a "human clinical trial research product" which contained "Clinically Researched Formulation Technology". The packaging also claimed it was tested on 800 patients. Also featured prominently on the external packaging of the product were the names of the entities associated with developing and marketing it: The Central Council for Research in Ayurvedic Sciences, Ministry of Ayush, National Research Development Corporation, the Department of Science and Technology, the Ministry of Science and Technology and the Government of India. The product was priced at ₹300 for 60 tablets and each tablet contained aqueous extracts of "Amra, Karela, Gudmar, Jamun and Shudh shilajit" along with preservatives such as Sodium Methylparaben, Sodium Propyl Paraben and approved excipients. All in all, the product was packaged to convey an image that it had the official blessings of the Government of India. Kudos also kicked off a very vocal marketing campaign describing IME-9 as "India's first wonder drug to treat diabetes globally" and that "IME-9 Tablets bring sugar under complete control".[26]

Other companies launched Ayush-82 under their own brand names. The launch of Ayush-82 in its various avatars immediately drew attention because of the grand claims being made during the marketing campaigns for the drug. Once journalists and scientists began digging into how the drug was approved, it was discovered that there were no published, peer-reviewed double-blind RCT studies documenting the therapeutic efficacy of the drug, as is usually the case for new drugs seeking approval.[27] Even worse were the complaints being posted online by patients who had consumed the drug. They complained of sugar levels having shot up, constipation, blood in the stools etc. with some patients even being rushed to the hospital in an emergency situation.[28]

Ultimately, the advertizing blitz launched by Kudos for IME-9 was brought to a halt by the Advertising Standards Council of India (ASCI), an industry watchdog. In correspondence, between ASCI and Kudos that we accessed under the RTI Act, it was clear that a number of complaints had been received by ASCI from the general public about the advertisements featuring IME-9. Kudos finally informed the ASCI that it would modify its advertisements to drop claims that the IME-9 would bring "sugar under complete control" and that it was the "first wonder drug to treat diabetes globally".[29] It even changed its packaging to remove any reference to diabetes or insulin management.

By the time these changes were implemented, drug inspectors from the Maharashtra Food and Drug Administration had already initiated a criminal prosecution against Kudos Laboratories under the Drug and Magic Remedies (Objectionable Advertisement) Act 1954 which prohibits advertisements that claim to cure or prevent certain medical conditions, including diabetes. On 27 August 2018, the proprietor of Kudos Laboratories pled guilty before the Chief Judicial Magistrate of Ahmednagar on charges of violating the Drug and Magic Remedies (Objectionable Advertisement) Act 1954, and was slapped with a paltry fine of ₹15,000 even though the legislation provides for imprisonment for violation of the law. The judge reasoned that since the proprietor had pled guilty and the advertisement in question had been rectified, a simple fine was sufficient.[30] And so ended a saga that began at the publicly funded CCRAS.

In addition to the Ayush-64 and Ayush-82 controversies was the BGR-34 controversy, which was brewing in the labs of the Council of Scientific and Industrial Research (CSIR), a consortium of 37 laboratories researching subjects ranging from molecular biology to the latest in chemical technology. Many of the laboratories in the CSIR network, like the National Chemical Laboratory (NCL) and the Centre for Cellular and Molecular Biology (CCMB) enjoy excellent reputations in their respective fields. Unlike the research councils under the Ministry of Ayush which research into the past, CSIR is tasked with conducting cutting edge research into modern science. Yet here it was, researching a supposed Ayurvedic cure for diabetes.

The drug sold under the BGR-34 brand name was developed jointly by the National Botanical Research Institute (NBRI) and Central Institute of Medicinal and Aromatic Plants (CIMAP), both of which function under the CSIR network. It contained six Ayurvedic ingredients, namely Daruharida, Vijaysar, Giloy,

Majeeth, Methika and Gudmar. A box containing 100 tablets was priced at ₹505. According to the claims made by CSIR in the press, the drug released 34 active phytoconstituents to help manage sugar levels for patients afflicted with diabetes.[31]

As per information provided to us under the RTI Act by CIMAP, both labs generated efficacy and safety data on small animals. In industry parlance, such a study would be classified as a pre-clinical study. Thereafter, both labs licenced the technology to a private company called AIMIL Pharmaceuticals (India) Ltd which then conducted a very small clinical trial on 56 patients (typically new diabetes medication would be tested on hundreds if not thousands of patients).[32] The results of the study were then published in a journal which was later discovered by journalists to be a "predatory journal".[33] These are low quality, pay-to-publish journals that are generally avoided by the scientific community.

As with IME-9, when BGR-34 reached the market, its packaging prominently featured the names of CSIR labs along with claims that the product had been scientifically validated through clinical trials. Similar to IME-9, the launch of the product was coupled with a very vocal publicity campaign. In 2016, the product even received a mention from Prime Minister Modi at an event held by CSIR.[34]

As with Ayush-82, the launch of BGR-34 met with a fair deal of public criticism in the media. The fact that the drug was targeted at diabetic patients rang alarm bells because of the potential health implications for patients consuming diabetes medication that was not properly tested. Even commentators otherwise sympathetic to Ayurveda, expressed their alarm over the boisterous claims that these Ayurvedic "cures" would cure diabetes.[35]

These concerns were not unfounded. In the months following the launch of BGR-34, scientists and journalists tracking the usage of the drug reported that the most common complaint from patients was that the drug was quite simply ineffective in controlling the levels of blood sugar, which in the case of diabetes, is a serious problem.[36] Patients also complained that the drug caused gastric problems and severe allergies.[37]

After the backlash in the press, AIMIL Pharmaceuticals appears to have rebranded BGR-34 as a "carbohydrate metaboliser" that can prevent "long term complications and tone body functions", apart from checking "over-fatigue and weakness".

The story does not end with drugs targeting diabetes. Another CSIR lab, called the Central Drug Research Institute (CDRI) had licenced a drug called DalZbone for rapidly healing bone fractures to a private company specializing in Ayurvedic products. The product is made of the extract from leaves of *Dalbergia sissoo* and was tested in a clinical trial on merely 28 patients. As per CDRI's claims, the drug would reduce the healing time of fractures by 30%–40%. In a press interview, the lead investigator of that clinical trial admitted that the trial was too small to prove the drug's efficacy.[38] Yet, CDRI had licenced out the product to a private company that began selling it in the open market.[39]

There are several more examples of CCRAS and CSIR labs commercializing vague products that have not been properly validated through rigorous double-blind RCTs. The private companies to whom research is transferred do not appear to be conducting any rigorous clinical trials either.

The question now is how did these drugs get to the market without going through rigorous clinical trials? The rather shocking answer is the fact that "patent and proprietary" traditional drugs, unlike new modern drugs, are subject to the ambiguously worded Rule 158B of the Drugs and Cosmetics Rules 1945. As discussed in the earlier chapter, Rule 158B is really unclear on the nature of clinical trials required to launch these "patent and proprietary" Ayurvedic medicine in the market. At one point in 2013, the government interpreted Rule 158B as requiring clinical trials, only to walk back on this requirement in 2018 when it declared that Rule 158B did not require clinical trials. There is no scientific rationale for excluding these "patent and proprietary" traditional medicine from rigorous clinical trials. These are essentially new drugs that should be tested rigorously through double-blind RCTs.

The original sin, in our opinion, that led to the flooding of the market with these dubious "patent and proprietary" drugs was the amendment in 1982 that opened the door to "patent and proprietary" medicine. Any attempt at reform should begin with doing away with the concept of "patent and proprietary" Ayurvedic and Unani medicine and subjecting all new drugs to the same regulatory pathway.

Bureaucrats in the Ministry of Ayush responsible for regulation in this area are quite aware of these regulatory shortcomings. In an interview to the media, after all the above mentioned controversies, the Secretary of the Ayush Ministry counselled consumers to take the claims made by manufacturers of new proprietary Ayurvedic cures with a "pinch of salt".[40]

Of heavy metals and adulterated Ayurvedic drugs

Quite contrary to the common perception in India that Ayurvedic "cures" are less toxic than modern medicine because they are herbal in nature, many Ayurvedic "cures" have been found to contain toxic heavy metals.

The rampant presence of heavy metals in Ayurvedic "cures" was first exposed in the United States after a scientific study published in the *Journal of the American Medical Association (JAMA)* in the year 2004 reported that 20% of primarily "Made in India" Ayurvedic Herbal Medicinal Products (HMPs) that were sampled by the authors had the presence of potentially harmful levels of lead, mercury, and/or arsenic.[41] The study went on to warn, that the level of these heavy metals could be potentially harmful to humans. Another study published in *JAMA* in 2009 with a sample size of 193 Ayurvedic "medicines" manufactured both in India and the United States (77 from India, 115 from the United States, and one from Canada), reported finding unsafe levels of heavy metals such as lead, arsenic, and mercury in 20.7% of the samples.[42]

There are two reasons for the presence of heavy metals in Ayurvedic "cures". The first is that a branch of Ayurveda called rasa shastra prescribes the use of heavy metals in conjunction with herbs to treat diseases.[43] Other traditional medicinal systems have also prescribed the similar use of heavy metals for medicinal purposes. The second reason for the presence of heavy metals is likely contamination in the sourcing of ingredients and the manufacturing process.

Over the last two decades, doctors across the world, from British Columbia[44] to Europe[45] to the United States have documented cases of primarily Indian origin patients falling sick due to heavy-metal poisoning after consuming Ayurvedic "medicines" or "supplements".

After the publication of the first study in *JAMA* in the year 2004, the Department of Ayush under the Ministry of Health and Family Welfare issued an order dated 14 October 2005, under Section 33 EEB of the Drugs and Cosmetics Act 1940, fixing the permissible limits of heavy metals that can be present in each container of Ayurvedic "cures" at the levels recommended by the WHO in its publication "Quality Control Methods for Medicinal Plants & Materials".[46] The wholesale adoption of a WHO standard, that was drafted in a different context, by the Government of India in the context of an India-specific problem was a strange way to deal with this issue. At the very least, the Indian government should have examined the problem in the Indian context and formulated India-specific rules. In any event, once the notification came into effect on 14 October 2005, any violation of the new standards would have resulted in jail time of six months and a paltry fine of ₹10,000. We are yet to hear of a single prosecution for a violation of this direction.

The new order and resulting penalties did not solve the problem. Proof of this lies in the results of a unique study published in 2017 where the investigators reached out to a community of Indians in the United States, known to consume Ayurvedic "cures" and herbal supplements that were sourced from a particular clinic in India, offering to test both the products and the blood samples of volunteers against standards for heavy metal consumption as set down by the Environmental Protection Agency (EPA) in the United States. In approximately 50% of the 252 samples tested, the levels of lead, mercury, arsenic, silver, and cadmium exceeded the recommended daily exposure limits in the United States. The key findings of the study are reproduced below:

> Two hundred and fifty-two samples of Ayurvedic products and herbal supplements were analyzed between the first and third quarter of 2011. Lead was the most common element found in 65% ($N = 164$) of all samples with maximum level of 43,200 mg/kg. However, half of the samples had Pb levels of 4.9 mg/kg and below (Table (Table2).2). Mercury and arsenic were each found in over one-third of the samples with median level of 53.0 mg/kg and 8.4 mg/kg and maximum levels of 279,000 mg/kg and 44,800 mg/kg of product, respectively. Antimony, barium, chromium, nickel, and silver were each found in less than one-fifth of the samples. Cadmium was present in only one product analyzed in this study.[47]

Some of these samples exceeded the exposure limits for heavy metals by a factor of several thousands.

These researchers also tested the blood of 115 persons

from this community which was consuming the aforementioned Ayurvedic "cures". The researchers found that 46 of these 115 persons had elevated levels of lead in their blood, i.e. greater than $\geq 10.0\,\mu g/dl$. Four individuals were found to have elevated levels of mercury, i.e. greater $\geq 10.0 ng/ml$.[48] These were worrying findings from a public health perspective.

Apart from these foreign studies, Indian doctors continue to report with regular frequency in scientific publications, social media as well as the Indian press, cases of metal poisoning in patients with a history of consuming Ayurvedic "cures".[49] A particularly vocal doctor on social media is Dr Cyriac Abby Philips, a hepatologist who is based out of Kerala. Tweeting under the monicker @theliverdr, Philips regularly posts anecdotes about the quality of Ayurvedic "cures" consumed by his patients who mostly suffer from liver damage.[50] He has proven to be particularly effective in riling the Ayurvedic industry, with many of them complaining to the government that they are being defamed by Philip's legitimate criticism.[51]

By any measure, this issue is a public health crisis that can be easily tackled with governmental intervention. Despite the ongoing nature of this threat to Indian public health, the issue receives relatively little attention in the Indian government. At the very least, the government should conduct a survey to ascertain the size of the problem before cracking down on the Ayurvedic industry with an iron fist.

Ayurveda's dangerous adulteration problem

A problem that is far more serious than the heavy metal problem is the relentless adulteration of Ayurvedic "cures" with modern medicine which cannot otherwise be administered without the prescription of a qualified doctor. Such adulteration of Ayurvedic "cures" is a crime under the Drugs and Cosmetics Act 1940, although the penalties are relatively light. At most, a fine of ₹20,000 and a maximum prison term of one year can be imposed on a person found to be selling adulterated Ayurvedic "cures".[52] On the other hand, selling adulterated modern drugs can be punished with anywhere between three years to a maximum of life in prison and an accompanying fine of ₹10 lakhs or three times the value of the consignment.[53]

The most rampant kind of adulteration appears to be the surreptitious mixing of steroids such as Betamethasone, Dexamethasone, and Prednisolone with Ayurvedic "cures". Steroids have the effect of reducing the activity of the immune system which results in reducing inflammation and pain, without actually "curing" the disease. Many of these Ayurvedic "cures" can be quite expensive. As per one report, a family member reported spending ₹75,000 to purchase an Ayurvedic "cure" for a cancer-stricken relative which did provide some instant relief for a few days after which it stopped acting.[54] It is very likely that the "cure" was adulterated with steroids, which would not have cost more than ₹100. We were able to trace one successful prosecution in Punjab where an Ayurvedic product called "Body Grow Fast Powder" and "Cough Less Powder" tested positive for Prednisolone, which is a steroid. This case ended with the conviction of the manufacturer who was sentenced to imprisonment for three years, but in our experience, such prosecutions are rare.[55]

The second common type of adulteration of Ayurvedic "cures" is the surreptitious mixing of Sildenafil, better known as Viagra; the brand name for Pfizer's blockbuster treatment for male erectile dysfunction. These Ayurvedic "cures" are then advertized as treating all kinds of sexual disorders. In one particular Indian case that we tracked, there were two Ayurvedic remedies called "3X Men Capsules Morning & Evening" and "3X Men Syrup 3 Times Passion for Intimate Moments" manufactured by the same firm in Rajasthan. Samples of both the capsules and syrup had been drawn from a chemist's shop in Mumbai by a drug inspector of the Maharashtra FDA and sent for testing to a government analyst in a drug control laboratory of the state government. The labelling of both the tablet and the syrup, indicated that the drugs contained a number of ingredients common to Ayurvedic "cures", such as Makardhwaja, mucuna pruriens, sida cordifolia, swarnmakshik bhasma, Amla, Ashwagandha, Kesar, Kaunch Beej etc. However, when the samples were tested, the government analyst discovered that the capsules contained between 18.65mg and 21.27mg of Sildenafil Citrate per capsule, while the syrup contained 15.44 mg of Sildenafil Citrate per 15 ml of the sample syrup! The firm that manufactured these samples denied the charges. The ensuing investigation which took the drug inspector till Rajasthan revealed that the firm actually held licences from the Rajasthan Drug Control Organization to manufacture the capsules, although the "ingredients" approved in the licence are not clear. Since the samples were declared to be spurious, the Maharashtra FDA launched a criminal prosecution against the company before a criminal court in Mumbai.[56] As per the e-court records, this case which was filed in 2016 was yet to be decided as of 2022.

The third common type of adulteration in the Ayurvedic market is where unscrupulous market players mix Ayurvedic "cures" with powerful painkillers. We tracked at least one case, where drugs inspectors from the Maharashtra FDA in Ahmednagar drew a sample of a drug called ARTIN Pluse Ayurvedic Capsules from a medical and general store. As per the labelling on this Ayurvedic "cure", it was priced at ₹150 and contained standard ingredients found in Ayurvedic "cures" such as guggul, bhasm and pannage ras and that it was "most effective in chronic joint pains". These ingredients were packaged in half-red, half-black hard gelatin cylindrical capsule. As is the practice, the drug inspector sent this sample for testing to the government analyst at the drug testing laboratory run by the state government. On testing the ingredients of the gelatin capsules, the analyst allegedly discovered that the sample contained 62.32 milligrams of Nimesulide, a powerful chemical painkiller that can be bought only with a prescription.

Nimesulide has been a controversial drug because of its alleged toxic side-effects on the liver and is prohibited in certain countries.[57] In India, the drug is prohibited for children but can be prescribed for adults.[58] To conceal such a powerful painkiller, without disclosing it on the labelling is a serious issue. During the investigation by the drug inspector who drew the sample, it was discovered that the manufacturer mentioned on the packaging, as well as one of the distributors in the supply chain, were fake entities and simply did not exist! The drug inspector eventually filed a criminal case under the Drugs and Cosmetics Act 1940 against only the shopkeeper and one of the distributors in the supply chain charging them with the offence of selling spurious Ayurvedic cures.[59] As per the e-court records, this case which was filed in 2016 was yet to be decided as of 2022.

A fourth type of adulteration of Ayurvedic "cures" that we were able to track were Ayurvedic skin creams claiming to be natural but were in reality adulterated with chemical agents. One particular sample drawn by the drug inspectors of the Maharashtra FDA was a skin cream which on its labeling indicated only natural ingredients such as aloe vera etc. for the purpose of treating hyperpigmentation and scars. When the sample was tested by the government analyst, it was discovered to contain Hydroquinone, a chemical depigmentation agent![60] Since the drug inspector in charge of the investigation declined to share information with us under the RTI Act, we are not sure whether the case was prosecuted before a criminal court.[61]

As things stand today, we know that Ayurvedic "cures" have a dangerous adulteration problem and that Indian patients are being duped and harmed by such adulteration. This is not just a regulatory issue but a law and order issue involving dangerous criminal elements. The problem however is that we do not know how serious the problem is on the ground. We dug out the above information after conducting painful and excruciating searches of government databases and filing requests for information under the RTI Act 2005. The government can easily publish consolidated figures based on the random sampling conducted by its drug inspectors to indicate the extent of this problem but it has not lifted a finger in this regard. The fight against unscrupulous firms indulging in adulteration of Ayurvedic "cures" is left largely to individual doctors, drug inspectors, and their sense of duty towards protecting public health.

The paradox of traditional medicine practitioners claiming the right to prescribe modern medicine

If the manner in which the Ayurvedic industry manufactures and markets its products is not troubling enough, there is also the issue of practitioners of traditional medicine prescribing modern medicine like antibiotics and painkillers despite not holding the qualifications required to practice modern medicine. This, despite the fact that many in the community of traditional medicine practitioners claim the superiority of their system over modern medicine. They likely feel the need to prescribe modern medicine because of a demand from their patients. As per the Health and Family Welfare Statistics in India released by the Ministry of Health in 2019–20 the percentage of ailments treated with modern medicine in India was approximately 95% in both rural and urban areas. Less than 5% of the population in both rural and urban areas depended on traditional Indian medicine.[62] Academics who used household data from the National Sample Survey Organization (NSSO) estimated that not more than 30% of

Indian household used traditional medicine, although this number varies widely across Indian states.[63] Simply put, if practitioners of traditional medicine have to compete with doctors practicing modern medicine, they have little choice but to prescribe modern medicine. The important question however, is whether this practice is legal or not.

Strangely, in India, this issue of who exactly can prescribe modern medicine has been litigated not under the laws regulating the practice of the medical profession such as the Indian Medical Council Act 1956 or the Indian Medicine Central Council of India Act 1970. The first was meant to regulate the awarding of MBBS degrees for doctors to practice what is commonly understood as modern medicine, as well as create a regulatory mechanism for the profession. The second is a legislation that was created to regulate the practitioners of Indian medicine and it created uniform educational standards for degrees like Bachelors in Ayurvedic Medical Sciences (BAMS) or Bachelors of Unani Medicine and Surgery (BUMS) and also a registration process for practitioners of traditional medicine.

Instead, the issue of who can prescribe what medicine came to be litigated under the Drugs and Cosmetics Rules 1945. This is because in 1959, the Drugs and Cosmetics Rules 1945 were amended to introduce Rule 2(ee) defining the phrase "registered medical practitioner" whose prescriptions would be required for the sale of specific categories of drugs. In addition, these "registered medical practitioners" also get some exemptions in Schedule K, which allows them to store and sell drugs without a pharmacy licence. This definition in Rule 2(ee) is anything but straightforward since it includes not just doctors holding qualifications under the Indian Medical Council Act 1956 but also persons "registered in a medical register of a State meant for the registration of persons practicing the modern scientific system of medicine" or "registered in a medical register" by virtue of a "general or special order made by a State Government" declaring that a "person is practicing modern scientific system of medicine for the purposes of this Act". The first of these two categories was a likely concession to the federal nature of the Indian Medical Council Act 1956 which recognized the rights of states to enact their own qualification criteria to practice medicine. The rationale for the second category which has proven to be the fountainhead of much litigation, is much more difficult to identify. In fact, we were unable to identify the rationale for the existence of this category in the definition of "registered medical practitioner". But here is what happened because of this provision.

Multiple state governments like those in Punjab and Rajasthan began issuing notifications in the decade of the 1960s under Rule 2(ee) declaring practitioners of traditional medicine as practicing modern scientific system of medicine thus giving them the legal status of "registered medical practitioners" for the purpose of the Drugs and Cosmetics Rules 1945. This meant that they could now prescribe modern medicine as well as store and sell modern drugs without a pharmacy licence.

The matter eventually landed up in litigation before different High Courts. One High Court declared Rule 2(ee) unconstitutional on the grounds that the Government of India lacked the power to formulate such a rule, while another High Court struck down a notification issued by a State Government permitting practitioners of traditional medicine to be recognized as "registered medical practitioners" under Rule 2(ee).

These cases were appealed till the Supreme Court of India rendered a judgment on the point in 1998 in the Mukhtiar Chand[64] case. The practitioners of traditional medicine invoked the definition of "Indian medicine" in the Indian Medicine Central Council Act 1970 to claim the right to practice modern medicine on the grounds that this definition includes "modern advances" as may be declared by the Central Council of Indian Medicine under that law from time to time. The Supreme Court did not accept this argument on the grounds that "modern advances" at most meant that these practitioners of Indian medicine could use modern diagnostic tools and nothing more.

On the more substantive question regarding the rights of traditional medicine practitioners to prescribe modern medicine, the Supreme Court pointed out that the Medical Council of India Act 1956 and the Indian Medicine Central Council Act 1970 created distinct regulatory regimes. On a "harmonious reading" of both laws, the court concluded "that there is no scope for a person enrolled on the State Register of Indian medicine or Central Register of Indian Medicine to practise modern scientific medicine in any of its branches unless that person is also enrolled on a State Medical Register within the meaning of 1956 Act". In the court's understanding, the right to "prescribe" particular medicine would be synonymous with the right to practice that system of medicine.

The above conclusion should have been the end of the matter but the court then went ahead to muddy the waters by also concluding that practitioners with qualifications in "integrated medicine" could be recognized as "registered medical practitioners" if the state in which they were resident, recognized such a qualification under state law as sufficient to get registered on the State Register for modern medicine. "Integrated medicine" is a controversial concept that can be traced back to the Committee on Indigenous Medicine in 1948 which called for integrating the best elements of traditional and modern medicine. The IMA, which represents practitioners of modern medicine, has consistently ridiculed the idea of "integrative medicine" and rightly so. There is little to reconcile between theories of modern medicine like the "Germ Theory" and "Tridosha theory", which is central to Ayurveda. In any event, this judgment should have brought the matter to a close after more than a decade of litigation. Unfortunately, that did not happen.

This was because a number of states continue the practice of issuing notifications under Rule 2(ee)(iii) only for the same to be challenged before the High Courts which then regularly declare such notifications to be illegal and contrary to the holding in *Mukhtiar Chand*. For example, in 2016, the Delhi High Court declared illegal a notification issued by the Delhi government in 1961 under Rule 2(ee)(iii) allowing practitioners of traditional medicine to prescribe modern medicine.[65] The local government of Delhi had tried to exploit the "integrated medicine" exception created by the Supreme Court in Mukhtiar Chand by enacting a law recognizing "integrated medicine" courses but the Delhi High Court was clearly not impressed. In 2017, the West Bengal government issued a notification under Rule 2(ee)(iii) of the Drugs and Cosmetics Rules 1945 allowing certain practitioners of traditional Indian medicine to prescribe particular modern medicines. The list included powerful antibiotics as well as antacids, antimalarials etc.[66] In other states like Karnataka, for example, the government withdrew a notification it had issued in 2017 after it was legally challenged before the Karnataka High Court.[67] In 2019, the Chhattisgarh High Court stayed a notification issued by the Chhattisgarh government in the same year under Rule 2(ee)(iii) allowing practitioners of traditional medicine to prescribe modern medicines.[68]

The sheer volume of litigation on this issue is stunning and indicative of the political might of the practitioners of traditional Indian medicine. The main justification offered by state governments for such policies is that they are facing a shortage of doctors, especially those willing to serve in rural areas and that allowing practitioners of traditional medicine to prescribe modern medicine would help deliver better medical services in those areas. There are civil society organizations which support these policies on the grounds that it will help increase access to medicine. During the litigation before the Delhi High Court, a NGO called Sankalp intervened in favour of the practitioners of traditional Indian medicine.

In fact, in some circles of civil society, it has become politically incorrect to even suggest that modern medicine is superior to traditional Indian medicine both in terms of theory and outcomes. Too many public health professionals in India have romanticized notions of integration between modern medicine and traditional medicine. However, as argued by the IMA, such policies end up promoting quackery and nothing else because the practitioners of Indian medicine barely have any exposure to the rigours of modern medicine during their training.[69] The only viable solution is for the government to increase its investment in medical colleges so that India produces more doctors qualified in modern medicine.

On the policy front, the Government of India can easily initiate steps to end this chaos and litigation by amending Rule 2(ee)(iii) of the Drugs and Cosmetics Rules 1945 to limit the definition of registered medical practitioners to only those doctors with MBBS degrees and dentists. Surprisingly, the Government of India does little to nothing in regard. Even in the Mukhtiar Chand case, when the Supreme Court had to hear the appeal against the decision of the High Court declaring Rule 2(ee) to be unconstitutional, the Government of India chose not to present any arguments before court. The Supreme Court was forced to note that "...we are constrained to observe that the stand taken by the Central Government shows utter bewilderment inasmuch as the authority which framed rule is not interested in supporting the legality and the validity of the rule nor does it want to do away with the Rule whole heartedly".

The Government of India had a fresh chance to look at this issue when it introduced legislation in 2019 and 2020; to replace the Medical Council of India Act 1956 with the National Commission for Medicine Act 2019, and the Indian Medicine Central Council Act 1970 with the National Commission for Indian System of Medicine Act 2020. Instead of making it impossible for practitioners of Indian medicine to prescribe modern medicine, the original draft of the National Commission for Medicine Bill 2017 had initially proposed making it legal for these practitioners to prescribe modern medicine after completing a bridge course in modern medicine. Thankfully, this provision was deleted from the final version of the bill after significant opposition from the IMA and even some state governments.[70]

Separate from the policy issue is the enforcement aspect. To what extent are states actually cracking down on practitioners of Ayurveda or Unani prescribing modern medicine? Going by daily reporting in newspapers, it appears that at least in urban India some municipal corporations conduct "anti-quackery" drives where they end up prosecuting practitioners of Indian medicine for practicing and prescribing modern medicine. While statistics on such prosecutions are not easily available, it does appear to be a serious problem, per the reporting in the press. The only occasion on which the issue gets prominent attention is when practitioners of traditional Indian medicine end up causing the deaths of patients under their care.

The future of regulating the traditional medicine industry

Regulating the traditional medicine industry is clearly an uphill task but given the danger posed to public health, there is no other alternative. On issues such as the presence of heavy metals and adulteration with modern medicine, the Ministry of Health has to create a national action plan mapping out the scale of the problem before coordinating a nation-wide response to stamp out the problem. Aggressive prosecutions can solve this problem successfully.

The more complex problem is the one emanating from the immense public-funded research establishment for traditional medicine. The researchers at these establishments are under pressure to demonstrate results while their overseers in the Ministry of Ayush need to justify their own existence. Reversing this trend of half-baked remedies being pushed into the market will require "patent and proprietary" traditional medicine to go through the same regulatory pathway as modern medicine. This is easier said than done. There is an ecosystem in the country that actively promotes poorly designed clinical studies, publications in predatory journals, and aggressive promotion of unestablished therapeutic claims all with the explicit intent to provide a veneer of respectability to this quackery using the "tools" of modern medicine. Once again, this is an issue that can be resolved only if the political class has the courage of conviction to follow the science on the matter. Let us not delude ourselves with notions of Indian, or for that matter, Hindu "exceptionalism". Ayurvedic medicine, like modern medicine must stand the test of the gold standard—well designed, double-blinded RCTs.

Lastly, with regard to practitioners of Indian medicine prescribing modern medicine, there are simple solutions to this problem provided the Government of India has the political will to act on the same. Leaving it to the courts to sort out these issues is quite simply a terrible approach to governance. Thankfully on this count, the IMA has been vociferous and effective in challenging notifications by the state governments.

Notes

1. Government of India, Planning Commission, *1st Five Year Plan* (ch 32: Health, 1951).
2. ibid.
3. Government of India, Planning Commission, *3rd Five Year Plan* (ch 32: Health and Family Planning, 1966).
4. Government of India, Ministry of AYUSH, Central Council for Research in Ayurvedic Sciences, *Glimpses of CCRAS contributions (50 Glorious years): Clinical Research and Drug Development* (Vol I, 2018) 1.
5. Shailaja Chandra, 'Status of Indian Medicine and Folk Healing: With a Focus on Integration of AYUSH Medical Systems in Healthcare Delivery' (2012) 33 Ayu 461 (Shailaja Chandra Report), ch 1: 'Historical Perspective', 13.
6. Aditya Kalra, 'India Gets Minister for Yoga and Traditional Medicine' *Reuters* (11 November 2014) <https://www.reuters.com/article/india-health-yoga-ministry-idINKCN0IV13J20141111> accessed 22 September 2021.
7. Government of India, Ministry of Health and Family Welfare/Ministry of AYUSH, *Demand for Grants* (2011–12 to 2021–22).
8. ibid.
9. Ewen Callaway and David Cyranoski, 'Anti-Parasite Drugs Sweep Nobel Prize in Medicine 2015' (2015) 526 *Nature*, 174; Xin-zhuan Su and Louis H Miller, 'The Discovery of Artemisinin and Nobel Prize in Physiology or Medicine' (2015) 58 *Science China Life Sciences*, 1175.
10. *Glimpses of CCRAS contributions* (n 4) 6.
11. Reply by the Minister of State (Ministry of AYUSH) Shri Shripad Yesso Naik to question raised by Shri D Kupendra Reddy, Rajya Sabha Deb 11 April 2017, Question No 4318, 87–92.
12. Reply by the Minister of State (Ministry of Health and Family Welfare) Kumari Saroj Khaparde to question raised by Dr G Vijaya Rama Rao, Lok Sabha Debate 3 December 1987, Question No 4143, 316–317.
13. Reply by the Minister of State (Ministry of Health and Family Welfare) Kumari Saroj Khaparde to question raised by Dr G Vijaya Rama Rao, Lok Sabha Debate 1 March 1989, Question No 1027, 72.
14. M.V. Chari and others, 'A Double Blind Clinical Trial With Ayush-64 an Ayurvedic Drug in P. Vivax Malaria' (1982) VI *Journal for Research in Ayurveda and Siddha*, 105, 105–116.

15. ibid 110.
16. Reply by the Minister of State (Ministry of Health and Family Welfare) Dr C Silvera to question raised by Shri Vijoy Kumar Yadav and Shrimati Geeta Mukherjee, Lok Sabha Debate 12 December 1994, Question No 675, 116–117.
17. Shri Paban Singh Ghatowar in Lok Sabha Deb 10 May 1995, 27.
18. Neena Valecha and others, 'Comparative Efficacy of Ayush-64 vs Chloroquine in Vivax Malaria' (2000) 78 *Current Science*, 1120, 1122–1123.
19. Government of India, Ministry of Ayush, *Memorandum*, (F. No.T.13020/8/2021/Part-1-DCC(AYUSH), 9 May 2021).
20. Government of India, Ministry of Ayush, *Memorandum*, (F. T-18020/1/2020-DCC-Part(1), 27 April 2021)."
21. Government of India, Ministry of AYUSH, *Government Order* (F.No. T. 18020/1/2020-DCC(AYUSH), 5 May 2021).
22. 'Rijiju Launches Distribution Campaign of AYUSH-64 and Immunity Boosting Medicines' *The Arunachal Times* (11 June 2021) <https://arunachaltimes.in/index.php/2021/06/11/rijiju-launches-distribution-campaign-of-ayush-64-and-immunity-boosting-medicines/> accessed 1 October 2021.
23. Pankaj Bhardwaj and others, 'Efficacy and Safety of Ayurveda Intervention (AYUSH 64) as Add-on Therapy for Patients with COVID-19 Infections—An Open Labelled, Parallel Group, Randomized Controlled Clinical Trial' [2021] medRxiv 2021.08.10.21261836; The Wire Staff, 'COVID-19: Small, Preliminary Study Doesn't Find Proof of AYUSH 64's Efficacy' *The Wire Science* (19 August 2021) <https://science.thewire.in/health/covid-19-small-preliminary-study-doesnt-find-proof-of-ayush-64s-efficacy/> accessed 1 October 2021.
24. Press Information Bureau, Government of India, 'Ayush Ministry Strongly Condemns the Tirade Against AYUSH-64 by a Section of Media: "It is Misinterpreting the Facts, Lacking the Understanding of the Matter"' (26 August 2021) <https://pib.gov.in/PressReleaseIframePage.aspx?PRID=1749138> accessed 1 October 2021.
25. Government of India, Ministry of AYUSH, *Committee to Review the Functioning of Central Council for Research in Ayurvedic Sciences (CCRAS) and Peripheral Institutes under it: Report and Recommendations* (2017) 43.
26. As noted in the notice issued by Vice-Chairperson Abanti Sankaranarayan, Advertising Standards Council of India to Kudos Laboratories India Ltd dated 14 October 2016 (accessed via the RTI Act).

27. PTI, 'Quality Concern in Herbal Medicine Remains a Challenge: AYUSH Minister' *The Economic Times* (8 November 2016) <https://economictimes.indiatimes.com/industry/healthcare/biotech/healthcare/quality-concern-in-herbal-medicine-remains-a-challenge-ayush-minister/articleshow/55310370.cms?from=mdr> accessed 23 September 2021; Dr Sumaiya Shaikh, 'Are AYUSH Supported BGR-34 and IME-9 Drugs Safe and Effective for Diabetes?' *Alt News* (13 August 2017) <https://www.altnews.in/bgr-34-ime-9-drugs-safe-effective-diabetes/> accessed 23 September 2021; Anoop Misra, Seema Gulati and Atul Luthra, 'Alternative Medicines for Diabetes in India: Maximum Hype, Minimum Science' (2016) 4 *The Lancet Diabetes & Endocrinology*, 302.
28. Pratik Sinha, Sumaiya Shaikh & Arjun Sidharth, *India Misinformed—The True Story*, (Harper Collins India 2019) at 232.
29. Reply to RTI application dated 14 November 2017, Ministry of AYUSH (Application No AYUSH/R/2017/50378, 3 October 2017).
30. *State of Maharashtra vs Karan Goomar* R.C.C.No. 2646/2017 before the Court of Civil Judge, Aurangabad (27 August 2018).
31. PTI, 'Herbal Drug BGR-34 Helps Cutting down Heart Attack Risk: Study' *ET Healthworld* (19 May 2018) <https://health.economictimes.indiatimes.com/news/pharma/herbal-drug-bgr-34-helps-cutting-down-heart-attack-risk-study/64236137> accessed 23 September 2021.
32. Reply to RTI application dated 31 October 2017, CIMAP (Application No CIMAP/R/2017/50008, 3 October 2017); Reply to RTI application dated 9 January 2018, CSIR (Application No CSIRH/R/2017/00191, 3 October 2017).
33. Priyanka Pulla, 'Big Claims, Little Evidence' *The Hindu* (25 February 2018) <https://www.thehindu.com/sci-tech/health/big-claims-little-evidence/article22847068.ece> accessed 23 September 2021.
34. KS Jayaraman, 'Did CSIR's Anti-Diabetic Drug Deserve Modi's Praise?' *The Wire* (4 October 2016) <https://thewire.in/health/bgr-34-csir-modi> accessed 23 September 2021.
35. Shailaja Chandra, 'Bitter Medicine' *The Indian Express* (1 November 2016) <https://indianexpress.com/article/opinion/columns/ayush-ministry-ayurveda-medicines-education-3731440/> accessed 23 September 2021.
36. Pulla (n 31).
37. Sinha and others (n 26).
38. Pulla (n 31).
39. CDRI, 'Reunion' <https://cdri.res.in/pdf/Reunion.pdf> accessed 23 September 2021.

40. Anoo Bhuyan, '"As of Now the Standards for Licencing Proprietary AYUSH Drugs Are Pretty Lax"' *The Wire* (31 March 2017) <https://thewire.in/government/ayush-ministry-interview-ajit-sharan> accessed 23 September 2021.
41. Robert B Saper and others, 'Heavy Metal Content of Ayurvedic Herbal Medicine Products' (2004) 292 *Journal of American Medical Association*, 2868 (Of the 27 companies whose products were sampled, 26 were Indian and one was Pakistani).
42. Robert B Saper and others, 'Lead, Mercury, and Arsenic in US and Indian-Manufactured Ayurvedic "cures" Sold via the Internet' (2008) 300 *Journal of American Medical Association*, 915.
43. SS Savrikar and B Ravishankar, 'Introduction to "Rasashaastra" the Iatrochemistry of Ayurveda' (2011) 8 *African Journal of Traditional, Complementary, and Alternative Medicines*, 66.
44. Rob Gair, 'Heavy Metal Poisoning from Ayurvedic "cures"' (2008) 50 *BC Medical Journal*, 105.
45. A Raviraja and others, 'Three Cases of Lead Toxicity Associated with Consumption of Ayurvedic "cures"' (2010) 25 *Indian Journal of Clinical Biochemistry*, 326.
46. Government of India, Ministry of Health and Family Welfare, Department of Ayurveda, Yoga & Naturopathy, Unani, Siddha and Homeopathy (Order F.No.K-11020/5/97-DCC (AYUSH), 14 October 2005).
47. Marek A Mikulski and others, 'Toxic Metals in Ayurvedic Preparations from a Public Health Lead Poisoning Cluster Investigation' (2017) 23 *International Journal of Occupational and Environmental Health*, 187.
48. Laura Breeher and others, 'A Cluster of Lead Poisoning among Consumers of Ayurvedic Medicine' (2015) 21 *International Journal of Occupational and Environmental Health*, 303.
49. Radha Sharma and Paul John, 'Poison in Ayurvedic Drugs' *The Times of India* (31 March 2017) <https://timesofindia.indiatimes.com/life-style/health-fitness/health-news/poison-in-ayurvedic-drugs/articleshow/57934912.cms> accessed 13 September 2021; Haritha John, 'Ayurvedic Lead Poisoning: Is Bengaluru Man's Case an Isolated One?' *The News Minute* (15 June 2015) <https://www.thenewsminute.com/article/ayurvedic-lead-poisoning-bengaluru-mans-case-isolated-one-30056> accessed 13 September 2021; Uday Yanamandra and others, 'Lead Poisoning Secondary to Unprescribed Ayurvedic "cures" Intake' (2020) 13 *BMJ Case Reports*, e238576; A Raviraja and others, 'Three Cases of Lead Toxicity Associated with Consumption of

Ayurvedic "cures"' (2010) 25 *Indian Journal of Clinical Biochemistry*, 326; Sujay Khandpur and others, 'Chronic Arsenic Toxicity from Ayurvedic "cures"' (2008) 47 *International Journal of Dermatology*, 618; G Gnanashanmugam and others, 'Mercury Toxicity Following Unauthorized Siddha Medicine Intake—A Mimicker of Acquired Neuromyotonia—Report of 32 Cases' (2018) 21 *Annals of Indian Academy of Neurology*, 49; Krishna S Gunturu and others, 'Ayurvedic Herbal Medicine and Lead Poisoning' (2011) 4 *Journal of Hematology and Oncology* <http://www.scopus.com/inward/record.url?scp=83655197902&partnerID=8YFLogxK> accessed 13 September 2021.

50. Abhishek Anand, 'Surge in Self-Medication Leading to Liver Damage during Covid, Says Dr Abby Philips' *India Today* (13 April 2022) <https://www.indiatoday.in/coronavirus-outbreak/story/surge-in-self-medication-leading-to-liver-damage-during-covid-says-dr-abby-philips-1936969-2022-04-13> accessed 2 May 2022.
51. Preetu Nair, 'Kerala: Doctor Sees Bid to Defame Him Using "Toolkit"' *The Times of India* (11 June 2021) <https://timesofindia.indiatimes.com/city/kochi/doc-sees-bid-to-defame-him-using-toolkit/articleshow/83411333.cms> accessed 2 May 2022.
52. The Drugs and Cosmetics Act 1940, s 33EE read with s 33-I.
53. The Drugs and Cosmetics Act 1940, s 17A read with s 27.
54. Priyanka Deshpande, 'Steroid Use in Ayurvedic "cures"s Rampant' *Midday* (23 November 2011) <https://www.mid-day.com/news/india-news/article/Steroid-use-in-Ayurvedic-medicines-rampant-143478> accessed 14 September 2021.
55. *CBI vs Gurbachan Singh* R.C. No. 0282010A0009 before Special Judge CBI, Punjab SAS Nagar, Mohali decided on 31 October, 2017.
56. *FDA Maharashtra State vs Velaram Choudhary and others* R.C.C. No. 1500099/SW/16 before the Chief Metropolitan Magistrate 15th Court Mazagaon, Mumbai decided on 7 June 2016; Test report from government lab generated by the government analyst, FDA Maharashtra (Report No NSQ/MUM/36735/2014, 29 October 2014); Test report from government lab generated by the government analyst, FDA Maharashtra (Report No NSQ/MUM/36736/2014, 29 October 2014).
57. 'Nimesulide Must Be Withdrawn Worldwide Due to Serious Liver Damage' *Therapeutics Initiative* (4 February 2008) <https://www.ti.ubc.ca/2008/02/04/nimesulide-must-be-withdrawn-worldwide-due-serious-liver-damage/> accessed 14 September 2021.

58. Savita Verma, 'Govt Bans Nimesulide Banned over Adverse Effects on Liver' *India Today* (15 February 2011) <https://www.indiatoday.in/india/north/story/government-bans-nimesulide-128660-2011-02-15> accessed 14 September 2021.
59. *FDA Maharashtra State vs Mahavir Ratilal Kothari and others* R.C.C. No. 01/2016 before the District & Sessions Judge, Shrirampur, District Ahmednagar decided on 19 October 2016; Test report from government lab generated by the government analyst, FDA Maharashtra (Report No NSQ/MUM/48742/2015, 18 March 2015).
60. Test report from government lab generated by the government analyst, FDA Maharashtra (Report No NSQ/MUM/48830/2015, 5 March 2015).
61. Reply to RTI application dated 19 October 2017, Public Information Officer, Food and Drug Administration, Maharashtra (Letter No /504/2217/15, 6 November 2017).
62. Government of India, Ministry of Health and Family Welfare, *Health and Family Welfare Statistics in India 2019-20* (16 October 2020) 151.
63. R Srinivasan and V Raji Sugumar, 'Spread of Traditional Medicines in India' (2017) 22 *Journal of Evidence-based Complementary & Alternative Medicine*, 194.
64. *Dr Mukhtiar Chand & Ors vs The State of Punjab & Ors* (1998) 7 SCC 579 (8 October 1998) <https://indiankanoon.org/doc/484509/> last accessed 23 March 2022.
65. *Delhi Medical Association vs Principal Secretary (Health) & Ors* W.P.(C) No.7865/2010 (Delhi HC, 8 April 2016) <https://indiankanoon.org/doc/95645241/> accessed 22 March 2022.
66. Government of West Bengal, Health and Family Welfare Department (AYUSH Branch), *Government Notification* (Notification No HF/O/AYUSH/650/1A-44/11, 1 September 2017).
67. Afshan Yasmeen, 'Order Allowing AYUSH Practitioners to Prescribe Allopathic Medicines Withdrawn' *The Hindu* (8 September 2020) <https://www.thehindu.com/news/national/karnataka/order-allowing-ayush-practitioners-to-prescribe-allopathic-medicines-withdrawn/article32555965.ece> accessed 24 March 2022.
68. *The Indian Medical Association vs State of Chattisgarh* WPPIL No. 109 of 2017 before the High Court of Chattisgarh (17 November 2017).
69. Indian Medical Association, 'Anti Quackery' <https://www.ima-india.org/ima/free-way-page.php?pid=143> accessed 24 March 2022; Indian Medical Association, 'Ayush Cannot Prescribe Modern

Medicine Drugs' <https://www.ima-india.org/ima/archive-page-details.php?pid=245> accessed 24 March 2022.

70. Department Related Parliamentary Standing Committee on Health and Family Welfare, *The National Medical Commission Bill, 2017* (One Hundred Ninth Report) (RS 2018); Sumi Sukanya Dutta, 'Doctors Oppose the NMC Bill Proposal to Allow AYUSH Doctors to Practice Modern Medicine; Say Its Akin to Legalising Quackery' *The New Indian Express* (30 December 2017) <https://www.newindianexpress.com/nation/2017/dec/30/doctors-oppose-the-nmc-bill-proposal-to-allow-ayush-doctors-to-practice-modern-medicine-say-its-aki-1740519.html> accessed 24 March 2022.

CHAPTER NINE

The Chaos of Indian Pharmacies and their Supply Chains

On a hot summer afternoon in May 1970, a drug inspector of the Maharashtra FDA, acting on a tip from an official in the Indian Railways, seized 17 containers containing 17,000 tablets that were in the possession of Mohammed Shabir while he was at the Bhusawal Railway Station. The drugs tested NSQ in the government laboratory leading to the prosecution of Shabir. The tricky question of law in this case that made its way all the way to the Supreme Court from the Magistrate's court, was whether Shabir could be convicted for the offence of "stocking" these drugs without a licence, even if he could establish that the "stocked" drugs were not meant for "sale".

The outcome in this case eventually turned upon the placement of a comma in Section 18(c) of the Drugs and Cosmetics Act 1940, which made it an offence to "manufacture for sale, or sell, or stocks or exhibit for sale, or distribute any drug..." without a licence. In 1978 when the Supreme Court finally delivered a judgment in this case, it ruled in favour of Shabir, concluding that:

> The absence of any comma after the word "stocks" clearly indicates that the clause "stocks or exhibits for sale" is one indivisible whole and it contemplates not merely stocking the drugs but stocking the drugs for the purpose of sale...[1]

Simply put, the court held that no person could be convicted for merely "stocking" drugs without a licence unless it could be proved that the drug was "stocked" for the purpose of a "sale". This interpretation by the Supreme Court however also meant that the law had a huge loophole, in that persons could store drugs without procuring any licences as long as they were not selling it. This opened up the possibility of huge gaps in the supply chain as a drug transited from the manufacturer to the pharmacy through the hands of multiple transporters and distributors, none of whom who could be prosecuted for "stocking" the drug without a licence. From a public health perspective, this loophole in the law which is yet to be rectified, is very worrying because even drugs which meet quality standards at the site of manufacture can degrade if not stored properly especially in India, where large parts of the country experience high heat or humidity.

The truly astonishing aspect of the court's judgment in Shabir is not the outcome but the fact that the Supreme Court completely missed the fact that just four years earlier it had come to the exact opposite conclusion in the case of Swantraj v. State of Maharashtra[2]. The accused in that case who did have a licence to sell drugs, had temporarily stocked medicine at an unlicenced premises leading to his prosecution. This time, when the court was faced with two different possible interpretations of the law—one that gave the benefit of doubt to the accused and the other which protected public health—it chose an interpretation that favoured protection of public health. In the court's words:

> If any godown, depot or premises become the nidus of spurious, time-expired or unscientifically stored drugs, can they be allowed to escape the coils of the penal law on the plea that they are not to be sold there, without great peril to patients? Then legal shelter for spurious drug rackets would be judicially ensured. And this colours construction. Stocked

> for sale there and then, or to be sold certainly but elsewhere later, are the two alternatives flowing from the language of Sec. 18(1) (c). The former permits abuse through, loopholes, the latter tightens up but loads the dealer with expenses and need for more licences. Since risk to life and health is avoided by the latter interpretation, we hold that the storage, even though for short spells and on ad hoc basis and without intent to sell at that place but as part of the sales business, comes within the scope of storage for sale in Sec. 18(c) and R. 62. To loosen the law in its joints is to play with life and therefore anti-humanist.

The accused in this case was convicted of violating the Drugs and Cosmetics Act 1940, even though there was no evidence that he intended to sell the drugs from the unlicenced premises. It is not clear how the Supreme Court missed its own decision in the Swantraj case while deciding the Shabir case, but since both decisions were delivered by benches consisting of two judges, both are considered good law and binding on lower court judges. The absurd consequence of these conflicting judgments is that even in 2020, more than 42 years after the judgment in Shabir, prosecutors and defence lawyers cite only one of these judgments to the exclusion of the other to benefit their respective clients. An illustration of how this plays out on the ground can be seen in the following two judgments: In February 2020, an Additional Sessions Judge in Nizamabad, Telangana, acquitted a former pharmacist, found to be stocking drugs in his house, on the basis of the decision in the Shabir case.[3] In the same year, a Sessions Judge in Faridabad, Haryana, cited the Swantraj judgment to convict a person accused of stocking 144 drugs without a licence.[4] These are but two examples of many other such judgments.

These contradictory outcomes in cases with similar fact situations paints a poor picture of the Indian judiciary. But it paints a poorer picture of the Ministry of Health which has done little to resolve the ambiguity created by the judgments in Swantraj and Shabir despite having moved amendments in Parliament to the Drugs and Cosmetics Act 1940 on at least three occasions since 1978. Even worse is the complete indifference of the Ministry of Health towards the Supreme Court's warning in Swantraj that there was a glaring gap in Indian law on the issue of regulating the transport of drugs throughout the country. Writing for the court, Justice Krishna Iyer noted in pertinent part, the following gap in Indian law:

> ...it is a glaring deficiency that while the Rules visualise wholesale distribution licences the forms do not spell out licences for mobile vans or distribution depots so essential for a wholesale distribution system. There is no doubt that if a scientific system of over-seeing wholesale distribution and a viable scheme of protected distribution is to be devised, licences for large and well-equipped conveyances and storage depots is desirable, nay, necessary. Indeed, storage in transit must also be licensed so that medicines do not suffer in the process. At present, no rules take care of transit by road or rail. Actually, cold storage or air-conditioned facilities for sensitive medicines are scarce in nationalised and private transport services and the drugs legislation winks at it. Likewise, the forms do not provide for storage depots or medical vans for wholesale supplies. Social guilt attaches to legal lacunae, the community being the victim. Arguments in this case have exposed these shortfalls in the law and we state them for legislative attention.[5]

The honourable Justice hit the nail on the head with his diagnosis on the complete absence of a regulatory framework for drugs in transit. But what has the Ministry of Health done to address this issue pointed out by the Supreme Court in 1974? The answer is not very much. The Drugs and Cosmetics Rules 1945 has remained silent on the issue of mandating cold-chain equipment for the supply chain dealing in pharmaceutical drugs. In fact, even those provisions in the Drugs and Cosmetics Rules 1945 dealing with retail pharmacies are completely outdated. The technical requirements for starting a pharmacy are laid out in Schedule N to the Drugs and Cosmetics Rules 1945 and have remained largely unchanged since 1972 when the requirements were first introduced into the law. It is entirely silent on cold-chain storage requirements, the maintenance of sterility, mechanisms for adverse event reporting, recall etc. Even Rules 64 and 65 of the Drugs and Cosmetics Rules 1945, which lay down the licencing requirements for retail pharmacies and wholesalers are silent on the technical requirements or management practices to be followed by owners of such establishments to ensure that drugs are maintained at the required temperature and humidity in a sterile environment. At most, Rule 64 requires pharmacies to maintain sales records and for premises to be "equipped with proper storage accommodation for preserving the properties of the drugs to which the licence applies". The law is silent on what exactly qualifies as "proper storage accommodation".

From a scientific and legal standpoint, these are poorly drafted regulations for a country that has climatic conditions varying from Himalayan cold to soaring heat in the rest of the country. In peak summer, the temperature across most parts of India can easily touch 40 degrees Celsius. Schedule P to the Drugs and Cosmetics Rules 1945 does specify some storage conditions for some drugs, from a labelling perspective and some of the prescribed storage conditions in Schedule P can be achieved only through cold storage conditions. In such a scenario, the law should specifically mandate cold storage equipment as a requirement of all pharmacy licences because a drug formulated to be stable till 25–30 degrees Celsius will most certainly degrade at 40 degrees Celsius.

The other truly appalling aspect of the Drugs and Cosmetics Rules 1945 when it comes to storage conditions is its complete silence on the issue of humidity control which again is a huge issue in many coastal states where humidity can rise beyond the average, affecting the stability of the drug. The WHO guidelines for example require humidity sensors and alarms to be installed in storage units for drugs.[6] Indian law sadly is completely silent on the issue.

The lack of such detail in the Indian law regulating pharmacies and wholesalers, especially with regard to storage conditions, is in sharp contrast to detailed regulations laid down by developed countries and international organisations like the WHO for storage and transport of drugs. This should truly terrify both the pharmaceutical industry and the medical community in India; since both of them are likely to face legal liability due to drugs that degrade in poor storage conditions.

The knight in shining armour in this story is once again the 59th report of the Parliamentary Standing Committee on Health which was tabled in 2012. This now famous and scathing report on the functioning of the CDSCO asked some relevant questions on the storage of drugs in pharmacies. These questions led to the CDSCO drawing up a set of Guidelines on Good Distribution Practices (GDP) for Pharmaceutical Products.[7] For the most part, these Guidelines bore close resemblance to the WHO's guidelines on good distribution practices for pharmaceutical products. While a good step forward, these Guidelines failed to incorporate the more specific WHO's model guidance for the storage and transport of time and temperature sensitive pharmaceutical products.[8]

However, even in its limited form, the GDP guidelines proposed by the CDSCO would have been an upgrade if given the force of the law that could be enforced against pharmacies. Unfortunately, these guidelines ran into trouble at the DCC. Originally, the DCC, in its 46th meeting held on 12 and 13 December 2013 was of the opinion that "guidelines on Good Distribution Practices for Pharmaceutical products

[are] the need of the hour as India is a vast country having major variations in temperature and climate" and it setup a sub-committee to recommend a path forward.[9] However, the very next year, the DCC rejected the recommendations of the sub-committee to give the GDP guidelines a binding legal status, on some rather absurd grounds, which are reproduced below:

> The sub-committee has laid stress on making provisions under the Drugs and Cosmetics Rules, for amending the various sale licences and bringing in the element of exercising control over the entire chain of distribution from end to end and registration of the transporter including amendments in the Act for the purpose. It was however, observed that there are over six lakh sale premises holding various sale licences. The amendment of these licences would be a momentous task and the attention of the Licensing Authorities in implementation of the present provisions under the Drugs and Cosmetics Rules 1945 to ensure the quality of drugs would be restricted. The members felt that judicious implementation of the present provisions can go a long way in ensuring that the patients get quality drugs than making more and more provisions which may be difficult to implement.[10]

In simple English, the DCC rejected the recommendation to amend the law to give a permanent legal character to the GDP guidelines because it would be too difficult for the state drug controllers to implement given the size of the supply chain and the number of pharmacies in India. Instead, it preferred to implement the existing regulations more "judiciously". From a public health perspective, this was an outrageous decision because it meant that the DCC were ready to risk degradation of drugs travelling through poor supply chains merely because an amendment to the law would create more work for the state drug controllers.

Surprisingly, however, four years later, in 2018, these GDP guidelines mysteriously made its way back onto the

DCC Agenda at its 53rd meeting. It is not clear why the GDP guidelines made it back to the agenda of the DCC but one possible reason is a surprise and well-publicized raid ordered by the Ministry of Health in 2017 on the infamous wholesale medical trading market at Bhagirath Palace, New Delhi. A retired joint secretary, K.L. Sharma, from the Ministry of Health recounts the raid and its shocking findings in his book on the state of drug regulation in India. This raid which involved 142 inspectors of the CDSCO, along with police protection, was conducted on 9 June 2017. According to Sharma, the inspection revealed a shocking state of affairs at the wholesale market including the storage of heat-sensitive drugs, which should have been stored at a temperature of 8–25 degree Celsius but instead were stored in a room whose temperature was 40 degrees Celsius. Many of the warehouses inspected during the raid were found lacking in cold-storage facilities and even in those where refrigerators were available, they were not always switched on. In one instance, the inspection team discovered a consignment of Tetanus Toxoid vaccines stocked in boxes containing icepacks or kept on open racks and shelves. These vaccines were actually required to be stored at 2–8 degree Celsius and were most likely degraded because of the poor storage conditions. Further, the inspections team discovered that none of the outlets had power backups in case of a failure of electricity.[11]

Sharma also narrates a startling account of premises so cramped that staff had to walk on top of boxes of medicines to reach the other end of the premises. The staff apparently were not trained in the handling or storage of medicine. This is not at all surprising because unlike pharmacies which are expressly required by the law to be under the charge of a "registered pharmacist" (which requires a degree in pharmacy), the law provides wholesalers with the option of keeping their premises under the charge of either a "registered pharmacist" or a person who has passed the "matriculation examination or its equivalent with four years experience in dealing with drugs". This requirement, which was introduced into the law in 1980, was further diluted in 2000, when the following third category of qualifications was added to the rules: any person "who holds a degree of a recognised University with one year's experience, in dealing with drugs"[12]. In other words, a person with a Bachelor's in Horticulture could be placed in charge of a premises as long as he had a year's experience in handling drugs.

Even more worryingly, Sharma reveals that documentation and record keeping practices at these facilities were abysmal. The law clearly specifies certain record keeping requirements for wholesalers.[13] However, in 17 instances during this raid, wholesale dealers at Bhagirath Palace were unable to produce purchase bills raising doubts about the source of the drugs in question.[14] Summing up the results of the inspections, Sharma concluded:

> Whatever the inspection revealed, speaks very poorly of the storage and distribution practices in vogue and it poses a serious threat to millions of unsuspecting consumers. If this could happen in the capital city that also houses the national regulator, the position in far-flung areas can only be imagined.[15]

The fact that the above statement was made by the top bureaucrat responsible for drug regulatory policy should give us serious cause for worry.

It is possible that the shocking revelations from the inspection of Bhagirath Palace forced the DCC to put the GDP guidelines back on the agenda. At the next meeting in 2019, the minutes of the 54th meeting of the DCC record the following abrupt recommendation to give legal sanctity to the GDPs:

> DCC deliberated the proposal and found that there has been no comment received from the State Drug Controllers and recommended to make necessary provisions for Good Distribution Practice under the Drugs and Cosmetics Rules 1945.[16]

Pressure from individual states may have also played a role in shaping the above recommendation. For example, at the same meeting, states like Punjab specifically asked for a mandatory requirement for all pharmacies to have air-conditioning and power backup especially in the summer months when room temperature soars above 30 degrees Celsius, which is the outer-limit in the stability specification for drugs being sold in India.[17]

But as is the case with many of these recommendations by the DCC, there is many a slip between the cup and the lip. Three years later, as this book goes to print, the Ministry of Health is yet to introduce the required amendments to the Drugs and Cosmetics Rules 1945 to give legal force to the GDP guidelines. In other words, nothing really changed despite the official acknowledgment that the GDP guidelines require legal status in order to ensure the quality of medicine travelling through the supply chain.

Presumably, private pharmacies and distributors are not particularly keen on the GDP guidelines getting a legal character because it would increase their costs of business. A key factor contributing to their nonchalance on this issue is the fact that Section 19 of the Drugs and Cosmetics Act 1940 gives pharmacies complete legal immunity in cases where a drug purchased or stored at their premises fails quality testing. This immunity is contingent on their having procured the drug from a licenced entity after exercising "reasonable due diligence" and being able to prove that the drug was "properly stored". More often than not, we noticed a trend among drug inspectors giving pharmacies a free pass in prosecutions involving substandard drugs as long as they are able to show that the drug was purchased from a legitimate source. Removing or even diluting this immunity from prosecution may create pressure within the community of pharmacies and distributors to actively support the enactment of new regulations on storage and distribution of drugs.

Regardless of the indifference on part of the pharmacies and distributors, one would expect sustained public pressure to be applied on the government to reform this sector since a poorly regulated supply chain has significant implications for public health. However, there is barely a squeak in the Indian press or civil society on the delays in enacting these much-needed and long-delayed reforms.

Rather, much of the regulatory discussion on pharmacies in India is concentrated on the following issues: the necessity of mandating the presence of registered pharmacists in pharmacies, unlicenced sale of addictive drugs and the resistance against the e-pharmacy juggernaut which is threatening the existence of the "brick and mortar" pharmacies that form the backbone of the politically powerful All India Organization of Chemists and Druggists (AIOCD). Each of these debates have implications for public health and are explained in the following pages.

Do pharmacies require pharmacists?

When the Drugs Inquiry Committee submitted its report in 1931, it spent a fair deal of print on the issue of regulating pharmacies. At the time, there was no regulation of the profession of pharmacists and the committee clearly had a poor opinion of the crop of people in charge of pharmacies, as evident from the following extract of its report:

> The profession here is represented by a set of people known as compounders whose status, functions and duties are ill-defined and improperly understood. They carry on the compounding, dispensing and selling of drugs and chemicals from day

> to day. They handle drugs and poisons with the utmost ease and freedom and in many cases in ignorance of their properties and potency. They also, do work as dressers and laboratory assistants in some of the hospitals and dispensaries. Anesthetists and operation assistants are sometimes drawn from their ranks. The list of their manifold duties does not end there. In some places, they pose as physicians and surgeons and acquire a position and income by no means inglorious or negligible. In respect of qualifications justifying the role they fill, they have little or none to boast of. Their standard of education is low and not much is expected of them by way of professional training.[18]

Clearly dissatisfied with the functioning of the profession, the committee recommended a radical reorganization of the profession of pharmacy. It called for the enactment of a legislation to prescribe educational qualifications for pharmacists and regulation of the profession through a body that represented pharmacists.[19] Those recommendations translated into law 17 years later when the Pharmacy Act was finally enacted in 1948 by the Constituent Assembly. This law created the Pharmacy Council of India, as a self-regulatory body that could prescribe qualification, educational, and registration requirements for pharmacists in India. This legislation however did not immediately mandate all pharmacies to be run only under the supervision of this new class of registered pharmacists. This law allowed persons already in the business of compounding, preparing, mixing or dispensing drugs to continue doing so with the caveat in Section 42 of the legislation that individual states could fix cut-off dates, after which only pharmacists registered under the Pharmacy Act 1948 could engage in the aforementioned acts of compounding or dispensing drugs. Presumably, this power had been delegated to states because each state needed time to invest in the training, education and creation of this new class of professional pharmacists.

Separate and apart from the Pharmacy Act 1948, the Drug Rules 1945, as originally notified on 21 December 1945, had already forayed into laying down the criteria for "qualified persons" required to be employed by those seeking licences to operate pharmacies. The three categories recognized in the definition of qualified persons for the territories administered directly by the Government of India (at the time individual provinces had the right to have separate licensing rules for pharmacies) were *first*, persons holding degrees in pharmacy or pharmaceutical chemistry in an institution approved by the licencing authority under the Drugs Act, *second*, if they were a member of the Pharmaceutical Society of Great Britain, and *third*, if they had not less than "four years practical experience" which "in the opinion of the authority" was "adequate".[20] As is obvious, the last category basically opened the door to almost anybody running a pharmacy and was counter-productive to the intent behind the enactment of the Pharmacy Act 1948.

The states made slow progress in enforcing Section 42 of the Pharmacy Act. Commenting on the situation in 1954, the Pharmaceutical Enquiry Report, setup by the Government of India, had this to say:

> It is not enough, if the Pharmacy Act is extended on paper to all the States in the country. Excepting for a very few States, the progress made by other States in the enforcement of the Drugs and Pharmacy legislation has been very poor. The State Governments have not realized the urgent need for starting institutions for providing courses of study in pharmacy.[21]

A decade later, the situation vis-à-vis the enforcement of Section 42 by the states was no better as evidenced from a tense discussion in the Rajya Sabha during Question Hour in September 1965, where Arjun Arora, a MP from Uttar Pradesh, accused the Deputy Minister of Health of misleading the House on the status of enforcement of the Pharmacy Act

1948. In his oral statement, P.S. Naskar, the Deputy Minister for Health, had informed the house that all states and union territories, except for five, had "enforced the Pharmacy Act, 1948 in varying degrees".[22] However, the statement tabled by the Deputy Minister had indicated that only the state of Uttar Pradesh had enforced Section 42 of the Pharmacy Act 1948, restricting the profession of pharmacy to pharmacists registered as per the Pharmacy Act 1948. When the government was accused by the MP who raised the question, of "seriously misleading" the House, the Health Minister was quick to explain that "many of the states" lacked qualified pharmacists and hence could not enforce Section 42.[23]

Finally in 1970, some much-needed legal reforms were executed by the Union Government. To begin with, Rule 65 of the Drugs and Cosmetics Rules 1945 (which post 1955, applied across the country, after states were stripped of their rule making power under the Drugs and Cosmetics Act) was amended to fix 31 December 1969 as the relevant date after which licences for pharmacies would mandatorily require the business of dispensing drugs to be carried out under the supervision of a registered pharmacist. No longer could someone with four years of experience in "dealing with drugs" be considered a "qualified person" for the purpose of running a pharmacy. A more wide-ranging reform was enacted in 1975 when the Ministry of Health introduced in Parliament, a legislation to amend Section 42 of the Pharmacy Act 1948. This amendment aimed at deleting the earlier wording that allowed state governments to decide the cut-off date beyond which only registered pharmacists could dispense drugs and instead, replaced it with a deadline of five years, after which, all states would have to ensure that only "registered pharmacists" could engage in the business of mixing, dispensing, or compounding drugs.

During the debates preceding the vote on the bill in the

Rajya Sabha, the Minister of State in the Ministry of Health, Chaudhary Ram Sewak, explained that although the Pharmacy Act 1948 had been in force for 27 years, only three states and the Union Territory of Delhi had enforced the mandate of Section 42 i.e., restricting the business of pharmacy to "registered pharmacists" who had the qualifications prescribed under the Pharmacy Act and were registered with the Pharmacy Council of India.[24] Given the inaction on the part of the states in notifying cut-off dates under Section 42, the Union Government had moved the bill under discussion to fix a cut-off date of five years for the enforcement of Section 42 across India. The Bill breezed through Parliament in 1976 with little opposition and literally so, since Prime Minister Indira Gandhi had jailed most of the Opposition after declaring an Emergency in 1975. The enactment of this amendment meant that only pharmacists registered with the Pharmacy Council of India could practice the profession of pharmacy from September 1981 onward.

A few years after the enactment of this amendment, in 1978, the DCC discussed concerns raised by many states that due to a shortage of pharmacists, there was a shortage of pharmacies in rural areas thereby limiting access to medicine. This was in context of the rule change carried out in 1969 to limit the grant of pharmacy licences to only registered pharmacists. As a result, many states were pressing for some kind of relaxation of the rule which made the presence of a registered pharmacist compulsory for all pharmacies.[25] Only some states like Goa and Tamil Nadu resisted any dilution of standards. The drug controller from Tamil Nadu even disputed the reasoning offered by some state drug controllers regarding the shortage of pharmacies in rural areas. According to him, the real reason was the lack of doctors in rural areas because of which there was little interest in opening pharmacies in rural areas. At the end of the meeting, the DCC resolved to drop the "registered pharmacist" requirement for opening and operating a pharmacy for towns with a population of less than 20,000 persons and instead allow anyone who has "passed a matriculate examination with science or any other equivalent examination, and who has also passed a 6 months training course approved by the State Government" to open a pharmacy.[26] It is not clear whether this decision was actually implemented by a rule change but the discussions provide a flavour of the policy making process in that era where decisions were taken mostly on the basis of anecdotal evidence rather than empirical evidence.

Ultimately the deadline of 31 August 1981, prescribed in the 1976 amendment to the Pharmacy Act 1948, was crossed with no extension being granted despite widespread concerns regarding a shortage of pharmacists in many states. Surprisingly, three months after the deadline was crossed, in November 1981, the Ministry of Health moved yet another legislation in Parliament to further extend the deadline by an additional three years because "representations" had been received from various quarters about the inadequacy of trained pharmacists. This new bill in 1981 sought to amend the law in order to extend the existing deadline to 1 September 1984. This time around, the Minister of Health, B. Shankaranand, who described the legislation as a "very simple bill" came under withering criticism from MPs in both the Rajya Sabha and the Lok Sabha. These MPs questioned not just the logic of extending a deadline three months after it had recently expired, but also the guarantee that the supposed shortage of pharmacists would be resolved in a period of 3 years.[27] Some MPs also strongly resisted pushing the deadline any further on the grounds that allowing untrained persons to dispense medicine posed a serious danger to public health. One MP, M.M.S. Siddhu, a doctor from Uttar Pradesh, emphasizing the importance of having trained pharmacists in charge of dispensing drugs, summed up the situation prevailing at that time in the following words:

> The pharmacist is an important link in dispensing. Especially the Minister may think over this. The opinion of the Government is that the doctors should prescribe the drugs by approved or generic name. But these persons are unable to read even the prescription of the doctor. They are going to dispense drugs which they don't understand. They dispense a prescription and say it is a similar drug, it has got the same action. Such persons are dangerous to the patients and the persons to whom the drugs are supplied.
>
> Meanwhile, take the number of chemists and druggist shops which have been opened. You will find that in most of them the untrained pharmacists are working there. The trained pharmacists are getting unemployed because they demand better salaries. So, in order to get cheap labour, the doctors as well as the hospitals and nursing homes, other than those of the Government, want untrained pharmacists to work with them. The result is that untrained people who are not conversant with sterilization, drugs, the incompatibility of drugs, the mode of action of drugs and storage of drugs are assisting them and dispensing drugs. That is dangerous. The untrained pharmacists are working in chemists shops and other places where the Drugs and Cosmetics Act also is applicable.[28] (sic)

Notwithstanding this opposition to any more extensions, the Parliament voted in favour of extending the deadline for Section 42 by another three years to 1 September 1984. In the following years, the existing lobby of "chemists and druggists", who qualified for pharmacy licences in the pre-1970 era, protested and even went on a strike against the upcoming deadline in 1984, the reverberations of which were felt even in Parliament as at least one MP took up the issue in Parliament.[29] In any event, the deadline of 1 September 1984 was not extended any further, thereby officially closing the door to anybody but "registered pharmacists" to be in charge of dispensing drugs at pharmacies.

Through the entire course of the aforementioned policy-making exercise, the Ministry of Health never once produced any report with empirical evidence stating the number of "registered pharmacists" available in India or the supposed shortage faced in different states. As a result, no measures were instituted to help states that did actually face a shortage of pharmacists. It was therefore not surprising when in the following decades, some states like Bihar have repeatedly complained about the lack of "registered pharmacists". The most recent such complaint from Bihar was at the meeting of the DCC held in July 2020, when the drug controller from the state once again asked for a relaxation in the criteria to start a pharmacy. The DCC for its part dismissed the demand on the grounds that there was no shortage of pharmacists in the country.[30] Once again, the DCC did not cite any empirical evidence to back its claim. It is important for the government to tackle such issues with empirical evidence because even a prosperous state like Maharashtra "confessed" at a DCC meeting that 34% of the pharmacies in the state did not have registered pharmacists![31] While accurate figures are not available, we noticed quite a few prosecutions in states against pharmacies being run without pharmacists. It is not clear whether this is due to a shortage of pharmacists or because the owners of pharmacies are trying to maximize their profits by hiring unqualified staff in lieu of registered pharmacists.

The main pushback to Section 42 from its opponents has taken place in the form of constitutional litigation in High Courts across the country. These challenges were mostly brought about by small businesses who wanted to engage in the drug trade, given its very profitable margins, without having to incur the cost of hiring a registered pharmacist. The Allahabad High Court alone heard four such cases in the decade of the 90s. In the last of these cases, Ramesh Giri Prop. M/S Goswami Medical Stores v. State of U.P & Ors.[32] a bench of the Allahabad High Court categorically rejected a constitutional challenge mounted by a petitioner who claimed that his fundamental right to trade under Article 19(1)(g) of the Constitution was being arbitrarily curbed by Section 42 of the Pharmacy Act 1948. A second line of argument advanced by the petitioner was that the law, as it stood, did not require a "registered pharmacist" if drugs were being sold in their original packaging. This argument was based on the fact that Rule 65(19) of the Drugs and Cosmetics Rules 1945 required a registered pharmacist to be present any time drugs were being sold in a container other than the one in which it was originally sold by the manufacturer. The petitioners drew a negative inference from this rule to claim an exemption from the requirement of having "registered pharmacists" present on occasions where drugs were being sold in their original packaging. Such constitutional challenges against regulatory law rarely succeed and the Allahabad High Court dismissed the challenge on the grounds that public interest weighed in favour of regulating the drug trade. One such pertinent observation of the court is reproduced as follows:

> ...the supply of medicines against a prescription essentially requires certain skill for correct interpretation of generally illegible routine prescriptions, checking the doses prescribed and detailing the same properly to the patient. It is also correct that frequently certain Latin terms are also used in the prescriptions detailing about drugs and food items which is only possible to follow through a qualified person. Such kind of job cannot be left open to be performed by an unqualified person. The framers of law are experts of the subject and they know better what steps are required for maintaining health of members of the society and to prevent any kind of health hazards by sale of spurious and sub-standard drugs. It

> is difficult to accept the contention raised that the restrictions are in any way against public interest.[33]

Despite the law being settled on the issue, a similar challenge was mounted in Bihar before the Patna High Court in 2012. The petitioner once again questioned the prohibition on selling drugs in the same packaging as produced by the manufacturer. The logic fueling these challenges is that unlike in the past where pharmacies would actually compound drugs, modern-day pharmacies only sell packaged drugs. In a judgment delivered in December 2016, the Patna High Court dismissed this challenge on the basis of the Ramesh Giri judgment of the Allahabad High Court.[34]

The Schedule K crisis

One of the peculiar aspects of law making in India is that every law will always have that one provision granting the government the discretion to create exemptions. In case of the Drugs and Cosmetics Act 1940, that provision is Schedule K, which basically exempts certain categories of drugs handled by certain categories of people from different legal requirements that generally apply to pharmacies. For example, government hospitals are exempted from the requirement of applying for sales licences like private pharmacies, although they are still required to ensure that drugs are stored properly. Similarly, registered medical practitioners are allowed to store and dispense drugs for their patients without the requirement for applying for sales licences, provided the drugs are stored properly.

In 1961, an exemption was created in Schedule K for pharmacies in villages with less than 1,000 people allowing them to stock 15 "household remedies" that included Aspirin, "syrups, lozenges, pills and tablets for cough", and tablets of Quinine Sulphate without being subject to any of the regular licencing requirements that applied to other pharmacies. Along the years, the government continued amending Schedule K to include more categories such as ophthalmic ointments required to be distributed as part of the National Trachoma Control Programme or Chloroquine tablets required to be distributed as part of the National Malaria Eradication Programme. Unlike the earlier conditional exemptions granted to government hospitals or doctors (subject to storage conditions), these were unconditional exemptions with no mention on how the drugs in question were to be stored.

The list of exemptions in Schedule K was expanded in 1980 to the following categories of medical workers for drugs being supplied by either the central or state governments: multipurpose workers attached to primary health centres/sub-centres, community health volunteers under the Rural Health Scheme; nurses, auxiliary nurses, midwives, and health visitors attached to urban family welfare centres, and PHC and anganwadi workers (added in 1989).[35] All of these workers were given an unconditional exemption from Chapter IV of the Drugs and Cosmetics Act 1940, which dealt with licencing requirements for pharmacies, meaning that they were not even required to adhere to proper storage conditions.

This trend of widening Schedule K continues. As late as 2019, the Ministry of Health proposed expanding Schedule K further to include primary healthcare centres and wellness centres in urban areas and Accredited Social Health Activist (ASHA) workers.[36] As originally envisaged under the National Health Mission, the ASHA worker, whose minimum qualification is to be literate or preferably pass 10th grade examinations, was supposed to be a "depot holder" for essential drugs like Oral Rehydration Therapy, Iron Folic Acid Tablet, Choloroquinine, oral pills, and condoms so that they could be made available to people in the community.[37]

These kind of exemptions in Schedule K, prior to 1984,

would have allowed these government health workers to dispense medicine despite lacking the qualification of a registered pharmacist. However, these exemptions in Schedule K could not extend to dispensing drugs, once Section 42 of the Pharmacy Act 1948 came into effect in 1984. This is because a provision of the Drugs and Cosmetics Rules 1945 cannot create an exemption to the provisions of a completely different law like the Pharmacy Act. This fact, however, appears to have missed the attention of the policymakers in the Ministry of Health and also the state governments, both of whom continue to seek cover under Schedule K to justify their decisions to allow government health workers to prescribe drugs despite them not being registered pharmacists.

The only pushback to these proposals including the one made by the Ministry of Health in 2019 to include ASHA workers in Schedule K, was from the Pharmacy Council of India (PCI) and other associations of pharmacists on the grounds that such an exemption would violate Section 42 of the Pharmacy Act and that the government should just hire more registered pharmacists since there was no shortage of pharmacists in the country.[38]

Ultimately, the government walked back on its proposal to include ASHA workers but it did include Community Health Officers in Schedule K. These health workers, who were a new category of "mid-level health provider" created under a new government health scheme called Ayushman Bharat are not trained doctors but anybody with a Bachelors in Science in Community Health, a Nurse or an Ayurvedic practitioner trained and certified through a university![39] There is a case to argue that none of these "medical" workers can dispense drugs given the bar in Section 42.

These exemptions in Schedule K need to be understood in the larger political context of poorly designed national health policies which are so centered on grand pronouncements of making healthcare more accessible and affordable, that policymakers forget to pay the necessary attention to legal and logistical details. Once legal issues such as the storage or dispensing of drugs are flagged during the implementation process, the Drug Regulation Section of the Ministry is likely forced by its overlords in the Ministry of Health to issue notifications under Schedule K to overcome all such legal hurdles, with little attention being paid to the original intent that informed the regulation of pharmacies under the Drugs and Cosmetics Act 1940 or Section 42 of the Pharmacy Act. This is typical of lawmaking in the country.

The situation is no better with public health programs run by state governments; which often leads to strikes, legal notices, and litigation. In 2012 in Rajasthan, nurses went on a strike because the state government tried to get them to dispense prescription drugs for a government scheme.[40] The nurses complained that they would be liable for violation of Section 42 of the Pharmacy Act 1948 if they dispensed drugs. From statements made to the press by an official in the state government, it appears that they were under the impression that nurses would be covered under the exemption in Schedule K. This was incorrect. In Kerala, the All Kerala Pharmacists Unions has litigated extensively against the government over the involvement of nurses in dispensing of drugs.[41] Similarly in Haryana, pharmacists accused government-run hospitals and primary health centres of violating Section 42 of the Pharmacy Act 1948 by not employing registered pharmacists.[42]

At some point, the Ministry of Health has to tackle this issue of medical professionals other than pharmacists dispensing drugs. This should be done through a rigorous, well-planned survey aimed at capturing the extent to which pharmacies and hospitals in India in both the private and public sector are staffed with pharmacists, the extent of the alleged shortage of registered pharmacists and the reasons for such shortage.

Such an exercise is essential to protect public health in India. Poorly qualified personnel in charge of pharmacies are bound to make mistakes in filling prescriptions or substituting drugs based on their generic names or even playing the role of first medical provider as is often the case with most pharmacies in India. If there is indeed a shortage of pharmacists, the Ministry of Health must come up with a plan to address the shortage, preferably by investing more in pharmacy colleges and training people. The current haphazard approach which is centered on tinkering with Schedule K is unacceptable.

Cracking the whip on illegal pharmacies, drug peddlers, and fake doctors: Of the good, the lenient, and the incompetent

Thanks to the skeletal licensing requirements in the Drugs and Cosmetics Act 1940, a licenced pharmacy cannot really violate many regulations, but even those few skeletal legal requirements are flouted regularly in India. The principal categories of prosecutions launched against pharmacies include the stocking or sale of drugs without the required licences (these include instances of moving premises without changing the address on the licence), flouting licence conditions by not having a registered pharmacist at the pharmacy during working hours, the failure to maintain necessary documentation of purchases or sales and lastly, dispensing certain drugs without a prescription. The most serious offence, however, from a public health perspective is the first category i.e., stocking or selling drugs without a licence. In a good percentage of such cases, the drugs in question are "habit forming" drugs, as addictive drugs are often described in judgments delivered by Indian courts.

In the state of Punjab, which has been in the middle of a drug addiction crisis for the last decade, drug inspectors have been very active in raiding and prosecuting establishments storing and selling drugs without having the relevant pharmacy licences under the Drugs and Cosmetics Rules 1945. Unlike many other states, the accused in these cases actually spend time in jail until the trials for these offences are concluded. Through the e-courts website, we were able to find at least 230 cases that were prosecuted by drug inspectors across Punjab over the last decade for violation of the provisions relating to stocking and selling drugs. In 124 of these cases, the drug inspectors managed to secure convictions against the persons accused of violating the law related to the stocking and selling of drugs. Most of these cases pertained to stocking and selling of drugs without the required licences. The punishments handed out by judges in these cases were surprisingly tough. In several cases, the accused were actually given the statutory minimum punishment of three years, along with the minimum fine of ₹1 lakh.[43] In most of these cases, though the accused had either already served time in prison awaiting their trial or alternatively if they were first time offenders, the court would release them on probation meaning that they could find their way back to jail to complete the sentence if they were found breaching the terms of their probation. In some cases, judges rejected the request for probation "because of the fact that in the State of Punjab, there is hue and cry regarding the youth becoming addicts day by day and if the unauthorised persons are allowed to keep and sell the drugs, more and more persons will be becoming users and addicts of the drugs".[44]

The quality of prosecutions, rate of convictions, and the speed of the trials in Punjab would have made for an impressive tale except that we discovered that at least 153 of these cases were heard by wrong judges due to a poorly drafted amendment to the Drugs and Cosmetics Act 1940 in 2008. This amendment had originally sowed confusion across the country regarding the courts of competent jurisdiction that could try certain categories of offences under the Drugs and Cosmetics Act 1940. Due to the confusion, most new prosecutions as well as existing prosecutions were being filed before the Sessions Court instead of Judicial Magistrates as was the case till 2008. In any event, this confusion was cleared by the Kerala High Court in the case of Zest Pharma v. Drug Inspector[45] in 2013 when it clarified that only cases involving offences such as spurious and adulterated drugs would be triable before Sessions Judges, while all other offences would be triable by Judicial Magistrates as was the case earlier. Even in Punjab, some of the Sessions Judges cited the decision in Zest Pharma to transfer cases to Judicial Magistrates. Surprisingly in other districts of Punjab, Sessions Judges continued to try and decide such cases even after 2013. From the data we were able to gather, a total of 153 cases (and possibly more) involving pharmacies were heard wrongly by Session Judges with 107 of these cases ending in conviction! In many of these 107 convictions, the judges awarded the statutory minimum punishment that included imprisonment of up to three to five years. Legally speaking, all these sentences should be set aside and the accused cannot be tried again because of the constitutional safeguard against trying people for the same offence more than once.

Punjab is not the only state to witness such gaffes. West Bengal is another state that experienced a different kind of gaffe at the prosecution stage. We were able to access approximately 95 judgments in West Bengal through the e-courts system for the time period between 2015 and 2019. In 61 of these cases which were filed before the Session Judges in Darjeeling and Malda, the state was prosecuting persons found to be "stocking" without a licence, large quantities of habit-forming, addictive drugs including fixed-dose-combinations that contained Tramadol (an opiate prone to abuse), sleeping medication that contained Benzodiazepam (a psychoactive drug) and an assortment of cough syrups that contained Codeine, which is an opiate and known to be heavily abused in India. The problem, however, was that in all these cases, it was the police which was conducting raids, arresting persons, and prosecuting them before Sessions Judges. The Drugs and Cosmetics Act 1940 is very clear that only drug inspectors notified by the state in the official gazette can institute prosecutions for offences under this legislation. As a result, in all 61 cases, the Sessions Judge acquitted the accused on the grounds that the police had no jurisdiction to prosecute cases under the Drugs and Cosmetics Act 1940. In another 22 cases that were prosecuted by drug inspectors who had the jurisdiction under the law to do so, the courts acquitted the accused due to poor investigations or procedural irregularities.

Far away in Maharashtra, we were able to access 62 judgments delivered in prosecutions filed between 1990 and 2017 against unlicenced pharmacies for "stocking" drugs or pharmacies breaching the terms of their licences (maintenance of records and having a registered pharmacist). Unlike in West Bengal, these prosecutions were at least filed by the correct authorities and before the correct courts resulting in 26 convictions and 36 acquittals. Unlike in West Bengal and Punjab, the prosecutions in Maharashtra did not appear to be targeted at persons stocking "habit forming" drugs. Also, unlike in Punjab, where prosecutions are quite speedy, the successful convictions in Maharashtra were achieved in a time frame ranging from three years to 18 years. Even then, the sentencing was exceptionally lenient. Of the 26 cases that ended in conviction, in 19 cases, the Judicial Magistrates awarded a sentence of "Simple Imprisonment Till the Rising of the Court", meaning that the convicted persons could leave the court soon as the judge rose for the day. This virtual non-punishment was accompanied by small fines ranging from ₹5,000 to ₹30,000.

In neighbouring Andhra Pradesh, we were able to access 55 prosecutions pertaining to the violations of laws that apply to pharmacies. Convictions were secured in only 14 cases, while there were acquittals in the remaining 41 cases. A small number of these cases involved "habit forming" drugs. In most of the other cases, a large variety of modern drugs were seized indicating that the persons in question were running unlicenced pharmacies. For example, in one case a total of 249 different drugs were seized.[46] In the 14 cases where convictions were secured, courts in Andhra Pradesh delivered sentences of up to three years imprisonment in six cases, along with fines ranging from ₹1,000 to ₹1,20,000.

The last state that warrants a discussion is Haryana, where the state government has been using the Drugs and Cosmetics Act 1940 to crack down on fake doctors and unregistered medical practitioners. While practicing medicine without being registered is an offence under the laws regulating the practice of modern medicine and traditional Indian medicine, we suspect that the state finds it quite difficult to prove beyond reasonable doubt that these unlicenced medical practitioners were actually practicing medicine. In such cases, it may be easier to successfully prosecute them on the grounds that they were storing drugs illegally. We came across at least 27 such prosecutions in Haryana, 17 of which ended in convictions for unlawfully stocking drugs without a licence. In most cases, the court awarded imprisonment of three to four years accompanied with fines of ₹1 lakh.

Take for example, the case of State of Haryana v. Dr. Mohinder Kumar[47] where the defendant was supposedly running a clinic in Panipat. A raid by a drug inspector found him to be stocking at least 20 different types of "allopathic drugs". When asked to produce proof of his registration, the accused was unable to do so. If he was a registered medical practitioner of either modern or Indian medicine, he could have taken benefit of Schedule K which allows such practitioners of medicine to store drugs without the requirement of a pharmacy licence. He was unable to provide such evidence and was hence found guilty of violating the provisions of the Drugs and Cosmetics Act 1940 that require licences to be procured for stocking or selling drugs and was sentenced to three years in prison along with a fine of ₹1 lakh.

The common thread running through the above discussion is that the Drugs and Cosmetics Act 1940 is used primarily to prosecute illegal pharmacies, drug peddlers, and fake doctors. All these prosecutions concentrate on the persons stocking or selling drugs or the maintenance of sales records. Zero attention is being paid to the issue of how exactly drugs are stored in order to maintain their potency, especially in hot and humid climates. This is because of the original sin of the Drugs and Cosmetics Rules 1945 not prescribing legal requirements that mandatorily require pharmacies to maintain cold storage equipment, power-backups, and alarms that can warn of humidity and temperature crossing certain limits. If there is no law regulating these issues, it cannot be broken. From a public health perspective, the silence on storage requirements across the supply chain is a disaster.

The policy paralysis on regulating online pharmacies and a chance to reform the regulation of pharmacies and supply chains

The Indian drug market is currently witnessing an epic clash between the traditional brick and mortar pharmacies, which are mostly small businesses and new online pharmacies, which sell drugs through the internet; i.e., they accept orders and payments through apps on smart phones and deliver the drugs ordered directly to the consumer. Most online pharmacies are owned by big corporations and are currently attracting billions of dollars in investment from foreign funds and big Indian businesses. The populist tendency in such battles is to side with small businesses, except that in the case of "brick and mortar" pharmacies, there have been several findings by the Competition Commission of India (CCI) that these businesses regularly colluded with each other, under the umbrella of trade associations, in order to raise the prices of drugs instead of competing with each to provide the consumer with medicines at the lowest possible price.[48] On occasion, pharmacists have also required pharmaceutical manufacturers to take "no object certificates" from their trade associations before appointing "stockists", failing which all pharmacists in an area would refuse to buy from the "stockist". Such carterlization is illegal under the Competition Act and over the years, the CCI has repeatedly ruled against different trade associations comprising pharmacists for engaging in anti-competitive behaviour that hurts consumer interests. The hope of many, including the CCI, is that online pharmacies with their venture capital backing and eagerness to capture market share through deep discounts, can disrupt these old cartels in the pharmacy sector and lower prices of drugs for the final consumers.[49]

As a part of their advocacy campaigns against online pharmacies, trade associations of "brick and mortar" pharmacies have adopted fear as their primary tactic, claiming that online pharmacies will open the door to drug abuse and sale of substandard and counterfeit medicine. They have also exploited the lack of a specific legal framework for online pharmacies to litigate before the courts seeking injunctions against online pharmacies.[50] However, these tactics have not worked to deter investors as can be witnessed by the huge investments being made by private capital in online pharmacies.[51] The Covid-19 pandemic further gave a boost to this sector when the Ministry of Health invoked its special powers under Section 26B of the Drugs and Cosmetics Act 1940, to allow all pharmacies to accept prescriptions through email and also deliver the drugs to the doorstep of the consumer.[52]

Apart from the above notification, the government for its part is doing precious little to lay down regulations specifically for online pharmacies. At most, in 2017 it did publish a set of draft rules to regulate online pharmacies but never notified them into law.[53] In any case, these draft rules were completely inadequate to deal with the issue of possible prescription abuse. Under the Drugs and Cosmetics Rules 1945, a prescription once filled, has to be physically marked by the pharmacist to prevent its reuse.[54] Since online pharmacies typically deal with photographed prescriptions, it is not possible for pharmacists to physically mark the prescription. The solution as devised in other countries like the United States is to create a system of electronic prescriptions that can be electronically verified by pharmacies. Apart from reducing the possibility of abuse, electronic prescribing in the United States has also increased the efficiency and accuracy of pharmacies.[55] The Indian government needs to seriously consider a similar initiative before prescription abuse becomes a huge problem with online pharmacies.

But more importantly, apart from tackling the issue of prescription abuse, the Ministry of Health must seriously consider using this opportunity to dramatically upgrade the current bare-boned licencing requirements to open and run a pharmacy or engage in the whole-sale trading of drugs. The entire supply chain is in the middle of a churn and big capital investing in online pharmacies is eventually going to reorder the manner in which drugs reach consumers from pharmaceutical manufacturers. These new businesses have the capital to invest in far better storage systems and human resources. There could be no better time for the Ministry of Health to completely rethink the regulation of pharmacies in a manner that guarantees better storage of drugs during transit and distribution while protecting against prescription abuse and guaranteeing supply chain integrity. More importantly, lawmaking in the Ministry must move to a data and evidence driven process, rather than the haphazard way in which loopholes are intentionally inserted into statutes to provide the government with a way to reconcile absurd provisions across multiple regulations.

Notes

1. *Mohd. Shabir vs State Of Maharashtra* 1979 SCR (2) 997 (17 January 1979).
2. *Swantraj vs State of Maharashtra* 1974 SCR (3) 287 (5 February 1974).
3. *Drug Inspector, Nizamabad vs Kaleru Subash* Drug SC No. 10 of 2014 before the Court of I Additional Sessions Judge, Nizamabad decided on 3 February 2020.
4. *State of Haryana through Drug Control Officer vs Harish Kumar* Sessions Case No. 54 of 2019 before the Court of the Additional Sessions Judge, Faridabad decided on 27 January 2020.
5. *Swantraj* (n 2) [para 6].
6. World Health Organization (WHO), *WHO good distribution practices for pharmaceutical products* (WHO Technical Report Series, No. 957, 2010).
7. Government of India, Drugs Controller General (India), *Notice: Draft Guidelines on Good Distribution Practices for pharmaceutical products-Reg.* (File No: 15-14/2018-DC, 25 September 2018).
8. World Health Organization (WHO), *Model guidance for the storage and transport of time- and temperature-sensitive pharmaceutical products* (WHO Technical Report Series, No. 961, 2011).
9. Drugs Consultative Committee (DCC), *'REPORT OF THE 46TH MEETING OF THE DRUGS CONSULTATIVE COMMITTEE HELD ON 12TH AND 13TH NOVEMBER, 2013 AT THE HOTEL METROPOLITAN NEW DELHI-110001'* (2013) 15 <https://cdsco.gov.in/opencms/opencms/system/modules/CDSCO.WEB/elements/common_download.jsp?num_id_pk=ODA4> accessed 8 April 2022.
10. Drugs Consultative Committee (DCC), *'REPORT OF THE 47TH MEETING OF THE DRUGS CONSULTATIVE COMMITTEE HELD ON 30TH AND 31ST JULY, 2014 AT NEW DELHI'* (2014) 28 <https://cdsco.gov.in/opencms/opencms/system/modules/CDSCO.WEB/elements/common_download.jsp?num_id_pk=ODA5> accessed 8 April 2022.

11. K.L. Sharma, *Healing the Pharmacy of the World: An Inside Story of Medical Products Manufacturing and Regulation in India* (Notion Press 2021)109–111.
12. Government of India, Ministry of Health & Family Welfare, *GSR 681(E)* (*Gazette of India Extraordinary*, Part II—s 3(i), 5 December 1980)—Rule 64 of the Drugs and Cosmetics Rules 1945; Government of India, Ministry of Health and Family Welfare, *GSR 351(E)* (*Gazette of India Extraordinary*, Part II—s 3(i), 26 April 2000)—Drugs and Cosmetics (Third Amendment) Rules, 2000.
13. The Drugs and Cosmetics Rules 1945, Rule 65(5)(1).
14. Sharma (n 11).
15. ibid 111.
16. Drugs Consultative Committee (DCC), '*REPORT OF 54TH MEETING OF DRUGS CONSULTATIVE COMMITTEE HELD ON 30TH JULY, 2018 AT NEW DELHI*' (2018) 5 <https://cdsco.gov.in/opencms/opencms/system/modules/CDSCO.WEB/elements/common_download.jsp?num_id_pk=ODE2> accessed 8 April 2022.
17. Drugs Consultative Committee (DCC), '*REPORT OF 54TH MEETING OF DRUGS CONSULTATIVE COMMITTEE HELD ON 30TH JULY, 2018 AT NEW DELHI*' (2018) 19 <https://cdsco.gov.in/opencms/opencms/system/modules/CDSCO.WEB/elements/common_download.jsp?num_id_pk=ODE2> accessed 8 April 2022.
18. Government of India, *Report of the Drugs Enquiry Committee* (1931) 73.
19. ibid 102.
20. The Drug Rules 1945, Rule 65(15).
21. Government of India, Ministry of Commerce and Industry, *Report of the Pharmaceutical Enquiry Committee* (1954) 212, para 6.1.8.
22. The Deputy Minister in the Ministry of Health, Rajya Sabha Debate 15 September 1965, 4036.
23. ibid 4037, 4040.
24. The Minister of State in the Ministry of Health and Family Planning on The Pharmacy (Amendment) Bill 1975, Rajya Sabha Deb 12 May 1976, 162.
25. Drugs Consultative Committee (DCC), '*MINUTES OF THE 20TH MEETING OF THE DRUGS CONSULTATIVE COMMITTEE HELD AT NEW DELHI ON THE 4th & 5th JULY. 1978*' (1978) 11-12 <https://cdsco.gov.in/opencms/opencms/system/modules/CDSCO.WEB/elements/common_download.jsp?num_id_pk=ODUz> accessed 8 April 2022.

26. ibid 27.
27. Discussion on Pharmacy (Amendment) Bill, Lok Sabha Debate 29 April 1982, 388–89; Discussion on Pharmacy (Amendment) Bill, Rajya Sabha Debate 1 December 1981, 242–243.
28. Dr MMS Siddhu (MP, Uttar Pradesh), Rajya Sabha Debate 1 December 1981, 245.
29. Shri Ratansinh Rajda (MP, Bombay South), Rajya Sabha Debate 7 August 1984, 480–81.
30. Drugs Consultative Committee (DCC), '*MINUTES OF 58TH MEETING (VIRTUAL) OF DRUGS CONSULTATIVE COMMITTEE HELD THROUGH WEB CONFERENCE ON 14TH JULY, 2020 AT CDSCO (HQ)*' (2020) 3 <https://cdsco.gov.in/opencms/opencms/system/modules/CDSCO.WEB/elements/common_download.jsp?num_id_pk=MTI1NQ==> accessed 8 April 2022.
31. Drugs Consultative Committee (DCC) (n 10) 5.
32. *Ramesh Giri Prop. M/S Goswami Medical Stores vs State of U.P & Ors.* 1996 SCC Online ALL 1012 (Allahabad HC, 29 January 1996).
33. ibid para 19.
34. *Lallan Kumar vs Chairman, Pharmacy Council of India* Civil Writ Jurisdiction Case No. 23771 of 2012 before the Patna High Court decided on 16 December 2016.
35. Government of India, Ministry of Health and Family Welfare, *GSR 540(E)* (*Gazette of India Extraordinary*, Part II—s 3(i), 22 September 1980); Government of India, Ministry of Health and Family Welfare, *GSR 784(E)* (*Gazette of India Extraordinary*, Part II—s 3(i), 28 August 1989).
36. Government of India, Ministry of Health and Family Welfare, *GSR 827(E)* (*Gazette of India Extraordinary*, Part II—s 3(i), 6 November 2019)—Drugs and Cosmetics (Amendment) Rules, 2019.
37. Government of India, National Rural Health Mission (NRHM), *Guidelines on Accredited Social Health Activists (ASHA).*
38. Pharmacy Council of India, *Objections of Pharmacy Council of India to proposed amendment in Schedule K against serial number 23 of the Drugs and Cosmetic Rules, 1945* (Ref No: 14-150/2015-PCI/6703-08, 27 November 2019); Peethaambaran Kunnathoor, 'OPIF Urges Health Ministry Not to Proceed with Its Plan to Amend Schedule K of D&C Rules' *Pharmabiz*, (17 December 2019) <http://www.pharmabiz.com/NewsDetails.aspx?aid=119983&sid=1> accessed 9 April 2022; Peethaambaran Kunnathoor, 'Legalising Nurses and Community Health Workers to Dispense Drugs an Open

Challenge against Pharmaceutical Care: TGPA' *Pharmabiz* (27 November 2019) <http://pharmabiz.com/NewsDetails.aspx?aid=119607&sid=1> accessed 9 April 2022.
39. Government of India, National Health Systems Resource Centre, *AYUSHMAN BHARAT: Comprehensive Primary Health Care through Health and Wellness Centers—Operational Guidelines* (2018) 39, s4.1.
40. Syed Intishab Ali, 'Over 400 SMS Nurses Strike Work' *The Times of India* (3 March 2012) <https://timesofindia.indiatimes.com/city/jaipur/over-400-sms-nurses-strike-work/articleshow/12118805.cms> accessed 9 April 2022.
41. *All Kerala Pharmacists Union & Ors vs State of Kerala* WP(C). No.33715 OF 2019(L) before the Kerala High Court decided on 25 February 2021.; *All Kerala Pharmacists Union & Ors vs State of Kerala* W.A. No. 495/2021 before the Kerala HC decided on 13 January 2022).
42. Peethaambaran Kunnathoor, 'Legal Notice Served to Health, FDA Authorities in Haryana for Breach of Section 42 of Pharmacy Act' *Pharmabiz* (3 September 2019) <http://www.pharmabiz.com/NewsDetails.aspx?aid=117908&sid=1> accessed 9 April 2022.
43. Drugs and Cosmetics Act 1940, Section 27(b)(ii).
44. *State through Drug Inspector vs Inderjit Singh* S.C. No.2 of 2015 before the Special Court, Ludhiana decided on 17 February 2016.
45. *Revision vs Zest Pharma* Crl.Rev.Pet.No. 1475 of 2013 before the Kerala High Court decided on 24 April 2013.
46. *State of Andhra Pradesh vs Jaggurothu Rambabu* CC No. 146 of 2009 before the Court of the Judicial Magistrate of I Class, Palakol decided on 27 April 2016.
47. Case No. 5 of 2018 before the Court of the Additional Sessions Judge, Panipat decided on 6 June 2018. An appeal against the conviction and sentencing is pending before the High Court. The conviction and sentence have been stayed pending the outcome of the appeal. Crl. Appeal No.S-2562-SB of 2018 before the High Court of Punjab and Haryana.
48. Ajay Bhaskarabhatla et. al., 'Hit Where It Hurts: Cartel Policing Using Targeted Sales and Supply Embargoes' (2016) 59 *The Journal of Law and Economics*, 80; Ajay Bhaskarabhatla et. al., 'Mitigating Regulatory Impact: The Case of Partial Price Controls on Metformin in India' (2017) 32 *Health Policy and Planning*, 194.
49. Competition Commission of India, *Policy Note: Making Markets Work for Affordable Healthcare* (October 2018); Prashant Reddy T,

'The Correct Prescription' *The Hindu* (26 February 2019) <https://www.thehindu.com/opinion/op-ed/the-correct-prescription/article26368011.ece> accessed 10 April 2022.

50. *Dr Zaheer Ahmed vs The Union of India* W.P.(C) 11711/2018 & CM APPL. 45307/2018 (Delhi HC, 12 December 2018); *The Tamil Nadu Chemists and Druggists Association vs The Union of India* W.P.No.28716 of 2018 (Madras HC, 17 December 2018); *Practo Technologies (P) Ltd vs Tamil Nadu Chemists and Druggists Assn* 2018 SCC OnLine Mad 3577 (Madras HC, 20 December 2018).
51. Saritha Rai, 'India's E-Pharmacy Segment Mints Its First Unicorn, Raises $350 Million' *Business Standard India* (7 April 2021) <https://www.business-standard.com/article/companies/india-s-e-pharmacy-segment-mints-its-first-unicorn-raises-350-million-121040700228_1.html> accessed 10 April 2022; Gireesh Babu, 'Online Pharmacies See Record Funding in 2019, Investments Double to $321 Mn' *Business Standard India* (18 January 2020) <https://www.business-standard.com/article/companies/online-pharmacies-see-record-funding-in-2019-investments-double-to-321-mn-120011800340_1.html> accessed 10 April 2022.
52. Government of India, Ministry of Health and Family Welfare, *GSR 220(E)* (*Gazette of India Extraordinary*, Part II—s 3(i), 26 March 2020).
53. Government of India, Ministry of Health and Family Welfare, *GSR 817(E)* (*Gazette of India Extraordinary*, Part II—s 3(i), 28 August 2018).
54. The Drugs and Cosmetics Rules 1945, Rule 65(11)(c).
55. Amber Porterfield, Kate Engelbert and Alberto Coustasse, 'Electronic Prescribing: Improving the Efficiency and Accuracy of Prescribing in the Ambulatory Care Setting' (2014) 11 *Perspectives in Health Information Management*, 1g.

CHAPTER TEN

Of Drug Advertisements, Promotions, and Trademarks

In 2008, Indian television witnessed the launch of an unprecedented advertizing campaign for "i-Pill", an emergency contraceptive pill (ECPs) for women looking to avoid pregnancies after unprotected sex. The advertisements featured women of differing ages and marital status worrying about a possible pregnancy before they are reassured by a companion or the voiceover that they could avert a pregnancy by consuming ECPs.[1]

While ECPs had already been available over the counter in India for a few years, the advertizing campaign in 2009 was justified by pharmaceutical companies as a way to empower women to take decisions about their sexual health by educating them about the existence of ECPs.[2] Sure enough, the sales of ECPs reportedly shot through the roof after that advertizing campaign—increasing four times from 2008 to 2013![3] Clearly, the pharmaceutical industry had tapped into an unmet need amongst Indian women.

However, not everyone was happy with the advertizing campaign for ECPs. There was an outcry from doctors who were the traditional information intermediaries between the pharmaceutical industry and patients. Many doctors worried about the tone and tenor of the advertisements, which they felt could mislead young women into thinking that ECPs could be used as substitutes for regular contraceptives leading to the improper use of these pills and possible side-effects.[4] There is some evidence from surveys to justify this argument made by doctors about a significant number of women mistaking ECPs as a regular contraceptive without understanding the possible side-effects of long-term use.[5] Separate and apart from the ethical and medical issues, the ECP advertisements also ran into legal questions and a temporary ban because of an ancient law called the Drugs and Magic Remedies (Objectionable Advertisements) Act 1954.[6]

This string of controversies over advertisements for ECPs provoked a rare public conversation in India on the many issues surrounding the advertisement of drugs. The regulatory framework for advertisements by the pharmaceutical industry has remained largely unchanged since 1954, despite the nature of medicine, the Indian pharmaceutical industry and the mode of advertisements undergoing a revolution of sorts in the last six decades.

The early debates on regulating drug labelling and advertizing

Historically, drug advertizing has been one of the focal points of governments looking to regulate the pharmaceutical industry because it is through these advertisements that the general public, doctors, and their elected representatives noticed the extravagant claims made by the pharmaceutical industry. In India, the issue was debated in the Council of States in 1927, especially in context of advertisements for "patent and proprietary" medicine which at the time were basically secret remedies whose ingredients were not publicly disclosed and known only to the manufacturer.[7] Due to the secrecy regarding the composition of these drugs it was difficult for independent experts to confirm the veracity of the claims made by the manufacturers.

In 1931, when the Drugs Inquiry Committee under Lt Col

Ramnath Chopra submitted its final report to the government, it documented in detail over five whole pages, numerous examples of astonishingly absurd advertisements made by manufacturers of various cures.[8] Here are a few examples:

> Cures snake bites on inhalation only.
>
> It cleans the blood, purifies it and infuses strength-giving properties into it. To those who had left youth behind and feel its want, this tonic will bring back good health quickly, positively and permanently.
>
> Cures menstrual disorders of every kind, hysteria, rheumatism, sterility, etc., improves the general state of the blood. Most effective in bringing the reproductive functions of women into perfect order.
>
> Sure remedy for helping expectant ladies to give birth to male children only. Male offspring guaranteed.
>
> To increase sex power. Stands unique. A dose or two invigorate and rejuvenate the weak and the impotent.
>
> Become young again. Sensational discovery by German scientist. It gives youthful freshness, energy and appearance once more, puts an end to sexual trouble, mental fatigue, nervous breakdown and neurasthenia in man and they can be retained for years in certain circumstances.
>
> Latest wonderful discovery for unyielding urinary diseases. Specific for gonorrhea.
>
> Diabetes cured at last. Amazing cure endorsed by thousands of eminent doctors.

All of these advertisements were clearly fraudulent for that era. In fact, most of them would be fraudulent even today despite the progress of modern science.

Apart from advertizing in the mass media, the purveyors of drugs in that era, also advertized in medical journals such as the *Indian Medical Gazette* whose main readership comprised the medical community. Yet another marketing tactic was for salespersons to visit the offices of doctors and provide them with promotional literature featuring fantastical claims and patient testimonials about individual drugs.

Given the nature and volume of these advertisements, it was no surprise that the Drugs Inquiry Committee received significant feedback on the issue leading it to conclude that "Rigid control over advertisements is a point over which there is unanimity."[9] The committee looked at these advertisements as not just a public health issue that could mislead citizens but also as an issue of vulgarity and obscenity that offended public morals. The committee stated in pertinent part, "The disgust and annoyance aroused by the advertisements is nothing compared to the untold harm they inflict on the people".[10]

The Drugs Inquiry Committee therefore had to decide how best to regulate these advertisements. It had received suggestions ranging from an outright ban to prior censorship by the government, to prior vetting of the claims made in these advertisements by doctors with expertise in the area. Surprisingly, the Committee took a very restrained view on the issue of regulating drug advertisements, most likely because of its view that "control over advertisements" could lead to "undue interference in legitimate trade in certain cases".[11] As a result, the committee made only two recommendations with regard to regulation of advertisements of "patent and proprietary" medicine.

The first recommendation was a complete prohibition on any advertisements relating to "aphrodisiacs, venereal diseases, remedies for the diseases of women, cures for cancer, leprosy and tuberculosis". The first three categories appear to be inspired by a need to regulate "obscene" advertisements. The United Kingdom had similar restrictions under a law called the Venereal Diseases Act 1917, which prohibited the publication of advertisements of any potions or drugs for venereal diseases, which the law defined as "syphilis, gonorrhea, or soft chancre".[12] The latter three categories of diseases in the committee's recommendation—cancer, leprosy, and tuberculosis—were most likely included out of concern for public health, since it was well-known that there existed no cures or treatment, at that point in time, for these diseases.

The second recommendation made by the committee was a prohibition on "false, misleading or exaggerated claims... on the labels, wrappers or advertisements".[13] The committee was entirely silent on how such a determination would be made and more importantly, how it would be enforced. Was the government to create a system of vetting all medical advertisements or was the issue to be determined by courts after the advertisements were published? Unlike today, in 1931, there was no requirement for pharmaceutical companies to submit clinical data regarding safety and efficacy data for new drugs. So how then was anybody, whether government or the courts, to determine the accuracy or lack thereof of a certain claim made in an advertisement? Such major policy issues were left unanswered by the Drugs Inquiry Committee in its final report that was submitted in 1931.

Nine years later, after one failed attempt in 1937, the Government of India introduced a new Drugs Bill in the Federal Legislature in 1940. In the intervening years, stakeholders like the All India Medical Conference had continued to pressure the government to enact legislation prohibiting the "publication of obscene literature and advertisements advocating the claims of the efficacy of various drugs and appliances", "controlling and regulating the public advertisements of patent and proprietary medicines" etc.[14]

When the Drugs Bill 1940 was introduced in the legislature, more than one legislator raised the issue of regulating drug advertizing. Speaking in the Council of States, Y.N. Sapru who was a legislator from the United Provinces explained the magnitude of the problem:

> One has got only to read the advertisements that appear in Indian newspapers—even leading Indian newspapers—to realise how quackery succeeds and works in this country. I wish, Sir, there was some law which would check these disgusting advertisements—which disfigure even our leading newspapers—regarding the efficacy and potency or virtue of this or that drug on this or that part of the human system. They indicate how widespread the evil is in this country.[15]

Another legislator, Muhammad Nauman from Patna, Chotta Nagpur, and Orissa, actually moved an amendment to the Drugs Bill that would have required one of the statutory boards being setup under the new law to lay down a procedure for regulating the advertisement of medicine. He explained:

> The object of my amendment is merely that the Board should also undertake to direct manufacturers, merchants and agents, in what way they should advertize. We have noticed not only exaggerations but also false statements as regards the efficacy of certain drugs; moderation is necessary. It has been very common in this country; and this has not been limited only to the productions of this country but also to the products imported from Europe. They also do not use caution in saying what they should say. That is my simple purpose and I hope the Government will see the necessity of using caution in the matter of advertisements.[16]

The government, however, pushed back on his proposed amendment, claiming that it had very carefully considered the issue of advertisements and had already incorporated provisions in the bill to tackle the issue. Specifically, reference was made to two clauses in the bill.[17] The first was a provision on misbranding, which made it an offence for a drug to feature on its labelling any "statement, design or device which makes any false claim for the drug or which is false or misleading in any particular".[18] A second provision in the Bill delegated to the Federal Government (for import) and Provincial Governments (for domestic manufacture) the power to make rules specifying "the diseases or ailments which a drug may not purport or claim to cure or mitigate and such other effects which a drug may not purport or claim to have".[19] This power eventually translated into Rule 106 of the Drugs and Cosmetics Rules 1945 which forbade any drug from claiming to cure any of the 34 categories of diseases/ailments mentioned in Schedule J to the Drugs Rules 1945. On receiving the government's assurance that these provisions were adequate to regulate drug advertisements, Nauman withdrew his amendments and the Bill was voted into law.

The fact of the matter, however, was that the Drugs Act 1940 did not create an effective enough framework to regulate drug advertisements. To begin with, a large loophole in the Drugs Act 1940 was that it entirely excluded Ayurvedic and Unani cures from the definition of "drug". This meant that purveyors of Ayurvedic and Unani cures could make all kinds of unsubstantiated claims without attracting any penalties under the law.

The second problem with the Drugs Act 1940 was that the "misbranding" provision was limited to only the labelling of the drug and would technically not cover advertisements in the press. Even with respect to inflated claims on the labelling of drugs, it would have been practically quite difficult to prosecute such cases before criminal courts because the government would have to collect and prove, beyond a reasonable doubt, through scientific evidence that such claims were exaggerated.

Third, the wording of Rule 106 was strange in that it did not specifically prohibit advertisements. Rather, it prohibited a "drug" from purporting or claiming to cure the 34 listed diseases/ailments. To further complicate matters, given the scheme of the Drugs Act 1940 prior to 1955, each province was free to draft its own version of Rule 106 (which applied only to imports) meaning that India did not have a uniform scheme that was applicable across the country despite being a common market through which goods could move easily.

The failure of the Drugs Act 1940 to create an effective framework to govern advertisements became obvious when a few years after its enactment, the DTAB, which was a newly created statutory board under the Drugs Act, conveyed to the government, "the necessity for legislation to prevent advertizing" of secret remedies including Ayurvedic and Unani medicine in the press and cinema.[20]

Even medical journals, like the prestigious *Indian Medical Gazette*, lamented about the quality of advertisements that it was receiving from the pharmaceutical industry during the war years when there was a general shortage of supplies. It complained, in 1943, as follows:

> We will quote a few examples of advertisements which have recently been rejected by this journal. Some have been 'infallible cures' of malaria but containing 'no quinine or arsenic'. One remedy was guaranteed 'to cure every case of dysentery' within a few days. One remedy was an arrowroot preparation said to be an excellent food for infants. Others have been 'sovereign remedies' for 'all respiratory diseases' including, one supposes, tuberculosis. One advertisement stated that the product cured most fevers, but if the fever had not subsided after a few weeks' treatment, a doctor should be consulted! Some advertisements have been rejected, not because the remedy appeared to be useless, but because the claims made for it were grossly exaggerated and un-scientific.[21]

The editorial ended with a plea to advertizers, asking them to send for publication only "good, simple, straightforward, informative and attractive advertisements" but refrained from asking the government to enact any legislative measures in this regard.[22]

It would take another decade for India to enact a new law regulating drug advertisements—this time under a new Constitution adopted by a newly independent India in 1950.

A new law and a constitutional challenge

In 1953, independent India's first Minister for Health, Oxford-educated Amrita Kaur who was from the Kapurthala royal family and a close friend and one-time secretary of Mahatma Gandhi, introduced in the Rajya Sabha a new legislation called the Drugs and Magic Remedies (Objectionable Advertisements) Bill 1953 to regulate drug advertisements.[23] In her introductory remarks before the Rajya Sabha she explained the reason for introducing such a Bill in Parliament with the following words:

> In recent years there has been a great increase in the number of objectionable advertisements relating to certain diseases and these advertisements border on the obscene—in fact they are obscene—and in addition they cause the ignorant and the unwary to resort to self-medication with very harmful drugs and appliances and even to resort to quacks who indulge in such advertisements and offer treatment which causes very great harm.[24]

As evident from the Minister's introduction, the primary purpose of the legislation was to deal with obscene advertisements while protecting public health remained a secondary objective. Except the issue of obscenity could have easily been dealt under the Indian Penal Code 1860 rather than through a law whose primary concern should have been protecting public health. The nature of the proposed prohibitions gives a clearer picture of the priorities of the government of the day. The Bill specifically prohibited three categories of advertisements.

The first category of prohibited advertisements included those making false or misleading claims about any drug and its effects. In reality, it would likely have been difficult for a drug inspector to prove such a claim before a criminal court because it would involve building a scientific case, with scientific experts and proving the same beyond reasonable doubt. To complicate matters further, the management or proprietor of a pharmaceutical company can invoke their fundamental right to not testify against themselves in criminal court. Cumulatively, all these factors would have made it quite difficult for drug inspectors to secure convictions for "false or misleading" claims under this law.

A second category of prohibited advertisements were those publicizing "magic remedies", which was defined in the law as any "talisman, mantra, kavacha and any other kind of charm" claiming to "possess miraculous powers". This prohibition had a rational basis and was likely motivated by public health concerns and patient welfare.

The third category of prohibited advertisements were for those drugs promising "the procurement of miscarriage in women or prevention of conception in women", "the maintenance or improvement of the capacity of human beings for sexual pleasure", "the correction of menstrual disorder in women", and "the diagnosis, cure, mitigation, treatment or prevention of any venereal diseases or any other disease or condition which may be specified in rules made under this Act".[25] The prohibitions in this category unlike the earlier two categories were not contingent on the "falsity" or "obscenity" of the advertisements. So, what then was the rationale for prohibiting these advertisements?

One possible answer is that the prudish Indian state presumed that any advertisement for a drug dealing with "sexual pleasure" or "menstrual disorders" or abortion or "contraceptive" or "venereal diseases" was going to be obscene and vulgar and hence deserving of a complete prohibition. If this indeed was the justification, then it was quite obvious that the Indian state was more concerned about protecting public morals than public health because by 1954, when this law was enacted, there were a whole range of antibiotics to treat venereal diseases like syphilis, gonorrhea etc. Clearly, the lack of proven treatment was not the reason for prohibiting advertisements for these specific diseases.

The other possible reason for prohibiting advertisements of drugs for the "procurement of miscarriage in women" was likely the fact that abortion was and continues to be a punishable offence under the Indian Penal Code 1860. Although, it should be noted that even during colonial rule, the provision of the Indian Penal Code 1860 penalizing abortions was rarely enforced unless the abortion resulted in the death of the lady.[26]

The ban on advertizing contraception in women is a little more difficult to explain since contraception was never illegal in India. In fact, India at the time was looking for ways to control the growth of its population through measures like contraception as was evident from the first Five Year Plan formulated by the Planning Commission.[27] Unlike in the West, where feminist movements were some of the greatest supporters of contraceptives because they viewed it as a means of "women empowerment", in India the government's family-planning policy supported contraceptives purely as a means to control the growth of population.[28] The only rational explanation for the prohibition of advertisement of contraceptives is that drafters of the Bill, like many conservative elements at the time in Indian polity, were guided by the age old fear that contraception would open the doors to "immoral men and women to satisfy sexual lust without the fear of pregnancy".[29]

When the Bill was introduced in the Rajya Sabha, the debate around the Bill showcased a remarkable variety of thought and opinion amongst the MPs. A MP from Madras, H.D. Rajah, opposed the bill on the principled ground that any battle against superstition and faith had to be won through education by the government rather than punitive measure such as the Bill under consideration which could imprison citizens as a punishment.[30]

Most of the remaining MPs who spoke in the Rajya Sabha were broadly supportive of the Bill and deeply critical of the press for publishing "objectionable advertisements". Rama Rao, a MP from Andhra, criticized newspapers for publishing regressive and superstitious advertisements at a time when "the country is trying to march on and on from medievalism to modernity".[31]

The other practical issue raised in the Rajya Sabha was the workability of this law on the ground. In particular, Kishen Chand, a MP from Hyderabad, said it was necessary for the government to specify an "agency which will examine all the drugs to find out whether those drugs are really efficacious and whether the claims made for them are true or not".[32] This was an important issue, referenced by two other MPs, including Khwaja Inait Ullah from Bihar and Rama Rao, who pointed out that the question of "false claims" was a question of fact that could be established only in a laboratory and that the law made no provision for an agency to vet such claims.[33]

Despite three MPs raising the issue of an agency or laboratory to test the falsity of a claim under this law, neither the Health Minister nor the Law Minister who participated in the debate addressed the issue during their rebuttal. One possible solution, proposed by an MP from Bombay, T.R. Deogirikar, was to enact a new law compelling all manufacturers of drugs to submit their products for examination and certification at a government laboratory.[34]

Deogirikar hit the nail on the head with his recommendation, since less than a decade after his comments, many countries starting with the Kefauver-Harris amendment in the United States in 1962, required pharmaceutical companies to submit proof of safety and efficacy of drugs as a condition to secure marketing approval. In any event, notwithstanding the rocky debate, the Bill was passed by the Rajya Sabha after which it was taken up in the Lok Sabha for a vote.

The Bill's passage in the Lok Sabha was significantly smoother. Most of the speakers supported the Bill and its objectives, often recounting instances of both bizarre advertisements and instances of quackery that they had witnessed across the country. One MP spoke of a boy in Travancore who offered magic cures, of a man who offered "cure-all" medical powder to treat children's diseases, of an advertisement for kumari pills offering assistance to kumaris who missed their menses, and lastly an advertisement for a stimulant that would provide for gradual and complete rejuvenation for old people.[35] Other MPs described advertisements of tonics that promised old people that they would become young and that the ugly would become beautiful, oils that would turn white hair into black etc.[36]

The government, however, faced at least three skeptics in the Lok Sabha who deserve a mention.

The first was a MP, S.S. More from Sholapur, who raised the same question asked by so many of his counterparts in the Rajya Sabha—how exactly would the law determine the efficacy or lack thereof of any medicine during the course of implementation of this legislation? He asked, "I sincerely request the hon. Health Minister to point out what is the apparatus by which it can be definitely known that a particular drug is a spurious drug, that it is a magic remedy."[37]

A second opponent of the Bill in the Lok Sabha was a MP from Mysore, M.S. Gurupadaswamy, who pointed out that advertisements were a major source of revenue for the press and that the bill would make major inroads into such revenue because neither editors nor the "advertisement managers" would be knowledgeable enough to take a call on drug advertisements. More pertinently, he warned against the wide-ranging powers under the law allowing government officials to conduct search and seizures.[38] In its present form, he felt that the Bill could not be supported "on the ground that it will make a positive inroad into the liberty of the Press".[39]

It is surprising that more MPs did not raise this issue of press freedom since a penal law to regulate advertisements could easily be misused by vindictive governments. Independent India had already witnessed government bans on publications like the left-leaning *Crossroads* and the right leaning *Organiser* and eventually the curtailment of the fundamental right to free speech through the enactment of the First Amendment to the Constitution in 1951 by Nehru's government.[40] Given that the Drugs and Magic Remedies (Objectionable Advertisements) Bill 1953 was being discussed merely two years later, one would have expected far more skepticism about a governmental effort to regulate advertisements that were the lifeblood of the press.

A third MP who categorically opposed the Bill was R.K. Chaudhari, the MP from Gauhati, who questioned the rationality of a blanket ban of advertisements for venereal diseases or drugs that promised improvement of sexual power, without first analyzing the ingredients of the drug in question.[41] Unlike many of his colleagues, Chaudhari preferred to let everything be advertized so that people may use their "good senses to make up their own minds".[42]

As was the case in the Rajya Sabha, the Minister for Health simply did not address many of the issues raised by opponents to the Bill during her rebuttal speech. On the point of press freedom and liberty, she merely pointed out how the scope of the bill was rather limited in the type of advertisements that were being banned and that editors should be happy that the government was trying to improve the quality of newspapers through the imposition of such restrictions on derogatory advertisements.[43] To be fair to the Minister, at least one M.P. in the Rajya Sabha who was from a journalistic background had supported the restrictions since it would give editors a legal handle to reject objectionable advertisements being pushed by the marketing department of the newspaper.[44]

In any event, the Bill was passed by the Lok Sabha and received presidential assent thereby giving India a second law on drug regulation after the Drugs and Cosmetics Act 1940. Most notably however, unlike the former, the Drugs and Magic Remedies (Objectionable Advertisements) Act 1954 applied to even Ayurvedic and Unani medicines since the definition of "drug" in this law (unlike the one in the Drugs and Cosmetics Act 1940) did not specifically exclude traditional medicine. This was perhaps the most significant aspect of this bill because it brought in for the first time some form of regulation of a previously unregulated sector that had so far been allowed to escape any liability for making all kinds of unsubstantiated claims.

After the law was enacted and enforcement actions picked up, two entities—Hamdard Dawakhana, a manufacturer of Unani remedies and Sadhana Ausadhalaya, a manufacturer of Ayurvedic medicine—were the first to challenge the constitutionality of the Drugs and Magic Remedies (Objectionable Advertisements) Act 1954 before the Supreme Court.[45]

Both the petitioners argued that the Drugs and Magic Remedies (Objectionable Advertisements) Act 1954 curtailed their right to advertize their products and infringed on their fundamental right to free speech, enshrined in Article 19(1)(a) of the Constitution of India. They also argued that it was unconstitutional for Parliament to delegate to the government the power to decide the list of diseases for which advertisements could be banned, without laying down any parameters to guide the exercise of this power by the government.[46] This latter provision prohibited advertisements for drugs aimed at the treatment of any venereal diseases and also "any other disease or condition which may be specified in rules made under this Act".[47] The last leg of the challenge was directed at Section 8 of the Act which gave the government wide and untrammeled search and seizure powers while enforcing the law.

In its defense, the government argued that that this law was meant "to prevent people from self medicating with regard to various serious diseases" since self-medication had "a deleterious effect on the health of the community" and that it was in the "interest of public health" to regulate drug advertisements.[48] While this defense did have some basis in the "statement of objects and reasons" appended to the Bill when it was introduced in Parliament, the tone of the debate in both the Lok Sabha and Rajya Sabha would have led a common observer to believe that the Health Minister was actually more concerned with combating obscene and vulgar advertisements.

In a typical case involving a constitutional challenge, the court will have to determine the "reasonableness" of the restriction imposed by the state. The Supreme Court, however, did not get into the "reasonableness" of the restrictions imposed by the Drugs and Magic Remedies (Objectionable Advertisement) Act 1954 because it concluded that commercial advertisements did not qualify as the type of "speech" that was protected in Article 19(1)(a) of the Constitution. In the court's words:

> Freedom of speech goes to the heart of the natural right of an organised freedom-loving society to "impart and acquire information about that common interest". If any limitation is placed which results in the society being deprived of such right then no doubt it would fall within the guaranteed freedom under Art. 19(1)(a). But if all it does is that it deprives a trader from commending his wares it would not fall within that term.[49]
>
> In the present case therefore (1) the advertisements affected by the Act do not fall within the words freedom of speech within Article 19(1)(a); (2) the scope and object of the Act, its true nature and character is not interference with the right of freedom of speech but it deals with trade or business; and

> (3) there is no direct abridgement of the right of free speech and a mere incidental interference with such right would not alter the character of the law.[50]

The court, however, took a dim view of two other provisions of this law that had been challenged. The first was Section 3(d)—this provision gave the government blanket power to prohibit drug advertisements for diseases and conditions not already mentioned in the law. The court found this provision to suffer from the vice of excessive delegation i.e., Parliament had delegated power to the government without providing it with any guidance on how to exercise such power.[51] This provision was thus struck down.

The second provision of this law struck down by the Supreme Court was Section 8 which gave the government untrammeled powers to search and seize drug advertisements that were in violation of the Drugs and Magic Remedies (Objectionable Advertisements) Act. The court ruled as follows:

> In our opinion this portion of the section goes far beyond the purpose for which the Act was enacted and, the absence of the safeguards which the legislature has thought it necessary and expedient in other statutes, e.g., the Indian Drugs Act, is an unreasonable restriction on the fundamental rights of the petitioners and therefore the first portion of the section, i.e., "any person authorised by any of the provisions of this Act" is unconstitutional. What then is the consequence of this unconstitutionality? If this portion is excised from the rest of the section the remaining portion is not even intelligible and cannot be upheld. The whole of the section must therefore be struck down.[52]

Thus, although the law was upheld and the Supreme Court rejected the industry's contention that the fundamental right to speech included commercial speech, it ended up striking down two crucial provisions.

Four years after the court struck down the two provisions,

the government moved the Drugs and Magic Remedies (Objectionable Advertisements) Bill 1963 in Parliament. This Bill introduced a new Section 3(d) which allowed the government to notify through the rules, medical conditions or disease for the treatment of which advertisements for drugs could not be published subject to two conditions. First, the medical condition should be one that usually required timely medical treatment in consultation with a doctor or for which it was accepted that there were no normally accepted remedies. Second, the government was required to consult the DTAB for its expert opinion before notifying a particular disease for which advertisements could no longer be published. The Bill also contained a Schedule listing 54 diseases and medical conditions preselected by the government, under Section 3(d) for which advertisements could not be published.

This time when the Bill was debated in Parliament, the government was less focused on the issue of the obscenity and vulgarity of advertisements and more focused on the dangers of self-medication that was bound to follow if unfiltered advertisements were allowed to be published.[53] Despite some skeptical MPs in Parliament, both the Lok Sabha and Rajya Sabha voted in favour of the Bill which then received Presidential assent on 7 December 1963.[54]

Parliament has neither revised nor debated this law since 1963 despite the pharmaceutical industry and technology having radically changed the way drugs are marketed to doctors and patients.

The enforcement of the Drugs and Magic Remedies (Objectionable Advertisements) Act 1954

Since its enactment, the Drugs and Magic Remedies (Objectionable Advertisements) Act has been enforced against a range of advertisements for bewildering products. For instance, in 1975, the Supreme Court heard a case involving an advertisement in the Hindi newspaper *Sanmarg* in West Bengal, for a "machine of science and electric treatment" to treat amongst other conditions weakness, laziness, oldness in youth etc. The conviction and penalty of ₹100 imposed by the lower courts was upheld by the Supreme Court.[55]

In 1982, the Bombay High Court heard an appeal against the conviction of the proprietor of a store called "Breast Beauty Stores" because he had advertized a device called "Bust Developer" for the "proper development of breasts of a woman". This was in violation of Sr. 21 of prohibited diseases/conditions contained in the schedule to the Drugs and Magic Remedies (Objectionable Advertisements) Act, which read as follows: Form and structure of the female bust. The Bombay High Court actually set aside the conviction by the lower court on the grounds that the very concept of objectionable advertisement had changed from 1954 when the law was enacted and that courts had to keep in mind the "new environment of permissive culture emerging around us".[56]

In a case heard by the Madras High Court in 1990 involving an advertisement in the Tamil weekly "Kalkandu" for a "Durka Ayurveda Tumbler" wherein it was claimed that water drunk from the tumbler was capable of controlling diabetes, blood pressure, weakness etc.[57] The court refused to stay the investigation by the drug inspector in this case.

In states like Kerala, this legislation has served as a useful, though not always successful, handle for public spirited NGOs and individuals to campaign against the sale of products like "Musli Power Xtra" which was marketed as a means to increase sexual pleasure.[58] For example, in 2017, a public interest litigation was filed before the Kerala High Court, impleading the Drug Controllers of Kerala along with many popular print and broadcast media organizations, asking the court to issue orders for rigorous enforcement of the law against unscientific and misleading advertisements. The government responded by informing the court that it was enforcing the law and that 137 actions under the Drugs and Magic Remedies (Objectionable Advertisements) Act were pending before various trial courts in Kerala.[59]

In one case in Delhi, the Delhi High Court simply refused to allow the prosecution of an advertisement in the *Hindustan Times* for a new technology developed by Bosch and Lomb to treat "cataract" which is Sr. No. 7 in the schedule to the Drugs and Magic Remedies (Objectionable Advertisements) Act which contains a list of conditions for which advertisements are not permitted. The court reasoned that the law was meant to prevent self-medication and that it was impossible for prospective patients to self-medicate with the technology being advertized.[60]

All of the above examples are mostly judgments rendered by High Courts hearing appeals. It is much more difficult tracking prosecutions before trial courts as these orders unlike High Court orders are not reported in private law journals and databases. To complicate matters further, various drug controllers do not proactively disclose their prosecutions on their websites. However, we did manage to get our hands on a set of approximately 85 judgments from trials courts, through the e-courts database, mainly in Andhra Pradesh, Kerala, and Maharashtra, delivered in prosecutions under the Drugs and Magic Remedies (Objectionable Advertisements) Act. These judgments were mostly delivered over the last decade.

Of the 24 judgments from Maharashtra that we could access, in 15 cases, the accused pled guilty to the charges and were fined between ₹1,000 to ₹50,000. None were sentenced to imprisonment. This was true even for the case where the seized products had labels claiming to be able to "control" cancer, cardiac conditions, blood pressure, malaria, typhoid, and improve the central nervous system. The accused in this case, who was the proprietor of Cura Pharmaceuticals, voluntarily pled guilty to the charges but was let off with a fine of ₹5,000 per product seized, totaling ₹40,000.[61] This despite the law allowing for an imprisonment of up to six months for first-time offenders and up to one year for repeat offenders.

In another case, where two firms were charged with violating the Drugs and Magic Remedies (Objectionable Advertisement) Act 1954 because they were advertizing and selling a tablet for the cure of AIDS, a syrup to improve memory in children, and an oil for sexual pleasure, the accused declined to plead guilty and faced a criminal trial before the Chief Judicial Magistrate, Pune. The court found both firms guilty of the offences.[62] As with the cases where the accused voluntarily pled guilty, the court in this case too imposed a paltry fine of ₹40,000 without sentencing anybody to prison.

In another judgment against Lupin Laboratories, the company was being prosecuted for a product called "U-Sedate" which was marketed by its Natural Product Division as useful treatment for the "Management of Menorrhagia, Metrorrhagia and dysfunctional uterine bleeding". The Judicial Magistrate at Aurangabad eventually found the company guilty in 2009, 12 years after the case was first filed. In particular, the labelling was found to violate the prohibitions in Sr. 12 (disease of the uterus), 13 (disease of menstrual flow) and 18 (female diseases) of the Schedule to the Drugs and Magic Remedies (Objectionable Advertisement) Act 1954. Despite concluding that the guilty company deserved the maximum punishment permissible under the law, the Judicial Magistrate imposed only a monetary fine of ₹50,000 refusing to sentence anybody in the management to imprisonment. Strangely, the magistrate reasoned that a company could not be imprisoned and hence only a monetary fine could be imposed. However, like most other laws, the Drugs and Magic Remedies (Objectionable Advertisement) Act 1954 has a provision allowing for the person in charge at a company to be imprisoned for offences committed under this law.[63]

We noticed similar trends in cases that were prosecuted in Andhra Pradesh. Of the 33 randomly selected judgments from this state, there were 12 convictions after trial, while in the remaining 21 cases the accused pled guilty. In all of these cases the courts only fined the accused between ₹3,000 to ₹60,000 without sending a single offender to prison. This was true even in cases involving products claiming to treat serious conditions like diabetes, ulcers, kidney stones, asthama.[64]

In one set of cases, the court of the Judicial Magistrate in Atmakur, in Nellore District of Andhra Pradesh found the same firm—Ayurgen Herbals—guilty of violating the Drugs and Magic Remedies (Objectionable Advertisements) Act 1954 in 11 cases that were simultaneously filed against it by a drug inspector for selling an assortment of tonics, extracts, and capsules for a range of conditions that included diabetes, asthama, menstrual disorders, rheumatism, ulcers, fever, weight loss, and impotence. Despite this gross violation of the law including clearly false advertizing for serious conditions like diabetes and asthama, the magistrate only imposed a fine of ₹5,000 in each case, thereby totaling ₹55,000.[65]

Things were no different in Kerala. In all 15 judgments that we were able to access, the courts found the accused guilty of the offences charged under the Drugs and Magic Remedies (Objectionable Advertisements) Act but the only penalty slapped on the accused were minor fines. In only one case did the judicial magistrate sentence a person to serve three months in prison (in addition to a fine of ₹10,000) for stocking and selling a drug "Musli Power Xtra" which described itself on the label as an "aphrodisiac" capable of solving "erectile problems".[66] On appeal, however, the Sessions Judge set aside the sentence of imprisonment on the grounds that the fine was sufficient.[67]

There are four aspects that really stand out from a reading of these judgments. First, that almost all the cases involve Ayurvedic or "natural" drugs, some of which were even licensed by drug controllers in different states, second, that the management and editors of newspapers in which advertisements are published are almost never prosecuted, and third, that almost nobody is sentenced to imprisonment under this law, despite being found guilty of gross violations of the law—including in cases where false claims were made of treating serious life-threatening diseases such as cancer, AIDs etc. A fourth observation is that in the absence of legislative guidance on the issue of fines, judges are imposing arbitrary fines without providing any reasoning. In civil cases, the theory of damages can alternate between compensatory damages which seek to make the plaintiff whole once again and account of profits which seeks to disgorge any profits made by the defendant. In criminal cases, it is generally common for the legislation to fix both the minimum and maximum amount that can be imposed as a fine but the Drugs and Magic Remedies (Objectionable Advertisement) Act 1954 does not provide a range of fines. In such a scenario, where the judge is given complete discretion by the legislature, the former should ideally develop a theory to justify the fines being imposed under this law. One possible theory could be that fines imposed under this law should be punitive in order to deter the publications of such advertisements in the future. Based on this theory, the court can develop a formula linking the fine to the value of the batch manufactured by the guilty company. For example, if the batch is worth ₹1,00,000 the fine could be twice the value of the batch, at ₹2,00,000 so as to really punish the guilty party which may have already profited from partial sale of the batch.

A draft bill published by the Ministry of Health in 2020 for public comments proposes an increase in the term of imprisonment for first time offenders up to two years with a fine up to ₹10 lakhs and for repeat offenders a prison term of up to five years and a fine up to ₹50 lakhs.[68] The Bill has not yet been introduced in Parliament. As usual, the Ministry of Health never published a white paper or a background paper explaining the rationale for the provisions contained in the draft bill.

The loophole for drug advertisements in promotional literature directed at the medical practitioners

When the Drugs and Magic Remedies (Objectionable Advertisement) Act 1954 was enacted, it contained a large carve out for drug advertisements that were published in medical journals or drug promotional literature that is sent directly to medical practitioners in a confidential manner. These two categories of advertisements are entirely excluded from the purview of the Drugs and Magic Remedies (Objectionable Advertisement) Act 1954.[69] The rationale for this exclusion appears to have been that doctors cannot be fooled by pharmaceutical companies.

These advertisements in journals and drug promotional literature supplied directly to doctors are critical cogs in the marketing efforts of pharmaceutical companies since it is doctors at the end of the day who prescribe drugs to patients. If a pharmaceutical company can convince a doctor of the efficacy and safety of its new drug, it would result in additional sales because the doctor is likely to prescribe the drug to more patients.

A consistent problem, however, with drug advertisements in medical journals and drug promotional literature in India is the fact that much of the information in these publications is either incomplete or inaccurate. According to the WHO's guidelines for ethical drug promotion, all advertisements targeted at doctors should contain the following information:

the name of the active ingredient or the International Non-Proprietary Name (INN), the approved generic name of the drug, the brand name, the content of active ingredient per dosage form, name of other ingredients known to cause problems, approved therapeutic uses, dosage form, side-effects and major adverse drug reactions, precautions, warnings and contraindications, major interactions, name and address of manufacturer or distributor, and reference to scientific literature as appropriate.[70] A significant portion of drug advertizing and promotional literature in India fails to meet this criteria and there is no shortage of studies documenting this problem.

In 1992, in a small study published in the *Indian Journal of Physiology and Pharmacology* by researchers from the Mahatma Gandhi Institute of Medical Sciences, the authors studied 903 drug advertisements published in Indian medical journals to discover that only 8.86% of the advertisements referenced the possible side-effects and major adverse reactions; while only 9.63% of the advertisements mentioned the "precaution, contra-indications and warnings" and only a pitiful 2.77% mentioned the "major interactions".[71]

In 1997, a group of researchers from the renowned Jawaharlal Institute of Postgraduate Medical Education and Research conducted another small study on drug advertisements published in the Indian edition of the *British Medical Journal*, which study was then published in the *British Medical Journal*. The study demonstrated how advertisements in the Indian edition of the *BMJ* were likely to be more misleading and make more unsubstantiated claims, when compared to the British edition of *BMJ*.[72] The researchers also picked 10 advertisements at random and sent them to international experts for a review. The response of these experts revealed the serious magnitude of misleading advertisements even in reputed journals like the *BMJ*. For example, for a drug called Pentoxifylline, an advertisement in the Indian edition made therapeutic claims that the manufacturer did not dare make in America or Britain. For another drug called Diclofenac, the manufacturer claimed the drug was gentle on the gastrointestinal tract despite it being well-known that the drug had a high incidence of gastrointestinal side-effects. In another advertisement for Ciprofloxacin, the advertisement claimed "super power in your hands" without providing basic information like contra-indications or side-effects.[73]

In their response, the editors of the Indian edition of the *BMJ*, outlined the three-fold challenge they faced while dealing with advertisements from the Indian pharmaceutical industry. The first was the lack of laws in India as they existed in the United States where the accuracy of drug advertisements is regulated; the second was the lack of effective consumer watchdog groups, and third, the large presence of ayurvedic and other traditional medicines which are widely used despite the lack of adequate scientific data supporting the claims they make. The editors also explained their efforts to instruct advertizers on the editorial policy of the *BMJ* and how internal review committees were setup to vet advertisements leading to rejections of advertisements. Ultimately, they simply passed the buck to doctors who were the final consumers of such advertisements by making a case for doctors and medical students to be educated so as to increase their ability to recognize misleading advertisements.[74]

At least part of the problem appears to be lax editorial standards at Indian journals. A study in 2016 found that non-compliance with ethical standards of advertizing was more common in advertisements published in Indian journals when compared to foreign journals.[75] Stronger editorial standards could help fix this issue.

The situation appears to be significantly worse in the case of drug promotional literature provided directly to doctors by pharmaceutical salespersons.

In a study on drug promotional literature that was published in the *Indian Journal of Pharmacology* in 2010, researchers studied 134 promotional leaflets that were given to medical practitioners. An analysis of the claims made in the drug promotional literature found that 20% of the claims were exaggerated, 32% were inconclusive, 17% were false and only 21% were authentic. The study concluded that its findings were similar to other studies in developing countries and that there was a dire need for the supply of unbiased information to medical practitioners.[76]

In a study published in 2014, researchers at the Government Medical College, Amritsar, collected 50 printed drug advertisement brochures from different out-patient departments of the hospital attached to the medical college and scrutinized them for the accuracy of information. Of the 209 claims made in these 50 advertisements, the researchers reported that only 46% were true, 21% were false, 16% vague, 7% were exaggerated and 10% were controversial. The study concluded that information in drug promotional literature was often "biased, incomplete, unauthentic, and unreliable with references exhibiting questionable credibility".[77]

Two years later, in 2016, a study by researchers at Sri Devraj Urs Medical College, Kolar, which examined 200 pieces of drug promotional literature collected from various departments at the attached medical hospital, found that 69% of the advertisements met only 50% of the WHO's ethical advertizing guidelines. Contraindications and adverse effects were listed only in 34.5% and 32.5% of the advertisements, respectively.[78]

To be certain, the issue of providing unbiased information to medical practitioners is not unique to India. It is a global problem. Pharmaceutical companies often devise deceptive "promotional literature" under the guise of providing medical education to doctors. Common transgressions are to highlight marginal improvements in outcomes based on a small or a limited clinical study without disclosing the study design. The problem is exacerbated in India due to lack of regulatory oversight and lax editorial standards for domestic publications.

Despite the fact that these advertisements in journals and promotional literature are widely published, it hardly features on the reform agenda of the government which is yet to commission a single official study on the issue. In 2014, a voluntary marketing code called the Uniform Code for Pharmaceutical Marketing Practices (UCPMP) was brought in by the Department of Pharmaceutical, Ministry of Chemicals & Fertilizers for the pharmaceutical industry. The Department is entirely silent on the law which gives it this power to introduce such a voluntary code. That said, this Code includes the WHO's criteria for ethical advertizing. But given that it is voluntary, it is also toothless and has little effect on the ground. Even as of 2020, the government in response to a parliamentary question has indicated that it was not going to make the UCPMP compulsory for the pharmaceutical industry.[79] And so the issue continues to fester unaddressed.

The regulatory vacuum around confusing pharmaceutical brand names in India

One of the key components of any marketing campaign by a pharmaceutical company for a new drug is the trademark/brand name adopted by a pharmaceutical company. An easy-to-remember brand name is all the more important in the case of the pharmaceutical industry since the chemical/biological name or even the "International Non-Proprietary Name" (INN) chosen by the World Health Organization (WHO) is often too complicated for the general public to remember.

Patients are more likely to remember the brand name "Crocin" coined by Glaxosmithkline, rather than "paracetamol" which is the INN. The INN will always be complex because it has to reflect certain chemical characteristics of the drug as per the naming conventions adopted by WHO.

For example, all drugs of a certain class may share the same "stem" as a suffix. All, cancer drugs which are Tyrosine Kinase inhibitors will have "tinib" as a suffix and all anti-virals will have "vir" as a suffix. Marketing departments of pharmaceutical companies are not bound by similar naming conventions and can pick and choose fancy brand names that work better from a marketing perspective. All these brand names will generally be protected as registered trademarks and depending on the commercial success of the drug and the marketing campaign around it, the trademark in itself can become a valuable asset for a pharmaceutical company.

Given the centrality of the brand name in the marketing process, most developed countries have very strict regulations on the type of names that can be chosen by pharmaceutical companies to brand their products. The USFDA has two divisions to carry out this analysis: the Division of Medication Error, Prevention and Analysis (DMEPA) which conducts a safety review to prevent possible confusion with other drug names and the Office of Prescription Drug Promotion (OPDP) which evaluates proposed proprietary names to determine "if they are overly fanciful, so as to misleadingly imply unique effectiveness or composition".[80] The USFDA also releases detailed guidance documents for the industry explaining the factors that must be kept in mind while choosing a brand name.[81] The EMA has a "name review group" to perform reviews of brand names submitted by pharmaceutical companies from a safety and promotional aspect.[82] Both regulators take this issue of brand names very seriously. At one point, the EMA was rejecting more brand names than it was accepting.[83] Similarly, the USFDA at one point was rejecting around 50% of the brand names submitted to it.[84]

The reasons that the Americans and Europeans take this issue so seriously is the fact that errors in medications due to confusion between brand names could have dire consequences for patients.

Unlike in the United States and Europe, the Indian drug regulator does not perform any review of the brand names/ trademarks of pharmaceutical products being sold in India. This is because the Ministry of Health has not put in place any regulations requiring the Indian drug regulator to conduct such a review. This despite thousands of pharmaceutical trademarks being registered in India every year by the Trade Mark Registry under the Trade Marks Act 1999. The annual reports of the Intellectual Property Office reveal that the annual number of trademarks registered under Class 5, which pertains to pharmaceuticals, increased from 2,634 in 2002–03 to 41,351 in 2020! The total number of pharmaceutical trademarks registered under the Trade Marks Act 1999 between 2002 and 2020 stands at 327,681. In addition, it is possible that some pharmaceutical companies do not register their brand names under the Trade Marks Act 1999 because there is no legal necessity to do so under the law. The above numbers should be understood in context of the National List of Essential Medicines (NLEM) announced by the Government of India in 2011 which contains only 348 medicines.

The sheer volume of registered trademarks for pharmaceuticals are an indication of intense competition in the Indian pharmaceutical market but who exactly is reviewing these trademarks from a medical perspective? It is no secret that the review performed by the Trade Mark Registry is very limited and not thorough since the Registry has been understaffed with a huge backlog. Even in theory, this review is limited to similarity of the proposed mark to existing ones in the Registry's database and the likelihood of confusion caused by the similarity to the average patient and not a medical review of the brand name as conducted by regulators in Europe and the United State.

It should then be no surprise when different Indian pharmaceutical companies end up using the same or similar brand names for marketing different drugs. Our research assistant managed to compile the following list of identical brand names being used by pharmaceutical companies for entirely different medications:

Brand Name	*Indication*
Zita Vital	Zita Vitamin (Premium nutrition for 28–40 week pregnancy).
Zita (100 mg)	Treats type 2 diabetes mellitus in adults
AZ (10 mg)	An antihistamine, used for allergic reactions.
AZ Plus Suspension (10ml)	Used to treat infections caused by worms.
AZ (500 mg)	Antibiotic for treating bacterial infections such as the infections of the middle ear, typhoid, and chancroid etc.
Visol eye drops	Used to relieve dry, irritated eyes.
Vizole capsules	Prescribed for Cancer treatment.
Ofloren eye drops	Used in treating infections of the urinary tract, nose, throat, skin and soft tissues, and lungs (pneumonia).
Ofloren (200 mg) tablets	Use is the same as that of Ofloren eye drops, however, the dosage is very different.
Clomine (25 mg) tablet	Used in adults to treat obsessive-compulsive disorder (OCD).
Clomin Drops	To treat stomach pain, bloating, and abdominal cramps, and pain associated with excessive acidity, gas, infections, and gastrointestinal tract diseases.

Medzole 400 (tablets)	Used to treat infections caused by worms.
Medzole-40	Gas relief tablets
Medzol (1 mg) injection	Used for sedation in intensive care units and to obtain anesthesia in elderly people before undergoing any surgical procedure.

The above list of examples is not exhaustive and covers only cases where the brand names are identical. The list of cases where the brand names are only similar and not identical likely runs into hundreds. The King Edward Memorial Hospital in Mumbai has compiled a helpful list of few of the similar sounding brand names for different drugs, which is reproduced below.[85]

Brand name	*Generic drug*	*Clinical use*
Tab. Aldactone Inj. Aldarone	Spironolactone Amiodarone	Diuretic Anti-arrhythmic
Inj. Amicom Inj. Amicor	Amikacin Amrinone	Anti microbial Congestive heart failure
Bactroban cream Batrafen cream	Mupirocin (2%) Ciclopirox oleamine	Topical anti-microbial Topical anti-fungal
Tab. Cadolac Tab. Carloc	Ketorolac Carvedilol	NSAID Non-selective beta blocker
Tab. Cetrine Inj. Cytarine	Cetrizine Cytarabine	Anti histaminic Anti neoplastic
Tab. Combutol Tab. Carbatol	Ethambutol Carbamazepine	Anti-tubercular Anti-convulsant
Cap. Dilantin Tab. Dilcontin	Phenytoin Diltiazem	Anti-convulsant Anti-hypertensive

Tab. Epitril Tab. Enapril	Clonazepam Enalapril	Anti-convulsant Angiotensin converting enzyme inhibitor
Cap. Moclox Cap. Macox	Amoxacillin + cloxacillin Rifampicin	Anti-microbial Anti-leprotic
Cap. Neurontin Tab. Nitrocontin	Gabapentin Glyceryl trinitrate	Anti-convulsant Anti-anginal
Tab. Opam Cap. Opaz	Pioglitazone Omeprazole	Oral anti-diabetic Proton pump inhibitor
Inj. Oframax Inj. Okavax	Ceftriaxone Live attenuated vaccine of varicella zoster	Anti microbial Vaccine
Tab. Rapilin Tab. Ranitin	Repaglinide Ranitidine	Anti-diabetic Histamine receptor 2 antagonist
Tab. Rokcin Tab. Roxin	Roxithromycin Thyroxine	Anti-microbial Hormone
Tab. Tricort Tab. Tricox	Triamcinolone Rifampicin + Isoniazid + Pyrazinamide	Corticosteroid Anti-tubercular
Inj. Vasopin Tab. Vasoprin	Vasopressin Isosorbide mononitrate + Aspirin	Bleeding esophageal varices Vasodilator + platelet inhibitor
Tab. Zetop Inj. Zyrop	Cetrizine Erythropoietin	Anti-histaminic Haemopoietic

Even worse is when the same pharmaceutical company uses the same brand name for different drugs. Take for example, the case of I-Pill which was initially marketed as an ECP to prevent conception. After the thumping success of the advertizing campaign around I-Pill, the same company began to use the brand name "I-Pill Daily" to market a daily birth control pill. An ECP is completely different from a daily birth control in that it is taken after unprotected sex in order to prevent pregnancy, while a daily birth control pill stops ovulation. Confusing these two drugs could result in unwanted pregnancies.

As a result of the entire Indian pharmaceutical industry using similar brand names, the industry endlessly litigates against each other on the issue of trademark infringement. The obvious problem with using identical or similar sounding brand names for different drugs that contain different active ingredients is that it increases the possibility of errors in prescriptions. In a country like India where self-medication is rampant and most of the population is not familiar with the English language (which is the most commonly used language for pharmaceutical brand names in India), the consequences of using similar sounding brand names can be dire.

Despite being alerted to this issue by both the Supreme Court and the Parliamentary Standing Committee on Health and Family Welfare, the Ministry of Health has been dragging its feet on regulating the use of brand names by pharmaceutical companies in India.

In 2001, the Supreme Court in a judgment—Cadila Healthcare Ltd. v. Cadila Pharmaceuticals Ltd.[86]—deciding a case about infringement of a pharmaceutical trademark, had urged the government to put in place a mechanism to ensure that the drug regulator evaluated brand names for drugs before granting manufacturing licences. The court also recommended putting in place a coordination mechanism between the Trade Marks Registry and the drug regulator's office to share information. The court reasoned as follows:

> Keeping in view the provisions of Section 17-B of the Drugs and Cosmetics Act, 1940 which inter alia indicates an imitation or resemblance of another drug in a manner likely to deceive being regarded as a spurious drug it is but proper that before granting permission to manufacture a drug under a brand name the authority under that Act is satisfied that there will be no confusion or deception in the market. The authorities should consider requiring such an applicant to submit an official search report from the Trade Mark office pertaining to the trade mark in question which will enable the drug authority to arrive at a correct conclusion.

In 2012, the Parliamentary Standing Committee on Health and Family Welfare in its scathing review of the functioning of the CDSCO flagged the problem of similar sounding brand names for entirely different drugs blaming it on the fact that different state regulators were approving brand names without coordinating with each other. The committee made the following pertinent observations:

> New drugs are approved by CDSCO under their generic (chemical/salt) names. The brand names are decided by the manufacturers and intimated to State Drug Authorities. Due to lack of coordination between various State Drug Authorities, many identical brands are being used for different medicines by various manufacturers located in different States. For example, Lona is being used for low sodium salt as well as for clonazepam (anti-epilepsy drug); AZ brand is being used for azithromycin (antibiotic), albendazole (for worms) and alprazolam (for anxiety). Needless to say this is a highly dangerous situation where wrong medicine can be sold and consumed leading to serious injury. CDSCO has expressed its inability to resolve the issue due to lack of rules and powers.[87]
>
> The Committee strongly recommends that all such cases should be thoroughly reviewed in close coordination with

> State Drug Authorities. Specific procedures may be framed for approval of brand names. The procedure adopted by the Registrar of Newspapers to avoid duplication may be worth emulating. As a beginning, a data bank of all branded pharmaceutical products along with their ingredients should be uploaded on the CDSCO website and regularly updated.[88]

The above diagnosis by the committee of the problem was not entirely correct. In 2012 there were no regulations that gave state drug authorities the power to approve brand names. Hence there was no question of different state drug authorities coordinating with each other on the issue of brand names. The committee's prescription for reform was however on point. The Ministry of Health should have ideally drafted new regulations requiring state licencing authorities to conduct a safety and promotional review of proposed brand names as is the case in the United States and Europe. Instead, what followed was bewildering to say the least.

The government referred this issue to the DCC. At its 44th meeting, the DCC decided that the state drug controllers would stop the practice of issuing manufacturing licences in the brand names and instead issue such licenses in the generic names of the drug.[89] This was a strange recommendation because issuing manufacturing licences in the generic name does not stop manufacturers from using brand names subsequently on the packaging and it certainly did not stop manufacturers from using similar sounding brand names. In any event, this suggestion was then implemented by the Ministry of Health by issuing directions under Section 33P of the Drugs and Cosmetics Act to state drug controllers that licences should only be issued using generic names and not the brand names.[90] These directions were then reported in the "Action Taken Report" sent by the Ministry of Health to the Parliamentary Standing Committee along with other vague assurances of a "data-bank" being setup by the government and of the

DCGI being "sensitized" in this regard.[91] In other words, the Ministry of Health did not even attempt creating a mechanism as suggested by the Parliamentary Standing Committee to prevent confusion in brand names used by pharmaceutical companies for different drugs.

This inaction by the government continued till 2018 when the government received a gentle judicial nudge from Mrs Justice Pratibha M. Singh, an intrepid judge of the Delhi High Court, who impleaded on her own motion, the DCGI and the Ministry of Health into a pharmaceutical trademark infringement lawsuit that she was adjudicating. She then pushed the Ministry of Health into implementing the Supreme Court's suggestion in the Cadila case while reminding the government that:[92]

> The issue of pharmaceutical preparations and medicines being sold under identical brand names has been a concern in a large number of disputes. The said issue is not just one which concerns statutory rights or trademark rights of a particular IP owner, but has a larger impact on the health of the patients.[93]

This time around, after the judicial nudge from the Delhi High Court, the DTAB made a recommendation to implement the Supreme Court's recommendation in the Cadila case and the DCC agreed with the recommendation.[94]

On 6 November 2019, the Ministry of Health notified a mutilated version of the Supreme Court's recommendation into law via the Drugs and Cosmetics (Thirteenth Amendment) Rules 2019.[95] As per these new rules, pharmaceutical companies would now have to submit an undertaking to the state drug controller issuing the manufacturing licence, informing them of the brand/trade name they intended to use to market the drug and that their chosen brand name to the best of their knowledge, was not similar to the name of any existing drug being sold in India, as per a search that they had conducted in databases maintained by the trademark registry, the CDSCO and also in existing literature, reference books and the internet.

The problem with this reform measure is two-fold. First, the CDSCO never created the "central database" of pharmaceutical tradenames mentioned in the amendments introduced in 2019. We asked them in a RTI application filed in December, 2021 to provide us a weblink to this database. We received a one-line answer from the CDSCO stating "No such information is maintained presently".[96]

The second problem with this reform measure is that it failed to impose any obligation on the CDSCO or state drug controller to conduct a review of the brand name from a safety and promotional perspective and reject the use of specific names on the grounds of confusion or safety. There is nothing stopping a pharmaceutical company from submitting an undertaking that it is of the opinion that its chosen brand name is not confusing or deceiving when compared to existing brand names since the question of similarity is a question of law, not fact. Two different people can have different opinions on the similarity of a name, which is why we see so much litigation on trademark infringement around the world. This is exactly why an impartial sovereign authority like a drug regulator must be made responsible for conducting a review of proposed pharmaceutical brand names from a safety and promotional perspective instead of leaving it to the pharmaceutical companies to self-regulate themselves on this aspect. Given the Health Ministry's inaction on this issue, it is likely that the Indian market will continue to see a flood of similar, if not identical sounding pharmaceutical brand names. The ensuing confusion will certainly lead to medication errors and unnecessary harm to patients. The reluctance of the Ministry of Health to tackle the situation with well thought out reforms, despite being alerted to the problem by Parliament and the Supreme Court is telling of its weak commitment to protect public health.

Inter-ministerial chaos on India's drug advertizing policy

The Government of India is well aware of the problems with drug advertizing in the country but instead of developing and enforcing an integrated policy on the issues of misleading advertisements, promotional literature, labelling, and confusing brand names, three different ministries have been announcing different policy initiatives on these issues, often in a piecemeal manner.

The first initiative was announced by the Department of Pharmaceuticals, Ministry of Chemical and Fertilizers in the form of the Uniform Code of Pharmaceuticals Marketing Practices (UCPMP) in 2014.[97] The UCPMP was supposed to be a voluntary self-regulating code to regulate advertizing by the pharmaceutical industry. It is not clear why the Department of Pharmaceuticals, which is responsible for the growth of the pharmaceutical industry, took up a public health issue like advertizing which is within the purview of the Ministry of Health. In fact, the notification by the Department of Pharmaceuticals does not even mention the law under which it is ordering the pharmaceutical industry to adopt the UCPMP.

Then in 2015, the Ministry of Health amended the Drugs and Cosmetics Rules 1945 to introduce a prohibition on advertizing any prescription drugs mentioned in Schedule H, H1 and X without the "previous sanction of the Central Government", except, the rules are entirely silent on the procedure to secure such prior sanction and the grounds on which such sanction may be granted or denied![98] Six years after this amendment was notified, when we asked the Ministry of Health, in an application under the RTI Act, the procedure to seek its prior sanction for such advertisements, it informed us that it had "no information available" with it and transferred the application to the CDSCO to respond to us.[99] This despite the fact that it is the Ministry and not the CDSCO that has the power to make rules. The CDSCO then replied informing us that it had no "additional information" to provide.[100] So basically, nobody in the government knows how exactly to grant sanction for the advertisement of a prescription drug despite the law allowing for advertisement after receipt of previous sanction from the government.

The third measure was brought in by the Ministry of Ayush when in 2016 when it published draft amendments to the Drugs and Cosmetics Rules 1945 to regulate the advertisements of Ayush drugs. This was a Ministry created only in 2014 when the government upgraded the erstwhile Department of Ayush under the Ministry of Health to a full-fledged Ministry. The creation of this new Ministry, led to the odd situation of two different Ministries amending the same rules at different times towards a similar policy objective. As explained elsewhere in this book, these amendments in 2016 were pushed by the Ministry of Ayush after facing immense pressure from the Parliamentary Standing Committee on Health which was shocked by new age Ayush drugs like IME-9 and BGR-34 that were being advertized by private Ayurvedic industry in conjunction with government funded laboratories to treat diabetes. However, the draft amendments proposed in 2016 by the Ministry of Ayush also faced immense pushback from the industry and it was not until 2018 that the Ministry of Ayush was able to amend the rules to require all Ayush advertisements to be vetted by state drug controllers before publication.[101] These rules also laid down the criteria for rejection of advertisements by state drug controllers. Unfortunately, the constitutionality of the rules was challenged before the Delhi High Court by the entire Ayurvedic industry on the ground that the rules violated their fundamental right to speech.[102] Final arguments in the matter and the inevitable appeal to the Supreme Court will likely take a few years if not longer.

The fourth measure taken by the Ministry of Health was in

2019 when it amended the Drugs and Cosmetics Rules 1945 as discussed in the previous section, requiring pharmaceutical companies to self-certify the fact that their own brand names were not similar or causing confusion. This was a pointless measure, as explained earlier.

Apart from these four policy initiatives, the Ministry of Health in 2020 introduced a draft bill to amend the Drugs and Magic Remedies (Objectionable Advertisements) Act 1954 to expand the application of the law to the internet, expand the list of diseases covered by the law and to increase the penalties that can be levied on offenders. This Bill is yet to be introduced in Parliament.

This fragmented approach by different ministries is reflective of a chaotic approach to policy making in India. It is clear that the government is simply tying itself up in knots on a crucial issue that deserves an integrated approach through a single legislation.

The path to future reform and the fundamental right to speech

As is obvious from the above, the Government of India needs a consolidated policy and an integrated law that covers all aspects of advertizing by the pharmaceutical industry, whether it is targeted at doctors or consumers.

A key issue that will determine the contours of any law regulating drug advertizing is the constitutional question of the extent to which the government can regulate drug advertizing. This question is contingent on whether the judiciary continues to uphold the ruling in Hamdard Dawakhana where a bench of five judges of the Supreme Court held that commercial speech does not come within the purview of the fundamental right to free speech and expression in Article 19(1)(a) of the Constitution. There are at least two judgments delivered by benches of three judges of the Supreme Court which have disagreed with the interpretation of Article 19(1)(a) in the Hamdard Dawakhana judgment.

The first judgment is Indian Express v. Union of India[103] where the bench of three judges hearing the case, after pointing out that the American precedents relied upon in the Hamdard Dawakhana judgment had been over-ruled even in the United States, concluded that "the observations made in the Hamdard Dawakhana's case (supra) are too broadly stated" and that it was "of the view that all commercial advertisements cannot be denied the protection of Article 19 (1) (a) of the Constitution merely because they are issued by businessmen."

The second judgment was delivered a decade later by another bench of three judges of the Supreme Court in the case of Tata Press v. Mahanagar Telephone Nigam Ltd.[104] This time around, the court conclusively broke with the precedent in Hamdard Dawakhana. In pertinent part, this judgment held as follows:

> The combined reading of Hamdard Dawakhana's case and the Indian Express Newspapers's case leads us to the conclusion that "commercial speech" cannot be denied the protection of Article 19(1) (a) of the Constitution merely because the same are issued by businessmen.

The court's reasoning for this conclusion was that advertizing was a critical component for any economic system in a democracy, not just for the market to perform its job of delivering quality goods at the lowest prices but also for the survival of the free press whose financial lifeline were advertisements. The judgment then goes even further to hold that the fundamental right to free speech includes not only the right of businesses to advertize their wares but also the right of consumers to receive such information through advertisements. It states in pertinent part:

> Examined from another angle, the public at large has a right to receive the "Commercial speech". Article (19) (1) (a) not only guarantees freedom of speech and expression, it

> also protects the rights of an individual to listen, read and receive the said speech. So far as the economic needs of a citizen are concerned, their fulfilment has to be guided by the information disseminated through the advertisements. The protection of Article 19(1)(a) is available to the speaker as well as to the recipient of the speech. The recipient of "commercial speech" may be having much deeper interest in the advertisement than the businessman who is behind the publication. An advertisement giving information regarding a life saving drug may be of much more importance to general public than to the advertizer who may be having purely a trade consideration.

This judgment of the Supreme Court was influenced in large part by a precedent of the Supreme Court of the United States (SCOTUS) in the case of Virginia State Board of Pharmacy v. Virginia Citizens Consumer Council Inc.[105] where the court struck down a ban on pharmacists advertizing prescription drug prices, on the grounds that such a ban violated the fundamental right to free speech contained in the First Amendment to the United States Constitution.

Now, the problem with both the above judgments in Indian Express and Tata Press is that they were delivered by benches smaller than the five judge bench that delivered Hamdard Dawakhana. By convention, a smaller bench cannot over-rule a larger bench of the Supreme Court. However, given the weak foundations of Hamdard Dawakhana and the unequivocal pronouncements in Indian Express and Tata Press, there is a possibility that a larger bench will eventually overrule Hamdard Dawakhana. This outcome is however far from certain since the court also has to navigate other questions which were not dealt with in Indian Express and Tata Press namely the question of whether companies can even claim fundamental rights.

These issues are likely to be litigated over the next few years as a result of the ongoing constitutional challenge before the

Delhi High Court against the new advertizing rules brought in by the Ministry of Ayush in 2018. If and when this litigation reaches the Supreme Court, it may be asked to conclusively overrule its previous ruling in Hamdard Dawakhana.

If this prediction comes true, it would become impossible for the Ministry of Health to impose a blanket prohibition on drug advertisements. It can, however, enact regulations to restrain the publication of misleading or harmful advertisements. The court in Tata Press was absolutely clear on this aspect when it concluded that, 'Commercial speech' which is deceptive, unfair, misleading and untruthful would be hit by Article 19(2) of the Constitution and can be regulated/prohibited by the State."[106]

The question now is what exactly is the best mode of regulating drug advertisements in a manner that protects public health. The current mode of regulation under the Drugs and Cosmetics Act 1940 and the Drugs and Magic Remedies (Objectionable Advertisements) Act 1954 wherein pharmaceutical companies can get away with making all kinds of unsubstantiated claims in advertisements or promotional literature, until after a drug inspector prosecutes them before a court is inefficient and does not serve the interests of public health. A more efficient system of regulation could be achieved by putting in place regulations that require all pharmaceutical companies to submit all advertisements, promotional literature and brand names to the national drug regulator for its permission before communicating the same to the general public. The drug regulator would need to create internal capacity to screen all such material thoroughly from a public health perspective. This is a task that can easily drown any regulator unless it is given adequate resources to conduct the job in an efficient manner. Executing such reforms will require immense political will on the part of the government given that it is likely to face an exceptional pushback from the pharmaceutical industry.

Notes

1. Vishakha Talreja, 'Morning after, Men Try to Find What's i-Pill', *The Economic Times* (29 September 2007) <https://economictimes.indiatimes.com/industry/healthcare/biotech/pharmaceuticals/morning-after-men-try-to-find-whats-i-pill/articleshow/2413553.cms?from=mdr> accessed 1 December 2021; 'i-pill emergency contraceptive pill', Youtube (16 October 2008) <https://www.youtube.com/watch?v=9m1-xAiGC8Y> accessed 1 December 2021.
2. Radhieka Pandeya and Priyanka Mehra, 'Morning after Pill Ads Come under Drug Regulator Lens' *Mint* (23 September 2009) <https://www.livemint.com/Consumer/FnjyYJnbO8d6aC0C4qaVmO/Morning-after-pill-ads-come-under-drug-regulator8217s-len.html> accessed 2 December 2021.
3. Anvita Dixit, ME Khan and Isha Bhatnagar, 'Mainstreaming of Emergency Contraception Pill in India: Challenges and Opportunities' (2015) 40 *Indian Journal of Community Medicine: Official Publication of Indian Association of Preventive & Social Medicine*, 49.
4. Pandeya and Mehra (n 2).
5. Maria Thomas, 'A Shocking Proportion of Indians Have Got Morning-after Pills All Wrong' *Quartz* <https://qz.com/india/1408192/indias-overuse-of-i-pill-reveals-a-crisis-of-sex-education/> accessed 1 December 2021.
6. Kounteya Sinha, 'Ban on Morning-after Pills' Ads Lifted', *The Times of India* (15 October 2011) <https://timesofindia.indiatimes.com/india/ban-on-morning-after-pills-ads-lifted/articleshow/10360543.cms> accessed 1 December 2021.
7. Council of State Debates 9 March 1927, vol I, 520–522.
8. Government of India, *Report of The Drugs Enquiry Committee* (1930–31) 378–382.
9. ibid 114.
10. ibid 116.
11. ibid.
12. The Venereal Diseases Act, s 2.
13. *Report of The Drugs Enquiry Committee* (n 8) 116–117.
14. 'Medical News' (1939) 74 *The Indian Medical Gazette*, 172, 173.
15. Council of State Debates 10 April 1940, vol I, 560.
16. Legislative Assembly Debates 5 April 1940, vol III, 2234.
17. ibid 2235.
18. The Drugs Act 1940, s 9(f) and s 17(f).
19. The Drugs Act 1940, s 12(2)(d) and s 33(2)(f).

20. Drugs Technical Advisory Board (DTAB), '*MINUTES OF THE 3RD DRUGS TECHNICAL ADVISORY BOARD MEETING HELD IN THE OFFICE OF THE DIRECTOR GENERAL, INDIAN MEDICAL SERVICE, NEW DELHI FROM 23 JANUARY 1945 TO 26 JANUARY, 1945*' (1945) 20.
21. 'Advertisements' (1943) 78 *The Indian Medical Gazette*, 347.
22. ibid 348.
23. Adrija Roychowdhury, 'Rajkumari Amrit Kaur: The Princess Who Built AIIMS' *The Indian Express* (27 August 2020) <https://indianexpress.com/article/research/rajkumari-amrit-kaur-the-princess-who-built-aiims-6570937/> accessed 1 December 2021; Explained Desk, 'Who Was Rajkumari Amrit Kaur, Named in TIME's Magazine List of 100 Influential Women?' *The Indian Express* (7 March 2020) <https://indianexpress.com/article/explained/explained-amrit-kaur-time-magazine-power-women-100-list-6302654/> accessed 1 December 2021.
24. Amrita Kaur, Minister of Health on the Drugs and Magic Remedies (Objectionable Advertisements) Bill 1953, Rajya Sabha Debate 16 February 1954, 75-76.
25. The Drugs and Magic Remedies (Objectionable Advertisements) Act 1954, s 3.
26. Mitra Sharafi, 'Abortion in South Asia, 1860–1947: A Medico-Legal History' (2021) 55 *Modern Asian Studies*, 371.
27. Government of India, Planning Commission, *1st Five Year Plan* (ch 32: Health, 1951).
28. Kiran Kumbhar, 'The History of Birth Control in India Was Never About Empowerment' *The Swaddle* (8 July 2018) <https://theswaddle.com/the-history-of-birth-control-in-india-was-never-about-empowerment/> accessed 1 December 2021.
29. Mausumi Manna, 'Approach towards Birth Control: Indian Women in the Early Twentieth Century' (1998) 35 *The Indian Economic & Social History Review*, 35, 37.
30. Debate on the Drugs and Magic Remedies (Objectionable Advertisements) Bill 1953, Rajya Sabha Debate, 16 February 1954, 77–78.
31. ibid 87.
32. ibid 82.
33. ibid 90, 118.
34. ibid 110.
35. Debate on the Drugs and Magic Remedies (Objectionable Advertisements) Bill 1953, Lok Sabha Debate 26 April 1954, 5737, 5740.

36. ibid 5744.
37. ibid 5757.
38. ibid 5759.
39. ibid 5761.
40. Tripurdaman Singh, *Sixteen Stormy Days* (Penguin 2020) 12–19.
41. Debate on the Drugs and Magic Remedies (Objectionable Advertisements) Bill 1953, Lok Sabha Debate (n 35) 5751.
42. ibid 5751–5752.
43. ibid 5765.
44. Debate on the Drugs and Magic Remedies (Objectionable Advertisements) Bill 1953, Rajya Sabha Debate (n 30) 83.
45. *Hamdard Dawakhana (Wakf) Lal Kuan, Delhi & Anr vs Union of India and Others* (1960) 2 SCR 671 (18 December 1959) <https://indiankanoon.org/doc/591481/> accessed 22 December 2021.
46. ibid para 3, 5.
47. The Drugs and Magic Remedies (Objectionable Advertisements) Act 1954, s 3(d) (as originally enacted and before its amendment in 1963).
48. *Hamdard Dawakhana* (n 45) para 4.
49. ibid para 17.
50. ibid para 19.
51. ibid para 33.
52. ibid para 35.
53. Dr Sushila Nayar, Minister of Health on the Drugs and Magic Remedies (Objectionable Advertisements) Bill 1963, Rajya Sabha Debate 10 September 1963, 3525; Dr D.S. Raju, Deputy Health Minister on the Drugs and Magic Remedies (Objectionable Advertisements) Bill 1963, Lok Sabha Debate 27 November 1963, 1822.
54. Arjun Arra, MP from Uttar Pradesh on the Drugs and Magic Remedies (Objectionable Advertisements) Bill 1963, Rajya Sabha Debate 10 September 1963, 3523.
55. *Zaffar Mohammed vs State of West Bengal* [1976] 2 SCR 782.<https://indiankanoon.org/doc/1148857/> accessed 23 December 2021.
56. *Smt Kantirani Jayanarayan Mangal vs State of Maharashtra* 1982 Cri LJ 1454 <https://indiankanoon.org/doc/1705154/> accessed 23 December 2021, para 20.
57. *TK Kuppuswamy vs Union of India* AIR 1991 Mad 17 (6 April 1990) <https://indiankanoon.org/doc/1385012/> accessed 23 December 2021.

58. *ASP Kurup vs Union of India & Ors* AIR 1983 Ker 259 (15 February 1983) <https://indiankanoon.org/doc/740590/> accessed 23 December 2021; *KC Abraham vs State of Kerala* WP(C) No 11410 of 2011 (Kerala HC, 27 June 2011) <https://indiankanoon.org/doc/117903436/> accessed 23 December 2021.
59. *G Jayaprakash vs State of Kerala* WP(C) No 5740 of 2017 before the Kerala High Court decided on 15 January 2021 <https://indiankanoon.org/doc/70232357/> accessed 23 December 2021.
60. *Amit Singh vs The State* MANU/DE/2191/201.
61. *State of Maharashtra vs Mr Hemant Kumar Sharma, Proprietor of Cura Pharmaceuticals* R.C.C. No. 267/2017 before the Court of Judicial Magistrate First Class at Vashi, District Thane, Maharashtra decided on 9 April 2018.
62. *State of Maharashtra vs Pramod Sakharam Arolkar, Anandi Pharmaceuticals* R.C.C. No. 770 of 2007 before the Court of the Chief Judicial Magistrate at Pune, Maharashtra decided on 29 April 2014.
63. *State of Maharashtra vs Lupin Laboratories* S.C.C. No. 36 of 1997 before the Court of Judicial Magistrate First Class, Aurangabad, Maharashtra decided on 9 September 2009.
64. *State of Andhra Pradesh vs S Vijaya, Proprietor of Balaji Natural Remedies, Apollo Medicare Agencies & Ors* C.C. No. 243 of 2012 before the Court of the IV Addl. Judicial Magistrate of 1st Class, Chittoor, decided on 20 September 2014. (The case involved the advertisement and sale of ASTHMA-ex capsules to give relief for Asthma); *State of Andhra Pradesh vs Shived Herbals, Vign Aayurceuticals & Ors* C.C. No. 902 of 2016 before the Court of Metropolitan Magistrate, Vijaywada, decided on 14 February 2017. (The case involved the advertisement and sale of Pramehnil Liquid for the treatment of diabetes).
65. *State of Andhra Pradesh vs Ayurgen Herbals & Anr* CC. No. 339, 340, 341, 342, 343, 345, 346, 347, 348, 349 & 350 of 2017 before the Court of the Judicial Magistrate of First Class at Atmakur, Nellore District decided on 12 December 2017.
66. *State represented by Drug Inspector vs Kunnath Pharmaceuticals* C.C. No. 640 of 2007 before the Court of the Judicial First Class Magistrate—II, Ernakulam decided on 1 August 2016.
67. *Kunnath Pharmaceuticals vs State represented by Drug Inspector* Crl. Appeal No. 241 of 2016 before the Court of the IInd Addl. District & Sessions Judge, Ernakulam decided on 18 January 2018.
68. Government of India, Ministry of Health and Family Welfare, *Draft*

of the Drugs and Magic Remedies (Objectionable Advertisements) (Amendment) Bill 2020 (F.No. A. 11035/133/2014-DFQC/DRS, 3 February 2020).

69. Drugs and Magic Remedies (Objectionable Advertisement) Act 1954, s 14.
70. World Health Organization, *Ethical criteria for medicinal drug promotion* (1988), 7–8.
71. A Lal and ML Sharma, 'Drug Advertisements in Indian Medical Journals' (1992) 36 *Indian Journal of Physiology and Pharmacology*, 139.
72. B Gitanjali et al., 'Are Drug Advertisements in Indian Edition of BMJ Unethical?' (1997) 315 *British Medical Journal*, 459.
73. ibid.
74. GG Christo and R Balasubramaniam, 'Commentary: Advertizing Adversities' (1997) 315 *BMJ* (Clinical research ed.), 460.
75. Pooja M Vachhani, Manish N Solanki and Mira K Desai, 'An Evaluation of Drug Promotional Literatures Published in Scientific Medical Journals' (2016) 8 *Journal of Pharmacy & Bioallied Sciences*, 248.
76. Mangala Bhaskar Murthy and Bhaskar Krishnamurthy, 'Authenticity of Claims Made in Drug Promotional Literature' (2010) 42 *Indian Journal of Pharmacology*, 59.
77. Gurpreet Kaur Randhawa and others, 'A Critical Analysis of Claims and Their Authenticity in Indian Drug Promotional Advertisements' (2015) 2015 *Advances in Medicine*, 469147.
78. Puttaswamy Ganashree, Krishnaswamy Bhuvana and Narayana Sarala, 'Critical Review of Drug Promotional Literature Using the World Health Organization Guidelines' (2016) 5 *Journal of Research in Pharmacy Practice*, 162.
79. Rema Nagarajan, 'No Plan for Mandatory Pharma Code, Says Government' *The Times of India* (24 September 2020) <https://timesofindia.indiatimes.com/business/india-business/no-plan-for-mandatory-pharma-code-says-govt/articleshow/78285961.cms> accessed 8 December 2021.
80. The United States Food and Drug Administration (USFDA), *How FDA Reviews Proposed Drug Names*. <https://www.fda.gov/files/drugs/published/How-FDA-reviews-drug-names.pdf> accessed 23 December 2021.
81. The United States Food and Drug Administration (USFDA), *Best Practices in Developing Proprietary Names for Human Prescription Drug Products: Guidance for Industry* (December 2020).

82. European Medicines Agency, *Mandate, objectives and rules of procedure for the Name Review Group (NRG)* (EMA/411943/2014, 7 October 2019).
83. Ian Schofield, 'High Rejection Rate of Proposed Brand Names On EMA Radar' *Pink Sheet* (19 May 2017) <https://pink.pharmaintelligence.informa.com/PS120676/High-Rejection-Rate-of-Proposed-Brand-Names-On-EMA-Radar> accessed 23 December 2021.
84. Laura Helbling, 'FDA Rejecting Fewer Proprietary Names' *Pink Sheet* (2 January 2015) <https://pink.pharmaintelligence.informa.com/PS079808/FDA-Rejecting-Fewer-Proprietary-Names> accessed 23 December 2021.
85. 'Sound Alike Drug Names in the Indian Market' (*King Edward Memorial Hospital*) <https://www.kem.edu/sound-alike-drug-names-in-the-indian-market/> accessed 23 December 2021.
86. *Cadila Healthcare Limited vs Cadila Pharmaceuticals Limited* 2001 PTC 541 (SC).
87. Department Related Parliamentary Standing Committee on Health and Family Welfare, *The Functioning of The Central Drugs Standard Control Organisation (CDCSO)* (Fifty-Ninth Report) (RS 2012) para 11.1.
88. ibid 11.2.
89. Drugs Consultative Committee (DCC), *'REPORT OF THE 44TH MEETING OF THE DRUGS CONSULTATIVE COMMITTEE HELD ON 20TH JULY, 2012 IN THE COMMITTEE ROOM, FDA BHAVAN, KOTLA ROAD, NEW DELHI—110002'* (2012) 20-21 <https://cdsco.gov.in/opencms/resources/UploadCDSCOWeb/2018/UploadCommitteeFiles/44dcc.pdf> accessed 23 December 2021.
90. Government of India, Ministry of Health & Family Welfare, *FINAL ACTION TAKEN REPORT ON THE OBSERVATIONS/RECOMMENDATIONS CONTAINED IN THE 59TH REPORT OF THE DEPARTMENT RELATED PARLIAMENTARY STANDING COMMITTEE ON HEALTH & FAMILY WELFARE ON THE FUNCTIONING OF THE CENTRAL DRUGS STANDARD CONTROL ORGANISATION (CDSCO)* (X.11035/32/2012-DFQC, 28 December 2012), 31.
91. Government of India, Ministry of Health & Family Welfare, *OBSERVATIONS/RECOMMENDATIONS ON THE FUNCTIONING OF THE CENTRAL DRUGS STANDARD CONTROL ORGANISATION (CDSCO)* (File No X11035/32/2012-DFQC, 12 September 2012).

92. *Curewell Drugs and Pharmaceuticals vs Ridley Life Science Private* CS (COMM) 1071/2018 (Delhi HC, 6 February 2019) <https://indiankanoon.org/doc/188331718/> accessed 23 December 2021.
93. ibid para 11.
94. Drugs Technical Advisory Board (DTAB), '*MINUTES OF THE 81ST MEETING OF DRUGS TECHNICAL ADVISORY BOARD HELD ON 29TH NOVEMBER, 2018 AT DGHS, NIRMAN BHAWAN, NEW DELHI*' (2018) 6 <https://cdsco.gov.in/opencms/resources/UploadCDSCOWeb/2018/UploadCommitteeFiles/dtab29nov18.pdf> accessed 23 December 2021; Drugs Consultative Committee (DCC), '*MINUTES OF 55TH MEETING OF DRUGS CONSULTATIVE COMMITTEE HELD ON 31ST JANUARY & 01ST FEBRUARY, 2019 AT NEW DELHI*' (2019) 21, Agenda No 15 <https://cdsco.gov.in/opencms/opencms/system/modules/CDSCO.WEB/elements/common_download.jsp?num_id_pk=ODMz> accessed 23 December 2021.
95. Drugs and Cosmetics (Thirteenth Amendment) Rules 2019.
96. Reply to RTI application dated 12 January 2022, CDSCO (Application No. CDSCO/R/E/21/00594, 13 December 2021).
97. Government of India, Ministry of Chemicals and Fertilizers, *Uniform Code of Pharmaceuticals Marketing Practices (UCPMP)* (F No 5/3/2009-PI-I/PI-II (Vol. III), 12 December 2014).
98. Government of India, Ministry of Health and Family Welfare, *GSR 289(E)* (*Gazette of India Extraordinary*, Part II—s 3(i), 15 April 2015), 2.
99. Reply to RTI application dated 10 December 2021, Ministry of Health and Family Welfare (Application No MOHFW/R/E/21/06748, 19 November 2021).
100. Reply to RTI application dated 12 December 2021, Central Drug Standard Control Organisation (Application No MOHFW/R/E/21/06748, 19 November 2021).
101. Government of India, Ministry of AYUSH, *GSR 1230(E)* (*Gazette of India Extraordinary*, Part II—s 3(i), 21 December 2018).
102. *Reckitt Benckiser India vs Union of India* W.P.(C) 321 of 2019, C.M. Appl. No. 1529-1530/2019 before the Delhi High Court heard on 15 January 2019. <http://delhihighcourt.nic.in/dhcqrydisp_o.asp?pn=6336&yr=2019> accessed 23 December 2021.
103. 1985 SCR (2) 287.
104. 1995 SCC (5) 139.
105. 425 U.S. 748.
106. *Tata Press* (n 104) para 17, 18, 25.

CHAPTER ELEVEN

The Politics and Levers of Reforming India's Drug Regulatory Framework

The path to reforming India's drug regulatory framework is a minefield of competing interests. It includes not just the obvious stakeholders like the powerful Indian pharmaceutical industry but also the state and union governments, the bureaucracy, and public health activists. The first and foremost challenge in the journey towards reform is for India to accept that its pharmaceutical industry has a quality problem which its regulator is unable to address. This would require the country to accept that the woes of the Indian pharmaceutical industry are not a "conspiracy theory" against the country by foreign drug regulators acting on behalf of foreign pharmaceutical companies. Once it accepts this problem, India has to consciously choose to protect the public health of its people over the growth, employment, and export dollars provided by the Indian pharmaceutical industry.

Presuming the country places public health over and above the commercial interests of the industry, it will have to resolve intense politics on the issue of federalism between the union and state governments, as well as inter-ministerial politics that is opposed to the idea of creating an independent regulator. Then there is intra-bureaucracy politics wherein the cadre of drug inspectors made of primarily pharmacists will do everything in their power to resist surrendering their position and significant powers to more qualified medical professionals. There also exist other levers of reforms, such as increased transparency, a guarantee of public participation, and an overhaul of public procurement procedures for drugs that can generate excellent dividends for public health.

While this journey towards reform may appear overwhelming if not impossible, we are confident that when citizen advocacy is combined with intrepid journalism and watchful parliamentarians, Indian democracy will triumph in forcing the interests of pharmaceutical companies to surrender before the needs of public health of the country. In this chapter, we explain some of these politics of reform along with the levers through which India can hopefully overhaul its drug regulatory framework.

Conspiracy theories and the "victim card"

13 May 2013 was one of the most important days in the history of the Indian pharmaceutical industry. It was on this day that Ranbaxy Laboratories, the "crown jewel" in the growth story of the Indian pharmaceutical industry, pled guilty before an American court to seven felony counts and also agreed to pay penalties of $500 million for manufacturing violations at two of its facilities located at Paonta Sahib and Dewas, both in India.[1]

In most countries, a scandal such as the guilty plea entered by one of the country's largest pharmaceutical company, Ranbaxy Laboratories, before an American court would have prompted some national soul-searching with citizens and political parties questioning the effectiveness of their own national regulator. Not so in India. This, despite the fact that all of Ranbaxy's manufacturing facilities that were at the center of the scandal were located in India and subject to the scrutiny of Indian law and its regulators. Save for a few individual hospitals and pharmacy chains that expressed concern in the press about the continued consumption of Ranbaxy's drugs by Indian patients, there was little outrage or calls for accountability in the Indian media.[2] In fact, some prominent members of the medical community like Dr Devi Prasad Shetty actively defended the company on television.[3] This muted criticism of Ranbaxy or the country's drug regulator was because the Government of India, the Indian pharmaceutical industry and public health activists all worked in tandem to paint the case against Ranbaxy as a conspiracy to defame the Indian pharmaceutical industry despite the fact that Ranbaxy pled guilty to all the charges!

Here is an account of the events that followed the news about Ranbaxy's guilty plea. The Ministry of Commerce, which has nothing to do with drug regulation in India, published a boisterous press release, on 3 June 2013 mere weeks after Ranbaxy's guilty plea propagating this conspiracy theory. An extract of the press release is reproduced below:

> There are reasons to believe that vested interests are raking up isolated issues reported regarding technical deficiencies on manufacturing and GMP. India is enjoying a unique position of low cost manufacturing and highest quality medicine, best of both the worlds. Government has strong reason to believe that some of the spurious drugs detected in the international markets, alleged to be exported from India, are desperate attempts by other countries getting affected by the strength of Indian pharma industry.[4]

So, who according to the Government of India were these "vested interests" raking up "isolated issues"? The answer to that question can be found in an earlier statement by the Health Secretary Naresh Dayal in 2008 when the USFDA first announced an import ban on drugs from Ranbaxy into the United States after an inspection revealed serious issues at the company's manufacturing plant. Dayal was quoted in the Indian press, blaming the ban on Ranbaxy on both the American government and the American pharmaceutical industry. He had said:

> The FDA never had problems with the same drugs earlier. The moment the House (US Congress) committee on trade, commerce and energy created a ruckus, FDA started having problems. All these are non-tariff barriers. There is a huge and growing market for Indian generic drugs in the US and drug lobbies there never want this to happen. Clearly, they are putting pressure on FDA. You have to understand there is a vested commercial interest in this.[5]

In effect, Dayal was accusing the USFDA of dancing to the tune of the American pharmaceutical industry; a serious accusation of corruption against a foreign regulator despite there being no evidence to substantiate such an accusation. While the Commerce Ministry in 2013 stopped short of naming the American government, the timing of its statement, close on the heels of the Ranbaxy scandal, was a clear indication that it was continuing the same strategy of blaming all of Ranbaxy's woes on the "foreign hand".

Indian public health activists were not very far behind the government when it came to deflecting the blame towards the "foreign hand". The *Hindu Business Line* ran a report titled "Public Health Activists smell conspiracy against Indian pharma" stating:

> the convenor of Jan Swasthya Abhiyan, B. Ekbal, said attempts were being made by multinational drug companies to belittle Indian drug-makers engaged in generic drug trade. Calling India the pharmacy of Third World countries, he said, "Though Ranbaxy is no more an Indian company, the targeting of Indian companies is part of a strategy".[6]

An influential public health activist, the late Amit Sengupta, who worked with the Jan Swasthya Abhiyan and other NGOs, while accepting that Ranbaxy was guilty of falsifying regulatory data, dismissed the magnitude of the plea on the grounds that the definition of "adulteration" in American law included not just drugs that failed quality tests but also drugs manufactured without following proper documentation procedures as required by the code of GMPs. According to Sengupta, "The fact that Ranbaxy provided false documents does not prove that its drugs were of bad quality, and by extension it is definitely not evidence that Indian generic drugs are generally of poor quality."[7] He then concluded that that the Ranbaxy episode was being used unfairly by "Big Pharma" and "its supporters in the corporate controlled media" to unfairly "demonize" the entire generic pharmaceutical industry in India.[8]

This argument that Ranbaxy was only guilty of not maintaining proper documentation was a common excuse being trotted out at the time by Ranbaxy and the Government to explain the fine of $500 million penalty and the guilty plea. Arun Sawhney, who was Ranbaxy's CEO at the time, had given similar interviews stating that:

> An incomplete understanding of the word 'adulteration' would have caused some to believe that the drugs are not safe, when in fact it was (simply) a question of (improper) documentation.[9]

The Minister of Health, Ghulam Nabi Azad, too gave a similar answer in Parliament when questioned by anxious MPs to explain the implications of Ranbaxy's guilty plea for Indian patients. When asked whether the Health Ministry could assure the country that Ranbaxy was not selling any adulterated drugs in India, the Health Minister chose to respond by outlining the differing legal definition of adulteration in India and in the United States:

> As per the US Law, any drug is considered adulterated, if it is not manufactured, processed, packed, etc. in conformity with

> the Current Good Manufacturing Practice (GCMP) regulations of the USFDA. However, as per Drugs and Cosmetics Act and Rules, in India, manufacturing of drugs not in conformity with Good Manufacturing Practices (GMP) is viewed as non-compliance to GMP under the said Act and Rules.[10]

In all three statements, by the noted public health activist, the CEO of the guilty pharmaceutical company, and the Union Health Minister, the aim was to portray the Ranbaxy plea as a "documentation issue" wherein the company failed to maintain proper records of its manufacturing process rather than a case where the company actually sold drugs of questionable quality to unsuspecting patients. These assertions were, however, completely factually incorrect because Ranbaxy had pled guilty to selling drugs in the American market even after it had knowledge that the drugs had failed certain quality tests. As explained by the Department of Justice press release outlining the guilty plea by Ranbaxy:

> Ranbaxy USA further admitted to failing to timely file required reports known to FDA as "field alerts" for batches of Sotret and gabapentin that had failed certain tests. With respect to Sotret, Ranbaxy USA was aware in January 2003 that a batch of Sotret failed an accelerated dissolution stability test but continued to distribute the batch into the United States for another 13 months. With respect to gabapentin, Ranbaxy USA was aware at various times between June and August 2007 that certain batches of gabapentin were testing out-of-specification, had unknown impurities, and would not maintain their expected shelf life. Nevertheless, Ranbaxy USA did not notify FDA and institute a voluntary recall until October 2007.[11]

By pleading guilty, Ranbaxy admitted to the charge of selling adulterated medicine in the United States. But even the issues dismissed as so called "documentation issues" were actually of a very serious magnitude since Ranbaxy had basically pled guilty to fabricating data with respect to crucial quality tests and making false statements in this regard to the USFDA. Two of the accusations to which Ranbaxy pled guilty as explained in the Department of Justice press release:

> Ranbaxy USA also admitted to making false, fictitious, and fraudulent statements to the FDA in Annual Reports filed in 2006 and 2007 regarding the dates of stability tests conducted on certain batches of Cefaclor, Cefadroxil, Amoxicillin, and Amoxicillin and Clavulanate Potassium, which were manufactured at the Dewas facility. Ranbaxy USA was found to have conducted stability testing of certain batches of these drugs weeks or months after the dates reported to FDA. In addition, instead of conducting some of the stability tests at prescribed intervals months apart, the tests were conducted on the same day or within a few days of each other. This practice resulted in unreliable test results regarding the shelf life of the drugs. Ranbaxy USA also acknowledged that drug samples waiting to be tested were stored for unknown periods of time in a refrigerator, which did not meet specified temperature and humidity ranges for an approved stability chamber, and that this was not disclosed to the FDA.[12]

These false statements and the inconsistencies in conducting the required tests at the prescribed time to ensure quality of its product were a cause for serious concern since stability testing is crucial in order to guarantee the therapeutic efficacy of a drug, which is why such testing is mandated in the GMPs code of most countries. A drug that is stable at the six months mark post manufacturing may begin to degrade at the eight months mark if it is not formulated properly which is why such regular testing is mandated. Without such testing, no company can guarantee the quality of their product until its labelled expiration date and hence the presumption in American law that drugs not tested as required by the GMPs are adulterated. Thus, the tendency to dismiss the failure to conduct quality tests as a mere "documentation issue", equivalent to the misfiling of documents in the wrong folder is a dangerously misconceived and a misleading exercise. Yet, that is exactly how the CEO of Ranbaxy, the Minister of Health, and the public health activist chose to dismiss the magnitude of Ranbaxy's guilty plea.

As the USFDA ramped up scrutiny of pharmaceutical manufacturing facilities in the years following the Ranbaxy scandal by issuing a number of warning letters to the Indian pharmaceutical industry, Indian public health activists doubled down on conspiracy theories centered around the "foreign hand". One such activist from the All India Drug Action Network (AIDAN), an influential collective of public health activists, directly imputed in an opinion editorial in a national newspaper that the USFDA was acting as a proxy for the western pharmaceutical industry:

> The USFDA's warning letters are no doubt the handiwork of the MNC. This is more a political battle than just the quality of few medicines and so it needs a political stand and solution. The Indian government should acknowledge the unique contribution and should not bend to the forces and strategies of the MNCs. This is not the first time that this lobby has tried this. Eternal vigilance and lobbying against such vested threats are the only way out.[13]

Rarely did the Indian government or Indian public health activists attempt to get into the weeds of the allegations made by foreign regulators despite regulators like the USFDA publishing all of its regulatory observations on its website, in a document called Form 483.

Less than two years after the controversy over Ranbaxy's guilty plea before an American court, came a new scandal at GVK Bio, a clinical research organization (CRO). The scandal at GVK Bio, as discussed elsewhere in this book, began after the French drug regulator was contacted by a whistleblower, who was a former employee of GVK Bio, and turned over evidence of data fabrication at the company. A detailed investigation by the French regulator, resulting in a long investigation report, accused GVK Bio of fabricating certain patient data as a result of which the regulator declared that it had no faith in any of the data generated by the CRO. On the basis of the French regulator's findings, the EMA cancelled the marketing approvals it had granted to 700 drugs because the drugs in question were approved on on the basis of regulatory data generated at GVK Bio.

Despite both Indian and foreign drug companies being affected by this decision of the EMA, the Indian government once again played the victim card. The DCGI, G.N. Singh, told the *Hindu* "...one must understand that there is a bigger game being played out here. I have repeatedly stated that multinational pharmaceutical companies constantly use incidents like this to bring disrepute to Indian generic drug makers".[14] The generic industry's top lobbyist, the late Mr D.G. Shah, who spoke for the Indian Pharmaceutical Alliance (IPA) was not far behind, telling the *Hindu* that the manner in which the European regulator went about the ban "... only leaves doubt about its intention".[15] Neither the drug regulator nor the industry lobbyist provided any factual evidence to substantiate their claims that the EMA was acting on behalf of foreign pharmaceutical companies.

The Ministry of Commerce then got into the fray by not just threatening to sue the European Union before the World Trade Organisation (WTO) for unfair trade practices but also cancelling pending trade talks with the European Union on a possible free-trade agreement with India. The Minister for Commerce, Nirmala Sitharaman, claimed that the decision had been taken at the highest level of government, implying that it had the blessings of the Prime Minister's Office.[16] The top rungs of the government appeared to be convinced that there was a conspiracy against India. Quoting the then Commerce Secretary Rajiv Kher, the *Hindu Business Line* reported, "The Secretary said that there were just a few big multinationals that were driving an agenda against the generic (off-patent drug) industry, affecting India's annual drug exports of $15 billion."[17] Once again, a senior government official was basically accusing the EMA of acting on behalf of a "few big multinational" without any evidence of the same. Once tempers cooled and the issue fell off the front pages, India quietly restarted the trade talks and never approached the WTO. All the bluster somehow vanished into thin air.

These conspiracy theories are not limited to instances where foreign regulators take action against Indian pharmaceutical companies but also extend to instances where foreign academics have published studies on the quality of Indian drugs. One such study in 2014, funded by the National Bureau of Economic Research (NBER) and authored by a team of American and Canadian academics had collected 1470 samples of "Made in India" drugs from Indian cities and also from cities in middle-income countries and Africa for the purpose of testing the drugs.[18] Amongst other conclusions, the study also concluded that the samples drawn from poorly regulated countries in Africa were more likely to fail quality testing thereby implying that Indian pharmaceutical companies were exporting poorer quality drugs to Africa.[19] This is not completely unbelievable; according to the Government of India's own survey report of drug quality published in 2017 pegs the quantity of NSQ drugs in government hospitals at 10.02%, which is three times the 3.16% detected by the survey in the open market.[20] The likely reason for this is because the Indian pharmaceutical industry knows that the public procurement system in India is inefficient, meaning that they are more likely to get away with cutting corners when selling to government agencies. It is therefore not unbelievable that the Indian pharmaceutical industry would apply less rigorous quality standards to drugs that were exported to poorly regulated markets in Africa as concluded by the NBER study.

The NBER report provoked a huge backlash from the Indian government, industry lobbyists, and Indian public health activists. A public health activist belonging to the All India Drug Action Network (AIDAN) condemned the report as "an attempt by Western pharmaceutical companies to malign the reputation of Indian generic drug makers".[21] The India Brand Equity Foundation (IBEF), which is a trust setup by the Government of India to promote the "Made in India" brand and headed by the Commerce Secretary, asked the government to sue the academics! In a statement released by the government run trust, the following allegations were made against the authors of the study:

> It seems that the effort is to tarnish the image of the Indian pharma industry, which it has painstakingly developed over the years and is often recognised as "Pharmacy of the World"
>
> The study has not been reviewed by any of the authors' peers as is the gold standard in serious academic publishing. The study cites anecdotal evidence and hearsay, quoted earlier in the authors' other publications, as facts with established academic provenance.
>
> Realising the serious damage that such an irresponsible report is trying to make, the pharma industry has asked the Government of India to initiate legal proceedings against all concerned.[22]

The late D.G. Shah, who at the time was the top lobbyist for the Indian Pharmaceutical Association (IPA) made similar noises, alleging that, "[The research paper] tarnishes the image of the Indian pharmaceutical industry. It would be to the advantage of our adversaries as they can then sell more expensive drugs to the poor countries."[23]

The fact of the matter however is that a number of

developing countries in Africa and Asia, such as Ghana, Mozambique, Vietnam, and Sri Lanka have officially complained to the Government of India about the quality of drugs being exported to their respective countries by Indian pharmaceutical companies. In 2014, the same year as the NBER study, Vietnam blacklisted a record 45 Indian companies and prohibited them from exporting to Vietnam because of quality concerns.[24] These complaints by African and Asian countries have been quietly acknowledged in government meetings.[25] Ultimately, the Government of India never sued the authors of the NBER study for defamation, the study was published in a peer review publication and the controversy faded away.

The conspiracy theories and ad-hominem attacks, however, continued to be used against critics of the Indian pharmaceutical industry. In 2016, when one of us, Dinesh Thakur, filed a public interest petition before the Supreme Court asking for regulatory reform, the DCGI, Dr G.N. Singh had this to say: "We welcome whistleblowers, we have got great respect, but their intentions should be genuine, should be nationalistic... I don't have any comment on this guy."[26] The imputation being that Dinesh was anti-national for questioning, before the highest court of the land, the functioning of the CDSCO which is headed by the DCGI.

Similarly, when Katherine Eban's best-selling book, *Bottles of Lies: The Inside Story of the Generic Pharmaceutical Boom*, was published in 2019, exposing the details of the scandals at Ranbaxy and other generic pharmaceutical companies in India, the CDSCO reportedly sent a note to the Ministry of Health recommending that the Government of India take "appropriate action to counter the allegations made in the book".[27]

According to the *Print*, which broke the story, the CDSCO's note stated that, "A brief perusal of the book reveals that there is no co-relating data available in the representing story and statements have been made based on the assumptions," and that the author's allegations were "fiction-filled stories" and that such allegations have been made "time to time attempting to malign Indian pharmaceutical industries due to their strong presence globally".[28] This despite the fact that Eban had extensively substantiated her reporting by citing primary sources. Ultimately, *Bottle of Lies* became a bestseller in both the United States and India.

This pattern of ad-hominem attacks and conspiracy theories which blamed all regulatory woes of Indian pharmaceutical industry on foreign regulators and foreign companies is reflective of a governance culture in India that is used to blaming domestic problems on some "foreign hand" or the "other". That many prominent public health activists in India have sided with the government's position has only lent credibility to these conspiracy theories. All of this has happened despite the Parliamentary Standing Committee on Health and Family Welfare roasting the CDSCO for doing an abysmal job in ensuring drug quality in India just a year before the guilty plea by Ranbaxy.[29]

Playing the victim card, intentionally distracting attention from real issues, and making empty threats seems to be a familiar trope of the Indian pharmaceutical industry and the Government of India anytime they are called to explain their misdeeds in public.

The first step thus to any meaningful reform of India's drug regulatory framework is for the Government of India to stop believing in and regurgitating the conspiracy theories spouted by lobbyists for the Indian pharmaceutical industry and accept that the Indian pharmaceutical industry and the Indian regulator have serious problems when it comes to ensuring quality of "Made in India" drugs. The rest will follow.

In 2017, the new draft pharmaceutical policy announced by the government actually admitted to serious quality issues within the Indian pharmaceutical industry. A relevant paragraph from the policy is extracted below:

> The quality assurance of indigenously manufactured drugs is another area of concern. While the drugs that get exported have a stringent quality assurance system, put in place and insisted by the importing countries internal requirements; concerns have been raised on the quality surveillance of the indigenously manufactured drugs for domestic consumption. There are not enough Nationally Accredited Laboratories (NABL) for conducting frequent and regular tests. The record of regular audit of these NABLs itself is also not very encouraging. The manufacturing permission for established drugs (already in market for more than 4 years) is given by State Drug Administrators without any Bio-Availability and Bio-Equivalence test of the claimed products. The inspection of the manufacturing premise and processes are, many a times perfunctory or absent. Many manufacturing units are not compliant with the World Health Organisation's (WHO) Good Manufacturing Practices (GMP) or the Good Laboratory Practices (GLP). All these severally and in combination give rise to grave quality concerns in pharmaceutical industry.

These serious admissions in the Draft Pharmaceutical Policy 2017 never acquired the stamp of official acceptance since the Government of India never finalized the draft pharmaceutical policy. The draft policy however reflects the fact at least some bureaucrats in the government were wise to the yarns being spun by the lobbyists of the Indian pharmaceutical industry.

Growth of the pharmaceutical industry v. public health: What is the job of the drug regulator?

In the race for economic growth, countries like India tend to put "development" and "economic growth" front and center of the national agenda. In the context of the pharmaceutical industry, this often means promoting growth of the industry at the cost of public health. In India, the key stakeholders in the regulatory framework are quite transparent about diluting regulatory standards that stand in the way of the growth and profitability of the domestic pharmaceutical industry. Take, for example, the decision taken by the Government of India in 2004, to dilute GMP standards that had been introduced in Indian law merely three years ago in 2001. The Minister of Health admitted in Parliament that the government was diluting the GMP standards because it had received a memorandum from 34 MPs asking the government to delay enforcement of the new GMP standards on the grounds that "thousands of small scale pharmaceutical units" would shut down if the new GMP standards were enforced.[30] This despite the fact that enforcement of the new standards introduced in 2001 had already been delayed by three years.

This attitude at the highest level of the government is reflected down the chain of command. For example, the CDSCO for the longest time had a mission statement that seemed to indicate it was more interested in the growth of the pharmaceutical industry than it was in protection of public health. This was pointed out by no less an authority than the Parliamentary Standing Committee on Health and Family Welfare in its 59th report. The committee noted with shock that the status report submitted by the Ministry to Parliament defined the regulator's mission as meeting "the aspirations ... demands and requirements of the pharmaceutical industry".[31] As rightly noted by the Parliamentary Committee, most national drug regulators put the interests of public health, not the pharmaceutical industry, at the front and center of their mission statement. The following conclusion of the Parliamentary Committee on the priorities of the CDSCO deserves to be read in its whole:

> The Committee is of the firm opinion that most of the ills besetting the system of drugs regulation in India are mainly

> due to the skewed priorities and perceptions of CDSCO. For decades together it has been according primacy to the propagation and facilitation of the drugs industry, due to which, unfortunately, the interest of the biggest stakeholder i.e. the consumer has never been ensured. Taking strong exception to this continued neglect of the poor and hapless patient, the Committee recommends that the Mission Statement of CDSCO be formulated forthwith to convey in very unambiguous terms that the organization is solely meant for public health.[32]

After this indictment, the CDSCO did redefine its "mission" statement. The new statement is as follows: "To safeguard and enhance the public health by assuring the safety, efficacy and quality of drugs, cosmetics and medical devices." Unfortunately, changing bureaucratic attitudes is not as easy as changing mission statements. Take for example, the minutes of the DCC meeting held in 2015, which recorded the following statement by a senior official in the Ministry of Health, to whom the CDSCO reports, on the role of the drug regulator:

> Dr Jagdish Prasad, D.G.H.S. in his address stated that the role of the Drug regulator is to be a facilitator to the industry. There should be no harassment and simultaneously no compromise on patient safety.[33]

That a top bureaucrat in the regulatory machinery should make the claim that the regulator is to play the role of the "facilitator to the industry" says it all. Drug regulators around the world consider themselves to be watchdogs protecting public health rather than "facilitators" for industrial growth. In India, the job of "growing" the pharmaceutical industry is actually the responsibility of another department called the Department of Pharmaceuticals. The CDSCO need not worry about growing the pharmaceutical industry.

In the years after foreign drug regulators began discovering massive violations of GMPs in India by Indian pharmaceutical companies, we noticed a trend of senior bureaucrats from the Ministry of Commerce attending the meetings of the DCC, constantly reminding the gathering of state drug controllers the importance of ensuring constant growth of the pharmaceutical industry and how regulators should work towards reducing delays.[34] At first glance, this may seem innocent but it is important to remember that the Commerce Ministry is obsessed with only the growth and exports of the pharmaceutical industry. Very often it acts as a mouthpiece for the pharmaceutical industry and is the most likely to repeat conspiracy theories spun by industry lobbyists. To have bureaucrats from this Ministry present at meetings of state drug controllers is unlikely to have a benign effect.

Post 2014, things have become even worse on this front because of the new government's obsession with improving "ease of doing business in India". In its original form, this slogan was meant to dismantle the red-tape that made doing business in India difficult. The pharmaceutical industry, however, is unlike other industries. Safety regulation cannot be viewed as bureaucratic red-tape. Yet, the DCGI, while citing the "ease of doing business" slogan, actually asked the pharmaceutical industry to submit its wish list of demands to reduce its "regulatory compliance burden"[35]. In response, the Indian Drug Manufacturers Association (IDMA), which represents the small and medium pharmaceutical manufacturers, asked the DCGI to make the GMP standards in Schedule M voluntary and not mandatory![36] While this demand was thankfully not accepted, the government did make moves to increase certification periods and ensure the grant of licences in perpetuity.[37] These measures may sound innocent enough except for the fact that the power of the regulator vis-à-vis the industry was weakened. And of course, the words "public health" have rarely if ever been uttered by successive DCGIs during the course of these discussions to "improve ease of business".

At some point, there has to be a shift in these attitudes to recognize that public health should be at the front and centre of regulatory policies. Other departments can be responsible for the growth of the industry but the policy matrix of the Ministry of Health or the CDSCO should always be focused on protecting the public health of the people. These bureaucratic attitudes will change only when an elected Minister forces such a change. Until then we are only likely to witness new slogans rather than new attitudes towards public health.

The politics of federalism in the context of drug regulation

One of the central issues of drug regulation in India over the last century has been the issue of whether drug regulation should be the responsibility of the Union Government or the State Governments. This issue has been at the center of debates on regulatory reform since 1927. As discussed in Chapter 2, the colonial government in the pre-independence days often passed the buck on enacting a national drug regulatory law on the grounds that it fell under the legislative purview of the provinces under the Government of India Act 1919 and subsequently, the Government of India Act, 1935. The understanding at the time was that drugs were a public health issue and since public health fell within the purview of provincial legislatures, the federal legislature or its predecessor, the Indian legislature, could not enact a national legislation for the whole of British India. Eventually the Drugs Act 1940 was enacted by the federal legislature only when provincial legislatures passed resolutions empowering it to enact a law on their behalf. Although the Drugs Act 1940 was a single legislation, it created a federated regulatory mechanism delegating to each province the right to enact its own rules, set its own standards, and appoint its own drug inspectors to regulate domestic manufacture. Similar powers were delegated to the Federal Government to enact its own rules, set standards and prosecute cases related to the import of drugs.

Post-independence from the British, India adopted a new Constitution in 1950, which unlike the Government of India Act 1935, did not contain the word "federal". The new Indian Constitution considered India as a Union of states with a strong central character. Despite this, India is generally considered to be a "quasi-federal" country.[38] The new Constitution distributed legislative powers between Parliament and state legislatures. List I of Schedule VII to the Constitution contains subjects on which only Parliament could enact law, List II contained subjects on which only State Legislatures could enact law and List III contained subjects on which both the Parliament and the State Legislatures could enact laws. In case of any conflict between the two, Parliamentary law would take precedence. Unlike the Government of India Act 1935 which was silent on the issue of "drugs" because of which it was presumed "drug regulation" would fall within "public health" that was within the purview of provincial legislatures, the new Constitution specifically slotted "drugs" in Entry 19 of List III. This meant that both Parliament and the state legislatures could enact legislation on drug regulation but in case of a conflict, parliamentary law will override the state laws.[39]

The post-independence debate in this regard has concentrated on whether drug regulation should be further centralized. The first serious recommendation in this regard was made a few years post-independence in the report of the Pharmaceutical Enquiry Committee 1954. This committee had "strongly recommend[ed] that the administration of Drug Control should be centralised by bringing control on manufacture, sale and distribution, which is, at present exercised by the State Drug Controller, under the control of the Drugs Controller (India)".[40]

The main reason for this recommendation by the Committee was its finding that state drug controllers were doing a woefully poor job of enforcing the Drugs Act 1940 in their respective jurisdictions. The following observations of the Committee deserves to be read in its entirety:

> 6.4.2. In very many States, the Drugs Act is so poorly administered that we found that factories, which had been licenced were located in unsanitary places and their premises maintained in no better conditions. They also had no proper equipment for manufacture or testing and neither the manufacturers nor the State were exercising any control on the quality of the products made by them. The products of these factories were a menace not only to the particular State, in which they were located, but also to the neighbouring States, to whose market they found their way. The people of the neighbouring States were in no way benefitted in spite of the fact that the Act was being administered there in a better manner. When these points were brought to the notice of the State Drugs Controllers, they appeared to be helpless in the matter, either because they were afraid that by closing down such factories, it might lead to unemployment, labour unrest etc., or they had their own misgivings of the powers delegated to them under the Drugs Act to take such steps. It is, therefore necessary to centralise the administration of the Drugs Act to bring about a uniform implementation of the Drugs Act throughout the country for proper co-ordination with the working of the Industries (Development & Regulation) Act to be possible.[41]

The Government of India acted swiftly to implement a part of this recommendation by introducing a bill in 1954 to amend the Drugs Act 1940 so that it could centralize a number of functions that otherwise existed with state governments. This included licencing powers for manufacturing facilities. The Statement of Objects and Reasons to the Bill, which basically contains the government's policy reasoning for the law, provided the following justification for the bill:

> It has further been found necessary that with a view to maintaining uniformity throughout the States the power to make rules under Chapter IV with respect to the manufacture, sale and distribution of drugs, which is at present vested in the State Governments should be entrusted to the Central Government.

In order to achieve this goal, this legislation replaced the phrase "provincial government" in Section 33 of the Drugs Act 1940 with "Central Government" (aka Union Government). By doing so, Parliament basically stripped the state governments of their right to enact their own rules with respect to creation of standards, issuance of manufacturing licences, qualification of drug inspectors etc. leaving them only with the right to test drugs and prosecute manufacturers of NSQ drugs. Post the enactment of this law in 1955, the Union Government had control over the setting of uniform standards across India and more importantly the power to appoint licencing authorities.

Surprisingly however, after having moved Parliament to appropriate these powers for itself, the Union Government in 1960 once again delegated the power of appointing the licencing authority to the state governments via an amendment to Rule 69 of the Drugs and Cosmetics Rules 1945! This meant that state governments continued to exercise the power to appoint licencing authorities, thereby going against the very rationale of the amending law introduced in 1954 on the recommendations of the Pharmaceutical Enquiry Committee to centralize drug licencing.

This delegation of power by the Government of India to the State Governments was in fact illegal. According to the administrative law principle captured in the Latin maxim *delegatus non potest delegare*, power once delegated to an authority cannot be further delegated. Therefore, if Parliament had delegated to the Union Government the power to appoint a licencing authority (who could issue and suspend manufacturing licences) the Union Government cannot give away this power to state governments. Such further delegation would go against the Parliamentary mandate and could be struck down by a court of law. It is not clear as to why the Union Government gave away these powers but we suspect it was because it lacked the human resources and regulatory infrastructure to take over the function of licencing manufacturing facilities across the entire country.

Surprisingly, the sleight of hand with regard to Rule 69 was not noticed by subsequent expert committees setup by the Union Government to advise it on drug regulation. The first of these committees was the Hathi Committee which submitted its report in 1975. This committee acknowledged the varying standard of enforcement of the Drugs and Cosmetics Act 1940 across the country, but did not recommend any centralization of powers. It instead made recommendations to beef up the resources available to state drug controllers and for better coordination between different state and union authorities responsible for drug regulation.[42] The second report prepared many decades later was by a committee headed by Dr Mashelkar. This committee which submitted its report in 2003, focused extensively on the issue of centralizing licencing powers with a strengthened drug regulator called the Central Drug Administration (CDA).[43] The Mashelkar committee noted that state drug controllers and the IDMA opposed switching over to a centralized licencing system.[44] Opposition from state drug controllers was predictable since they would be losing their licencing powers over manufacturing units, which was their main source of power. Stripped of their powers to issue manufacture licences, these state drug controllers would only have the power to issue pharmacy licences and perhaps some enforcement powers to prosecute manufacturers of NSQ drugs.

Since the Mashelkar Committee's recommendation in 2003, there have been two legislative attempts focusing on centralization of licencing powers with the central drug regulator. The first was one in 2007 (for all drugs) and another in 2013 (for 17 categories of advanced drugs). Both legislations were examined by the Parliamentary Standing Committee on Health and Family Welfare which noted the existence of severe opposition to the idea of centralization, primarily by the small and medium members of the pharmaceutical industry.[45] The first committee that examined the 2007 bill wholeheartedly supported the move to centralize while the second committee was ambivalent about recommending centralized regulation for 17 categories, and calling upon the government to "reconsider" its views on centralizing licencing.[46]

In reality, if the Government of India had sought and received competent legal advice, it would have realized that it did not have to move a legislative amendment in Parliament to centralize licencing powers. As we pointed out above, the Drugs (Amendment) Act, 1955 had already given the Government of India the power to appoint licencing authorities for the country via the amendment to Section 33. It was the Union Government which had inexplicably given away this power to the state governments via an amendment, in 1960, to Rule 69 of the Drugs and Cosmetics Rules 1945. Given this position of law, one of us—Dinesh Thakur—filed a constitutional challenge against Rule 69 before the Supreme Court via the route of a public interest litigation (PIL). Typically, in PILs, the *locus standi* requirement is relaxed thereby allowing people not directly impacted by a particular law or legal action to litigate the issue in public interest.

It was our case that Rule 69 should be struck down on the grounds that it offended the principle of *delegatus non podest delegare* and that the Union Government could not further delegate powers that had been delegated to it by Parliament Since the law enacted by Parliament in 1955 delegated the power to appoint licencing authorities to the

Union Government, we argued that this power could not be further delegated to the state governments. Simply put, the Union Government necessarily had to discharge the powers that were delegated to it by the Parliament. Unfortunately, despite the strength of our argument, the court was reluctant to hear the matter; as a result of which we withdrew the petition with liberty to petition the government.[47]

Even though the court did not hear our argument, it appears that someone in the Ministry of Health did eventually look at our argument and realized that they did not have to go to Parliament to seek the power to regulate manufacturing facilities. We say this because in 2017, the Ministry of Health notified the Drugs and Cosmetics (Tenth Amendment) Rules, 2017 inserting new rules into the Drugs and Cosmetics Rules 1945 to create a requirement for joint inspections by both central and state drug inspectors once in three years or before the issuance of a new manufacturing licence or a new pharmacy licence. The rules are silent on how differences between state and central drugs inspectors are to be resolved.

This new arrangement had the potential to disrupt the cosy arrangements between the state drug inspectors and the pharmaceutical industry, which was long been used to dealing with only state level officials. Not surprisingly, an association of state drug controllers called the All India Drugs Control Officers Confederation, along with the Pharmaceutical Manufacturers Association of Tamil Nadu, filed a constitutional challenge against the new rules on a variety of grounds, including that the said rules were arbitrary, *ultra vires* the Drugs and Cosmetics Act 1940 and against the federal scheme of the Constitution of India.[48] These were weak arguments. As explained earlier, the Parliament had actually given the Union Government the power to appoint licencing authorities in 1955 when it amended Section 33. Hence, there was no question of the recently amended rules being *ultra vires* the parent legislation.

The federalism argument was even weaker. The subject of "drugs" is clearly mentioned in Entry 19 of List III, meaning that the Parliament was competent to enact a legislation on drug regulation. There are also other arguments to justify the sole right of Parliament to enact laws on drug regulation. For instance, Parliament has the sole right to enact legislation on "inter-state trade and commerce" (Entry 42, List I) as well as establishment of standards for goods subject to interstate trade or export (Entry 51, List I). Under these entries, the Parliament has the overwhelming right to enact laws on drug regulation for drugs involved in interstate commerce. Yet, the petitioners in this case tried arguing that drug regulation fell within Entry 27 of List II which deals with the production, supply and distribution of goods. The Madras High Court rejected their argument on the grounds that "Drugs" fell within Entry 19 of List III.[49] Hence, the challenge by the drug control officers and the pharmaceutical industry failed.

The more interesting aspect of this litigation was the very fact that both state drug controllers and pharmaceutical manufacturers challenged these amendments mandating joint inspections by both the central and state drug inspectors. What was the impetus for both these lobbies to challenge the legality of the regulation allowing for the central drug inspectors to join inspections of manufacturing facilities? Our guess, as mentioned earlier, is that central drug inspectors had the potential to disrupt the existing cosy relationships between state drug inspectors, the local pharmaceutical industry and local politicians. Whether this has actually happened is an issue that deserves further study.

The larger question to ask is whether further centralization of various aspects of drug regulation is the path forward?

Our own research indicates that the findings of the Pharmaceutical Enquiry Committee, 1954 continue to be true even in 2022. Not all state governments are enforcing the

Drugs and Cosmetics Act 1940 with equal vigour and this is true across various indicators ranging from the volume of testing to the rate of prosecution of pharmaceutical companies found to be manufacturing NSQ drugs.

Data provided to us by different state laboratories indicates that while Tamil Nadu tested close to 57,567 drug samples between the years 2016–22, West Bengal tested only 2,637 between the years 2016–22.[50] States like Bihar and Himachal Pradesh had abysmal, almost non-existing testing facilities which meant that they could not carry out the whole suite of pharmacopeial testing mandated by the law.[51] Similarly, while states like Tamil Nadu and Maharashtra regularly prosecute companies found to be manufacturing NSQ drugs, Nagaland has not prosecuted a single pharmaceutical manufacturer in the last five years.[52]

There is also a lot of data available to indicate that states like Himachal Pradesh and Uttarakhand are the fountainhead of the NSQ problem in India. For instance, the Maharashtra drug controller while responding to one of our queries under the RTI Act about the state which was the largest contributor of NSQ drugs in Maharashtra for the time period between 2012 and 2017, specifically named Himachal Pradesh as the "biggest manufacturer of spurious/NSQ drugs in this time period". As per the data provided to us by the drug controller for this time period, Himachal Pradesh and Uttarakhand accounted for 552 and 253 NSQ drugs, respectively, out of a total of 1,654 NSQ drugs detected by the state laboratories in Maharashtra.[53] Similarly, we analyzed the drug alerts on the CDSCO's website, which features NSQ drugs detected by central government laboratories and for the years 2019 through 2022, Himachal Pradesh and Uttarakhand accounted for 282 and 188 NSQ drugs respectively, out of a total of 1,078 NSQ drugs detected by these laboratories.[54] There are two reasons for these two states accounting for most of the

NSQ drugs detected in other states. First, is the fact that both Himachal Pradesh and Uttarakhand account for the lion's share of pharmaceutical manufacturing in India due to certain tax incentives put in place by the Union Government to facilitate industrialization in these states. The second is the fact that neither state is doing a very good job at enforcing the Drugs and Cosmetics Act 1940 after having succeeded in attracting pharmaceutical manufacturing facilities to their respective states. We suspect this is because neither state has an incentive to improve the quality of drug regulation lest it adversely affect local investment in the state by the pharmaceutical industry and local employment.

However, since India is a common market where goods manufactured in one state can travel across the country, the abysmal state of drug regulation in Himachal Pradesh and Uttarakhand has a deleterious effect on public health across the country. States like Karnataka and Tamil Nadu, with relatively better drug regulators, have to allow entry to drugs manufactured in poorly regulated states like Himachal Pradesh or Uttarakhand. In the best-case scenario, where drug inspectors in these better-regulated states detect substandard drugs manufactured in other states, they can only initiate a criminal prosecution against the out-of-state manufacturers but these prosecutions can take years before Indian courts. These better-regulated states lack the powers to cancel manufacturing licences of out-of-state companies because of which they cannot stop these companies from continuing to manufacture and ship poor quality drugs to other states. Only the state drug controllers in Himachal Pradesh and Uttarakhand can cancel the manufacturing licences of facilities located in their jurisdiction. As a result, the entire country will have to suffer a flood of NSQ drugs because a few states lack the incentive to rigorously regulate pharmaceutical manufacturing facilities located within their jurisdictions.

But will greater centralization under a single authority necessarily improve the quality of drug supply especially when the functioning of the CDSCO itself has been excoriated by no less of an authority than the Parliamentary Standing Committee on Health and Family Welfare? There is every possibility that an incompetent central regulator can make things worse. There is then also the question of democratic accountability. How responsive will a central regulator be to the local demands of states? To what extent will a central regulator head quartered in New Delhi respond to the needs and demands of citizens in Tamil Nadu? Will centralization lead to a sort of a democratic deficit by reducing accountability of regulators to citizens?

From a strictly theoretical viewpoint, we believe that drugs subject to interstate trade and commerce across India should be subject to oversight by a centralized regulator not just because it is likely to ensure a more uniform application of the law across a country that is a common market but also because drug regulation is a "national public good" for the entire country. In such a scenario, where the entire country is affected by poor regulation, the burden of that regulation should not fall on individual states. It is only fair that resources for such an exercise be funded from the union's pool of taxes which will then naturally have to be controlled by an authority answerable to the Union Government, which in turn is answerable to Parliament that comprises of elected representative from across the country. An additional advantage of centralization is that the Union Government has far deeper pockets than states, meaning that it will be in a better position to finance the operation of a central regulator. In fact, during our research, we discovered that the newly created central drug testing laboratories are far better equipped than most state testing laboratories and were also buying larger numbers of reference standards from the Indian Pharmacopeia Commission indicating that they were conducting more rigorous testing when compared to state laboratories.[55]

On the point of accountability, there is certainly merit in the argument that greater centralization will likely impact accountability of the regulator to individual states and their citizens but then again, the situation is much worse under the present system when neither citizens nor their elected representatives from states like Karnataka or Tamil Nadu have any possibility of influencing politics or regulators of Himachal Pradesh and Uttarakhand. At least a central regulator could be subject to some kind of accountability from Members of Parliament across all states. In any event, one way to mitigate this problem of accountability of the central regulator to localized concerns is by creating councils in each state, with representatives from both the central regulators and state government, so that there is a constant feedback loop informing the central regulator about local concerns in different states.

An alternate model of reform is to centralize only the licencing function with a central regulator but retain the current split in the law with regard to prosecution powers; wherein both the union government and state governments can appoint drug inspectors to draw market samples, test the same and conduct prosecutions of manufacturers of NSQ drugs. Additionally, state governments should be given the power to block certain companies from selling their drugs in their respective states if it has concerns about the track record of the company based on test reports etc. Such a model will ensure that state governments act as a check on the central regulator since the former's sampling of drugs will act as a form of a quality audit of the central regulator's licencing and inspection function. If state regulators detect larger amounts of NSQ drugs during their sampling surveys, it would necessarily mean that the central regulator is doing a poorer job at guaranteeing GMP compliance. This split of powers may also be more palatable for the large lobby of incumbent state drug inspectors who otherwise risk losing their jobs in the event that Parliament transfers all powers of state drug inspectors to a central regulator. We, however, anticipate that sections of the pharmaceutical industry will recoil with horror at the prospect of having to deal with two different sets of regulators, each working under a different political dispensation. In either of the above scenarios, centralization of the manufacturing licencing function is inevitable.

Who makes for a good DCGI?

A key stakeholder in the quest to improve the quality of drug regulation is the bureaucracy which constitutes the backbone of the CDSCO and state drug regulators. Traditionally, the qualification criteria for the leadership position in both—the Drugs Controller General of India (DCGI) who heads the CDSCO—as well as the rank and file consisting of drug inspectors (employed by the State drug regulators) has been skewed in favour of pharmacy graduates despite the qualification criteria for these positions recognizing a wide pool of educational degrees such as medicine, microbiology etc. Pharmacy graduates, however, enjoy an advantage despite this wide pool of recognized educational degrees because the qualification criteria for the post of drug inspector also includes an "experience" component that requires those applying for the post to either have experience working in pharmaceutical manufacturing for 18 months or experience working in a testing laboratory for 18 months.[56] Only pharmacists are likely to have such work experience since doctors are unlikely to ever work in pharmaceutical manufacturing or testing laboratories.

Similarly, to be appointed as the DCGI or the state drug controller, there is a compulsory "experience" requirement of have worked in the manufacture or testing of drugs or having worked in the enforcement of the Drugs and Cosmetics Act 1940 for a period of at least five years.[57] (The period of experience required for appointment to the post of the DCGIs was increased to 15 years in 2011).[58] Once again medical doctors are unlikely to have this experience. Only drug inspectors (who once again are pharmacists) with 15 years experience in enforcing the drugs law are likely to meet the qualification criteria for DCGI or state drug controllers. Since the qualification criteria for drug inspectors favour pharmacists, it is almost certain that only a pharmacist will wind up in the post of either the DCGI or state drug controller.

Such qualification criterion that leans heavily in favour of pharmacists is completely outdated because pharmacists are basically trained in the formulation chemistry of drugs. They have perfunctory understanding of the human body or how medicine is metabolized by the human body. A doctor of medicine has a far more detailed understanding of how medicine acts on the human body and that is an important skill for a person heading a national drug regulator. A doctor qualified in public health and who understands the wider contours of public health is even more valuable as the leader of a national drug regulator.

This existing qualification criterion in the Drugs and Cosmetics Rules 1945, especially for the post of DCGI, has been the subject of harsh criticism by the Parliamentary Standing Committee of Health and Family Welfare in its 59th report, tabled in 2012. The committee pointed out that, "The stumbling block is the requirement that DCGI should have experience in the manufacture or testing of drugs or enforcement of the provisions of the Drugs and Cosmetic Act for a minimum period of five years." This requirement virtually excludes even highly qualified medical doctors from occupying the post of DCGI."[59] The committee pointed out that most developed countries like the United States and the United Kingdom have a practice of appointing highly qualified doctors or scientists with a deep understanding of pharmaceutical research and development and/or public health as heads of their national drug regulators.[60] This criticism by the Standing Committee was on point. Manufacturing is only one aspect of a very complicated pharmaceutical industry that has a huge impact on public health. The far more complicated aspects of this industry include clinical trials, bioethics and the launch of new drugs. In such a scenario, it is absolutely necessary that the leadership of a drug regulator be vested in persons who have a broader understanding of clinical research, pharmacology of drugs, bioethics, and the impact of the pharmaceutical industry on public health.

Post the criticism by the Parliamentary Standing Committee in 2012, the Ministry of Health and Family Welfare did setup an "expert" committee to revise the qualification criteria for the post of the DCGI. This committee comprised of a former Secretary of the Department of Personnel and Training, a former Secretary of the Department of Biotechnology, a former professor of Pharmacology and two former DCGIs. The final recommendation of the committee did recommend widening the experience requirement to persons who had experience in clinical research or clinical trials or any research in any related disciplines but was silent on deleting the existing criteria that allowed pharmacists to be appointed to this post.[61] This recommendation to allow persons with experience in clinical research to be appointed as the DCGI was promptly opposed by professional associations of pharmacists like the Delhi Pharmaceutical Trust (DPT).[62] In one of its representations, the DPT made the following rather absurd analogy that deserves to be read in its entirety:

> A post graduate surgeon is in fact as far away from understanding pharmaceutical sciences as an airline captain is from understanding the intricacies of cruise ship. Therefore the

> existing Recruitment Rules have taken a very conscious and thoughtful view of this fact. A proposal to make a surgeon or a doctor the chief of the army under that belief that after all army involves health of serving and wounded soldiers and no one can manage them better than that the doctor...[63]

The DPT apparently argued that only those qualified in pharmacy understood the process of manufacturing drugs and that the focus in India unlike in the United States or United Kingdom was not on new drug approvals but manufacturing licences. This could not have been a more flawed assessment. Not only was it incorrect, it represented a completely outdated understanding of drug regulation. The DPT clearly views the task of drug regulation as merely issuing manufacturing licences and conducting inspections of manufacturing facilities. There appears to be no understanding that modern drug regulation involves clinical trials, bioethics, and approval of new drugs based on their benefits for public health. As we demonstrated elsewhere in this book, there is ample evidence of successive DCGIs personally mucking up the process of approving applications for marketing of new drugs. Not all of these controversies can be attributed to corruption. The series of controversies over the approvals of new drugs and vaccines during the COVID pandemic further reinforces our argument that the leadership of the CDSCO is not well-versed with the nuances of drug development, clinical research, evidence-based medicine, or public health. Views like those voiced by the DPT represent entrenched lobbies of pharmacists who want to retain control of not just the post of the DCGI but also the posts of drug inspectors because those qualifications too will come under scrutiny once the qualification criteria for the DCGI is changed.

In any event, the Ministry of Health and Family Welfare has not taken any measure to change the recruitment criteria as per the recommendations of the Parliamentary Standing

Committee or its own expert committee. Unless India's drug regulator has a leadership with a proven track record of excellence in clinical research and public health, we are unlikely to witness the scientific rigour that is so necessary to establish the credibility of the regulatory processes of the Indian drug regulator.

A related, if not bizarre, controversy that has been brewing in two southern states—Telangana and Andhra Pradesh—pertains to the appointment of officers from All India Services as the head of the state drug control organization. Both states have in the recent past appointed officers from the Indian Administrative Service, Indian Police Service and Indian Revenue Service to the top post of the state drug control administration. It is not clear how this practice has continued since the Drugs and Cosmetics Rules 1945 which lays down the qualifications for "controlling authority" does not include IPS, IAS, or IRS officers. Yet the practice continues, despite opposition from the drug control officers associations in both states.[64]

Upgrading the CDSCO's administrative status and the turf war with the DGHS

One of the truly strange aspects of the CDSCO is its relatively low position in the overall pecking order of government hierarchy. Unlike other sectoral regulators like the Securities Exchange Board of India (SEBI) and Telecom Regulatory Authority of India (TRAI), the CDSCO is not a creation of a statute that has an existence independent of the Government of India. Rather, it is a subordinate office of the Directorate General of Health Services (DGHS) which is one of the many departments operating under the Ministry of Health and Family Welfare. The DCGI who heads the CDSCO is answerable to the Director General of Health Services (DG-DGHS) who in turn is answerable to the Secretary of Health, who in turn is accountable to the Minister of Health and Family Welfare, an elected politician. As a consequence of this arrangement, the DG-DGHS, who heads the DGHS has significant operational control over the functioning of the CDSCO. This in itself would not be a problem if it were not for the fact that the DGHS is a massive department with multiple areas of responsibilities ranging from the execution of national disease control programs for leprosy, vector-borne diseases, and tuberculosis to looking after infrastructure of hospitals owned by the central government to collecting health statistics from across the country to setting up public health standards. These are only few examples of the vast responsibilities vested in the DG-DGHS. In such a scenario it is unlikely that a DGHS can give sufficient attention to the functioning of the CDSCO. Since the DCGI is rather far from the Secretary, who is the main centre of power in the Ministry, it is unlikely that the DCGI has a direct line to this most important power centre in the Ministry.

Further, unlike TRAI or SEBI, which have the powers to "make law" via rules and regulations, the CDSCO has no law-making powers. All the rules made by the executive under the Drugs and Cosmetics Act 1940 or the Drugs and Magic Remedies (Objectionable Advertisements) Act 1954 are actually formulated by the Drug Regulation Section of the Ministry of Health and Family Welfare, which itself operates under a Joint Secretary (who is generally a non-specialist IAS officer) answerable to the Secretary of Health and Family Welfare. This is unlike the situation in other countries like the United States, where the USFDA itself has been given some rule making power by the US Congress. The advantage of such delegation of power is that it makes the regulator more flexible and powerful thereby enabling it to deal with emerging issues in a nimble manner without having to cut through multiple layers of red-tape.

There have been several calls to upgrade the administrative status of the CDSCO. For example, the Mashelkar Committee which submitted its report on reforms to India's drug regulatory framework in 2003, had recommended that the CDSCO be renamed the Central Drug Administration (CDA) and made "into an independent office under the Ministry of Health and Family Welfare as is the case in most of the countries".[65] Subsequent to that recommendation the Ministry of Health made two legislative attempts, one in 2007 and another in 2013 to give statutory backing and an independent corporate identity to a CDSCO that was to be renamed as the CDA. Neither legislative attempt was put to vote in Parliament.

In 2015, an expert committee setup by the government to relook the qualification requirements of the DCGI recommended that the CDSCO "be upgraded from the status of a Subordinate Office of the DGHS to an Attached Office of the Department of Health and Family Welfare and given substantial functional freedom".[66] In other words, the committee recommended that the DGHS be removed as a layer between the CDSCO and the Secretary of the Ministry.

In his book on the Indian drug regulatory system, K.L. Sharma, recounts that there have been multiple recommendations to upgrade the status of the CDSCO as an attached office of the Ministry of Health and Family Welfare but that the proposal never moved "beyond discussion" despite the fact that the Cabinet can change the departmental status of the CDSCO by itself without the need for legislation.[67] In his words, "the issue of strengthening the CDSCO continues to be discussed and deliberated, including at the level of Cabinet Secretary whenever there is a crisis".[68] As a result, meaningful reform continues to elude the CDSCO and its status within the government.

Our recommendation in this regard would be to recast the CDSCO as a modern regulator, by giving it legislative sanctity through a law enacted by Parliament. As any other modern regulator in India, the CDSCO in its new avatar should have an independent corporate identity along with the power to manage its own finances and enact its own regulations, subject to safeguards such as prior mandatory public consultation. This should include the power to conduct its own recruitment of professionals at market rates so that the CDSCO may benefit from the experience of professionals in the private sector. Such delegation of power will hopefully create a nimble regulator that has the flexibility to meet emerging challenges from an innovative industry. This recommendation is of course subject to reforming the qualification criteria for the post of DCGI and the institution of a transparent accountability framework that makes the DCGI publicly accountable to the people of India. Of the many reforms that are required, this will be the most difficult reform to enact due to possible turf wars within the Ministry of Health.

Democratizing regulation: Empowering citizens with information and the right to participate

The most important lever for reforming the drug regulatory system in India, in our opinion, is the Indian citizen's fundamental right to information.

Long before the enactment of the Right to Information Act, 2005, the Supreme Court of India interpreted Article 19(1)(a) of the Constitution which guarantees to every citizen the "right to free speech and expression" against the state, to include the "right to information".[69] The logic of reading this right to information into Article 19(1)(a) is that citizens cannot assert their fundamental right to free speech and expression unless they are informed of the internal functioning of the state. With the enactment of the RTI Act 2005, this fundamental right was operationalized in a practical manner. This legislation included not just a right to ask the state for information but also imposed a duty upon the state to proactively disclose information to its citizens. Such transparency is particularly important in context of drug regulation where bureaucrats are required to exercise highly discretionary powers.

Unfortunately, neither the CDSCO nor the state drug controllers have taken it upon themselves to publicly disclose any of their records. On the contrary, as demonstrated by the Parliamentary Standing Committee on Health and Family Welfare, the CDSCO struggles to maintain critical files regarding drug approvals in storage without losing them.[70] Even a crucial inquiry report like the Mohapatra Committee report that we requested a copy of went missing from the CDSCO's office.[71] It is unlikely that all of these disappearances were accidental. Missing files are the easiest route to escape accountability despite the fact that the Public Records Act 1993 requires an investigation into all missing public records.

Even when records are maintained, it can be very difficult for a common citizen to access them even under the RTI Act 2005. For example, when we tried sourcing data on prosecutions from state drug controllers, many states responded by transferring our request to each district in the state. Each district officer would then either send the information or request us to visit their office to inspect the files on the grounds that we asked for voluminous information. This is the reason we could not get consolidated aggregated statistics from most states on the rates of criminal prosecutions under the Drugs and Cosmetics Act 1940.

Similarly, the typical response from the CDSCO to our requests for statistical information is to transfer the same to its Zonal Offices, which in turn, after a considerable delay, either plead ignorance, provide incomplete information, or transfer the request back to the CDSCO. The entire process exists to frustrate the citizen and deny them any useful information that can be used to hold the regulator accountable to the people of the country.

One way to resolve the above problems and truly operationalize the "right to information" is to create a regulatory structure that guarantees transparency by design. Such an approach already exists in the law for a few regulatory actions. For example, Section 26A and Section 26B of the Drugs and Cosmetics Act 1940 requires the government to publish certain regulatory decisions in the *Gazette of India*. Similarly, the New Drugs and Clinical Trial Rules 2019 requires the registration of all clinical trials in the Clinical Trials Registry of India (CTRI), which is a publicly accessible register maintained online by the Indian Council of Medical Research (ICMR).

Such proactive disclosures however are not mandatory for most regulatory decisions under the current Drugs and Cosmetics Act 1940. For example, critical documentation regarding the approval of a new drug application is not proactively published by the DCGI's office. Similarly, inspection reports of manufacturing facilities are not publicly available because of which procurement agencies of the Government or those in the private sector do not have complete information while taking the decision to procure drugs from particular pharmaceutical companies. Unlike in India, regulatory authorities in other countries like the United States or the European Union proactively publish their internal reviews of all new drug applications on their respective websites. The USFDA also proactively publishes on its websites, its inspection reports of manufacturing facilities and clinical research organizations (CROs). These practices contribute immensely in building public confidence and trust in the regulator. Further, the functioning of the American regulator itself is subject to performance reviews by statutory bodies like the Government Accountability Office (GAO) in the US.[72] There is an urgent need for Indian law to be rewritten in a manner that proactively publishes all the information required by a common citizen to conduct a "social audit" of the functioning of the regulator so as to inform themselves of the regulator's effectiveness in enforcing the law.

Transparency in the context of a drug regulator, apart from facilitating accountability of the regulator to common citizens, also has direct implications for public health. For doctors prescribing new drugs, the primary source of information is the promotional material given to them by salespersons from pharmaceutical companies, which as we have explained in this book can often be misleading since pharmaceutical companies tend to downplay unfavourable information about their own drugs. A secondary source of information about new drugs for doctors can be published clinical trial studies in peer-reviewed journals but many of these journals are behind paywalls and incredibly expensive to access for most Indian doctors. In such a scenario, proactive publication of regulatory information that can be accessed for free by all doctors can be an important source of information for health professionals looking to make treatment decisions. Similarly, greater regulatory transparency can facilitate the procurement of quality drugs. Currently, drug procurement agencies in the public and private sector do not have access to either inspection reports of drug inspectors or a consolidated database of all NSQ drugs across the country while making decisions on bulk purchases. Some like the Indian Railways end up conducting their own "inspections" which, apart from being wasteful public expenditure, is also quite superficial. Other procurement agencies simply go by "self-declarations" made by pharmaceutical companies since there are no consolidated databases that can be used to verify the "self-declaration" made by the pharmaceutical company. This is not particularly efficient. If the CDSCO and state drug controllers made available such information from across the country in well-designed, searchable databases it would dramatically improve the efficiency of both public and private procurement of drugs.

Of all the reforms discussed in this chapter, measures to improve transparency will have a disproportionately large impact on the quality of regulation, enforcement and quality of care. But the right to information is in itself not useful unless it is accompanied with a right to participate in regulatory decisions. Given the amount and nature of power delegated to the bureaucracy in the course of drug regulation, it is impossible to rely only on parliamentary oversight to ensure the democratic accountability of regulators to the people. Any comprehensive regulatory reform must therefore create pathways for common citizens to participate and challenge regulatory decisions. This is not as ambitious as it sounds. Environmental law and land acquisition law already require the government to conduct public hearings and note public oppositions. In context of drug regulation, the law must have similar safeguards allowing citizens to question drug approvals, petition for specific regulatory action and comment on rules and regulations before they are finalized. In short, the people being affected by bureaucratic decisions must have legal pathways to question and contribute to those decisions.

Increasing accountability of public procurement

Another potentially powerful lever of reform that exists outside the drug regulatory system is the system of public procurement. While no consolidated figures regarding the volume of public procurement of drugs are available, we estimate that between the Government of India and the state governments, a significant sum of public funds are spent on procuring drugs for the public health system. This includes procurements by the Central Medical Service Society (CMSS) for central government hospitals, the Bureau of Pharma PSUs of India (BPPI) which procures for programs like the government's Jan Aushadhi program (aimed at funding generics only pharmacies across the country) and state level agencies like the Tamil Nadu Medical Services Corporation (TNMSC) which conduct bulk procurement for their respective state governments. In addition, public institutions that are large employers, like the Armed Forces and Indian Railways which have their own network of hospitals, also conduct their own procurement exercises for purchasing drugs.

The major problem with the public procurement process is that it is has a shockingly high percentage of NSQ drugs. This is obvious from the government's own survey data from 2017 which reported the percentage of NSQ drugs in government hospitals at 10.02%; three times the 3.16% in the general market.[73] Apart from this survey data, there is also anecdotal evidence to suggest a serious quality issue with drug supply in the public sector. For example, a report of the Comptroller and Auditor General (CAG) after an audit of the Armed Forces Medical Services Depot (AFMSD) which procures drugs for the Armed Forces reported that the rate of rejection of "locally procured" drugs by the AFMSD over a period of four years due to quality issues averaged at 24%![74] Think about it. One in four of locally procured drugs by the Indian Armed Forces is of poor quality. Similarly, CAG has pointed out quality issues in its audits of other procurement agencies ranging from the Ministry of Health[75] to the National Rural Health Mission[76] to state-level authorities like the Orissa State Medical Corporation Ltd and the Jharkhand Medical and Health Infrastructure Development and Procurement Corporation Ltd.[77]

The reason these figures are available is because most public procurement agencies in India conduct (or are supposed to conduct) their own testing on each batch that is procured before it is released to patients. The requirement for such testing is a sign of low trust even amongst the public sector about the quality of drug regulation in India but serves as a useful indicator of the quality of the procurement process.

The high percentage of NSQ drugs in government hospitals is indicative of not just a threat to persons being treated in these public hospitals but also conclusive proof of the waste of precious public funds on dubious manufacturers who have likely won bids for contracts by cutting corners and bribing public servants. There is no shortage of reports of corruption in procurement of drugs. A simple search for such reports will throw up allegations from across the country of mindboggling corruption during the public procurement process.[78]

One of the reasons for this abysmal state of affairs as pointed out by CAG in successive reports, is the lack of well thought out codified procedures and manuals to guide the procurement process. This leaves procurement authorities with immense discretion while making procurement decisions and corruption eventually follows. Even on the issue of blacklisting, academics have pointed out the lack of transparent criteria informing all participants of the grounds on which they can be blacklisted from supplying for future bids.[79] Moreover, as we discovered to our amazement, large purchasers like the Indian Railways do not have a consolidated blacklist for the entire organisation. When we asked the headquarters of the Indian Railways for a list of pharmaceutical companies blacklisted from participating in its procurement process for drugs, our application was transferred to each railway zone, each of whom provided us their own blacklist.[80] Similarly, the Government of India does not have a single blacklist covering all of the various procurement agencies operating under its auspices.

One simple solution to this problem is for Parliament to enact an over-arching public procurement law specifically governing the purchase of drugs by the Government of India or any other agency receiving funds that have been appropriated by Parliament. In fact, in April 2012 the Government of India had introduced a general public procurement law for all government purchases but it was never voted upon by Parliament.[81] A more specific public procurement law that focuses only on the purchase of pharmaceuticals can have an impact on the quality of drugs available in the public health system. Such a procurement law should lay down specific procurement criteria. It should also focus on mandating testing of each batch of drugs purchased before these drugs are released to patients. Drugs that fail such quality testing should result in blacklisting of the manufacturers. Once a pharmaceutical company is blacklisted by one procurement agency, it should automatically be prohibited from supplying to any government entity for the duration it is on the blacklist. This blacklist maintained by the Government of India will likely also be relied upon by state government agencies and large procurement agencies in the private sector such as pharmacy chains and hospital chains. Thus, even if the Government of India is unable to overhaul the Drugs and Cosmetics Act 1940 due to opposition from state governments, it can still rely on its enormous purchasing power to inflict significant punishment on pharmaceutical companies that are found to be supplying NSQ drugs by blocking them from lucrative markets.

Last but not the least, such a procurement law should mandate the creation of resources that can aid government agencies in assessing the quality track record of pharmaceutical companies across the country by forcing all relevant stakeholders to share information such as quality testing reports and inspection reports into a consolidated database that acts as a single source of truth for procurement officers in both the public and private sector.

Of drug regulation and public health activism

As a country, India is fortunate to have a very active civil society movement comprising of academics and activists who are willing to hold the government accountable. There is no shortage of public health activism in India but surprisingly little of this activism is directed towards improving the quality of drug regulation in India. Instead, most of this activism is directed towards the issue of "access to medicine", price control for drugs, or broader public health issues.

A part of the reason that there is little activism on drug regulatory issues, is the fact that "access to medicine" activism in India was premised on building bridges with the Indian generic pharmaceutical industry to oppose the new patent regime imposed by the Agreement on Trade Related Intellectual Property Right (TRIPs) and also individual patents on crucial drugs. In fact, one of the first meetings, in the 90s, between the generic pharmaceutical industry and public health activists in India to oppose TRIPs was held at the corporate offices of Ranbaxy.[82] Post 2005, when the new patent regime came into force in India, public health activists and Indian generic pharmaceutical companies were often challenging the same patents on crucial life-saving drugs. To take up issues related to drug quality in this context would have roiled a partnership that was otherwise very successful in achieving its goals of improving access to medicine.

The only group which has dedicated some space to the issue of drug regulation is the All India Drug Action Network (AIDAN), which describes itself as "an independent network of several non-government organizations working to increase access and improve the rational use of essential medicines".[83] This includes mainly Indian NGOs and some international NGOs like the *Médecins Sans Frontières* (MSF). This group has been active in public advocacy against untested, possibly dangerous Fixed Dose Combinations (FDC), against the arbitrary decision of the Ministry of Health to restrict the manufacture of Oxytocin in India and has also advocated for urgent measures to regulate drug advertising and promotion in India.[84]

However, AIDAN rarely dedicates similar bandwidth to issues that goes to the core of drug quality in India, such as the importance of bioequivalence and stability testing. One reason for this could be the fact that AIDAN as a voluntary activist group lacks the resources to advocate multiple causes. The other possibility is that AIDAN suffers from a severe conflict of interest given that one of its founding members is a public charitable trust called "Low Cost Standard Therapeutics", better known as LOCOST. By itself, LOCOST presents an interesting model of pharmaceutical manufacturing since it has been formed as a not-for-profit public charitable trust focused on making low-cost essential drugs. As a manufacturer of drugs, LOCOST and its trustees like S. Srinivasan and Dr Anant Phadke, who are also prominent public health activists in their own right, have little incentive to push for stricter enforcement of the Drugs and Cosmetics Act 1940 because it would directly impact them in their capacity as persons responsible for running a pharmaceutical manufacturing facility. This is not even a hypothetical scenario. In 2009, the Chief Judicial Magistrate, Pune convicted LOCOST, S. Srinivasan, and two other managerial personnel, under Section 18(a)(i) read with Section 27 of the Drugs and Cosmetics Act 1940 for manufacturing and selling a drug that failed quality testing in a government laboratory. The drug in question was Enalapril Maleate and is used to treat hyper-tension. The version manufactured by LOCOST was found to contain only 45.8% of the quantity advertized on the label. As a result, the drug was declared to be NSQ by the government analyst. After a trial, the Chief Judicial Magistrate found LOCOST, Srinivasan, and others guilty of manufacturing and selling NSQ drugs. The court sentenced them to pay a fine of ₹10,000 and suffer simple imprisonment till the rising of the court, after which they were free to go. As confirmed by Srinivasan in an email to us, the conviction was never appealed to a higher court. This conviction did not stop the erstwhile Planning Commission from including Srinivasan on expert groups studying the issue of drug regulation.[85]

Neither AIDAN nor any other public health NGO is likely to seriously take up the issue of tightening regulations on drug quality as long as they are allied with generic drug manufacturers. To do so would make life harder for their allies. There is a real need for the activist community to rethink its stand on the issue of drug regulation. Access to medicines is important but what good is access to a drug that does not work?

Citizen advocacy and political lobbying not the judiciary is the road to reform

Demands by the middle class for reform in India generally begin with the filing of public interest litigations (PILs) before the Supreme Court. PILs are a controversial procedural innovation by the Indian Supreme Court which significantly dilutes the *locus standi* requirement, allowing persons to challenge government action (or the lack of it) despite not being directly affected by the same. This procedural innovation, combined with a proclivity for a strain of activism that extends to forcing the government to follow judicial diktats present the theoretical possibility of achieving radical, albeit undemocratic, reform through the judicial route.

In reality, the Supreme Court's track record on PILs borders on completely arbitrariness as witnessed by the court's approach to two PILs filed by one of us, Dinesh Thakur, in 2016. A bench of the Supreme Court headed by the then Chief Justice of India, T.S. Thakur, expressed its reluctance to hear the PILs, citing amongst other grounds, the allegedly "academic nature" of the petition. In reality the PILs referenced the reports of the government's own committees, pointing out to a litany of unenforced regulatory decisions and their consequences for public health. One PIL challenged the constitutionality of a specific rule that created a federated drug licencing system despite the law being clear on the fact that Indian was to have a unified drug regulatory structure. What made the court's reluctance more baffling was the fact that the then Chief Justice of India, T.S. Thakur, in the months preceding this petition, had admitted absurd PILs to ban jokes about Sardars, to bring back the Kohinoor diamond from the United Kingdom and to reform the sports body in charge of the Indian cricket team![86] In any event, with the benefit of hindsight, we do not think this was a significant setback because the Supreme Court's track record on PILs pertaining to regulatory issues with clinical trials, biotechnology and nuclear technology is quite dismal. At most, the court grants temporary relief and has been unable to achieve systemic reform and understandably so. There is a separation of powers between the judiciary, legislature, and the executive. Unelected judges should be careful about the extent to which they take over the functions of the other two branches. The problem, however, with the Indian Supreme Court is that it is exceptionally inconsistent on this front.

In any event, effective reform, as we have learnt over the course of the last several years can be achieved only through sustained advocacy that educates not just parliamentarians and government bureaucrats about the shortcomings with the regulator but also educating civil society and convincing them for the need of change. Building a political consensus is a long and messy job but it is the only route to reform in a democracy. Luckily for India, there are a handful of individuals from the medical community, journalism, government, and Parliament who are doing their bit on this front. A few of them deserve a mention before we conclude this book.

First on the list is Dr Chander Gulati, the editor of the

Monthly Index of Medical Specialties (MIMS) who has blown the whistle on a number of half-baked approvals granted by the DCGI for drugs. For his comments on one particular drug called Deanxit, Dr Gulati has been prosecuted for criminal defamation by a company called Lundbeck.[87]

Second on the list is an outspoken doctor by the name Dr Abby Philips who runs a popular Twitter handle (@ theliverdr) regularly exposing the pseudoscience propagated by practitioners of traditional medicine in India. As a hepatologist, Dr Philips, in the course of his practice, often comes across patients suffering from serious ailments, especially liver diseases, after having consumed traditional medicine. He presents many of these case studies on Twitter for common citizens and doctors. The effectiveness of his advocacy is obvious from the fact that practitioners of traditional medicine have complained against Dr Philips to the Government of India on the ground that he is defaming their profession. Acting on these complaints, the Ministry of Ayush has actually threatened defamation proceedings against Dr Philips.[88] This threat has had no effect on Dr Philips and he continues to be relentless in his advocacy against the dangers of untested traditional medicine.

Amongst the community of journalists is Priyanka Pulla, a freelance journalist who has reported some of the most detailed and complicated issues pertaining to the state of drug regulation in India. These include stories on the state of investigations into the deaths of the 12 children in Jammu that we mentioned in the prologue, a shocking story about the contamination of generic Remdesivir manufactured by an Indian pharmaceutical company during the Covid-19 pandemic and the controversial approval of Covid-19 vaccines. For her reportage on a Covid-19 vaccine called Covaxin, Pulla has been sued for defamation by the vaccine's manufacturer—Bharat Biotech, along with the publication *Wire* and eight others.

A court in Hyderabad passed a temporary injunction against Pulla, *Wire*, and others in February, 2022 without so much as granting them a hearing.[89]

While much of this book is critical about Indian bureaucrats, we must point out that one particular bureaucrat, Mr K.L. Sharma, the former Joint Secretary of the Drugs Regulation Section of the Ministry of Health and Family Welfare deserves a special mention. After the Supreme Court declined to hear our PIL, one of us, Dinesh Thakur, met Sharma to present him with a report containing our recommendations. To his credit, Sharma heard all our concerns and began reforms based on not just our report but also other sources. During his time, the government finally acted on the prickly issues of illegal FDCs, the issue of mandatory bioequivalence, advertizing etc. The government "rewarded" Sharma by transferring him out to the post of Joint Secretary, National Commission for Women (NCW), from where he retired in October 2018 after an illustrious career in the Central Secretariat Services. Such transfers in the last year of service to institutions such as the NCW are generally considered to be "punishment" postings. In this case, Sharma's likely "crime" was to have the "temerity" to push through reforms that were unpopular with the Indian pharmaceutical industry but absolutely necessary from a public health perspective. On retirement Sharma penned a book—*Healing the Pharmacy of the World*—which is well worth a read for anybody interested in how the government machinery deals with policy making in the field of drug regulation.

This list of outstanding individuals contributing to the debate on drug regulatory reform would not be complete without a reference to the outstanding Parliamentarians sitting on the Parliamentary Standing Committee on Health and Family Welfare, especially those who authored the famous 59th report on the functioning of the CDSCO that has been cited throughout this book.[90] These MPs displayed the glory, brilliance and courage of Indian democracy with that one report hauling up the CDSCO for the shoddy job that it was doing with regard to drug regulation. Three MPs on the sub-committee that drafted the reports, deserve a special mention: Dr Jyoti Mirdha, Balbir Punj, and Dr Sanjay Jaiswal. Together with the Chairperson of the Committee Brajesh Pathak, these MPs demonstrated the power of parliamentary standing committees in holding the government accountable for their action and inaction. If only they did so more frequently.

Notes

1. The United States Department of Justice, Office of Public Affairs, *Generic Drug Manufacturer Ranbaxy Pleads Guilty and Agrees to Pay $500 Million to Resolve False Claims Allegations, cGMP Violations and False Statements to the FDA* (Press Release No 13-542, 13 May 2013).
2. TNN, 'Ranbaxy Drugs: Apollo Pharmacy Issues Advisory' *The Times of India* (8 June 2013) <https://timesofindia.indiatimes.com/business/india-business/Ranbaxy-drugs-Apollo-Pharmacy-issues-advisory/articleshow/20487741.cms> accessed 23 May 2022.
3. NDTV, *Ranbaxy under Fire: Will India's Pharma Industry Be Hit?* (2013) <https://www.youtube.com/watch?v=MwmXXWwUSMs> accessed 23 May 2022.
4. Government of India, Ministry of Commerce and Industry, Press Information Bureau, 'Clarifications on Reports of Malpractices of Pharma Manufacturing in India' (3 June 2013) <https://pib.gov.in/newsite/PrintRelease.aspx?relid=96366> accessed 22 May 2022.
5. Vikas Bhardwaj and Khomba Singh, 'India Sees US Lobbies behind FDA Ban on Ranbaxy Drugs' *The Economic Times* (16 October 2008) <https://economictimes.indiatimes.com/industry/healthcare/biotech/pharmaceuticals/india-sees-us-lobbies-behind-fda-ban-on-ranbaxy-drugs/articleshow/3600276.cms?from=mdr> accessed 23 May 2022.
6. 'Public Health Activists Smell Conspiracy against Indian Pharma' *The Hindu Business Line* (24 May 2013) <https://www.thehindubusinessline.com/companies/public-health-activists-smell-conspiracy-against-indian-pharma/article20617469.ece1> accessed 23 May 2022.
7. Amit Sengupta, 'Who Manufactures Dirty Medicines?' *NewsClick* (15

June 2013) <https://www.newsclick.in/who-manufactures-dirty-medicines> accessed 23 May 2022.
8. ibid.
9. Interview with Arun Sawhney (CEO & MD, Ranbaxy), '"It's Just Improper Documentation"' *Outlook* (5 February 2022) <https://www.outlookindia.com/magazine/story/its-just-improper-documentation/286855> accessed 23 May 2022.
10. Reply by the Minister of Health and Family Welfare Shri Ghulam Nabi Azad to question raised by Shri Anil Desai, Rajya Sabha Deb 6 August 2013, Question No 232, 138–139.
11. The United States Department of Justice (n 1).
12. ibid.
13. Dr Gopal Dabade, 'MNCs Play Proxy War against Indian Generics' *Deccan Herald* (9 January 2016) <https://www.deccanherald.com/content/522212/mncs-play-proxy-war-against.html> accessed 23 May 2022.
14. Vidya Krishnan, 'A Love Story That Cost GVK Its International Reputation' *The Hindu* (8 October 2015) <https://www.thehindu.com/news/national/A-love-story-that-cost-GVK-its-international-reputation/article60296519.ece> accessed 23 May 2022.
15. ibid.
16. P Vaidyanathan Iyer, 'Suspending EU Trade Talks "Unilateral", but Not "Unconsidered": Nirmala Sitharaman' *The Indian Express* (8 September 2015) <https://indianexpress.com/article/business/business-others/suspending-eu-trade-talks-unilateral-but-not-unconsidered-nirmala-sitharaman/> accessed 23 May 2022.
17. Amiti Sen, 'Data Manipulation: India Contests EU Charges against GVK Bio' *The Hindu Business Line* (5 April 2015) <https://www.thehindubusinessline.com/companies/data-manipulation-india-contests-eu-charges-against-gvk-bio/article21016776.ece1> accessed 23 May 2022.
18. Roger Bate and others, 'Poor-Quality Drugs and Global Trade: A Pilot Study' (2016) 2 *American Journal of Health Economics*, 373.
19. ibid 394.
20. Government of India, Ministry of Health and Family Welfare, 'National Drug Survey 2014–2016: SUMMARY & RECOMMENDATIONS On Possible Strategies and Implementation Plan to Address the Problems Identified' (Chapter 11, 2017) 215.
21. Dinsa Sachan, 'Indian Manufacturers Hit Back over Quality Claims' *Chemistry World* (17 October 2014) <https://www.chemistryworld.com/news/indian-manufacturers-hit-back-over-quality-claims/7869.article> accessed 23 May 2022.

22. Sanjeet Bagcchi, 'Indian Generic Drugs Debate Heats Up' (2014) 384 *The Lancet*, 1334.
23. ibid.
24. Maitri Porecha, 'Vietnam Shows the Door to 45 Indian Pharma Companies' *DNA* (21 April 2014) <https://www.dnaindia.com/mumbai/report-vietnam-shows-the-door-to-45-indian-pharma-companies-1980761> accessed 23 May 2022.
25. Drugs Consultative Committee (DCC), *'REPORT OF THE 47th MEETING OF THE DRUGS CONSULTATIVE COMMITTEE HELD ON 30TH AND 31ST JULY, 2014 AT NEW DELHI'* (2014) 19 <https://cdsco.gov.in/opencms/opencms/system/modules/CDSCO.WEB/elements/common_download.jsp?num_id_pk=ODA5> accessed 23 May 2022; Drugs Consultative Committee (DCC), *'REPORT OF 50TH MEETING OF DRUGS CONSULTATIVE COMMITTEE HELD ON 04 & 05TH NOVEMBER, 2016 AT NEW DELHI'* (2016) 2 <https://cdsco.gov.in/opencms/opencms/system/modules/CDSCO.WEB/elements/common_download.jsp?num_id_pk=ODEy> accessed 23 May 2023.
26. Zeba Siddiqui, 'Pharma Crusader Dinesh Thakur Takes India's Drug Regulators to Court' *Reuters* (7 March 2016) <https://www.reuters.com/article/india-pharma-whistleblower-idUSKCN0W90C8> accessed 23 May 2022.
27. Himani Chandna, 'Modi Govt Plans Action against US Writer Who Said Indian Drugs Are "Flea-Market Quality"' *ThePrint* (10 January 2020) <https://theprint.in/health/modi-govt-plans-action-against-us-writer-who-said-indian-drugs-are-flea-market-quality/347189/> accessed 23 May 2022.
28. ibid.
29. Department Related Parliamentary Standing Committee on Health and Family Welfare, *The Functioning of The Central Drugs Standard Control Organisation (CDCSO)* (Fifty-Ninth Report) (RS 2012).
30. Chittabratta Mazumdar and Dipankar Mukherjee on the "Revision of Schedule M of Drugs and Cosmetics Act", Rajya Sabha Debate 10 December 2004, Question No 874.
31. *The Functioning of The Central Drugs Standard Control Organisation* (n 29) at para 2.1.
32. *The Functioning of The Central Drugs Standard Control Organisation* (n 29) at para 2.2.
33. Drugs Consultative Committee (DCC), *'REPORT OF THE 48TH MEETING OF THE DRUGS CONSULTATIVE COMMITTEE HELD ON 24TH JULY, 2015 AT NEW DELHI'* (2015) 1 <https://

cdsco.gov.in/opencms/opencms/system/modules/CDSCO.WEB/elements/common_download.jsp?num_id_pk=ODEw> accessed 24 May 2022.

34. ibid; Drugs Consultative Committee (DCC), *'REPORT OF THE 46TH MEETING OF THE DRUGS CONSULTATIVE COMMITTEE HELD ON 12TH AND 13TH NOVEMBER, 2013 AT THE HOTEL METROPOLITAN NEW DELHI-110001'* (2013) <https://cdsco.gov.in/opencms/opencms/system/modules/CDSCO.WEB/elements/common_download.jsp?num_id_pk=ODA4> accessed 24 May 2022; Drugs Consultative Committee (DCC), *'REPORT OF THE 47TH MEETING OF THE DRUGS CONSULTATIVE COMMITTEE HELD ON 30TH AND 31ST JULY, 2014 AT NEW DELHI'* (2014) <https://cdsco.gov.in/opencms/opencms/system/modules/CDSCO.WEB/elements/common_download.jsp?num_id_pk=ODA5> accessed 24 May 2022.

35. Usha Sharma, 'DCGI Calls for Suggestions from Industry to Reduce Compliance Burden' *Express Pharma* (29 January 2021) <https://www.expresspharma.in/dcgi-calls-for-suggestions-from-industry-to-reduce-compliance-burden/> accessed 24 May 2022.

36. ibid.

37. Prabha Raghavan, 'CDSCO Increases WHO GMP Certificate to Three Years for Ease of Doing Business' *The Economic Times* (8 May 2018) <https://economictimes.indiatimes.com/industry/healthcare/biotech/healthcare/cdsco-increases-who-gmp-certificate-to-three-years-for-ease-of-doing-business/articleshow/64084982.cms> accessed 24 May 2022; Dinesh Thakur and Prashant Reddy, 'Deregulation of the Pharma Industry in the Time of Scandals' *The News Minute* (17 October 2016) <https://www.thenewsminute.com/article/deregulation-pharma-industry-time-scandals-51512> accessed 24 May 2022.

38. Louise Tillin, *Indian Federalism: Oxford India Short Introductions* (Oxford University Press 2019) 2–5.

39. The Constitution of India 1950, Article 254.

40. Government of India, Ministry of Commerce and Industry, *Report of The Pharmaceutical Enquiry Committee* (1954) 153, para 3.7.

41. ibid 164–165, para 6.4.2. z

42. Government of India, Ministry of Petroleum and Chemicals, *Report of The Committee on Drugs and Pharmaceutical Industry (Hathi Committee Report)* (1975) 190–201.

43. Government of India, Ministry of Health and Family Welfare, *Report of The Expert Committee on a Comprehensive Examination of Drug Regulatory Issues, including the problem of Spurious Drugs*

(Mashelkar Committee Report) (No Z.28015/112/2002-D/DMS&PFA, 2003) 36, para 5.7.3.
44. ibid 44, para 6.1.8.
45. The Drugs and Cosmetics (Amendment) Bill 2007; The Drugs and Cosmetics (Amendment) Bill 2013.
46. Department Related Parliamentary Standing Committee on Health and Family Welfare, *Drugs and Cosmetics (Amendment) Bill-2007* (Thirtieth Report) (RS 2008) 18-19, para 9.22-9.23; Department Related Parliamentary Standing Committee on Health and Family Welfare, *The Drugs and Cosmetics (Amendment) Bill, 2013* (Seventy-Ninth Report) (RS 2013) 52, para 68.
47. *Dinesh Thakur vs Union of India* WP(C) No. 137 of 2016 before the Supreme Court of India.
48. Special Correspondent, 'Drug Control Officers Challenge Amendment to Statutory Rules' *The Hindu* (6 January 2018) <https://www.thehindu.com/news/national/tamil-nadu/drug-control-officers-challenge-amendment-to-statutory-rules/article22388587.ece> accessed 24 May 2022.
49. *All India Drugs Control Officers Confederation vs The Government of India* WP.No.33924/2017 before the High Court of Madras (28 February 2020) <https://indiankanoon.org/doc/191958036/> accessed 24 May 2022.
50. Reply to RTI application dated 23 March 2022, Drug Testing Laboratory, Chennai, Government of Tamil Nadu (Application No 379/A1/2022, 17 February 2022); Reply to RTI application dated 7 March 2022, State Drugs Control and Research Laboratory, Government of West Bengal (Application No SDCRL/29, 17 February 2022).
51. Reply to RTI application dated 17 March 2022, Joint Food and Drugs Laboratory, Government of Bihar (Application No 709, 17 February 2022); Reply to RTI application dated 16 March 2022, Composite Testing Laboratory, Khandagat, District Solan, Directorate of Health Safety & Regulation, Government of Himachal Pradesh (Application No HSR-H (RTI) 2022-IX-9528, 17 February 2022).
52. Reply to RTI application dated 2 March 2022, Directorate of Health & Family Welfare, Government of Nagaland (Application No DHFW-13/DC/RTI/116/2013-14/12479, 10 February 2022).
53. Reply to RTI application dated 3 December 2017, Food and Drugs Administration, Government of Maharashtra (Application No RTI/518/232-17/15, 14 November 2017).
54. Government of India, Ministry of Health and Family Welfare, Central

Drugs Standard Control Organization (CDSCO), *Drug Alerts* <https://cdsco.gov.in/opencms/opencms/en/Latest-Alerts/> accessed 24 May 2022.

55. Reply to RTI application dated 5 May 2022, Indian Pharmacopoeia Commission (Application No CIPGZ/R/E/22/00020, 14 April 2022); Reply to RTI application dated 5 May 2022, Indian Pharmacopoeia Commission (Application No CIPGZ/R/E/22/00021, 14 April 2022).
56. The Drugs and Cosmetics Rules 1945, Rule 49.
57. The Drugs and Cosmetics Rules 1945, Rule 50A.
58. Government of India, Ministry of Health and Family Welfare, *GSR 425(E)* (*Gazette of India Extraordinary*, Part II—s 3(i), 14 June 2011) (Central Drugs Standard Control Organisation [Drugs Controller (India)] Recruitment Rules, 2011).
59. *The Functioning of The Central Drugs Standard Control Organisation* (n 29) at para 2.23.
60. ibid 7, para 3.2–3.3.
61. Government of India, Department of Health and Family Welfare, *Report of The Expert Committee Set Up to Suggest Recruitment Rules/Job Description for Senior Level Posts in Central Drugs Standard Control Organisation* (2015).
62. Nandita Vijay, 'DPT Urges Ministry of Health Not to Make Changes in Recruitment Rules for DCGI Post, Other Tops Jobs in CDSCO' *Pharmabiz* (Bengaluru, 19 January 2015) <http://www.pharmabiz.com/NewsDetails.aspx?aid=86219&sid=1> accessed 24 May 2022.
63. Ibid.
64. 'IPS Officers to Now Head Drugs Control Administration' *The New Indian Express* (1 February 2022) <https://www.newindianexpress.com/cities/hyderabad/2022/feb/01/ips-officer-to-now-head-drugs-control-admin-2413675.html> accessed 24 May 2022; Bureau, 'Drug Control Officers Demand Technically Qualified Persons to Head DCA in Telangana, AP' *Pharmabiz* (12 July 2014) <http://www.pharmabiz.com/NewsDetails.aspx?aid=82891&sid=1> accessed 24 May 2022.
65. Government of India, Ministry of Health and Family Welfare, *Report of The Expert Committee on a Comprehensive Examination of Drug Regulatory Issues, including the problem of Spurious Drugs (Mashelkar Committee Report)* (No Z.28015/112/2002-D/DMS&PFA, 2003) 41, para 5.9.4.
66. *Report of The Expert Committee* (n 61) 6.
67. KL Sharma, *Healing the Pharmacy of the World: An Inside Story of Medical Products Manufacturing and Regulation in India* (Notion Press 2021) 82.

68. ibid 83.
69. *SP Gupta vs Union of India* (1982) 2 S.C.R. 365. <https://indiankanoon.org/doc/1294854/> accessed 24 May 2022.
70. *The Functioning of The Central Drugs Standard Control Organisation* (n 29) at para 7.12.
71. *Prashant Reddy vs Ministry of Health & Family Welfare* Second Appeal No. CIC/MH&FW/A/2018/159460-BJ before the Central Information Commission (26 May 2020) <https://indiankanoon.org/doc/115080764/> accessed 24 May 2022.
72. United States Government Accountability Office, 'Drug Safety: FDA's Future Inspection Plans Need to Address Issues Presented by COVID-19 Backlog' (GAO-21-409T, 4 March 2021).
73. Government of India, Ministry of Health and Family Welfare, 'National Drug Survey 2014-2016 (Chapter 11, 2017) 215.
74. Comptroller and Auditor General of India, *Report on Performance of Medical Establishments in Defence Services* (Report No 18 of 2012-13, ch 5: Procurement of drugs and quality inspection, 14 December 2013).
75. Comptroller and Auditor General of India, *Performance audit of Procurement of medicines and medical equipment in the Ministry of Health and Family Welfare* (Report No 20 of 2007, 27 November 2007).
76. Comptroller and Auditor General of India, *Performance Audit of National Rural Health Mission of Union Government, Ministry of Health & Family Welfare* (Report No 8 of 2009, ch 7: Procurement and supply of medicine and equipment, 18 December 2009).
77. Comptroller and Auditor General of India, *Report of the Comptroller and Auditor General of India State Finances Audit Report for the year ended March 2021* (Report No 2 of 2022, ch II: Compliance Audit, 31 March 2022) 33; PTI, 'Expired Vaccines, Unutilised Funds: CAG Report Exposes Jharkhand's Health Infrastructure' *The New Indian Express* (17 March 2022) <https://www.newindianexpress.com/nation/2022/mar/17/expired-vaccines-unutilised-funds-cag-report-exposes-jharkhands-health-infrastructure-2431134.html> accessed 24 May 2022.
78. U Sudhakar Reddy, 'Telangana: Vigilance Unearths Drug Purchase Scam in ESI Hospitals' *The Times of India* (17 July 2019) <https://timesofindia.indiatimes.com/city/hyderabad/vigilance-unearths-drug-purchase-scam/articleshow/70252212.cms> accessed 24 May 2022.
79. Harleen Kaur, Ajay Shah and Siddhartha Srivastava, 'How Elements

of the Indian State Purchase Drugs' (xKDR 2021) 5 <https://ideas.repec.org/p/anf/wpaper/5.html> accessed 24 May 2022.

80. RTI case no.G.542/1/2015-16/HQ/14718 dated 03.2.2016 filed with Railways HQ and received on 09.3.2016.
81. PTI, 'Government Approves Public Procurement Bill' *The Hindu* (12 April 2012) <https://www.thehindu.com/news/national/government-approves-public-procurement-bill/article3306949.ece> accessed 24 May 2022.
82. Amiti Sen Gupta, 'B K Keayla: A Personal Reminiscence' (2010) 45 *Economic and Political Weekly*, 7.
83. 'About Us' (*All India Drug Action Network (AIDAN)*, 1 September 2008) <https://aidanindia.wordpress.com/about-us/> accessed 24 May 2022.
84. PTI, 'Government Approves Public Procurement Bill' *The Hindu* (New Delhi, 12 April 2012) <https://www.thehindu.com/news/national/government-approves-public-procurement-bill/article3306949.ece> accessed 24 May 2022.
85. Government of India, Planning Commission, *Report of The Working Group on Drugs and Food Regulation for The 12th Five Year Plan* (No 2(6)2010-H&FW, 9 May 2011).
86. 'SC Agrees to Hear PIL Seeking Ban on Websites Spreading "Sardar Jokes"' *LiveLaw* (30 October 2015) <https://www.livelaw.in/sc-agrees-to-hear-pil-seeking-ban-on-websites-spreading-sardar-jokes/> accessed 24 May 2022; Bhadra Sinha, 'Kohinoor Our Property, Govt Tells Supreme Court' *Hindustan Times* (20 September 2016) <https://www.hindustantimes.com/india-news/kohinoor-our-property-govt-tells-supreme-court/story-j1jqu8qSukJcyHBvDFLt0N.html> accessed 24 May 2022; Nagraj Gollapudi, 'Supreme Court Admits BCCI Petition' *ESPN* (7 August 2013) <https://www.espncricinfo.com/story/_/id/21871852/supreme-court-admits-bcci-petition> accessed 24 May 2022.
87. *M/s Lundbeck India Private Limited vs Dr Chandra M Gulhati* Criminal Petition No. 4683/2011 before the Karnataka High Court decided on 26 July 2012 <https://indiankanoon.org/doc/183428285/> accessed 24 May 2022.
88. Staff Reporter, 'Union AYUSH Ministry Threatens Defamation against Kerala Doctor' *The Hindu* (27 September 2021) <https://www.thehindu.com/news/national/kerala/union-ayush-ministry-threatens-defamation-against-kerala-doctor/article36696410.ece> accessed 24 May 2022.
89. Ayush Tiwari, 'Bharat Biotech Defamation Case: A Day after Court

Order, Wire Says No Notice Yet' *Newslaundry* (24 February 2022) <https://www.newslaundry.com/2022/02/24/bharat-biotech-defamation-case-a-day-after-court-order-wire-says-no-notice-yet> accessed 24 May 2022.

90. *The Functioning of The Central Drugs Standard Control Organisation* (n 29).

Acknowledgements

Books like this one are typically difficult to write in a country like India, given the opacity with which much of the drug regulatory structure carries out its duties. The main instrument of our research was therefore the RTI Act, 2005. We have filed more than 400 applications under the RTI Act with drug controllers and other government departments across the country to elicit information tucked away in the dark corners of government offices. While we are aware that the RTI Act has been the subject of many an obituary in the recent years, it does deliver results, often after a mind-numbing and frustrating process. It takes patience, some good luck, and the occasional public spirited "Public Information Officer" to ensure a meaningful reply but we have been able to collect hundreds of pages of useful information that form the basis of this book. This book would not have been possible without the RTI Act and for that we are grateful to the many ordinary and extraordinary people who made the RTI Act possible. We are also very grateful to those Public Information Officers who provided us with honest, helpful information in a timely manner, complying with both the letter and spirit of the RTI Act. Many of their colleagues were less than helpful and we continue our endeavour to hold them accountable.

The second set of people we would like to thank are the many law students who worked with us as research assistants on this project. Top of the list is Balaji Subramanian, who is now a lawyer in London. While a student at NALSAR

University of Law, he helped strategize and execute a pivotal round of RTI applications. It is thanks to Bala that we were able to corner the Ministry of Health and CDSCO on the missing Mohapatra Committee report. Both of us authors had missed key clues on the existence of the report until Bala's eagle eyes spotted a document that opened the can of worms for the government. The second research assistant to whom we are especially grateful is Harsh Tripathi, a student at NALSAR University of Law, who was our main pillar of support during the course of writing this book. Apart from being able to dig up obscure documents for us, including dated notifications published in the *Gazette of India*, Harsh also helped extensively with the referencing for every chapter of this book. We are also very grateful to Gayatri Gupta and Vishal Rakhecha, who while students at NALSAR University of Law, painstakingly read through a few hundred judgments of trial courts that we had collected from the e-courts website, to plot trends in prosecutions under the Drugs and Cosmetics Act 1940 and the Drugs and Magic Remedies (Objectionable Advertisements) Act 1954. It was a tough assignment and they executed it flawlessly. Vishal also helped with strategizing and filing RTI applications. We are also thankful to Khushi Mittal, a law student at NALSAR University of Law, for her research assistance on the tricky question of the rights of practitioners of traditional medicine and also for her assistance in digging out data on pharmaceutical trademarks in India. Lastly, we would like to thank law students Nipun Kalra, a student of NLU Delhi for his research on similar pharmaceutical tradenames and Revathi Thushara, a student of NLU-Orissa for her research on the rights of traditional medicine practitioners when it came to prescribing modern medicine.

We also thank Bhavesh Kaachhadiya for helping us scrape judgments related to the Drugs and Cosmetics Act 1940 off the e-courts website. We were able to read judgments from across a number of states thanks to his efforts. Studying these judgments gave us excellent insights into how the law is actually implemented in India.

A special thanks to our lawyer, Harsh Parashar, who apart from providing us with legal counsel and representation before the Delhi High Court also sportingly agreed to let us use his office address as the destination for replies to our many RTI applications. We owe an enormous debt of gratitude to his law clerk, Dharmendra Mishra, who diligently scanned and emailed us each RTI reply received from government offices across the country. We are also grateful to our lawyer Sai Vinod Nayani, who has helped us with pursuing many appeals under the RTI Act before the Central Information Commission and some lawsuits against the drug regulator.

Conversations, on different occasions, with Prof. Ajay Shah, Harleen Kaur, Priyanka Pulla, K.L. Sharma, Dhvani Mehta, and Shreya Shrivastava helped shape some of our thoughts and arguments in this book. We are very grateful to them.

We are also most grateful to Professor Lionel Bently at Cambridge University, a world-renowned academic in the field of intellectual property law, for providing us a copy of an old British law—the UK Food and Drugs Act, 1938—which we were unable to procure from any online sources. An email out of the blue asking Prof. Bently for advice on how we could access this old law resulted in his offer to personally look for it in the libraries at Cambridge and send us a copy. We are thankful for his generosity with his time.

We would also like to thank Gavin Morris for the wonderful cover that he has designed for this book. It was one of many fantastic covers that he sent us. Last but not the least, we would like to thank our editors at Simon and Schuster—Himanjali Sankar, Megha Mukherjee, and Sayantan Ghosh—for tolerating many busted deadlines, hand-holding us through the process of publication, and bringing out the book to the market in record time.

This book wouldn't have been possible but for my co-author, Prashant. As an Overseas Citizen of India, I am not allowed to file RTI requests in India (I have challenged this restriction before the Delhi High Court). Much of the data we collected and analyzed in this book was led by him. The analysis we present to bolster our views and the conclusions we draw are largely his work product. On many a occasion, his counsel and advice to temper my expectations given how bad the situation is with our drug supply was instrumental in the recommendations we make.

The credit for genesis of this book has to go to the Supreme Court of India and its former Chief Justice, T.S. Thakur. He dismissed two PILs that I had filed, after a year of painstaking research, on the grounds that it dealt with "academic issues"; this was the prime motive to prove to the citizens of India that this issue is anything but academic. Credit also should go to Dr Harsh Vardhan, the former Minister of Health, Union of India who agreed to meet with me, made me wait for hours outside his office and was distracted watching television for the brief time he gave me. Both these incidents informed me that the only way to affect change in the country was to educate its people, especially doctors, who prescribe medicine, not repose my faith in either the administration or the judiciary. I haven't been proven wrong during the last two years while authoring this book.

Lastly, this is an attempt to address the law-making process in the country. Much of the process of framing laws has become pedantic and ideological of late. We do not invest in empirical research, we don't frame regulations based on facts from the ground. Not only has the drafting process become perfunctory, much of the regulation is driven by lobbying from vested interests. No wonder we end up with laws that undermine each other and create loopholes for exploitation. This is an effort to educate the law makers, doctors and other stakeholders; an attempt to show why understanding how we got here is important in charting out the path for where we need to go as a country.

– Dinesh S. Thakur

~

My initial interest in drug regulation began in the context of pharmaceutical patent litigation since in India much of it gets embroiled in regulatory issues. The gamechanger in 2012 was a defamation lawsuit against my friend and mentor Prof. Shamnad Basheer, by a leading Indian pharmaceutical company in India for some of his comments about a patent infringement lawsuit involving the company that were published on SpicyIP, a leading blog on intellectual property law founded by him. As a fellow contributor to the blog, I believed that no "good deed" should go "unpunished", least of all a defamation lawsuit. Knowing that the pharmaceutical company in question had some skeletons in its "regulatory closet" I convinced Shamnad to extract the relevant information from the Ministry of Health using the RTI Act 2005. While the process took time, once we received the information from the government, we realized to our horror the absolute chaos of drug regulation in India. Based on this information, Shamnad, Sai Vinod Nayani, and I published a report, on SpicyIP on this issue. That report led to a long conversation on drug regulation in India with Prof. Amir Attaran at the University of Ottawa, who was then working on drug quality issues. Subsequently, Amir introduced me to Dinesh who was looking for a lawyer to help him dig into the chaos of Indian drug regulation. I ended up quitting my position at a law firm to work full time with Dinesh to unearth the dark secrets of India's drug regulatory system. If it was not for that pharmaceutical company suing Shamnad, it is unlikely that I would have paid much attention to drug regulatory law in India!

The main inspiration, though, for my decision to try and write more, including this book, has always been Shamnad. Several years my senior from law school, I had the privilege of writing with Shamnad on a number of issues pertaining to intellectual property law and I got a front-row seat to his style of thinking and writing. While Indian law schools can be exceptionally cynical places, too often seeding students with unhealthy cynicism, Shamnad was that rare Indian legal academic who, through his scholarship and advocacy, could inspire law students and lawyers alike into believing that the law, even in India, can be used for the greater good. I think working with Shamnad made me less cynical. It was shortly after we lost him in 2019 that I quit my job at a think tank and joined forces with Dinesh to work full-time on this book, fuelled by the memory of many conversations with Shamnad on drug regulation and the Indian pharmaceutical industry. I suspect he would have enjoyed reading this book.

A second academic figure I would like to thank is Professor Hank Greely at Stanford Law School. During the course of my LLM at Stanford, I got to take his courses on drug regulation and the intersection of law and the biosciences. As a student fellow at the Centre for Law and the Biosciences, headed by Prof. Greely, I also got exposure to a number of brilliant scholars who used to lecture at the university. This was the first and only formal education that I received on issues pertaining to drug regulation and it proved to be very useful while thinking through many of the issues in this book with Dinesh.

Last but not the least, I am very grateful to my family and friends. Writing a book outside an academic institution during the worst pandemic in a century can be an isolating and uphill venture, even if it is with a co-author as wonderful as Dinesh. My deep gratitude to Laasya and Suhas, who were my flatmates at different times in Bangalore during the first phase of the pandemic when we had just begun writing this book. They provided the company, food, and liquids to keep my spirits high. Also, thanks to my wonderful friends from law school: Harsh, Mukul, Subramanian, and Apurva for keeping me entertained on calls and messages, especially during the forced isolation of the pandemic. A special thanks to my school friends in Hyderabad—Aman, Kailash, Shashank, Kashyap, Keerti, and Abhishek who provided a much-needed respite from the book-writing process, after I shifted back to the city.

Amongst family, I am very grateful to my wonderful parents, Satya and Sudhakar, for ensuring I got all the opportunities in life that were not available to them. Mostly though I am just relieved that they have been surprisingly tolerant of my "trajectory-less" career spanning three universities, two law firms, one think tank, one whistle-blower, one philanthropic foundation, two books, and one masters program over a period of 14 years. I am also grateful to my brother Vikas and his wife Mrudulata. I have spent many comfortable, lazy Sunday family lunches with them, arguing over politics even when we agree with each other. Also, my gratitude to my lawyer niece, Shanu, who has done wonders in building my reputation amongst my extended family and hopefully she convinces all of them to read this book. A professional PR expert could not have done a better job.

Last but not the least, I am grateful to my co-author Dinesh Thakur. Co-authoring a book is never easy, especially with me, and especially on a topic as frustratingly complex as the working of India's opaque drug regulatory machinery. It takes a good deal of patience, coordination, optimism and a whole lot of trust. His bravery and integrity in blowing the whistle at Ranbaxy inspired me enough to give up a career in a law firm. It was a decision that I never regretted. While progress in effecting change to India's drug regulatory system has been slow, there has nevertheless been progress.

– *Prashant Reddy T.*

Glossary

AFMSD: Armed Forces Medical Services Depot
HMP: Herbal Medicinal Products
AIDAN: All India Drug Action Network
AIOCD: All India Organisation of Chemists & Druggists
AIDS: Acquired Immunodeficiency Disease (AIDS)
AMA: American Medical Association
ADMA: Ayurvedic Drug Manufacturers Association
API: Active Pharmaceutical Ingredient
ASCI: Advertising Standards Council of India
ASHA: Accredited Social Health Activist
AYUSH: Ayurveda, Yoga and Naturopathy, Unani, Siddha and Homeopathy
BA: Bioavailability
BAMS: Bachelors in Ayurvedic Medical Sciences
BCS: Biopharmaceutical Classification System
BE: Bioequivalence
BET: Bacterial Endotoxin Test
BMJ: British Medical Journal
BP: British Pharmacopeia
BPPI: Bureau of Pharma PSUs of India
BUMS: Bachelors of Unani Medicine and Surgery

CBER: Center for Biological Evaluation and Research

CBI: Central Bureau of Investigation

CCI: Competition Commission of India

CCMB: Centre for Cellular & Molecular Biology

CCRAS: Central Council for Research in Ayurvedic & Siddha

CCRH: Central Council for Research in Homeopathy

CCRIMH: Central Council for Research in Indian Medicine & Homeopathy

CCRUM: Central Council for Research in Unani Medicine

CCRYN: Central Council for Yoga & Naturopathy

CCRS: Central Council for Research in Siddha

CAG: Comptroller & Auditor General

CDA: Central Drug Administration

CDER: Center for Drug Evaluation and Research, USFDA

CDL: Central Drug Laboratory

CDRI: Central Drug Research Institute, USFDA

CDSCO: Central Drugs Standards Control Organization

CIC: Central Information Commission

CIMAP: Central Institute of Medicinal & Aromatic Plants

CMSS: Central Medical Services Society

CoA: Certificate of Analysis

CRO: Clinical Research Organization

CSIR: Council of Scientific and Industrial Research

CTRI: Clinical Trials Registry of India

DCC: Drugs Consultative Committee, is a statutory committee created under Section 7 of the Drugs and Cosmetics Act 1940. It has as its members representatives from all state drug controllers, the central drug regulator and also the Union Ministry of Health.

DCGI: Drugs Controller General of India

DEG: DiEthylene Glycol

DG: Director General

DGHS: Directorate General of Health Services

DMEPA: Division of Medication Error, Prevention & Analysis, USFDA.

DPCO: Drug Price Control Order

DPT: Delhi Pharmaceutical Trust

DTAB: Drugs Technical Advisory Board is a statutory board created under Section 5 of the Drugs and Cosmetics Act 1940. It consists of experts and is meant to advise the Union Ministry of Health on technical issues related to the law.

ECG: Electro Cardiogram

ECP: Emergency Contraceptive Pill

EMA: European Medicines Agency

EPA: Environmental Protection Agency

EPAR: European Public Assessment Report

EU: European Union

EUA: Emergency Use Authorization

FDA: Food and Drug Administration (the enforcement agency in Maharashtra)

FDC: Fixed Dose Combination

FDCA: Food and Drugs Control Administration

GAO: Government Accountability Office

GCP: Good Clinical Practice

GDP: Good Distribution Practices

GLP: Good Laboratory Practice

GMP: Good Manufacturing Practices

GC: Gas Chromatography

HCQ: Hydroxychloroquine

HPDCA: Himachal Pradesh Drugs Control Administration

HPLC: High Performance Liquid Chromatography

HIV: Human Immunodeficiency Virus

IBEF: India Brand Equity Foundation

ICMR: Indian Council of Medical Research

IDMA: Indian Drug Manufacturers Association

IMS: Indian Medical Services

IMA: Indian Medical Association

INN: International Non- Proprietary Name

IP: Indian Pharmacopeia

IPA: Indian Pharmaceutical Alliance

IPC: Indian Pharmacopeial Commission

IPC: Indian Penal Code

JAMA: Journal of the American Medical Association

Kg: Kilogram

LOCOST : Low Cost Standard Therapeutics

MoHFW: Ministry of Health and Family Welfare

MMIS: Monthly Index of Medical Specialities

MP: Member of the Parliament

MSF: Médecins Sans Frontières

NABL: National Accreditation Board for Testing and Calibration of Laboratories

NBER: National Bureau of Economic Research

NBRI: National Botanical Research Institute

NCL: National Chemical Laboratory

NCW: National Commission for Women

NGO: Non-Governmental Organization

NHM: National Health Mission

NIH: National Institutes of Health

NLEM: National List of Essential Medicines

NRA: National Regulatory Assessment

NRDC: National Research Development Corporation

NSAID: Nonsteroidal anti-inflammatory drug

NSQ: Not of Standard Quality

NSSO: National Sample Survey Organisation

NTI: Narrow Therapeutic Index

OPDP: Office of Prescription Drug Promotion, USFDA

OPPI: Organisation of Pharmaceutical Producers of India

PCI: Pharmacy Council of India

PD: Pharmacodynamics

PGIMER: Post Graduate Institute of Medical Education and Research

PIL: Public Interest Litigation

PK: Pharmacokinetics

RCT: Randomized Control Trial

RDTL: Regional Drug Testing Laboratory

RTI: Right to Information Act 2005

SCOTUS: Supreme Court of the United States

SEBI: Securities Exchange Board of India

SEC: Subject Expert Committee

SUGAM: An e-governance platform used by the CDSCO

TNMSC : Tamil Nadu Medical Services Corporation

TRAI: Telecom Regulatory Authority of India

TRIPs: Trade Related Intellectual Property Rights

QA: Quality Assurance

UCPMP: Uniform Code for Pharmaceutical Marketing Practices
USAN: United States Adopted Names
USFDA: United States Food and Drug Administration
USP: United States Pharmacopeia
WHO: World Health Organization
WTO: World Trade Organization